A TEXTBOOK OF ORGANISATIONAL BEHAVIOUR

WITH TEXT AND CASES

For the Students of Business Schools

Dr. C.B. GUPTA
M.Com., Ph.D., MIMA
Former Head
Department of Commerce
Shri Ram College of Commerce
University of Delhi, Delhi

S. CHAND
PUBLISHING

S Chand And Company Limited
(ISO 9001 Certified Company)

S Chand And Company Limited

(ISO 9001 Certified Company)

Head Office: Block B-1, House No. D-1, Ground Floor, Mohan Co-operative Industrial Estate, New Delhi – 110 044 | Phone: 011-66672000

Registered Office: A-27, 2nd Floor, Mohan Co-operative Industrial Estate, New Delhi – 110 044 Phone: 011-49731800

www.**schandpublishing.com**; e-mail: **info@schandpublishing.com**

Branches

Chennai	:	Ph: 23632120; chennai@schandpublishing.com
Guwahati	:	Ph: 2738811, 2735640; guwahati@schandpublishing.com
Hyderabad	:	Ph: 40186018; hyderabad@schandpublishing.com
Jalandhar	:	Ph: 4645630; jalandhar@schandpublishing.com
Kolkata	:	Ph: 23357458, 23353914; kolkata@schandpublishing.com
Lucknow	:	Ph: 4003633; lucknow@schandpublishing.com
Mumbai	:	Ph: 25000297; mumbai@schandpublishing.com
Patna	:	Ph: 2260011; patna@schandpublishing.com

First Edition 2014
Reprints 2018, 2019, 2020, 2021

Reprint 2022 (Twice)

ISBN: 978-81-219-4301-7 **Product Code:** H8ORB60BMGT10ENAA14R

PRINTED IN INDIA

By Vikas Publishing House Private Limited, Plot 20/4, Site-IV, Industrial Area Sahibabad, Ghaziabad – 201 010 and Published by S Chand And Company Limited, A-27, 2nd Floor, Mohan Co-operative Industrial Estate, New Delhi – 110 044.

PREFACE

In the rapidly changing environment, business as well as non-business organisations are finding it increasingly difficult to survive and grow. Improvements in performance at individual, group and organistional levels are essential for success of every organisation. The present book is a modest attempt to explain human behaviour at these three levels. The book is designed to meet the course content requirements of students of commerce, management and other disciplines. The text is divided into three broad parts — individual behaviour, group behaviour and overall behaviour. It is based on my teaching experience of more than four decades. Some of the distinctive features of the book are as follows :

- Chapter outline in the beginning of each chapter to provide a bird's-eye view of the contents.
- Comprehensive coverage of various topics.
- Tables and diagrams to illustrate the text.
- Examples from Indian industry.
- Test Questions culled from examinations of various business schools and universities at the end of each chapter.
- Case Study at the end of each chapter.
- Simple language and lucid style.

I am indebted to my teachers, colleagues and students at Delhi University and at various business schools in the NCR for their advice and assistance in the preparation of this book.

I am confident that the book will be found useful by the concerned students and teachers. Suggestions and critical comments for improvements in subsequent editions are welcome.

Dr. C.B. Gupta

Preface

In the rapidly changing environment, business as well as non-business organisations are finding it increasingly difficult to survive and grow. Improvements in performance at individual, group and organisational levels are essential for success of every organisation. The present book is a modest attempt to explain human behaviour at these three levels. The book is designed to meet the course content requirements of students of commerce, management and other disciplines. The text is divided into three broad parts — individual behaviour, group behaviour and overall behaviour. It is based on my teaching experience of more than four decades. Some of the distinctive features of the book are as follows :

- Chapter outline in the beginning of each chapter to provide a bird's-eye view of the contents.
- Comprehensive coverage of various topics.
- Tables and diagrams to illustrate the text.
- Examples from Indian industry.
- Test Questions culled from examinations of various business schools and universities at the end of each chapter.
- Case Study at the end of each chapter.
- Simple language and lucid style.

I am indebted to my teachers, colleagues and students at Delhi University and at various business schools in the NCR for their advice and assistance in the preparation of this book.

I am confident that the book will be found useful by the concerned students and teachers. Suggestions and critical comments for improvements in subsequent editions are welcome.

Dr C.B. Gupta

SYLLABUS

UNIVERSITY OF DELHI

B.SC. PROGRAMME – PART II
EL 210 (III) ORGANISATIONAL BEHAVIOUR

(50 Lectures) **Total Marks: 50**

The purpose of this paper is to provide the students of science, a basic understanding of the concepts and processes of organisational behaviour to equip them with the necessary skills to manage human behaviour at work.

Unit I: Introduction

Significance of Organisational Behaviour

Contribution of Psychology, Sociology and Anthropology to the field of Organisational Behaviour. Models of Organisational Behaviour. Basic Roles of Managers.

Unit II: Individual In the Organisation

Personality: Traits and Types. Attitudes and Values. Perception — Process and Factors. Rationality in Decision-Making. Motivation — Maslow and Herzberg Models. Role of Incentives.

Unit III: Interpersonal Behaviour

Transactional Analysis — Ego States, Life Positions. Interpersonal Conflicts, Interpersonal Communication.

Unit IV: Group Behaviour

Group Dynamics. Informal Organisation. Team Decision-making. Leadership — Concept and Styles.

Unit V: Contemporary Issues In Organisational Behaviour

Creating and Sustaining Organisational Culture. Managing Workforce Diversity. Managing Change and Creating Learning Organisation.

MBA
101 – MANAGEMENT PROCESS AND ORGANISATIONAL BEHAVIOUR

Objectives

The objective of this paper is to familiarise the student with basic management concepts and behavioural processes in the organisation.

Course Contents

Managerial Processes, Functions, Skills and Roles in Organisation — An Overview; Evolution of Management Theory: Systems Approaches for Understanding Organisation; Problem Solving & Decision Making Processes; Organisation Structure; Control Processes,

Foundations of Organisational Behaviour; Personality; Perceptual Processes; Learning; Values & Attitudes, Work Motivation; Interpersonal Communication; Group Dynamics; Coping with Frustration & Stress; Leadership and Influence Process.

MASTER OF COMMERCE (M.COM.)

COURSE 411 : ORGANISATIONAL THEORY AND BEHAVIOUR

Time : 3 Hrs. **Max. Marks: 75**

Objective

The objective of the course is to develop a theoretical understanding among students about the structure and behaviour of organisation as it develops over time. The course will also make them capable of realising the competitiveness for firms.

Course Outline

1. **Organisational Theories and Behaviour:** Classical, Neo-classical and Contemporary. Authority, power, status, formal and informal structure. Flat and Tall structures. bureaucratisation of organisations. Organisational Behaviour concepts, determinants, models, challenges and opportunities of OB, Transaction cost and organisational behaviours. Contributing disciplines to the OB. Individual Behaviour: Foundations of individual behaviour, values, attitudes, personality and emotions. Theory X and Theory Y, Chris Argyris behaviour patterns, Perceptual process.
2. **Group Decision-making and Communication:** Concept and nature of decision-making process, Individual versus group decision-making, Nominal group technique and Dolphi technique, models of communication, communication effectiveness in organisation, Feedback, TA, Johari Window.
3. **Motivation:** Need hierarchy, Maslow's Need Hierarchy, Two-factor theory, Contemporary theories of motivation (ERG, Cognitive evaluation, goal setting, equity) expectancy model. Behaviour modification, Motivation and organisational effectiveness.
4. **Leadership, Power and Conflict:** Concept and theories, Behavioural approach, Situational approach, Leadership effectiveness, Contemporary issues in leadership. Power and conflict, Bases of Power, power tactics, sources of conflict patterns, levels and conflict resolution strategies.
5. **Organisational Culture, Organisational Development and Stress Management:** Concept and determinants of organisational culture, Organisational Development: concept and intervention techniques. Individual and organisational factors to stress, consequences of stress on individual and organisation, management of stress.
6. **Case Studies:** Some cases of real business world are required to be discussed.

MASTER OF INTERNATIONAL BUSINESS (MIB)

PAPER 511 : MANAGEMENT CONCEPTS AND ORGANISATIONAL BEHAVIOUR

Objective

The main objective of this paper is to familiarise the students with the basic concepts of management and factors underlying organisational behaviour.

Contents

1. **Introduction to Management:** Meaning, nature and importance of management; Management functions; Co-ordination; Managerial skills; Principles of management; Major schools of management thought : An overview.
2. **Planning:** Importance of planning; Types of plans; planning and decision making process.
3. **Organisation and Control:** Process of organising; Organisational structure and design - vertical and horizontal dimensions.
4. **Organisational Behaviour:** Introduction to organisational behaviour in management; Foundations of individual behaviour — personality perception; learning; values, attitudes and job Satisfaction; ability and motivation.
5. **Group:** Foundations of group behaviour; Communication and group decision making; Leadership: power and politics, conflict.
6. **Organisation:** Foundations of organisation structure; Job design, work settings and job stress; Organisational culture: Meaning, importance and characteristics of organisation culture.
7. **Organisation Change and Development:** Significance of change; Forces of change; Resistance to organisational change; Management of change; Organisation development : Concept, characteristics and assumptions; Goals, approaches and techniques of organisation development.

MASTER OF HUMAN RESOURCES AND ORGANISATION DEVELOPMENT (MHROD)

ORGANISATIONAL BEHAVIOUR

Objective

To acquaint the students with the determinants of intra-individual, inter-personnel and inter-group behaviour in organisational setting and to equip them with behavioural skills in managing people at work.

Contents

Unit I – ***Introduction:*** Organisational Behaviour: Concept, Determinants and Models.

Unit II – ***Individual Behaviour:*** Personality, Learning, Perception and Individual Decision-making, Values and Attitudes.

Management's assumptions about people: McGregor's Theory X and Theory Y Chris Argyris' Behaviour Pattern.

Motivation: Maslow's Need Hierarchy, Herzberg's Two-Factor Theory, Vroom's Expectancy Theory. OB Mod.

Unit III – ***Interpersonal Behaviour:*** Communication and Feedback, Transactional Analysis (TA), Johari Window.

Unit IV – ***Group Behaviour:*** Group Dynamics, Cohesiveness and Productivity Resistance to Change.

Conflict: Sources, Patterns, Levels and Resolution. Organisational Politics.

Leadership: Concept and Styles, Fielder's Contingency Model, House's Path-Goal Theory, Leadership Effectiveness.

Unit V – ***Organisational Processes:*** Control: Process and Behavioural Dimensions of Control.

Organisational Climate: Concept and Determinants of Organisation Culture.

Organisational Effectiveness: Concept and Measurement.

Organisational Change: Emerging issues in Organisational Behaviour, Case Studies.

MBA
ORGANISATIONAL DEVELOPMENT

Course Code : MS 239 **L-3** **T-0** **Credits-3**

Objective

The objective of this paper is to prepare students as organisational change facilitators using the knowledge and techniques of behavioural science.

Course Contents

Organisation Change – An Overview; Approaches to Problem Diagnosis: Some Major Techniques of Planned Change; Steps in OD, General OD Competencies. OD Skills.

Designing Interventions – Interpersonal, Team, Intergroup and System: Evaluation of OD. Ethics of OD Professional, Future of OD.

MASTER OF BUSINESS ECONOMICS (MBE)
PAPER 4 : ORGANISATIONAL BEHAVIOUR AND DEVELOPMENT

Individual Behaviour at work - Perception, Learning and Reinforcement, Motivation and Performance, Personality, Personal Values and Ethics, Cultural and Social Differences.

Group and Inter-Group Relations, Group Dynamics.

Organisational Processes - Leadership, Communication, power and Politics in Organisation.

Conflict Management.

Organisational Change and Development.

Organisation Development and Human Resource Planning, Appraisal.

Training and Development in Indian Enterprises and MNCs.

POST GRADUATE DIPLOMA IN GLOBAL BUSINESS OPERATIONS
PAPER 1.6 — ORGANISATIONAL PSYCHOLOGY

The objective of this paper is to provide broad understanding about basic concepts and techniques related to the study of human behaviour in work - environment so as to equip the participants to manage behavioural aspects of international business.

1. **Concept and Nature of Psychology in behaviour in Organisations.** Psychological Foundations of Organisational Behaviour, Perceptual processes, learning, Values and Attitudes. Work Motivation, Stress, Leadership and Influence process.
2. **Systems Approach to understanding organisations.**
3. **Organisations Culture & Climate**
4. **Group Dynamics.** Organisational Change. Organisational Development. Conflict Management. Team Building, Stress Management.
5. **Organisational Creativity and Innovations.**
6. **Power and Politics in Global Corporations.** Behavioural issues in managing across cultures and countries.

GGS INDRAPRASTHA UNIVERSITY

MBA

Management Process & Organisational Behaviour

Course Code: MS 101 L - 4 Credits - 4

Objectives: This course is designed to expose the students to fundamental concepts of management, its processes and behavioural dynamics in organisations.

Course Contents

1. **Introduction:** Meaning and Nature of Management, Management Approaches, Processes, Managerial Skills, Tasks and Responsibilities of a Professional Manager. (12 Hours)
2. **Organisational Structure and Process:** Organisational Culture and Climate, Managerial Ethos, Organisation Structure & Design, and Managerial Communication. (13 Hours)
3. **Organisation Behaviour: An Introduction, Behavioural Dynamics:** Individual Determinants of Organisation. Behaviour: Perception, Learning, Personality, Attitudes and Values, Motivation, Job Anxiety and Stress. Group Dynamics and Interpersonal Relations, Management of Organisational Conflicts, Management of Change, Leadership and Theories and Styles. (16 Hours)
4. **Planning and Controlling:** Planning Types and Process, Management By Objectives, Decision-Making Types and Models, Problem Solving Techniques, Controlling: Process and Techniques. (15 Hours)

BBA 201: ORGANISATIONAL BEHAVIOUR

Objectives

The course aims to provide an understanding of basic concepts, theories and techniques in the field of human behaviour at the individual, group and organisational levels in the changing global scenario. The course must be taught using case study method.

Unit I Lectures:-10

Introduction: Concept and nature of Organisational Behaviour; Contributing disciplines to the field of O.B.; O.B. Models; Need to understand human behaviour; Challenges and Opportunities.

Unit II Lectures:-16

Individual & Interpersonal Behaviour: Biographical Characteristics; Ability; Values; Attitudes – Formation, Theories, Organisation Related Attitude, Relationship between Attitude and Behaviour;

Personality – Determinants and Traits; Emotions; Learning-Theories and Reinforcement Schedules,

Perception – Process and Errors. Interpersonal Behaviour: Johari Window; Transactional Analysis –

Ego States, Types of Transactions, Life Positions, Applications of T.A.

Unit III Lectures:-14

Group Behaviour & Team Development: Concept of Group and Group Dynamics; Types of Groups; Formal and Informal Groups; Stages of Group Development, Theories of Group Formation: Group Norms. Group Cohesiveness; Group Think and Group Shift. Group Decision Making, Inter-Group Behaviour, Concept of Team Vs. Group, Types of Teams; Building and Managing Effective Teams.

Unit IV Lectures:-12

Organisation Culture and Conflict Management: Organisational Culture – Concept. Functions, Socialisation; Creating and sustaining culture; Managing Conflict – Sources, Types, Process and Resolution of Conflict; Managing Change; Resistance to Change, Planned Change. Managing Across Cultures; Empowerment and Participation.

UNIVERSITY OF PUNE

MBA PART I/12

(101) ORGANISATIONAL BEHAVIOUR & PRINCIPLES & PRACTICE OF MANAGEMENT

Section – I

1. Organisational Behaviour - Definition - Importance - Historical Background - Fundamental Concepts of OB - 21st Century corporates - Different models of OB i.e. autocratic, custodial, supportive, collegial and SOBC (6)
2. Personality & Attitudes - Meaning of personality - Development of personality - Nature and dimensions of attitude - Job Satisfaction - Organisational Commitment. (4)
3. Motivation - Motives - Characteristics - Classification of motives - Primary Motives - Secondary motives - Morale - Definition and relationship with productivity - Morale Indicators; Theories of Work Motivation - Maslow's theory of need hierarchy - Herzberg's theory of job loading. (6)
4. Group Dynamics and Teams - Theories of Group Formation - Formal Organisation and Informal Groups and their interaction - Importance of teams - Formation of teams - Team Work. (6)
5. Conflict Management - Traditional vis-à-vis Modern view of conflict - Stress management, Constructive and Destructive conflict - Conflict Process - Strategies for encouraging constructive conflict - Strategies for resolving destructive conflict. (5)
6. Leadership - Definition - Importance - Leadership Styles - Models and Theories of Leadership Styles. (3)

Section - II

Principles and Practices of Management

1. Basic concepts of management - Definition - Evolution of management thought - Functions of management. (6)
2. Planning - Nature and purpose - Setting objectives - Management by objectives - Strategies, policies and planning premises. (6)
3. Organising - Nature and purpose - Departmentation - Line and Staff Authority - Decentralisation - Coordination. (6)
4. Controlling - Process of controlling - Control techniques. (6)
5. Decision-making - Nature and purpose - Principles. (6)

MBA PART II
(307E) HUMAN RESOURCE MANAGEMENT SPECIALISATION
ORGANISATIONAL DEVELOPMENT

1. Introduction Organisational Development (OD) - Defining OD, Important characteristics of OD, Value, Beliefs and Assumptions underlying the field of OD.
2. Foundations of Organisational Development - Models of Change Management, Systems Theory, Parallel Learning Structure, Action Research.
3. Process of Organisational Development - Diagnosis, Why diagnosis - Importance of correct diagnosis in success of OD, SIX BOX model, 7 S Framework, Organisational Iceberg Model, Force Field Analysis.
4. OD Interventions - Introducing the term "interventions" - thinking about OD Interventions and classifying OD Interventions. (Role focused Interventions) Types of Interventions - Structural Interventions, Sociotechnical systems, Work redesign, Quality of work life projects, Total quality management, Reengineering.
5. Applications of OD - OD in Healthcare, School Systems and the Public Sector, Future directions in OD, OD Consultants - Role, Competencies and Ethical issues in OD Consulting.

UNIVERSITY OF MADRAS

DEGREE OF MASTER OF BUSINESS ADMINISTRATION – MBA
(FULL-TIME & PART-TIME)
MBA 1003 - ORGANISATIONAL BEHAVIOUR

Syllabus

1. **Behaviour:** Personality, Perception, Learning, Values and Introduction of Organisational Behaviour - Foundations of Individual Attitudes.
2. **Motivation:** Early theories, Contemporary theories; Motivation at work - Designing Motivating jobs.
3. **Group Dynamics:** Group Behaviour, Communication and Group Decision Making, Intergroup Relations.
4. **Leadership:** Trait, Behavioural and Contingency Theories; Power and Politics; Transactional Analysis (T.A.); Work Stress.
5. **Organisational Structure and Design:** Organisational Change and Development; Organisational Culture and Climate.

   Organisational Conflict: Causes, Types of Conflict, Management conflict.

BACHELOR OF BUSINESS ADMINISTRATION (BBA)
CORE SUBJECT : VI – ORGANISATIONAL BEHAVIOUR

Unit – I

Need and scope of organisational behavior - Theories of organisation - Individual difference vs Group intelligence tests -Measurement of intelligence - Personality Tests - Nature - Types and uses of perception.

Unit – II

Motivation - Financial and non-Financial motivational techniques - Job satisfaction - meaning - Factors - Theories - Measurement - Morale - Importance - Employee attitudes and behaviour and their significance to employee productivity.

Unit – III

Work environment - Good housekeeping practices - Design of workplace - Fatigue - Causes and prevention and their importance - Leadership - Types and theories of leadership.

Unit – IV

Group dynamics - Cohesiveness - Co-operation - Competition - Resolution - Sociometry - Group norms - Role position status.

Unit – V

Organisational culture and climate - Organisational Development.

NAGARJUNA UNIVERSITY

M. COM.
PAPER – II : ORGANISATIONAL BEHAVIOUR

Organisational Behaviour: Meaning–Scope–Significance–Approach to Organisational Behaviour – Foundations – Historical Development – Contributing disciplines – Theory X & Theory Y.

Individual: Models of Man – Personality : Meaning-Theories of Personality - Determinants of personality-perception: concept – process - principales - Learning; Concept - Principles - Theories - Reinforcement and punishment - Organisational Behaviour modification. Value: importance-Types-Sources of value system. Attitudes concept-Sources-Functions-theories-Changing attitudes.

Group Dynamics: Group Development-Types-Informal groups-formal groups Norms Cohesiveness-Group Decision making techniques-Stress-learning-causes-Effects of occupational stress-coping strategies.

Quality of work life: Total quality management- Reengineering - Bench marking-Empowerment-Learning organisation. Meaning-types-Organisational Behaviour in learning organisations:

Conflict: Types – Causes – Conflict resolution – Organisational culture. Definition – Characteristic – Types – Creating and sustaining organisational culture.

Organisational Change: Concept-Change process-Causes of Resistance-Measures to overcome change. Organisational Development; changing face of organisations-Organisational Development approaches and techniques – Critical assessment.

Organisational effectiveness. Mature – Approaches-Criteria for effectiveness-Implications. Organisational Climate: definition – Factors – affecting – Measurement – Developing Sound organisational climate.

GUJARAT UNIVERSITY

MBA
ORGANISATIONAL BEHAVIOUR

Objectives

(*i*) To introduce the fundamentals of human behaviour within the context of organisations and their environment, (*ii*) To apply the concepts for understanding behaviours of individuals and groups in the organisational context.

1. Organisational behaviour — concept, myth or science, contributing disciplines.
2. Foundations of individual behaviour — values, attitudes and job satisfaction, perception, individual decision-making ability and learning, ethics in decision making, Personality, Transactional Analysis : Ego state, life positions, script, types of transactions.
3. Motivation — concept, theories, including expectancy model and Theory Z.
4. Foundations of group behaviour — Definition and types of groups, stages of group development, group structure and processes, group behaviour, sociometry (analysing group behaviour), group decision-making.
5. Work-teams — Team vs group, types of teams, creating effective teams, turning individuals into team players, contemporary issues in managing teams.
6. Leadership and Trust — Meaning and theories of leadership, contemporary issues in leadership.
7. Power and Politics — Definition and bases of power, power tactics, power in groups (coalitions) sexual treatment (unequal power in the workplace), politics (power in action), factors contributing to political behaviour, politicking.
8. Conflict and Negotiation — Definition of conflict, functional and dysfunctional conflict, the conflict process, managing conflicts, giving and receiving feedback effectively, Johari Window.
9. Organisational culture — concept, Hofstede's dimensions, creating and sustaining culture, how employees learn culture, matching people with culture.
10. Organisational change and stress management — work stress and its management, meaning and consequences of stress, sources of stress, managing stress.

CONTENTS

PART – I : INDIVIDUAL BEHAVIOUR

1. Fundamentals of Human Behaviour **3–14**

1.1 Concept of Human Behaviour 3
1.2 Characteristics of Human Behaviour 4
1.3 Process of Human Behaviour 5
1.4 Factors Influencing Individual Behaviour 6
1.5 Individual Differences 7
1.6 Models of Man or Individual Behaviour 9
• Test Questions 12
• Case Study 13

2. Personality **15–30**

2.1 Concept of Personality 15
2.2 Determinants of Personality 17
2.3 Development of Personality 19
2.4 Theories of Personality 22
2.5 Personality Traits Influencing Behaviour 26
2.6 Measurement of Personality 27
2.7 Implications of Personality for Management 28
• Test Questions 29
• Case Study 30

3. Perception **31–43**

3.1 Concept of Perception 31
3.2 Process of Perception 33
3.3 Factors Influencing Perception 35
3.4 Interpersonal Perception 37
3.5 Perceptual Errors and Distortion 37
3.6 Perceptual Constancy, Perceptual Context and Perceptual Defence 39
3.7 Managerial Applications of Perception 40
3.8 How to Develop Perceptual Skills 40
• Test Questions 41
• Case Study 43

4. Learning and Behaviour Modification **44–57**

4.1 Concept and Nature of Learning 44
4.2 Process of Learning 45
4.3 Factors Affecting Learning 46
4.4 Theories of Learning 47
4.5 Reinforcement 50
4.6 Organisation Behaviour Modification (OB Mod) 53
• Test Questions 56
• Case Study 57

5. Attitudes and Values **58–73**

5.1 Concept of Attitudes 58
5.2 Components of Attitudes 60
5.3 Attitudes and Individual Behaviour 60
5.4 Theories of Attitude Formation 61
5.5 Factors Influencing Attitude Formation 62
5.6 Measurement of Attitudes 63
5.7 Effects of Employee Attitudes on Organisational Behaviour 65
5.8 Attitude Change 66
5.9 How to Develop Positive Attitudes 67
5.10 Concept of Values 68
5.11 Difference between Attitudes and Values 69
5.12 Types of Values 69
5.13 Factors Influencing Value Formation (Sources of Values) 71
5.14 Effect of Values on Behaviour 71
• Test Questions 12
• Case Study 13

6. Motivation **74–95**

6.1 Concept of Motivation 74
6.2 Motivation and Behaviour 76
6.3 Motivation and Performance 76
6.4 Theories or Models of Motivation 77
• Test Questions 91
• Case Study 93

PART – II : GROUP BEHAVIOUR

7. Interpersonal Behaviour and Transactional Analysis **99–111**

7.1 Concept and Nature of Interpersonal Behaviour 99

7.2 Transactional Analysis 100

• Test Questions 91

• Case Study 93

8. Group Dynamics **112–128**

8.1 Concept of Group Dynamics 112

8.2 Concept and Nature of Group 113

8.3 Types of Groups and Cliques 113

8.4 Stages in Group Development 116

8.5 Theories of Group Formation 116

8.6 Reasons for Emergence of Informal Groups [Benefits to Employees] 118

8.7 Functions of Informal Groups [Benefits to Management] 119

8.8 Dysfunctions (Demerits) of Informal Groups 119

8.9 How to Deal with Informal Groups 120

8.10 Factors Influencing Group Behaviour 120

8.11 Group Norms 121

8.12 Group Cohesiveness 122

8.13 Relationship between Group Cohesiveness and Productivity 123

• Test Questions 125

• Case Study 126

9. Power, Politics and Status **129–143**

9.1 Concept and Nature of Power 129

9.2 Difference between Power and Authority 130

9.3 Sources of Power 130

9.4 Traits of Successful Power Users 131

9.5 Guidelines for Effective Use of Power 132

9.6 Mulder's Theory of Power Distance 132

9.7 Tactics Used to Gain Power 133

9.8 Concept and Nature of Organisational Politics 134

9.9 Causes of Politics in Organisations 135

9.10 Dysfunctions of Organisational Politics 136
9.11 Handling Organisational Politics 137
9.12 Concept of Status 137
9.13 Sources or Determinants of Status 138
9.14 Functions of Status System 138
9.15 Status Symbols 139
9.16 Problems Caused by Status System 140
• Test Questions 141
• Case Study 142

10. Leadership and Influence 144–174

10.1 Concept and Nature of Leadership 145
10.2 Difference between Leadership and Management 145
10.3 Formal and Informal Leaders 146
10.4 Importance of Leadership 146
10.5 Styles of Leadership 147
10.6 Continuum of Leadership Behaviour 150
10.7 Trait Theories of Leadership 151
10.8 Behavioural Theories of Leadership 152
10.9 Situational Theories of Leadership 158
10.10 Transactional Leadership 167
10.11 Transformational Leadership 168
• Test Questions 168
• Case Study 171

11. Control 175–186

11.1 Concept of Control 175
11.2 Nature of Control 176
11.3 Relationship between Control and Planning 176
11.4 Need and Significance of Control 177
11.5 Limitations or Dysfunctions of Control 177
11.6 Steps in the Process of Control 178
11.7 Kinds or Types of Control 179
11.8 Control of Human Element 180
11.9 Reactions of People to Controls 181
11.10 Behavioural Implications of Control 182

11.11 Reasons for Human Resistance to Controls 183
11.12 Overcoming Resistance to Controls 183
11.13 Management by Exception (MBE) 184
• Test Questions 184
• Case Study 185

12. Morale and Job Satisfaction 187–194

12.1 Concept of Morale 187
12.2 Nature (Characteristics) of Morale 188
12.3 Measurement of Morale 188
12.4 Factors Influencing Morale 189
12.5 Morale and Productivity 190
12.6 Building High Morale 191
12.7 Concept of Job Satisfaction 191
12.8 Importance of Job Satisfaction 192
12.9 Consequences of Job Dissatisfaction 192
12.10 Determinants of Job Satisfaction 193
• Test Questions 193
• Case Study 194

PART – III : OVERALL BEHAVIOUR

13. Nature and Types of Organisations 197–209

13.1 Need for Study of Organisations 197
13.2 Concept of Organisation 198
13.3 Characteristics of Organisations 198
13.4 Organisation as a System 199
13.5 Organisations and Biological Systems 201
13.6 Importance of Organisations 202
13.7 Typologies (Types) of Organisations 203
• Test Questions 207
• Case Study 208

14. Organisation and Environment 210–218

14.1 Concept of Environment 210
14.2 Nature of Environment 211
14.3 Emery and Trist Typology of Environment 212

14.4 Dimensions of Environment 213
14.5 Organisation-Environment Interface 214
14.6 Strategies to Deal with Environment 216
- Test Questions 217
- Case Study 218

15. Nature and Scope of Organisational Behaviour 219–230

15.1 Concept of Organisational Behaviour 220
15.2 Nature of Organisational Behaviour 220
15.3 Role of Organisational Behaviour 221
15.4 Foundations of Organisational Behaviour 223
15.5 Contribution of Behavioural Sciences 224
15.6 Models of Organisational Behaviour 225
15.7 Difference Between Organisation Theory and Organisational Behaviour 226
15.8 Determinants of Organisational Behaviour 227
- Test Questions 228
- Case Study 230

16. Organisational Goals 231–243

16.1 Concept and Nature of Organisational Goals 231
16.2 Importance or Functions of Organisational Goals 232
16.3 Types of Organisational Goals 232
16.4 Goal Setting Process 233
16.5 Organisation as a Coalition 234
16.6 Influence of Environment on Organisational Goals 235
16.7 Goal Succession 236
16.8 Goal Distortion 236
16.9 Goal Displacement 237
16.10 Conflict between Organisational Goals and Individual Goals 239
16.11 Integration of Individual Goals and Organisational Goals 241
- Test Questions 242
- Case Study 243

17. Organisational Change 244–259

17.1 Concept and Nature of Organisational Change 244
17.2 Factors or Forces in Organisational Change 246
17.3 The Process of Planned Change 247
17.4 Causes of Resistance to Change 249

17.5 Overcoming Resistance to Change 251
17.6 Group Dynamics for Change 252
17.7 Force Field Analysis 253
17.8 Change Agents 254
17.9 Organisational Growth and Change 255
• Test Questions 257
• Case Study 259

18. Organisation Development **260–282**

18.1 Concept of Organisation Development 260
18.2 Characteristics of Organisation Development 261
18.3 Difference between Organisation Development and Management Development 262
18.4 Objectives of Organisation Development 263
18.5 Benefits (Role) of Organisation Development 263
18.6 Limitations of Organisation Development 264
18.7 Assumptions of Organisation Development 265
18.8 Process of Organisation Development 265
18.9 Action Research Model of OD 266
18.10 OD Interventions or Techniques 267
• Test Questions 278
• Case Study 281

19. Organisational Climate and Culture **283–293**

19.1 Concept of Organisational Climate 283
19.2 Characteristics of Organisational Climate 284
19.3 Dimensions of Organisational Climate 284
19.4 Importance of Organisational Climate 285
19.5 Determinants of Organisational Climate 286
19.6 Improving Organisational Climate 287
19.7 Concept of Organisational Culture 287
19.8 Characteristics of Organisational Culture 288
19.9 Subcultures 289
19.10 Impact of Organisational Culture 289
19.11 Socialisation 290
• Test Questions 290
• Case Study 292

20. Organisational Conflict **294–307**

20.1 Concept of Organisational Conflict 294

20.2 Nature of Organisational Conflict 295

20.3 Stages in Organisational Conflict 296

20.4 Changing Views of Organisational Conflict 297

20.5 Functions (Positive Outcomes) of Organisational Conflict 297

20.6 Dysfunctions (Negative Effects) of Organisational Conflict 298

20.7 Levels of Organisational Conflict 298

20.8 Management of Organisational Conflict 303

- Test Questions 305
- Case Study 307

21. Organisational Effectiveness **308–319**

21.1 The Concept of Organisational Effectiveness 308

21.2 Effectiveness Versus Efficiency 309

21.3 Measurement of Effectiveness 310

21.4 Approaches to Organisational Effectiveness 311

21.5 Factors Influencing Organisational Effectiveness 316

21.6 Likert's Model of Effectiveness 317

21.7 Adaptive Coping Cycle 317

- Test Questions 318
- Case Study 319

PART – I
INDIVIDUAL BEHAVIOUR

1. Fundamentals of Human Behaviour
2. Personality
3. Perception
4. Learning and Behaviour Modification
5. Attitudes and Values
6. Motivation

CHAPTER

1

FUNDAMENTALS OF HUMAN BEHAVIOUR

CHAPTER OUTLINE

1.1 Concept of Human Behaviour
1.2 Characteristics of Human Behaviour
1.3 Process of Human Behaviour
1.4 Factors Influencing Individual Behaviour
1.5 Individual Differences
1.5.1 Nature
1.5.2 Causes
1.5.3 Implications
1.5.4 Whole Person
1.6 Models of Man or Individual Behaviour
1.6.1 Rational-Economic Man Model
1.6.2 Social Man Model
1.6.3 Organisation Man Model
1.6.4 Self-Actualising Man Model
1.6.5 Complex Man Model
- **Test Questions**
- **Case Study**

Every organisation consists of people or human beings. The main problem of an organisation is how to maximise the contributions its people make towards the accomplishment of organisational goals. These contributions depend primarily on the thinking and behaviour of human beings. Therefore, managers are always interested in understanding how and why people behave in organisational settings.

1.1 CONCEPT OF HUMAN BEHAVIOUR

Human behaviour means what human beings think, feel and do. It is of two types – overt and covert. **Overt behaviour** refers to the observable and measurable activity of human beings. It consists of mental process (*e.g.,* decision-making) and physical process (*e.g.,* handling a machine). **Covert behaviour** refers to behaviour that cannot be observed or measured. It consists of attitudes, feelings, perceptions of people. These may be favourable or unfavourable.

The two types of human behaviour are interdependent and interrelated. The covert behaviour shapes and influences the overt behaviour. The overt behaviour is a manifestation of covert behaviour. Therefore, it is necessary to understand the total human behaviour.

There are two contrary assumptions behind human behaviour. The traditional assumption is that human behaviour is autonomous or spontaneous. This assumption is based on cultural values which suggest that an individual is an autonomous moral agent and behaves largely in the context of cultural values. His behaviour may be good (right) or bad (wrong) depending on the particular culture. In case the behaviour of a person is consistent with the cultural values it is considered good, otherwise it is bad. According to a contrary (modern) assumption human behaviour is caused and it is not spontaneous. Human behaviour is systematic not random and orderly not arbitrary. Several factors within and outside a person influence his behaviour. A person's behaviour affects the behaviour of others and is affected by others' behaviour. In fact, a person's behaviour is the outcome of the total environment of which he is a part. In other words, a human being is not a self-contained entity. Rather he is a subsystem of a wider system – family, group or society. Therefore, human behaviour can be understood by analysing the causes behind it. Similarly, human behaviour can be directed and controlled by influencing the underlying causes.

Thus, there are two main implications for understanding human behaviour :

(*i*) Human behaviour can better be understood in terms of cause and effect relationship rather than in philosophical terms. Managers can better direct organisations towards goal accomplishment by analysing the causes of human behaviour.

(*ii*) Human behaviour is the outcome of several interrelated and ever changing factors. Therefore, human behaviour cannot be predicted perfectly. Managers have often to make limited generalisations about human behaviour in organisations on the basis of incomplete information.

1.2 CHARACTERISTICS OF HUMAN BEHAVIOUR

The foregoing description reveals the following characteristics of human behaviour.

(*i*) **Caused:** Human behaviour is caused, not spontaneous or autonomous. It can be understood by analysing the factors that cause it.

(*ii*) **Dynamic:** Behaviour of an individual is not static or stable. It keeps on changing from one situation or time period to another.

(*iii*) **Multidimensional:** Human behaviour has several dimensions and assumes different forms. Sometimes, it is observable and at other times non-observable.

(*iv*) **Complex:** Human behaviour is quite complex and difficult to understand. Complete information about the factors influencing it is not always available.

(*v*) **Partly Predictable:** It is not possible to predict human behaviour with full accuracy. It is influenced by a large number of variables which keep on changing.

(*vi*) **Controllable:** Human behaviour can be controlled to a great extent by controlling the causes affecting it.

(*vii*) **Goal-Directed:** People behave in order to protect and promote their interests and the interests of their near and dear ones.

1.3 PROCESS OF HUMAN BEHAVIOUR

Assuming that human behaviour is caused, it can be explained in the form of a process. Over the years, experts in behavioural sciences have developed three different models of the process of human behaviour. These are as follows :

1. **S–R Model:** The classical stimulus (S) Response (R) model suggests that human behaviour or Response (R) is caused by a stimulus (S) or certain variables. These variables are external environment (stimulus). A stimulus is an agent such as heat, cold, light, information, etc. that directly influences the activity of a person. No human action takes place without the stimulus. Stimulus is the total situation in which a person happens to be. Environmental forces or the situations shape and determine the behaviour of an individual at any given point of time.

   The S–R model is quite simple and easy to understand. But it offers an incomplete explanation of the factors causing human behaviour. It overlooks the role of internal feelings (motivation) in shaping a person's behaviour.

   The behaviour of a person is caused not only by external environment but also by the person's internal feelings. The situation interacts with the person before causing his/her behaviour. Thus, the SR model does not take into account all the causes of human behaviour.

2. **S–O–R Model:** In the S–R model the person (organism) is treated as passive and immobile. But in the S–O–R model, organisation (O) mediates between the stimulus and the response. It scans its surroundings, monitors its own actions, seeks certain conditions and avoids others. The organism also performs maintenance and adjustment functions. In the maintenance function, the organism ensures its health and growth. Maintenance organs are of three types — **receptors** (sense organs), **connectors** (nervous organs), and **effectors** (muscles and glands). In the adjustment function, the organism monitors its activities to satisfy its needs and overcomes obstacles.

   The S–O–R model is an improvement over the S–R model as it recognises the role of the human being. But S–O–R model is a simplistic and mechanistic approach that does not explain fully the complex nature of human behaviour.

3. **S–O–B–C Model:** This is a modification and extension of the S–O–R model. In this model, S represents the situation which consists of all aspects of the environment—stimulus, socio-cultural environment, physical environment, etc. O stands for the organism consisting of both physical and psychological being. B is the behaviour pattern, including both overt and covert behaviour. C stands for overt and covert consequences. Thus, the S–O–B–C model is more complex and comprehensive view of human behaviour than the earlier models. In the S–O–B–C model, behaviour is the outcome of interaction between situation (S), organism (O), behaviour pattern (B) and consequences (C) as shown in Fig. 1.1.

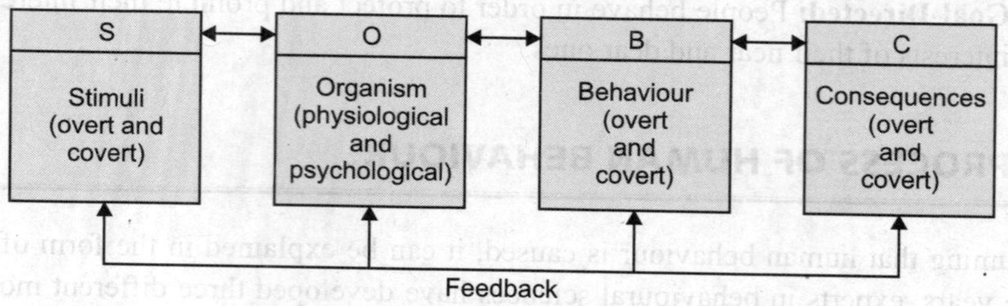

Fig. 1.1: S–O–B–C Model of Human Behaviour

There is complex interaction among different elements of this model of human behaviour. This complexity arises due to two main factors. **First**, each element of the model contains several variables. Different elements interact among themselves. Each element affects the other elements and is in turn affected by them [see double-headed arrows in Fig. 1.1). **Second**, the physiological and the psychological variables of the organism interact with the situation and exercise significant impact on the process of human behaviour.

No doubt S–O–B–C model is comprehensive. However, it presents a sketchy view of human behaviour.

Understanding of human behaviour is necessary for managers because they have to channelise individual behaviour towards organisational objectives. Such channelisation requires a good person-job fit. Such a fit occurs when the person's contributions (organisational loyalty, efforts, productivity, etc.) match the incentives (job security, pay, good working conditions, etc.) offered by the organisation. As an employee, each person wants to satisfy a specific set of needs and contributes a set of job-related behaviours. An organisation can achieve a good person-job fit by satisfying these needs fully and taking advantages of job-related behaviours of each employee. This is possible only when those managing the organisation understand and predict individual behaviour. In order to understand and predict human behaviour managers must understand the factors that influence individual behaviour.

1.4 FACTORS INFLUENCING INDIVIDUAL BEHAVIOUR

The factors that influence individual behaviour are often called the foundations of individual behaviour. These factors may be classified into two broad categories as shown in Fig. 1.2.

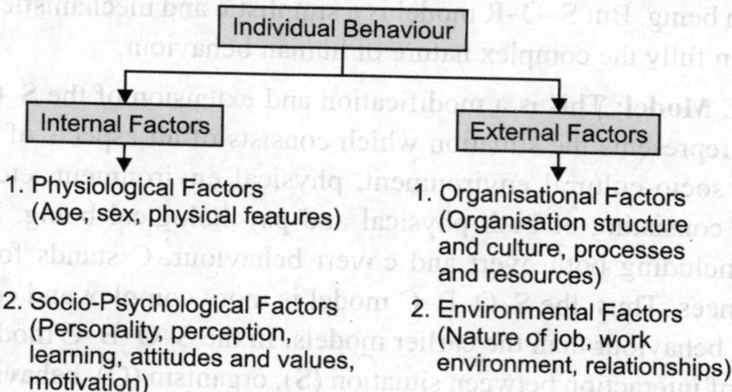

Fig. 1.2: Factors Influencing Individual Behaviour

Individual behaviour means some concrete action by a person. For example, how a teacher behaves in the class reflects his behaviour. The behaviour of an individual depends on several factors. Some of these factors lie within an individual (*i.e.*, personality, feelings, etc.) while some others lie outside him (*i.e.*, external environment). The environment acts as a stimulus and the person responds to it. The response depends upon the physiological and socio-psychological characteristics of the person. For example, a teacher's behaviour is affected by the behaviour of his students and in turn affects their behaviour. Thus, individual behaviour is not a self-induced phenomenon but is affected by a larger system (*e.g.*, family, society, etc.) within which an individual functions. Some of the factors influencing individual behaviour are described below:

1. **Personality:** Personality refers to personal traits, such as aggressiveness, persistence, dominance, etc. An individual's personality determines the type of activities that he or she is suited for and the effectiveness with which the person would perform the task. Managers should take into account the personality of an employee while assigning a job/position to him in the organisation.
2. **Perception:** Perception means the viewpoint by which a person interprets the given situation. For example, a teacher may perceive that the students sitting on front benches are more superior than those sitting on back benches. An individual's behaviour is influenced not by what the situation really is but by how the individual perceives it.
3. **Learning:** The behaviour of a person also depends upon his ability which means skills and capabilities. Ability is the outcome of learning. A person learns through education, training and experience. An able person tends to engage in behaviour required for effective performance of the job.
4. **Motivation:** Motivation refers to the forces operating within a person. These forces may be internal (*e.g.*, a challenging job) or external (*e.g.*, rewards). The attitudes, beliefs goals and values of a person also influence his motivation. Motivation causes a person to engage in certain kinds of behaviour than others. In spite of all facilities, a person may not work effectively unless he is motivated to perform well.
5. **Organisational Factors:** The systems and resources of an organisation influence the behaviour of its members. Systems such as organisational structure and hierarchy assist or constrain what individuals do and how they do it. The technology, finances, leadership and other resources of an organisation also influence individual behaviour.
6. **Environmental Factors:** The social environment of an individual refers to relationship with family members, friends, co-workers, superiors, etc. The behaviour of others influences an individual's behaviour. Similarly, the cultural background of a person in terms of his values and beliefs influences his behaviour.

1.5 INDIVIDUAL DIFFERENCES

The science of human behaviour is based on the assumption that every individual is different from others. Individuals differ in physical characteristics, personality, intelligence, attitudes, skills, etc. Such differences are reflected in their behaviour. There can be (*i*) differences in the behaviour of an individual over time (intra individual differences), and (*ii*) differences in the behaviour of individuals in the same situation (inter individual differences).

1.5.1 Nature of Individual Differences

With respect to work, people may differ in the following ways:

(*i*) People differ in their preference for working hours. Some people prefer to start the working day early and finish it early in the evening. Others prefer the opposite of this.

(*ii*) People differ in their preference for compensation plan. Some people like to work under piece wage system while others prefer time wage system.

(*iii*) People differ in the kinds of jobs they would like to perform. Some people prefer challenging jobs while others prefer routine and secure jobs.

(*iv*) People differ in the rewards they seek. Some people prefer financial rewards while others prefer non-financial rewards.

(*v*) People differ in their liking for the style of supervision. Some people prefer to depend upon the boss for decision making and like to work under autocratic leadership. Others want to be their own boss and seek democratic leadership.

(*vi*) People differ in their tolerance for stress and ambiguity. Some people perform better in stressful and ambiguous situations while others are not able to bear stress and ambiguity.

1.5.2 Causes of Individual Differences

Differences in the behaviour of individuals arise due to individual variables and situational variables.

1. **Individual Variables:** An individual is characterised by certain physiological and socio-psychological variables. Physiological characteristics like physical build-up, sensory organs and nervous system affect a person's behaviour. These characteristics change over time as a person gains maturity with age. Socio-psychological characteristics such as personality, perception, attitudes and values change over time due to learning. An individual continuously interacts with his social and cultural environment and thereby learns new behaviour patterns. Both physiological and socio-psychological variables together make an individual different from others. Therefore, the behaviour of one person tends to be different from the behaviour of others.

2. **Situational Variables:** In the context of an organisation, situational variables include organisation structure, organisational processes (*e.g.,* motivation, leadership, communication and control) and organisational culture. In the context of job, nature of job and the overall environment in which the job is performed are situational variables. All these situational variables exercise a significant influence on a person's behaviour.

1.5.3 Implications of Individual Differences

The principle of individual differences suggests that a manager should be careful while dealing with people. As individuals differ in their goals, feelings, attitudes, etc. they need to be treated differently. Management can secure the desired behaviour from people by understanding and appreciating individual differences. A good manager must possess a flexible approach and a range of skills to cater to different needs and motives of individuals.

An organisation requires people with different qualities and capacities to perform different jobs. Performance can be maximised only when each job is performed by the person best suited to perform it. Understanding of individual differences helps management in selecting the right person for each job, in assigning jobs to individuals, and in motivating and leading people. Such understanding also enables management to minimise employee absenteeism and employee turnover. Scientific techniques have been developed to identify and measure individual differences. These techniques can be used in selection and placement of right persons for various jobs.

Thus, the principle of individual differences is widely applicable in selection, placement, training, supervision, motivation and leadership of employees. In order to secure maximum cooperation from individuals, the type of motivation, the control system and the style of leadership must be such that can satisfy their different needs and motives.

1.5.4 The Whole Person

According to the concept of whole person, a person's behaviour at work cannot be understood in isolation. An individual comes to the workplace as a complete person. His background, sentiments, emotions, feelings, etc. cannot be separated from the skills he uses on the job. A person carries the problems of his private life to the workplace and these affect his work performance. Similarly, the environment at the workplace affects his private life. An individual may carry workplace problems and tensions at home and these affect his behaviour with his family.

Human beings are unlike other factors of production because they have a mind which thinks and a heart which feels. Therefore, individuals should be treated with respect and dignity.

1.6 MODELS OF MAN OR INDIVIDUAL BEHAVIOUR

While dealing with people, managers make some assumptions about their nature. Managerial effectiveness in dealing with people depends on the degree to which these assumptions fit the actual situation. Several models of man have been developed to explain and understand the behaviour of individuals. Each model is based on a separate set of assumptions. Edgar Schein[1] has identified four models – rational-economic man, social man, self-actualising man, and complex man. In addition, William Whyte[2] has suggested 'organisation man'. These five models are explained below:

1. **Rational-Economic Man:** This is the oldest model. According to this model, the rational-economic man strives to maximise his self-interest. His decisions are based on rationality because he takes into account the costs associated with his efforts and the benefits he will be getting from these efforts. The rational-economic man model is based on the following assumptions:

   (*a*) Man is motivated primarily by economic incentives. He will do what maximises his economic gain.

   (*b*) A man's feelings are essentially irrational and must be controlled so that these do not interfere with rationality and self-interest.

   (*c*) The organisation controls the economic incentives and man remains mostly passive. The organisation can manipulate, motivate and control man.

   (*d*) Organisations can and must be designed in such a way as to control man's feelings and unpredictable behaviour.

1 Edgar H. Schein, **Organisational Psychology,** Prentice Hall of India, New Delhi, 1979, pp 70-71.
2 William H. Whyte, **The Organisation Man,** Doubleday Anchor Books, New York, 1956, pp 7-8.

A rational-economic man is largely self-centred and this model is reflected in McGregor's assumptions of Theory X. The essence of this model is that people can be induced to produce more just by providing economic incentives. This model is based on classical organisation theory. The classical models of designing organisation structures and processes have several shortcomings and do not suit the present-day conditions. Economic incentives like piece-wage system can work as long as man is not reasonably satisfied with his money. The rational-economic man model ignores the human characteristics that all men possess. This model also overlooks contingent and environmental factors. The assumptions of this model constrain understanding and predicting human behaviour.

2. **Social Man Model:** According to this model, man is a part of the society. Therefore, he seeks satisfaction of those needs which help to maintain his social relationships. This model shifts the focus from the individual to 'groups' and 'society' in which the individual functions.

   Man is responsive to group pressures and is receptive to group problems and sanctions. The social man model is based on the following assumptions:

   (*a*) Man is basically motivated by his social needs and he strives to get satisfaction by maintaining relationship with others.

   (*b*) Man is more responsive to group pressures and sanctions than to the incentives and controls of management in the organisation. This is so because he gives more importance to social relationship than to economic gain.

   (*c*) Man will obey and comply orders of management so long as these are in conformity with satisfaction of his social needs and group goals.

   (*d*) Work has become meaningless and dull due to specialisation, rationalisation and industrialisation. Such work creates alienation, frustration and conflict. Therefore, managers should organise work in such a way that develops a sense of belonging among people.

   Social man model is the outcome of Elton Mayo's Hawthorne Experiments conducted during 1927-32. How does a manager motivate and control people depends on the assumptions he makes about them. The assumptions of the social man model have several implications for managers. **First**, managers should focus attention on social as well as economic needs of people. **Second,** managers should analyse and understand man's behaviour in terms of groups and not on individual basis. **Third,** economic incentives alone cannot motivate people and their feelings and social relationships need to be considered. More democratic and free organisation structures and processes are needed for this purpose. **Fourth**, managers should act as facilitators and sympathetic supporters rather than as creators of work and controllers of behaviour.

3. **Organisation Man Model:** William H. Whyte has suggested the concept of 'organisation man'. According to him, loyalty to the organisation and cooperation with fellow workers is most important for a person. Therefore, he is willing to sacrifice his individuality for the sake of the organisation. The organisation man model is based on the following assumptions:

   (*a*) The group is the source of creativity. The individual by himself is isolated and meaningless. Only when he collaborates with others does he create. Individual helps to produce a whole that is greater than the sum of its parts.

(*b*) Belongingness is the ultimate need of the individual. There should not be conflicts between man and society because what is normally considered conflict is merely misunderstanding and breakdown in communication.

(*c*) The science can achieve the goal of belongingness. By applying the methods of science, the obstacles to consensus can be eliminated and an equilibrium can be created where society's needs and the needs of the individual are one and the same.

According to the organisation man model, there is no conflict between organisation and individual. Even if there is any conflict, it can be overcome by sacrificing the individual interest in favour of organisational interest. This proposition is based on the assumption that the organisation will take care of the individual interest. The organisation man model is an extension of the social man model.

4. **Self-Actualising Man Model:** According to this model, man's inherent need is to create new things by making use of his skills and capabilities. He is characterised by high degree of dynamism and individuality. There is a conflict between self-actualising man and the formal organisation because the formal organisation does not allow him to satisfy his self-actualisation needs. The self-actualising man model is based on the following assumptions:

(*a*) Various needs of man can be arranged in hierarchy. For example, Maslow has arranged human needs in a hierarchy – physiological, safety, belongingness, esteem and self-actualisation. Any unsatisfied need motivates man. Since man attempts to satisfy his needs according to this hierarchy, self-actualisation becomes his ultimate goal. Therefore, man tries to make a sense and meaning in his work.

(*b*) Man moves from a state of immaturity to a state of maturity in the process of self-actualising himself.

(*c*) Man is essentially self-motivated and self-controlled. Therefore, any externally imposed incentive and control will threaten him and lead to less mature adjustment.

(*d*) There is an inherent conflict between traditional organisation structure and self-actualising man because such a structure is based on the assumptions of immature personality.

These assumptions are largely based on McGregor's Theory Y[3] and Argyris's immaturity-maturity theory[4]. Self-actualisation man model suggests that people in work organisations require more autonomy, incentives based on intrinsic factors, and participation throughout the organisational processes. These factors increase commitment to organisational goals, release the potential of people and induce them to work in pursuit of the goals.

5. **Complex Man Model:** The four models described above are based on simplistic assumptions about the nature of man and his behaviour. Human behaviour is not as simple as is assumed and man does not behave according to a set pattern. Several complex variables influence human behaviour and these variables are quite unpredictable. Moreover, everyone does not behave in the same manner in a given situation due to

3 Douglas McGregor, **The Human Side of Enterprise,** McGraw Hill, New York, 1960.

4 Chris Argyris, **Personality and Organisation,** Harper Collins, New York, 1955.

individual differences. The complex man model suggests that human beings are complex and their behaviour cannot be predicted accurately. The complex man model is based on the following assumptions:

(*a*) Man is motivated by several variables and there is no one universal hierarchy of needs. There are several overlapping needs and degree of satisfaction desired may differ from person to person.

(*b*) A man learns many motives through interaction with the organisation. Therefore, the need pattern depends both on the individual and his contacts with the organisation.

(*c*) Need pattern and behaviour differ from person to person. Therefore, the need for direction and control is not the same for all.

(*d*) There is no direct cause and effect relationship between needs and behaviour. For example, two persons showing the same set of needs may behave differently. Therefore, understanding of human needs does not provide full understanding of human behaviour.

(*e*) The same man responds and behaves differently in various situations. Therefore, there is no universal strategy to deal with him.

The complex man model suggests a contingency approach to management. Under this approach the style of motivation and leadership varies with the situation. The complex man model presents a more realistic picture of human behaviour. However, this model is quite complex.

TEST QUESTIONS

1. What do you understand by human behaviour? Distinguish between overt behaviour and covert behaviour.
2. "Human behaviour is complex". Do you agree? Give reasons.
3. "Behaviour is not always rational". Explain.
4. "Human behaviour is not spontaneous. It is caused, motivated and goal directed". Discuss.
5. Explain different models concerning the process of human behaviour. Which model would you suggest and why?
6. Describe the nature and causes of individual differences.
7. What are the implications of individual differences for management?
8. Explain the factors that influence the behaviour of individuals in an organisation.
9. Critically examine different models of individual behaviour in organisations.
10. Write short notes on:

    (*a*) Whole Person

    (*b*) Organisation Man

    (c) Complex Man
11. In the process of growing up people make assumptions about self and others in the environment. How do these assumptions affect the life positions of an individual? Identify and discuss the techniques to overcome the problems of stroke economy.

12. It is said, "In the process of growing up people make assumptions about themselves and other significant people in the environment". How do these assumptions get operationalised into life positions for an individual? Discuss the role of strokes in the development of life positions.
13. List out the similarities and differences among individuals.
14. From a managerial standpoint, why is it important to understand common patterns in behaviour rather than assuming each individual is unique?
15. Explain the relevance of individual differences.
16. How individual behaviour is different from group behaviour? Which factors influence individual behaviour?
17. "Behaviour of a person is always unpredictable"? Explain, giving reasons for your answer.

CASE STUDY

Sunder Chemicals was established in the year 1945 with about 40 workers and was manufacturing a couple of pharmaceutical products. After three years of initial crisis, the company found itself in a very prosperous situation. In 1965, the company employed about 25,000 employees working in 15 different departments.

Mr. Parikh was incharge of the Tablet department having about 30 workers. In the day shift, Parikh was assisted by Mr. Patel for the general supervision of the department.

Mr. Joshi was one of the workers in the Tablet department about whom Patel did not have a good opinion as Joshi was in the habit of remaining absent without leave. Patel often found him taking leave under false pretexts. Patel did not have any other complaint about Joshi.

One day Joshi approached Patel with a request to grant him leave for a week, as he wanted to go for a pilgrimage with his family. Patel this time flatly refused to grant leave to him saying that he was not prepared to believe him considering his past record. Joshi felt very sorry about this and seemed to be disturbed.

During the lunch break, he was not in a mood to talk with his co-workers with whom he otherwise talked very cheerfully. On observing this, Mr. Solanki, a very old worker who was with the company from its inception, asked Joshi if there was something wrong with him. Joshi narrated the matter and broke into tears saying that his old parents would be unable to go on a pilgrimage.

Solanki was very popular among the group and always helped his co-workers by representing their case to the management. He was in general very hostile towards the officers and they in turn did not have good opinion about him. Solanki assured Joshi that he would certainly get his leave granted.

Solanki went to see Patel on the same day and found him giving instructions to some workers. Throwing the leave application on Patel's table, Solanki very arrogantly asked him why he was not sanctioning leave to Joshi. Patel felt very bad about the manner in which Solanki asked this and that too in front of his subordinates. But, controlling his emotions, he simply told him to ask Joshi to discuss the same with him. Solanki said that Joshi had authorised him to discuss this matter. He further accused Patel by saying that he unnecessarily harassed workers and that he will have to give up this habit, or he should be prepared to face the consequences. Patel, feeling very much insulted, asked him (Solanki) to get out of the department. On hearing this Solanki reacted very furiously and pushing Patel physically, told him, "I will now straighten you." After saying this, he himself left the department. Immediately, Patel saw Parikh and briefed him about the incident. Parikh regarded this as a very serious matter, and informed the Personnel Officer, Mr. Amin, to take appropriate action in the matter. Considering this as a gross misconduct, Mr. Amin served Solanki with a charge-sheet. The company had a consistent policy for disciplinary action and in such cases the punishment would be that of discharge.

Solanki was a very active member of the representative union which had very good relations with the management. Management always supported this union against another union which was very aggressive and protested against all actions of the mangement. When workers of the department came to know that Solanki had been charge-sheeted, they all approached the Secretary (of the recognised union) and strongly requested him to see that Solanki did not lose his job. They all agreed that Solanki was, to some extent, at fault. The Secretary, after hearing the full story, remarked that Solanki should have rather taken the constitutional course to deal with the matter. The workers said that in any case Solanki should not lose the job, as he had fought for his co-worker and not for himself. Considering the insistence of the workers the Secretary decided to see Amin. In the meantime, a written petition was also handed over to Amin by the workers.

The Secretary met Amin and conveyed to him the feeling of the workers. He pointed out that this was the first time when workers had expressed their desire so forcefully. The Secretary further requested Amin to reconsider the case for the following reasons :

(*i*) All the workers were insistent and felt involved in the matter, and if they were dissatisfied, the popularity of the union may decline, thus paying way for the other obstinate union.

(*ii*) The Secretary assured that he would see to it that Solanki does not misbehave like this in future.

Amin had been until now very consistent with the policy and he thought that this may become a very significant deviation from the rules. On the other hand, he thought that it would be rather difficult for him to observe consistency in this case, as otherwise he will have to displease the workers and perhaps the other union might take up the opportunity to establish a footing in the company. In the meanwhile, Parikh telephoned Amin and said that his workers had approached him and requested him to consider the case sympathetically. He insisted that he considered this as a very serious thing and that no mercy may be shown in Solanki's case.

Questions

1. What is the problem in the case?
2. Indicate the individual, managerial and organisational causes that have led to the problem.
3. What other realistic alternatives did Patel, Parikh and Amin have which could have avoided the problem? How can you explain Patel's behaviour?
4. Discuss the alternatives now available to Parikh and Amin. Discuss the consequences of these alternatives for the organisation and the feasibility of enforcing these alternatives.

CHAPTER

2

PERSONALITY

CHAPTER OUTLINE

2.1 Concept of Personality
2.2 Determinants of Personality
2.3 Development of Personality
2.4 Theories of Personality
2.5 Personality Traits Influencing Behaviour
2.6 Measurement of Personality
2.7 Implications of Personality for Organisation and Management
- **Test Questions**
- **Case Study**

An organisation is a collection of people who have united to achieve certain common objectives. Individuals are the basic building blocks of an organisation. It is, therefore, necessary to study individual behaviour for understanding the organisation. The study of personality and its development provides an insight into individual behaviour. Individuals respond differently to organisational environment due to differences in their personality. Personality affects perception, learning, motivation and other psychological processes. An individual has no meaning without personality as it reflects the whole man concept. According to James,[1] "It is better to consider the individual aspects of a person's make-up as bricks, and personality as the whole house built of bricks, but held together with cement."

2.1 CONCEPT OF PERSONALITY

The term 'personality' is derived from the Latin word 'personnare' which means "to speak through". This Latin word denotes the masks which actors used to wear in ancient Greece and Rome.

Traditionally, personality is used to refer to how people influence others through their external appearance. However, mere external appearance does not constitute the whole personality. According to Ruch[2], personality consists of the following :

1 D.E. James, **Introduction to Psychology,** Constable, London, 1968, p 219.

2 Floyd L. Ruch, **Personality and Life,** Scott Fresman, Chicago, 1963, p 353.

(*i*) external appearance and behaviour;

(*ii*) inner awareness of self as a permanent organising force; and

(*iii*) the particular pattern or organisation of measurable traits, both inner and outer.

Some more definitions of personality are given below :

According to Glueck, "Personality is a pattern of stable states and characteristics of a person that influence his or her behaviour towards goal achievement. Each person has unique ways of protecting these states."[3] In the words of Allport, "Personality is the dynamic organisation within the individuals of those psychological systems that determine his unique adjustment to his environment."[4] Luthans defines personality as follows: "Personality means how a person affects others and how he understands and views himself as well as the pattern of inner and outer measurable traits, and the person-situation interaction."[5] Madi has given a comprehensive definition of personality: "Personality is a stable set of characteristics and tendencies that determine those commonalities and differences in the psychological behaviour (thoughts, feelings and actions) of people that have continuity in time and that may not be easily understood as the sole result of the social and biological pressures of the moment."[6]

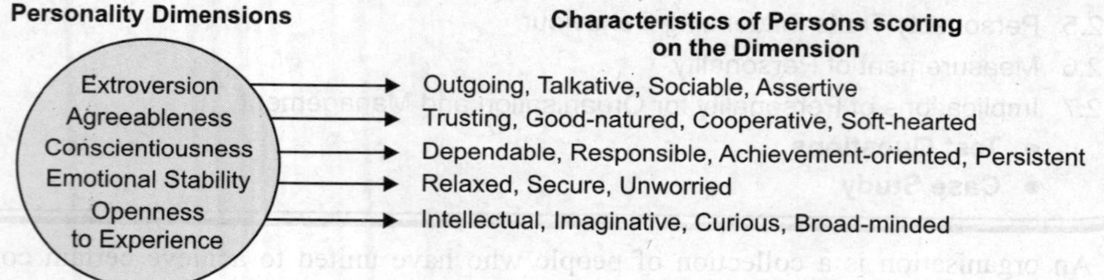

Fig. 2.1: Dimensions of Personality

Three dimensions of this definition need to be considered, *First*, personality refers to relatively stable characteristics which account for consistent patterns of behaviour. *Secondly*, an individual has certain similarities and differences with other individuals. *Thirdly*, it is necessary to consider such aspects of personality that induce people to behave in a manner as required by biological and social pressures. For example, a worker stops working and goes for lunch due to biological pressure. Similarly, a worker may do the job the way his boss likes due to social pressure. These behaviours do not require any explanation in terms of personality factors because the causes of such behaviour are clear.

Personality exercises a significant influence on job performance. Therefore, managers should ensure a good match between personality of a subordinate and the work assigned to him. In case of personality problems, a manager has three options. *First*, he can change the job of a person so that it suits his personality. *Secondly,* the person can be replaced so that personality matches the job requirements. *Thirdly,* the manager may modify personality traits and behaviour to make them more consistent with the needs of the job.

3 William F. Glueck, **Management,** Dryden Press, 1977, p. 90.

4 Gordon W. Allport, **Personality,** Henry Hot, New York, 1937, p 43.

5 Fred Luthans, **Organisational Behaviour,** McGraw Hill, New York, 1989, p 117.

6 Salvatore Madi, **Personality Theories – A Comparative Analysis,** Dorsey, Homewood, 1990, p. 10.

Fig. 2.2: Aspects of Self

2.2 DETERMINANTS OF PERSONALITY

The factors which shape the personality of an individual are given below :

1. Biological Factors

(*a*) *Heredity*: It implies the transmission of qualities from ancestor to descendant through a mechanism lying primarily in the chromosomes of the germ cells. An individual inherits physical stature, facial attractiveness, sex, temperament, etc. from his or her parents. However, the role of heredity differs from one personality trait to another. For example, heredity is generally more important in determining a person's temperament than his ideals and values.

(*b*) *Brain*: Brain is supposed to play an important role in the development of one's personality. However, no conclusive proof is available so far about the role of brain in personality formation.

(*c*) *Physical Features*: Height, weight, colour, facial features, etc. may have a great effect on man's personality. He influences others through his physical personality which in turn affects his self-concept. Rate of maturation may also affect personality because persons of varying maturity are exposed to different physical and social situations.

2. Family and Social Factors: Generally, an infant acquires those personality traits and behaviour patterns which are customary and acceptable to his family and the community. Parents and other family members exercise a strong influence on the personality development of children. In addition to family members and home environment, social groups such as co-students, friends and co-workers affect a person's personality. Family and social groups shape a person's personality through the process of socialisation and identification.

(*a*) *Socialisation*: It is a process by which an infant acquires from the enormously wide range of behaviour potentialities that are open to him at birth, those behaviour patterns that are customary and acceptable to the family and social groups. This process begins with initial contact between mother and her infant. Later on, other members of the family and social groups influence the socialisation process.

(*b*) *Identification*: This process occurs when a person tries to identify himself with some person whom he feels ideal in the family. Generally, a child tries to behave like his mother or father. The identification process can be examined from three different perspectives. *First*, it can be viewed as the similarity of behaviour (including feelings and attitudes) between the child and the model. *Secondly*, identification can be looked as the child's motives or desires to be like the model. *Thirdly*, it can be considered as the process through which the child actually acquires the attributes of the model.

In addition to the socialization and identification processes, the home environment influences the personality of an individual. The overall environment at home is critical to personality development. Family background and social class also influence the personality of an individual.

3. **Cultural Factors:** The culture within which a person has been brought up shapes his personality. For example, American culture fosters a spirit of independence and competition whereas Japanese culture reinforces attitudes of cooperation and team spirit. However, there is no linear relationship between culture and personality so that individuals within the same culture can differ in their personality and behaviour.

   Culture is the "complex of beliefs, values, and techniques for dealing with the environment which are shared among contemporaries and transmitted by one generation to the next."[7] Culture requires conformity to established mores through social pressure. Each culture expects its members to behave in the ways that are acceptable to the group.

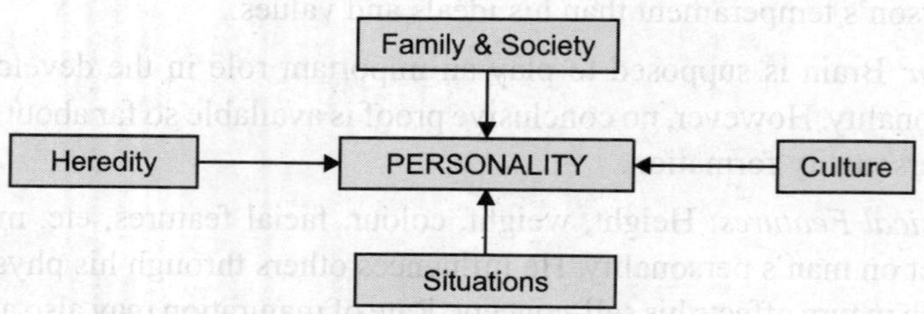

Fig. 2.3: Determinants of Personality

4. **Situational Factors:** Environment exercises a strong influence on human personality. A person interacts with his environment and acquires knowledge, skills and other traits through personal experience. The demands of different situations may call for different aspects of an individual's personality. Milgram's research study reveals that in certain circumstances, it is not so much the kind of person a man is, as the kind of situation in which he is placed, that determines his actions. For example, a very hardworking and ambitious person may appear lazy and trouble-maker because the bureaucratic work situation does not satisfy his need for achievement and power.

7 James D. Thompson and Donald Houton, **The Behavioural Sciences – An Interpretation,** Addison-Wesley, Reading Mass, 1970, p 22.

2.3 DEVELOPMENT OF PERSONALITY

There are several physiological and psychological stages that occur in the development of human personality. At each stage, an individual develops different aspects of personality. In fact, personality development is an ongoing process and it continues throughout life. Different psychologists have identified various stages in personality development. Two main categories are given below:

1. Freudian Stages

According to Sigmund Freud[8], there are five universal stages of psycho-sexual development which give rise to personality. These stages are as follows :

(*i*) **Oral Stage:** This stage continues from birth to 18 months of age. This stage may be divided into two periods – oral sucking and oral biting. Oral sucking period lasts from birth to 8 months. During this period, a child satisfies his sexual instinct by sucking from mouth, lips and tongue. In this condition, the child is totally driven by pleasure. In case he is not breast-fed properly, he satisfies himself by sucking his thumb or finger. Oral biting period is from 8 months to 18 months of age. The child enjoys in biting and if he is denied sucking or breast-feeding or biting, disturbances arise in personality development.

(*ii*) **Anal Stage:** This stage lasts from 18 months to three years. During this stage the focus of libidal energy shifts from mouth to the anal region. The child satisfies his sexual instinct by retaining and releasing urine and faeces. He expresses his anger by urinating and defecating at wrong places. In case proper attention is not paid to the child, he experiences stress which creates problems of personality development.

(*iii*) **Phallic Stage:** This stage is from 3 to 7 years. During this stage the child seeks sexual gratification by fondling his genitals. He observes and learns to discriminate genitals by observing other children. At this stage, the child is prone to develop complexes such as dedipus, electra, castration, penis envy, etc.

(*iv*) **Latency Stage:** This stage extends from 7 to 12 years. During this stage, the child suppresses his sexual instincts due to social fear. He seeks gratification from outside, *e.g.,* talking and playing with his friends. It is a period of social development as the child acquires knowledge and curiosity.

(*v*) **Genital Stage:** This stage lasts from 12 to 20 years. With growth of sex organs, there is revival of sexual and aggressive impulses. There is increasing interest in the opposite sex. The boys and girls start day dreaming, masturbating and may indulge in homo-sexuality. Freud believed that in order to attain the ideal genital character, an individual must learn to work, become responsible and above all assume a more active role in dealing with the problems of life.

Freudian stages of personality development are based on sexual gratification. Freud has provided some very basic insight for understanding personality development. But most of the modern psychologists do not agree on the focus on sexual instincts

---

8 Sigmund Freud, **Outline of Psychoanalysis** (translated by J. Strachery). Norton, New York, 1949.

as determinants of personality. Psychologists like Erik Erikson, Alfred Adler, Carl Jung stress upon the role of environment in personality development.

Erikson's Psychological Stages

Erikson[9] feels that social rather than biological factors should be given more attention in the development of personality. He has identified eight psychological stages of personality development. At each stage, a psychological crisis occurs and needs to be resolved for proper development of personality. However, these stages are not totally separable and the crisis at a particular stage is not fully resolved. The eight stages are described below:

1. **Infancy:** During the first year of life, a child tries to resolve the crisis of trust vs mistrust. An infant who is cared well develops trust in people. On the other hand, an infant who is not cared well develops mistrust. This stage makes a serious impact on the child that influences his behaviour throughout his life.
2. **Early Childhood:** In the second and third years of life, a child seeks independence. If the parents approve his behaviour, the child develops a sense of autonomy. If the elders constantly disapprove the child's behaviour, a sense of self-doubt and shame is likely to develop.
3. **Play Age:** In the fourth and fifth year of life, a child tries to discover how much he can do. If the child is encouraged to experiment and to achieve reasonable goals, he develops a sense of initiative. If the child is blocked and made to feel incapable, he develops a sense of guilt and lack of self-confidence.
4. **School Stage:** During 6 to 12 years of age, a child learns many new skills and social abilities. If the child experiences real progress at a rate compatible with his abilities, he develops a sense of enterprise. Otherwise, a sense of inferiority is developed.
5. **Adolescence:** In this teenage stage of life, the adolescent person tries to gain a sense of identity. He tries to establish himself as socially different from his parents. The autonomy, initiative, and enterprise developed at the earlier stage of life are very important in helping the teenager to resolve the crisis of identity vs. confusion and to prepare himself for the adulthood.
6. **Early Adulthood:** During the early 20s of life, a person tries to resolve the crisis of intimacy versus isolation. The sense of identity developed during the teenage stage helps the early adult to start developing deep and lasting relationships.
7. **Adulthood:** During the late 20s of life, the adult tries to resolve the crisis of generativity versus stagnation or self-absorption. Generative persons consider the society more important than themselves. For them productivity at work and societal advancement are more important. They try to become innovative and creative. On the other hand, self-absorbed persons never develop the ability to look beyond themselves. They remain preoccupied with their own career advancement and do not show concern for future generations and social welfare.
8. **Mature Adulthood:** At this stage, an individual faces the crisis of integrity versus despair. He acquires wisdom and develops the perspective that can guide the younger generations.

9 Erik Erikson, **Childhood and Society,** Norton, New York, 1963.

Table 2.1: Erikson's Psychological Stages

.	Stage of Personality Development	Age (Years)	Crisis
1.	Infancy	0-1	Trust vs. mistrust
2.	Early childhood	1-3	Autonomy vs. doubt
3.	Play age	3-5	Initiative vs. guilt
4.	School age	5-12	Enterprise vs. inferiority
5.	Adolescence	12-19	Identity vs. confusion
6.	Early adulthood	Early 20s	Intimacy vs. isolation
7.	Adulthood	Late 20s	Generativity vs. stagnation
8.	Mature adulthood	30s	Integrity vs. despair

Immaturity-Maturity Theory

Chris Argyris[10] argues that personality of an individual develops along a continuum rather than going through precise stages. Personality progresses along a continuum of immaturity as an infant to maturity as an adult. He identified seven dimensions in the continuum as given in Table 2.2.

Table 2.2: Immaturity-Maturity Continuum

Immaturity characteristics	Maturity characteristics
Passivity	Activity
Dependence	Independence
Capable of behaving in few ways	Capable of behaving in many ways
Shallow interests	Deep interests
Short-term perspective	Long-term perspective
Subordinate position	Superordinate position
Lack of self-awareness	Self-awareness and control

These seven dimensions continually change in degree from the infant to the adult end of the continuum. These dimensions are based upon latent characteristics of personality which may be quite different from the observable behaviour. Moreover, the seven dimensions represent only one aspect of the total personality. An individual's perception, self concept and adjustment to the environment are equally important.

Argyris believes that very few persons develop to full maturity due to organisational setting and management practices. Traditional formal organisations encourage people to be passive, dependent and subordinate. Classical organisations, based on the principles of task specialization, chain of command, unity of direction and span of management together with directive leadership and management controls, restrict initiative and creativity of individuals. Argyris suggests proper integration of organisational and individual goals. He advocates humanistic organisations and participative management to provide opportunity to individuals to become mature and to use their full potential for achieving organisational goals.

Argyris' model provides a useful method of describing and measuring the growth of any individual. However, it is only a construct and cannot predict specific behaviour.

10 Chris Argyris, *op. cit.*

2.4 THEORIES OF PERSONALITY

Various theories of personality may be described as follows :

2.4.1 Freud's Psychoanalytic Theory

Psychoanalytic theory is based on the belief that a person is motivated more by unconscious framework than by conscious and rational thought. Sigmund Freud[11] is the most known propounder of this theory. Carl Jung, Alfred Adler, Karen Horney and Eric Fromins have also contributed to psychoanalytic approach to personality. According to Freud, the unconscious framework of an individual consists of inter-related but conflicting elements — id, ego and super ego.

1. **The Id:** Id basically represents an individual's natural urges and feelings. It is the source of psychic energy. It seeks immediate gratification of biological or instinctual needs. Freud classified instincts into life-instructs and death-instructs. Life-instructs are hunger, thirst and sex and the energy involved in them is the libido. Id is primitive, pleasure driven, childish and irrational. Ego keeps a check on the id by channelling human activity into acceptable ways. An individual learns to control the id as he matures. However, id remains a driving force throughout life. It is an important source of thinking and behaving.
2. **The Ego:** The ego is the conscious and logical part of the human personality. While id represents the unconscious, ego is conscious and based on reality. Ego keeps the id in check through intellect and reason. Id wants immediate pleasure while ego requires postponement to a more appropriate time and place. The conflict between id and ego is resolved with support from the super ego.
3. **The Super Ego:** As an individual gains and absorbs parental and social values, he develops the super ego. The super ego represents personal and social norms. It represents the conscience and acts as an ethical constraint on behaviour. The super ego determines what is right or wrong. According to Freud, the ego mediates in the battle between id and super ego. A personality becomes disorderly when either id or super ego is dominant. An individual's personal development also suffers when ego consumes too much energy in mediating between the id and the super ego.

The psychoanalytic theory of Freud is structural as it consists of three basic dimensions — id, ego and super ego. It is also developmental in the sense that ego and super ego become stronger as one progresses through life. The theory is dynamic as it assumes that human actions result from psychic energy called libido. The theory is also deterministic as behaviour is assumed to be caused.

Freud's theory has been criticised on two main counts. *First,* the theory is based on a theoretical conception and cannot be verified scientifically. *Second,* the theory does not provide a complete picture of behaviour emerging from personality. However, the theory provides a useful insight into personality structure and unconscious motivation.

---

11 Sigmund Freud, *op. cit.*

2.4.2 Socio-Psychological Theory

According to socio-psychological theory, the personality of an individual is determined by the interaction between the individual and the society. The individual strives to meet the needs of the society and the society helps the individual to attain his goals. Thus, there is interdependence between the individual and the society.

There are two main differences between socio-psychological theory and psychoanalytic theory. **First,** social variables rather than biological instincts are assumed to shape personality. **Second,** conscious (needs and wants) rather than unconscious framework is considered as the motivator of human behaviour.

Socio-psychological theory offers some answers to the emergence of human personality. Managers can use the social factors in shaping the behaviour of their employees. However, the theory does not provide a total picture of how personality influences behaviour. Moreover, there is no immunity on the relative impact of social factors on personality. Fromin stresses the role of social context whereas Sullivan and Horney emphasise interpersonal orientations.

2.4.3 Trait Theory

Another useful approach to understanding human personality is by considering the traits a person possesses. A personality trait is an enduring attribute of a person that appears constantly in a variety of situations. According to the trait theory an individual's personality can be described in terms of traits. The theory is based upon the following assumptions:

(*i*) Individuals differ in terms of traits they possess *i.e.* traits distinguish one personality from another.

(*ii*) Traits are relatively stable and exert fairly universal influence on behaviour irrespective of the environmental situation.

(*iii*) Traits can be judged from the measurement of behavioural indicators.

Table 2.3: Some Personality Traits

1.	Reserved	Outgoing
2.	Less intelligent	More intelligent
3.	Affected feelings	Emotionally more stable
4.	Submissive	Dominant
5.	Serious	Happy-go-lucky
6.	Expedient	Conscientious
7.	Timid	Venturesome
8.	Tough-minded	Sensitive
9.	Trusting	Suspicious
10.	Practical	Imaginative
11.	Forthright	Shrewd
12.	Self-assured	Apprehensive
13.	Conservative	Experimenting
14.	Group dependent	Self-dependent
15.	Uncontrolled	Controlled
16.	Relaxed	Tense

The two most widely known trait theories are that of Allport and Cattell. Gordon Allport makes a distinction between common traits and personal dispositions. **Common traits** are used to compare people. He has identified six types of values – religious, social, economic, political, aesthetic and theoretical. Personal dispositions are completely unique to a person. These are cardinal (most pervasive), central (unique and limited in number) or secondary (peripheral). Each individual has values that emphasise common traits or orientations. For example, some individuals may be high in economic and low in other values. It is the profile of a person's values that defines his personality. Cattell[12] has identified two categories of traits – surface traits, and source traits. There are thirty-five surface traits that lie on the surface of the personality : wise-foolish, honest-dishonest, sociable-seclusive are examples of such traits. There are twelve source traits such as ego strength (maturity and realism) versus emotionality and hemoticism (maturity and evasiveness), dominance versus submissiveness, and so on.

Trait theory recognises the continuity of personality. It is based on research that attempts to find a relationship between a set of personality variables and assorted behaviour. However, trait theory suffers from several limitations :

(*i*) Trait theory focusses on isolated traits without specifying how these traits are organised within the personality. An individual's personality can be described adequately without knowing the relationship between different traits and their relative importance.

(*ii*) Trait theory is essentially descriptive rather than analytical.

(*iii*) Traits may be too abstract to be measured *e.g.* anxiety.

2.4.4 Self Theory

The theories described above represent the traditional approaches to understanding human personality. Self theory focuses on the organism as a whole and the interrelationship of all behaviours. Carl Rogers is most closely associated with this theory. According to Rogers[13], there are three basic ingredients of personality – the self concept, the organism, and the phenomenal field.

1. **Self Concept:** Rogers defines the self concept as "an organised, consistent, conceptual, gestalt composed of the characteristics of the 'I' or 'me' and the perceptions of the relationship of 'I' or 'me' to others and to various aspects of life, together with the values attached to these perceptions". Here "I" represents the personal self and "me" represents the social self. Personal self consists of a person's psychological processes such as perception, motivation, attitudes, etc., that result in a composed whole. Social self means the way a person appears to others and the way the person thinks he appears to others. There are four factors in self concept :

   (*a*) **Self Image:** Self image or personal self is the way one sees oneself. Every individual has certain beliefs about who or what he is. These beliefs together constitute a person's self image or identity.

   (*b*) **Ideal Self:** The ideal self represents the type of person an individual likes to be. It differs from the self image in the sense that the former indicates the ideal image

---

12 Raymond B. Cattell, **The Scientific Analysis of Personality**, Aldine Publishing, Chicago, 1965.

13 Carl C. Rogers, **Counselling and Psychotherapy; New Concepts in Practice,** Houghton, Boston, 1942.

while the latter indicates the real image as perceived by the person. The ideal self is important because an individual will select those stimuli which fit in with his ideal self.

(*c*) **Looking Glass Self:** It means the perception of an individual about how others perceive him. It emerges from face-to-face interaction with others. This interaction provides clue about how others see him as an individual. In other words, beliefs about self are largely a reflection of other's perception about the individual.

(*d*) **Real Self:** It implies what a person really is. If the ideal self is closer to the real self, the individual will be fulfilled and happy. On the other hand, if there is large discrepancy between the two, the individual is likely to be dissatisfied and unhappy.

2. **The Organism:** The organism is the locus of all experience.
3. **Phenomenal Field:** The totality of experience is the phenomenal field and it is known as frame of reference. It determines an individual's behaviour.

The main force that motivates a person is self actualisation or the tendency toward fulfilment. This force is under the influence of social environment right from childhood.

Self theory is organised around the concept of self. It recognises that the individual largely determines his personality and behaviour. Another positive aspect of self theory is that the internal frame of reference of the individual himself is the best vantage point for understanding personality.

A person's self concept provides him a sense of meaningfulness and consistency. The self concept plays a significant role in the analysis of organisational behaviour. A person perceives a situation according to his self concept. Different managerial practices are required for persons having different self concepts.

For example, authoritarian leadership, and monetary rewards may prove to be effective for insecure, unintelligent and indecisive workers. The same practices may prove in-effective for intelligent, independent and decisive workers.

Self theory is criticised on the ground that self concept and self actualisation are vague terms and of little use in predicting human behaviour. It is also not possible to measure accurately subjective experiences and self.

2.4.5 Social Learning Theory

According to the social learning theory, the actions of an individual in a given situation depend as much on the individual's appraisal of the situation as on the specific characteristics of the situation. The main focus of the theory is on the behaviour patterns an individual learns in coping with his environment. An individual learns by observing the actions of others and by noting the consequences of these actions.

The learned behaviour is strengthened by reinforcement which may be direct, vicarious, or self-administered. **Direct reinforcement** means social approval and their tangible rewards. **Vicarious reinforcement** refers to observation of someone else receiving reward or punishment for similar behaviour. **Self-administered reinforcement** implies evaluation of one's own performance with self-praise or reapproach. The social learning theory views human behaviour as reaction to the situation. But, it overlooks individual differences, and overstresses the role of situational factors in behaviour. However, the way a person perceives the situation is the most important determinant of behaviour. This fact cannot be ignored by behavioural scientists.

2.5 PERSONALITY TRAITS INFLUENCING BEHAVIOUR

Personality exercises a great influence on individual behaviour and work performance. Some characteristics of personality and their relationship with specific behaviour of an individual in work organisation are given below.

1. **Authoritarianism:** Authoritarianism refers to blind acceptance of authority. An individual with authoritarian personality believes in the legitimacy of formal authority, expects blind obedience to authority, adheres to conventional values and conforms to rules and regulations. Such persons prefer stable and structured work environment with clear rules and regulations. Similarly, authoritarian people prefer autocratic leadership and exhibit high respect for individuals in positions of authority. Such people make good followers and are more productive within rigid organisation structures.

   A closely related term to authoritarianism is 'dogmatism' which means the rigidity of a person's beliefs. A dogmatic person is close minded, highly radical in his views, intolerant towards others and believes in blind obedience to authority. Religious fanatics, hardcore communists and right-wing Nazis are examples of dogmatic personality.

2. **Bureaucratic Personality:** A bureaucratic person differs from an authoritarian person as his respect for authority is not blind but is based upon respect for organisational rules and regulations. Such a person values rules conformity, subordination and impersonal or formal relationships. He is not innovative, does not take risks and follows established directives. Bureaucratic people are better supervisors in routine and repetitive types of work.

3. **Machiavellianism:** This term is named after Niccolo Machiaveli who wrote in the 16th century on how people gain and manipulate power. People with high machiavellianism manipulate others for personal gains and believe that ends can justify means. Such people have high self-confidence and are cool and calculating. They do not feel guilty in using unethical means to serve their own interests. They are very successful in exploiting vulnerable people and unstructured situations.

4. **Problem Solving Style:** Individuals have their own style of making decisions and this style reflects their personality in certain ways. Some people are very thoughtful, meticulous and detail-oriented while others are impassive and intuitive. The former type prefer routine and structured situations whereas the latter type dislike routine and repetition. Thinking people are more logical and analytical in solving problems. On the other hand, impulsive persons depend more on feelings and judgements.

5. **Locus of Control:** A person has either internal locus of control or external locus of control. In the former case an individual believes that events are under his control whereas in the latter case he believes that events are determined by forces beyond his control. Internals are more active in seeking information to make decisions and are more active socially. On the other hand, externals are less satisfied with their jobs and less involved socially.

6. **Introvert and Extrovert:** Introverts are basically shy, prefer to be alone and have difficulty in communication. On the other hand, extroverts are gregarious and sociable. These two types of people have different career orientations and require different types of people, have different career orientations and require different types of work environment to maximise performance. Introverts are more likely to excel at tasks that require thought and analytical skills. Extroverts are more suitable for managerial positions and other jobs that require considerable interaction with others.
7. **Type 'A' and Type 'B':** People with type 'A' personality are impatient, aggressive and highly competitive. They work very hard and tend to be very productive. But they are not good team players and lack good judgement. People with type 'B' personality are easy going, laid back and non-competitive. They perform better on complex tasks involving judgement and accuracy rather than hard work and speed.

2.6 MEASUREMENT OF PERSONALITY

The main methods used to measure personality are given below:

1. **Observation Method:** Under this method, an individual's personality is assessed by observing his behaviour in different situations. This method is based upon the proposition that the behavioural pattern of a person reflects his personality. Therefore, overt behaviour of an individual provides clue to his personality. This method can yield good results provided the observers are able to relate behavioural pattern with personality. Observations have been used to identify many personality traits.
2. **Interview Method:** A formal and in-depth conversation with an individual can reveal his personality characteristics. Two types of interview are used to measure personality. In an **exhaustive interview,** questions are asked on various dimensions of personality. In **stress interview** an attempt is made to find out how the individual behaves in a stressful situation. A stressful situation may be created by asking questions too rapidly, criticising the individual, interrupting him frequently and so on. Interview provides opportunity for face-to-face interaction with the individual. Therefore, it is better than observation method. But highly skilled persons should conduct the interview.
3. **Case History Method:** In this method, information is collected from different sources to appraise the personality characteristics of an individual. Personal letters of the individual, diaries, his family members, relations and friends, work groups, etc. are these sources. The information collected about the individual is analysed to assess his personality. Psychiatrists use this method to treat abnormal people. Case history method is not scientific and there is lack of control in data collection. However, this method can be quite effective when the psychiatrists are fully trained.
4. **Personality Inventories:** Under this method both internal and external features of the individual are measured. Observations are used to measure external characteristics while internal characteristics are judged through questionnaire and other techniques. Two main personality inventories are as follows:

   (*a*) **Minnesota Multiphasic Personality Inventory (MMPI):** It contains 550 items each having three alternative answers — true, false and not known. Scoring is done on the basis of answers given by the individual. Personality characterisitcs are ascertained on the basis of scores.

(*b*) **Sixteen Personality Factor Questionnaire (16 PFQ):** In this test 16 personality traits are measured. Factor analysis is used to analyse the obtained scores. Personality traits are determined after such analysis.

(5) Projective Method: In this method an attempt is made to identify the basic personality structure of an individual by allowing him to respond to stimuli in a free manner. There is preconceived system of correct or incorrect answers for reference. Two widely used projective techniques are as under:

(*a*) **Rorschach Ink Blot Test:** This test is used to measure the cognitive, corrective and affective aspects of personality. The test consists of ten standardised cards. Five cards have black and white blots and the other five cards have coloured blots. An individual perceives these blots according to his personality structure. The personality characteristics of the person are identified on the basis of his perception of these blots. This test is quite effective in diagnosing personality and related problems. Motives, repressed desires, feelings and unconscious mind can also be studied with this test.

(*b*) **Thematic Appreciation Test (TAT):** This test is based on the fact that when confronted with an ambiguous situation, a person is likely to project and reveal his personality. The test consists of 31 cards of which 30 cards contain semi-structured pictures. One card is left blank. The personality characteristics are judged on the basis of how the individual describes the various pictures. The test may be administered on individual basis or group basis. This test is designed to reveal the traits that underlie individual behaviour as well as needs. The reliability coefficient of this test is 0.91. An Indian version of the test containing 14 pictures is now available.

2.7 IMPLICATIONS OF PERSONALITY FOR MANAGEMENT

Understanding of human personality is helpful in effective management of organisations. Some applications of personality are given below :

1. **Matching Jobs and Persons:** Every job requires some specific characteristics on the part of its performer. When the personality of the job performer matches with the requirements of the job, job performance and job satisfaction tend to be better. Therefore, personality tests and personal interview are used in employee selection. When a person is promoted, the nature of his job changes and new personality traits need to be developed through training and experience.
2. **Designing Motivation System:** Different incentives are needed to motivate different individuals due to differences in their personality. Some employees prefer financial incentives while others seek non-financial incentives. Knowledge and understanding of personality characteristics of people in the organisation is very helpful in designing an effective system of motivation.
3. **Designing Control System:** A control system is needed to ensure that members of the organisation make the desired contributions. Such a system may be flexible or tight.

Different people react differently to the same control system depending upon their personality. Such differences in personality must be considered while designing an effective system of control.

TEST QUESTIONS

1. Define Personality. How does the study of personality help in understanding Organisational Behaviour?
2. "Personality is an organised whole, without which an individual has no meaning". Comment.
3. Explain in brief the factors that shape the personality of an individual.
4. "People are similar, yet they are different". Comment.
5. What is personality? How does it influence the behaviour of an individual?
6. Explain Freudian stages of personality development.
7. Discuss the personality traits that shape the behaviour of individuals.
8. Explain the concept of personality. How is the study of personality useful for managers?
9. Critically examine Freud's psychoanalytic theory of personality.
10. Explain socio-psychological theory of personality.
11. Discuss trait theory of personality.
12. Explain self theory of personality.
13. Describe social learning theory of personality.
14. Discuss various methods used to measure an individual's personality.
15. Explain the implications of personality for management.
16. Explain the determinants of personality.
17. Explain the constructs that make up personality.
18. What are the factors that shape an individual's personality? How does the study of personality help in understanding organisational behaviour?
19. Examine the factors determining personality by citing relevant examples.
20. Discuss the major personality attributes that influence organisational behaviour and explain their ability to predict employee behaviour.
21. (*a*) What are the advantages and the risks associated with using information about personality as the basis for making important organisational decisions?

    (*b*) Describe the managerial implications of the attribution theory.

    (*c*) What comments do you have about your own personality type? What are the strengths and potential pitfalls?
22. What is the significance of personality in organisational settings?
23. What are the 'Big Five' personality traits? Which one seems to have the biggest impact on performance?
24. Explain Type 'A' and Type 'B' personality.

25. What personality traits are relevant from the point of view of OB?
26. "Personality can be ascribed and acquired depending upon how you look at it." Comment.
27. "Personality reflects individual differences. Though it is consistent and enduring, yet it can be changed." Explain, describing the impact of heredity and environment on personality.
28. How do biological factors influence personality?
29. Explain the personality traits that shape the behaviour of individual.
30. Describe the various factors which influence personality development of an individual.

CASE STUDY

In a socialization lecture of a leading private sector company, the Director (Personnel) advises a set of management trainees in the following lines :

(*a*) Never become 'chummy' with your subordinates.

(*b*) On promotion cut off your relationship/friendship with your old colleagues.

(*c*) Never call on your subordinates (or) accept their invitation for parties.

(*d*) Make friends with people at higher level.

(*e*) What you know is important : whom you know is more important.

(*f*) Whom you know on the higher levels and whom you have forgotten at your previous level takes you to places.

(*g*) Business ethics is a shade different from ethics in public life.

(*h*) You are judged by the more number of votes you get from the top and less number of votes you get from subordinates.

(*i*) What is said is important; who said it is more important.

(*j*) If policies is the act of possibilities, hypocrisy is the science of success in organizational politics.

Questions

1. Do you agree with the ten "Commandments"? If so, evaluate your success rate by marking against each.
2. If you do not agree on any, specify the reasons thereof.
3. What type of Personality you assign to Director (Personnel)?
4. What is the impact of this advice on management trainees?

CHAPTER

3

PERCEPTION

CHAPTER OUTLINE

3.1 Concept of Perception
3.2 Process of Perception
3.3 Factors Influencing Perception
3.4 Interpersonal Perception
3.5 Perceptual Errors and Distortion
3.6 Perceptual Constancy, Perceptual Context and Perceptual Defence
3.7 Managerial Applications of Perception
3.8 How to Develop Perceptual Skills
- **Test Questions**
- **Case Study**

Quite often people see the same phenomenon but derive different meanings from it. For example, workers may consider computerisation as a threat to their job security while management may view it as a method of improving efficiency of operations. Similarly, to the marketing department a quality improvement programme may be a means of increasing sales whereas the production department may view it as a cause of increase in the cost of production. These differences arise due to perception.

3.1 CONCEPT OF PERCEPTION

Perception may be described as a person's view of reality. It is the process of selecting, organising and attaching meaning to the events happening in the environment. According to Robbins[1], "Perception may be defined as a process by which individuals organise and interpret their sensory impressions in order to give meaning to their environment."

The main features of perception are as follows :

(*i*) Perception is the intellectual process by which a person selects data from the environment, organises it and derives meaning from it.

1 Stephen P. Robbins, **Organisational Behaviour,** Prentice Hall, New Delhi, 2003, p 123.

(*ii*) Perception is a psychological process. The manner in which a person perceives the environment affects his behaviour. The emotions, thoughts, feelings and actions of people are triggered by the perception of their surroundings.

(*iii*) People differ in their perception. Therefore, different people view the same world differently.

(*iv*) Perception is different from sensation.

Difference Between Perception and Sensation

Both perception and sensation are cognitive processes but the two are different from each other. Sensation is the response of a physical sensory organ to events in the environment. There are five physical senses – vision, hearing, touch, smell and taste. These senses receive stimuli continuously. The stimuli may be from both inside and outside the human body. A particular sense organ reacts to these stimuli: Reaction of eye to colour, ear to sound, nose to fragrance, fingers to burning coal and tongue to spicy food. These examples show that sensation deals with very elementary behaviour that largely depends upon physiological functioning. In the words of Berelson and Steiner, "All knowledge of the world depends on the senses and their stimulation, but the facts of raw sensory data are insufficient to produce or to explain the coherent picture of the world as experienced by the normal adult."[2]

Perception is a wider term than sensation. It correlates, integrates and comprehends diverse sensations and information from several organs of the body by means of which a person identifies things and objects. Perception classifies the stimuli on the basis of past experience (learning), feelings and motives. Thus, perception is determined by both physiological and psychological characteristics of the organism. But psychological factors such as learning and motives do not affect sensation. Sensation only activates the organs of the body. According to Dempey, "By means of my eye, I see, but it is not my eye but I who see, and I tend to see an object in its totality, a thing or event with certain qualities with a figure and form set against a background."[3] Thus, in seeing process, both sensation and perception are involved. Activation of eyes to see an object is sensation and the interpretation of what is seen is perception.

Thus, perception and sensation are different in the following ways :

(*a*) Sensation is a simple process whereas perception is comparatively a complex process as several variables affect it.

(*b*) Sensation only makes a person aware of the stimuli whereas perception gives meaning to the stimuli.

(*c*) During sensation only sensory organs of a person are active but during perception all parts of the body become active.

(*d*) Sensation is the first stage in perception. In other words, sensation is a part of perception.

---

2 Bernard Berelson and Gary A. Steiner, **Human Behaviour,** Harcourt Brace and World Inc; New York, 1964, p 87.

3 Peter J.R. Dempey, **Psychology and the Manager,** Pan Books, London, 1993, p 4.

3.2 PROCESS OF PERCEPTION

Perception is a process consisting of many subprocesses. It may be viewed as an input - throughput - output process.

1. **Perceptual Inputs:** The stimuli in the environment – objects, events and people – may be considered as the perceptual inputs. Everything in the situation where events occur or which make events happen can be called perceptual inputs. Thus, perceptual inputs include all stimuli that exist in the environment.

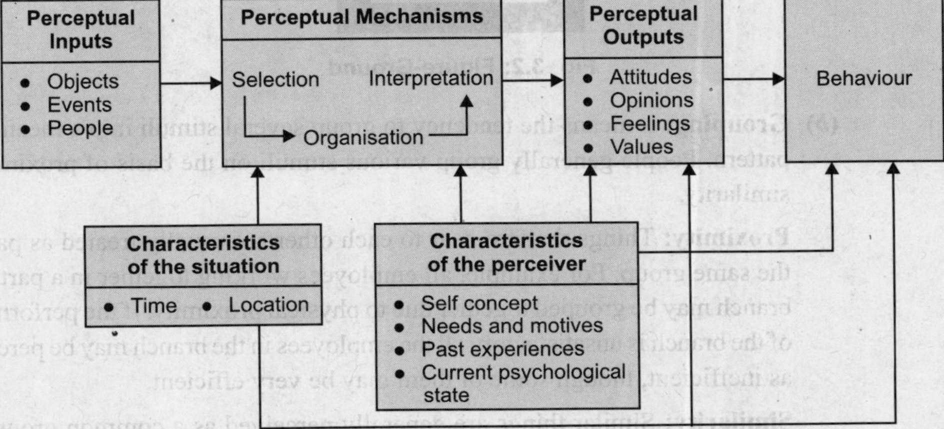

Fig. 3.1: The Process of Perception

2. **Perceptual Mechanisms:** The stimuli or inputs pass through the subprocesses of selection, organisation and interpretation.

   (*i*) **Selection:** Several things happen in the environment simultaneously. A person cannot pay equal attention to all these things. Only the most relevant things are selected for further processing and the other things are screened out. Several internal (related to the perceiver) and external (related to the stimuli) factors affect selection. These factors and their impact on the selection of stimuli are described in the next section of this chapter. Generally a person selects those aspects of the situation which relate specifically to his area of specialisation or field of activity.

   (*ii*) **Organisation:** After the data from the situation are selected, these are organised in some form in order to make sense out of it. Stimuli may be organised into a meaningful whole according to the following principles:

   (*a*) **Figure-Ground:** According to this principle, the significant and meaningful portion of the stimuli is called the "figure" and the insignificant and meaningless portion is known as the "ground". The purpose is to focus attention on the figure and less attention is paid to the background. For example, during the examination days students tend to focus complete attention on their studies and ignore other activities like sports, films, etc. Thus, the perceiver tends to organise only that information in the environment which is significant to him. What becomes 'figure' and what becomes 'ground' depends on the needs and expectations of the perceiver. For example, in Fig. 3.2 if you concentrate on black portion you notice white cup. On the other hand, if you concentrate on white portion you notice two faces facing each other.

Fig. 3.2: Figure-Ground

(*b*) **Grouping:** It means the tendency to group several stimuli into a meaningful pattern. People generally group various stimuli on the basis of proximity or similarity.

Proximity: Things that are near to each other are usually treated as parts of the same group. For example, all employees working together in a particular branch may be grouped together due to physical proximity. If the performance of the branch is unsatisfactory all the employees in the branch may be perceived as inefficient, though some of them may be very efficient.

Similarity: Similar things are generally perceived as a common group. For example, all the students sitting on back benches may be viewed as less serious though some of them may be very serious about studies.

(*c*) **Simplification:** Whenever a person is overloaded with information, he tries to simplify it to make it more meaningful and understandable. In the process of simplification, the perceiver ignores less salient information and concentrates on important information.

(*d*) **Closure:** When faced with incomplete information, the perceiver fills up the gaps himself to make the information meaningful. He may do it on the basis of past experience, past data or hunches. For example, when a manager has to select new employees from all the applicants, he may not have complete information about the suitability of candidates. In such a case, the manager may rely on his intuition.

(*iii*) **Interpretation:** Once the stimuli are organised, the perceiver assigns meaning to the same. Selection and organisation make no sense without interpretation. In fact perception takes place only after the information is interpreted. A person interprets the selected and organised information in terms of his own assumptions. Several factors such as characteristics of stimuli, situation under which perception takes place and characteristics of the perceiver affect interpretation. The physical, social and organisational settings in which an object is perceived also affect interpretation. In the process of interpretation, a person tends to become judgemental. He may commit mistake and distort what he has selected.

3. **Perceptual Outputs:** Interpretation creates perceptual outputs. These outputs may be in the form of covert actions such as attitudes, opinions and beliefs about the stimuli. These outputs together with other factors may result in overt behaviour. For example, when an individual observes a celebrity using a product (stimulus), he may perceive that the product is good. This perception alone may not lead the person to buy the product (overt behaviour). Several other factors like availability of the product, perceiver's need for a product, his capacity to buy the product, etc. also influence the purchase.

3.3 FACTORS INFLUENCING PERCEPTION

As stated above, a person selects only a limited amount of information in the environment. During selection phase, certain aspects of the stimuli are screened out. For example, a person reads only that part of the daily newspaper which interests him. This is known as **perceptual selectivity**. Several internal and external factors influence selectivity.

Internal Factors: These factors are related to the complex psychological make-up of the perceiver. These are as follows :

1. **Self Concept:** The way a person views the world depends largely on the concept or image he has about himself. Self concept plays a vital role in perceptual selectivity. One can see others more accurately if one knows oneself. A person tends to select only those aspects of the stimuli which he feels match with his own characteristics.
2. **Beliefs:** The beliefs of an individual have a profound influence on his perception. A fact is conceived not on what it is but what a person believes it to be. A person normally screens out stimulus inputs that disturb his existing beliefs. This is known as **'maintenance of cognitive consistency'.** Daniel Katz argues that (*a*) an individual self censors his intake of communications so as to shield his beliefs and practices from attack; (*b*) an individual seeks out communications which support his beliefs and practices; and (*c*) the latter is particularly true when the beliefs and practices in question have undergone attack or the individual has otherwise been made of them.[4]
3. **Expectations:** What a person perceives also depends upon the type of behaviour he anticipates from others. Expectations affect the perception of people even in the organisational settings. For example, the human resource manager in a company may expect rough language from union leaders.
4. **Inner Needs and Motives:** People with different needs usually experience different stimuli. For example, power seekers are more likely to notice power related stimuli. Similarly, people with different needs select different items to remember or respond to. Where a person is not able to satisfy his needs, he engages in wishful thinking. Such day dreaming is a way to satisfy the needs not in real world but in imaginary world. In such cases, an individual will perceive only those items which are consistent with his wishful thinking.

---

4 Daniel E. Katz, "On Reopening the Question of Selectivity in Exposure to Mass Communication", in R.P. Abelson, *et.al.* (eds.), **Theories of Cognitive Consistency : A Source Book,** Rand McNaily, Chicago, 1968, p 775.

5. **Personality:** Individual personality has a significant influence on perceived behaviour. For example, optimistic people perceive things in favourable terms (glass is half full) while pessimistic people perceive in unfavourable terms (glass is half empty). Research on the effects of individual personality on perception reveals the following:
   (*a*) Secure individuals tend to perceive others as warm, not cold and indifferent.
   (*b*) Thoughtful individuals do not expose by expressing extreme judgements of others.
   (*c*) Persons who accept themselves and have faith in their individuality perceive things differently.
   (*d*) Self accepting individuals perceive themselves as liked, wanted and accepted by others.
6. **Experience:** Knowledge and experience exercise a constant influence on perception. Successful experiences boost the ability to perceive accurately. On the other hand, unsuccessful experiences erode self-confidence and reduce the perceptive ability. For example, a person, who has been betrayed by his best friend, is likely to distrust any new friendship.
7. **Current Psychological State:** The emotional state of a person has a bearing on his perception. When a person is depressed he is likely to perceive the same situation differently than when he is elated. Similarly, a lady who has got scared by seeing a snake in the garden may perceive a rope under the bed as a snake.
8. **Context:** The situation in which a person sees objects or events is also important. Elements in the surroundings influence one's perception. Time, location, light, temperature are some of these elements.
9. **Status:** Status of an individual also influences his perception. For example, when a new employee is introduced to the departmental head and the supervisor, he is likely to remember the name of the departmental head than the name of the supervisor.

External Factors: These factors are related to the stimuli. These are given below :

1. **Size:** Size attracts the attention of a person. The bigger the size of the perceived stimulus, the higher is the probability that it is selected for perception. For example, letters of bigger size in newspapers are first selected for reading.
2. **Intensity:** The more intense the stimulus is, the more likely it is to be perceived. A bright light, a loud sound and a strong odour are noticed more as compared to a dim light, a soft sound and a weak odour. That is why TV commercials are slightly louder than the regular programmes.
3. **Repetition:** A frequently repeated stimulus is more likely to get attention than a single one. Repetition increases alertness or sensitivity of people to the stimulus. Advertisement of a product is repeated to attract the attention of people.
4. **Contrast:** Stimuli that stand apart from the surroundings or background receive more attention. For example, letters of bold types, uniquely dressed persons, and buildings of different colours in the same locality get more attention.
5. **Novelty and Familiarity:** A novel or a familiar stimulus gets more attention. New objects or events in a familiar setting or familiar objects or events in a new setting draw

better attention. For example, when an employee is transferred to a new job, he becomes more attentive.

6. **Motion:** A moving object draws more attention than a stationary object. For example, moving commercials on TV get more attention than advertisements in print media.

3.4 INTERPERSONAL PERCEPTION

Interpersonal perception means one person perceives another person. Individuals in an organisation constantly perceive one another. Managers perceive workers, workers perceive managers and so on. When the perceiver's expectations about the actions of other people are confirmed, there is smooth social interaction. Otherwise there is embarrassment and stress. For a better understanding of interpersonal perception, it is necessary to know the specific characteristics of the perceiver and the perceived. According to Zald Kind and Costello[5], the relevant characteristics of the perceiver are as follows :

(*i*) Knowing oneself makes it easier to see others accurately.

(*ii*) One's own characteristics affect the characteristics one is likely to see in others

(*iii*) The person who accepts himself is more likely to be able to see favourable aspects of other people.

(*iv*) Accuracy in perceiving others is not a single skill.

The relevant characteristics of the perceived are as follows :

(*i*) The status of the person perceived will greatly influence others' perception of him.

(*ii*) The person being perceived is usually placed into categories to simplify the viewer's perceptual activities. Two common categories are status and role.

(*iii*) The visible traits of the person perceived will greatly influence others' perception of him.

3.5 PERCEPTUAL ERRORS AND DISTORTION

Perception is distorted when errors arise in the perceptual process. The main causes of perceptual errors and distortion are as follows :

1. **Selective Perception:** People see only a part of the stimulus rather than the whole stimulus. They pay attention to those aspects of the situation which are in accordance with their needs, motives and interests. For example, after their journey in a railway compartment, the farmer noticed only the crops while the architect observed only the buildings on the way. Such selective view of the total situation creates errors in perception. Sometimes, people may distort meaning of the situation so that the same may fit with what they want.

2. **Projection:** An individual tends to project his own characteristics in others. For example, a dishonest person may see others as dishonest. A fearful person may interpret

5 Sheldon S. Zald Kind and Timothy W. Costello, "Perception : Some Recent Research and Implications for Administration", **Administrative Science Quarterly,** September 1962.

the behaviour of others as fearful or anxious[6]. Such projection can distort perceptual judgements about others. One can avoid this error in judging others by remaining conscious of differences among people.

3. **Stereotyping:** Judging a person on the basis of the characteristics of the group to which he belongs is known as 'stereotyping'. Some examples of stereotypes at the international level are : the Americans are materialistic, the Japanese are nationalistic, the Germans are industrious, the Chinese are inscrutable and the Italians are quick-tempered. Stereotypes are not always true and may distort perception. For example, all salespersons are not aggressive and all union leaders are not self-serving.

4. **Halo Effect:** It means the tendency to judge a person on the basis of a single characteristic such as intelligency or appearance. In such a case the halo serves as a screen keeping the perceived away from other characteristics of the perceived. Halo error occurs when a manager who evaluaties the performance of a subordinate is influenced by one aspect such as obedience. Research reveals that halo effect is more marked in the following conditions :

   (*a*) When the traits are unclear in behavioural expressions;

   (*b*) When the traits are not frequently used by the perceiver; and

   (*c*) When the traits have moral implications.

   One way to avoid the halo effect is to ask the manager to judge all his subordinates on a single factor or trait before taking up the next. In this manner, the rater can consider all the subordinates relative to a standard.

5. **Attribution:** When the perceiver gives cause and effect explanation to the observed behaviour, it is called attribution. People tend to attribute their own behaviour to the situations and the behaviour of others to their personal dispositions. For example, an employee who is bypassed in promotion may attribute his bypassing to others being close to the authorities rather than to his own incompetence.

   Attribution distorts perception on account of (*a*) fundamental attribution error, and (*b*) self-serving bias. While making judgements about others' behaviour, one tends to underestimate the influence of external factors and overestimate the influence of internal or personal factors. For example, a factory supervisor may attribute low production of workers to their laziness rather than to obsolete plant and machinery. This is called the **fundamental attribution error**. People also tend to attribute their success to internal or personal factors while putting the blame for failure on external factors like luck. This is known as **self-serving bias**.

6. **First Impression:** It is very common that a person evaluates others on the basis of first impression. Quite often the first impression is not based on adequate information. Therefore, it may not be true reflection of the person being perceived. This error can be corrected through more frequent interaction. However, it is not that easy to erase the first impression.

7. **Mental Set:** Also known as perceptual set, it means the previously held beliefs about objects and events. For example, a manager may have developed the general belief and

---

6 Jerome S. Bruner and R. Taguiri, "The Perception of People" in Gardner Lindzey (ed.), **Handbook of Social Psychology,** Addison-Wesley, Cambridge Mass., 1984, p 641.

attitudes that workers are lazy and shirkers. They want to gain whatever is possible from the company without giving their best to it. Such a manager will be harsh in his judgement about all workers.

8. **Status and Visibility of the Perceived:** Perception may be distorted when a person is perceived on the basis of his status rather than on the basis of his actual characteristics. For example, a person having high status may be perceived as having many desirable qualities which may not be true. Similarly, less visible traits like honesty and loyalty are likely to be perceived less accurately than more visible traits like physical appearance and voice.

3.6 PERCEPTUAL CONSTANCY, PERCEPTUAL CONTEXT AND PERCEPTUAL DEFENCE

1. **Perceptual Constancy:** The shape, size, colour, brightness and location of an object are reasonably and fairly constant irrespective of the information received by our senses. The principle of consistency makes the task of the perceiver easy. It enables the individual to interpret the changing environment in such a manner that the stimuli reflect with more or less accuracy the stability of objects and people.[7] Perceptual constancy does not arise from ignoring any particular cue but from responding to a pattern of cues.

2. **Perceptual Context:** Context is very significant in deriving meaning from objects, events and people. The principle of context can be explained with the help of doodles as shown in Fig. 3.3.

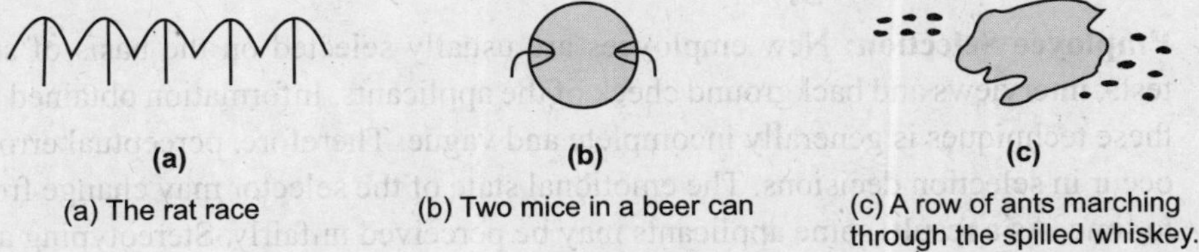

(a) The rat race (b) Two mice in a beer can (c) A row of ants marching through the spilled whiskey.

Fig. 3.3: Context of Perception

The visual stimuli without context is meaningless. But the doodles acquire meaning and significance when these are placed in a verbal context. In organisational settings, a raised eyebrow, a suggestive gesture, and a pat on the back will be meaningless without proper context. A pat on the back of an employee for superior performance becomes meaningful.

3. **Perceptual Defence:** People usually build defences against objects, events and people that are unacceptable, conflicting or threatening to them. Perceptual defence means screening out those elements of the stimuli that create conflict and threat for the perceiver. The defence mechanisms adopted by the perceived may be in the following forms:[8]

---

7 Merle J. Moskowitz and Arthur R. Orgel, **General Psychology,** Houghton Miffin Co., Boston, 1969, p 168

8 David Lawtess, **Effective Management,** Prentice Hall, New Jersey, 1992, pp 56-58.

(*a*) **Denial:** The perceiver may outrightly deny the existence or importance of conflicting information.

(*b*) **Modification:** The perceiver may modify the received information to match his existing beliefs.

(*c*) **Change in Perception:** The perceiver may acknowledge the received information but treat it as a non-representative exception.

(*d*) **Recognition:** The perceiver may accept the information.

3.7 MANAGERIAL APPLICATIONS OF PERCEPTION

Perception affects human behaviour. Everyone perceives the world differently. We react to what we perceive than to reality. Therefore, perception is very important in understanding human behaviour. Managers can avoid making errors in dealing with employees and events in the work setting through proper understanding of their perceptions.

Managers are primarily concerned with achieving organisational objectives through the efforts of other people. In order to influence others' behaviour in the desired manner, managers must understand the perception of employees. Perceptual understanding and accuracy is particularly useful in the following areas :

1. **Interpersonal Relationships:** Cordial interpersonal relations and teamwork are essential for achieving organisational objectives. When members of the organisation must share similar or at least compatible perceptions. Distorted perceptions create lack of mutual trust and conflict among people.
2. **Employee Selection:** New employees are usually selected on the basis of selection tests, interviews and background check of the applicants. Information obtained through these techniques is generally incomplete and vague. Therefore, perceptual errors often occur in selection decisions. The emotional state of the selector may change from time to time. As a result, some applicants may be perceived unfairly. Stereotyping and halo error may occur during preliminary interviews.
3. **Performance Appraisal:** A manager's perception affects the appraisal of subordinates' performance. A manager may over-evaluate those subordinates who are more liked or noticed. Performance appraisal may be faulty due to halo effect.

3.8 HOW TO DEVELOP PERCEPTUAL SKILLS

In view of the significance of correct perception, it becomes necessary that managers develop their perceptual skills. Some guidelines which can be helpful in developing perceptual skills are given below:

1. **Enhance Your Self Concept:** A positive self concept enables one to perceive others more accurately. A person can develop his self-esteem and self-respect by accomplishing things successfully. A person having self-regard is likely to respect others more and

perceive them better. Abraham Maslow argues that self-actualising individuals have more accurate perceptions than those who are not self-actualising.

2. **Perceive Yourself Correctly:** In order to perceive others accurately, a person must first of all perceive himself correctly. One who understands oneself better tends to better perceive others. Awareness about self can be increased with the help of Johari Window.

3. **Develop Positive Attitudes:** Managers can improve their perception by looking at things and events from a positive angle. They should make concerted efforts to get rid of their negative feelings and personal biases. They need to be objective minded.

4. **Be Empathetic:** You can understand others better by putting yourself in their shoes. You can see events and problems in the right perspective by looking at them from others' point of view. Therefore, one must be sensitive to the needs and problems of others.

5. **Communicate Openly:** Too much reliance on one-way communication and inadequate communication are the main cause of misperception in organisations. Managers must ensure that right message reaches to the right person at the right time and at the right place. A sound communication system will enable them to understand the events in the organisation in the right perspective.

6. **Avoid Perceptual Distortions:** People in an organisation must guard themselves against half effort, stereotyping, attribution and other perceptual distortions. This requires continuous efforts. Impressions, judgements and decisions should be formed only after careful analysis of information and situation.

TEST QUESTIONS

1. What is perception? How does it differ from sensation?
2. What do you mean by perception? Explain its nature.
3. Explain in brief the process of perception.
4. What are the elements of perceptual process? Describe the nature of interrelationship among these elements.
5. Why do two persons see the same thing but interpret it differently? Explain.
6. What is meant by perceptual selectivity? Describe the factors influencing it?
7. Explain interpersonal perception.
8. Discuss the factors that cause errors and distortion in perception.
9. (*a*) What characteristics of the perceiver affect perception?

   (*b*) What do you understand by attribution?

   (*c*) Briefly explain the figure-ground principle.
10. Discuss the concept of perception. Explain the process of attribution and the factors affecting it.
11. What do you understand by attribution? Discuss the errors which usually creep in while appraising the performance of employees. Also suggest measures to avoid these errors.
12. Discuss the steps which you would take as a manager to reduce perceptual errors as you appraise the performance of your subordinates.

13. Explain the managerial applications of perception.
14. Describe the various ways in which a perceiver may organise different stimuli under perception.
15. Describe the measures that can be taken for developing perceptual skills among managers.
16. "People's responses are always based on their perceptions." Explain.
17. "Perceptual errors can lead to lower employee performance, low morale and reduction in organisational effectiveness." Examine this statement critically.
18. Write short notes on :
    (*a*) Perceptual constancy.
    (*b*) Perceptual context
    (*c*) Perceptual defence
19. As the Human Resource Manager of a company you have been asked to inform that three workers in the factory have been laid off. What perceptual errors you will watch for while delivering the message to the workers.
20. Discuss ways to manage distortions at the stage of interpretation during the process of perception.
21. Find out about stereotypical images of people from a particular background. How are such stereotypes formed? Discuss how these can be broken for better social and interpersonal understanding.
22. Discuss the factors affecting perception.
23. Briefly explain the process of perception. What characteristics of the perceiver affect perception?
24. Define perception. How does perception affect attitude?
25. "Perceptual interpretation is more complex than perceptual selection and perceptual organisation". Explain.
26. Discuss Gestalt principles of perceptual organisation.
27. People do not experience the numerous stimuli they select from the environment as separate and discrete sensations, rather they tend to organise them into groups and perceive them as unified whole. In the light of basic principles of perceptual organisation, explain with suitable examples – figure-ground, grouping and closure.
28. Explain the concept of Halo Effect and Contrast Effect in Perception with suitable examples.
29. "Perception can be deceptive". Elaborate with suitable examples.
30. Write notes on:
    (*a*) Perceptual errors
    (*b*) Cognitive processes
31. What is perception? Write in detail about the Gestalt theory of perception. How is understanding of perception important for a manager?
32. What are the various implications of perception for management? How does management effect perception of people in the organisation?

33. Explain halo effect and its role in the formation of perception.
34. Explain the implications of perception for management.
35. Define perception. Discuss the processes involved in perception.

CASE STUDY

Rajesh is a supervisor in a commercial tool room in the machining section of Priyanka Industries Ltd. for the past seven years. He is a diploma-holder in Mech. Engg., and joined the present organisation as an apprentice engineer and has grown to be a supervisor. During all these years in the company, he had no occasion to attend any supervisory development programme and his concentration has been mostly on the technical aspects of the job. The present works manager (WM) has seen Rajesh grow from an apprentice to supervisor and is yet to reconcile with the change of responsibilities and designation of Rajesh.

On a particular day Rajesh had prepared schedule for the day for all machines and on the jig boring machine, the top priority was for a job from HAL. When Rajesh came for his round he was surprised to see that the operator had loaded some other job other than the job from HAL on the jig boring machine. At this Rajesh was annoyed and the following conversation took place:

Supervisor to Operator: Please take up this HAL job immediately. It is required on top priority.

Operator: WM has given me the other job. Only after finishing this I can take up the HAL job.

Supervisor: I don't want to hear all that. WM has only told me that anything else has to be stopped and the HAL job has to be taken up first.

Operator: Agreed—whenever you have said a job is urgent I have been taking that up immediately. But what you have done about my increment which has been due for over three months?

Supervisor: These things—I am not answerable. The management is responsible. However, you are not the only person with such a grievance, there are many more, I am helpless in this regard. I suggest you go and sort it out with the WM.

Operator: As a supervisor it is your duly to sort out my problems as I report to you.

Supervisor: Don't tell me my job. I am not interested and as I have already told you, you may sort out your increment problem with the WM and right now I don't even care whether you take up this HAL job or not. I will simply report to higher authorities about your misconduct of refusing my order. Let them do what they want. Don't come back to me crying again.

Questions

(*a*) "Individuals tend to project their own feelings and motives into their judgement of others." Comment on the statement from the point of view of the operator, the supervisor and the WM.

(*b*) What situational factors affect the perception of individuals?

(*c*) Recommend an action plan to prevent such an episode in the future.

CHAPTER

4

LEARNING AND BEHAVIOUR MODIFICATION

CHAPTER OUTLINE

4.1 Concept and Nature of Learning
4.2 Process of Learning
4.3 Factors Affecting Learning
4.4 Theories of Learning
- Classical Conditioning
- Operant Conditioning
- Cognitive Learning
- Social Learning

4.5 Reinforcement
- Types of Reinforcement
- Schedules of Reinforcement

4.6 Organisational Behaviour Modification (OB Mod)
- Steps in OB Mod
- Contributions (Utility) of OB Mod
- Criticism (Limitations) of OB Mod
- **Test Questions**
- **Case Study**

As compared to animals, human beings have greater mental capacity to learn and to adapt to changing environment. In fact, learning is an important psychological process that influences human behaviour.

4.1 CONCEPT AND NATURE OF LEARNING

According to Mitchell, "Learning is the process by which new behaviours are acquired. It is generally agreed that learning involves changes in behaviours, practising new behaviours, and establishing permanency in the change".[1]

---

1 T.R. Mitchell, **People in Organisations : Understanding Their Behaviour,** McGraw Hill, New York, 1994, p. 113.

Hilgard has defined learning as "a relatively permanent change in behaviour that occurs as a result of prior experience".[2] In the words of McGehee, "Learning has taken place if an individual behaves, reacts, responds as a result of experience in a manner different from the way he formerly behaved."[3]

Thus, learning means a relatively enduring change in behaviour brought about as a consequence of experience and reinforced practice. It involves acquisition of new behaviour. The definitions given above reveal the following features of learning :

(*i*) Learning involves a change in behaviour. This change is not necessarily an improvement over previous behaviour. For example, bad habits, prejudice, stereotypes, and work restrictions are also learned.

(*ii*) The change in behaviour must be relatively permanent. Any temporary change in behaviour due to fatigue or any other reason is not a part of learning. Temporary changes may be only reflective and eventually disappear in the absence of practice or experience.

(*iii*) The change in behaviour must occur as a result of experience or practice. Any behavioural change due to physical maturation is not learning.

(*iv*) The experience or practice must be reinforced in order for learning to occur. If reinforcement does not accompany the practice or experience the learned behaviour will eventually disappear. It is reinforcement that makes change in behaviour enduring by strengthening and intensifying it.

(*v*) Learning is reflected in behaviour. A change in the thought process or attitudes of an individual not accompanied by change in behaviour is no learning.

Table 4.1: Distinction Between Learning and Maturation

Learning	Physical Maturation
1. Learning requires efforts on the part of a person.	Maturation is a natural process and requires no efforts.
2. Changes occur only in the behaviour of the person who learns.	Changes occur in the behaviour of the entire race.
3. Learning requires practice.	Maturation does not require practice.
4. Learning can go on throughout life.	Maturation takes place up to the age of 25 years.
5. Learning is possible only in favourable conditions.	Maturation takes place under both favourable and unfavourable conditions.
6. Learning requires some form of motivation.	No motivation is needed for maturation.

4.2 PROCESS OF LEARNING

The learning process consists of the following elements :

1. **Drive:** Learning occurs due to some drive or strong stimulus that impels action. Drive arouses a person and keeps him ready to change. It provides the necessary motivation

2 E.R. Hilgard, **Introduction to Psychology**, Oxford & IBH, New Delhi, 1975, p. 196

3 W. McGehee, "Are We Using What We Know About Training? Learning Theory and Training" **Personnel Psychology,** Spring, 1958, p. 2.

for learning. Drives are of two types — (*a*) primary or physiological, and (*b*) secondary or psychological. These two types of drives often interact with each other.

2. **Cue Stimuli:** These refer to the objects existing in the environment and as perceived by the learner. Cue stimuli are of two types — generalisation and discrimination.
   (*a*) **Generalisation:** When a similar but new stimulus elicits a response, generalisation takes place. The principle of generalisation facilitates human learning by making human actions stable over time. An individual can borrow from past learning experiences for smooth adjustment to new learning situations. He need not completely relearn each of the new tasks confronting him from time to time. However, generalisation can lead to false conclusion.
   (*b*) **Discrimination:** It is the opposite of generalisation. It means an organism does not give the same response to a similar but somewhat different stimulus. For example, a bull may learn to respond to the red colour but not to the white. Discrimination can be applied in the management of human behaviour. For example, a sales officer can discriminate between two equally high performing salespersons. He responds positively to the salesperson who has built customer relationships and not to the salesperson who has failed to build such relationships. In the absence of positive response (reinforcement) the second salesperson may change his sales behaviour.
3. **Responses:** The stimuli yield responses which may be physical or psychological. Behavioural responses in terms of attitudes, perception, etc. are counted in learning.
4. **Reinforcement:** Reinforcement is essential for learning. No measurable change in behaviour takes place without reinforcement. Responses which are positively reinforced recur. All events in the environment which affect the probability of occurrence of responses are known as reinforcement.
5. **Retention:** Some of the learning is retained over time while others may be forgotten. Retention makes the learned behaviour stable over time.
6. **Extinction:** Extinction means loss of memory. It leads to loss of learned behaviour. Once something is learned, a part of it may be unlearned or disappear from memory.
7. **Recovery:** There may be spontaneous recovery of the extinct learning. This may happen when memory is regained or when the extinguished response is rewarded.

4.3 FACTORS AFFECTING LEARNING

The main factors affecting learning are given below :

(*i*) **Mental Set of the Learner:** Learning can occur only when the learner is mentally prepared to learn. Research reveals that a person's mental set activates him and such activation makes him inclined to acquire new attitudes, habits, knowledge and skills.

(*ii*) **Motivation:** Motivation refers to what moves a person to action and continues him in action. A person will learn only when he is willing to learn. When a positive behaviour developed through learning is rewarded, it tends to be repeated. For example, employees are likely to learn seriously when they are promised some financial and non-financial reward after successful completion of the training programme.

(*iii*) **Learning Material:** Learning tends to be quick when the learning material is easy and familiar. The shape, meaningfulness and serial position of the learning material also affect learning.

(*iv*) **Environment:** The environment in which learning takes place is very important. People learn faster and without much stress when the environment is supportive, cohesive and without pressure.

(*v*) **Practice:** Regular and continuous practice strengthens learning. The more an individual practises, the more he absorbs the learning contents.

4.4 THEORIES OF LEARNING

Major theories of learning are as follows:

1. **Classical Conditioning:** According to this theory, behaviour is learnt by repetitive association between a stimulus (S) and a response (R). In this type of conditioning an individual responds to some stimulus that would invariably elicit such a response. The research of the famous Russian physiologist and Nobel laureate Ivan Pavlov explains the process of classical conditioning[4].

   Pavlov conducted an experiment on a dog to study the relation between the dog's salivation and the ringing of a bell. A simple surgical procedure enabled him to measure accurately the amount of saliva secreted by the dog. When Pavlov presented a piece of meat (unconditional stimulus) to the dog, he noticed a great amount of salivation (unconditional response). On the other hand, when he merely rang a bell (neutral stimulus) the dog did not salivate. During the next phase, Pavlov offered meat along with ringing of the bell. On this the dog salivated. After that Pavlov rang the bell without offering the meat. The dog again salivated. The dog had become classically conditioned to salivate (conditional response) to the sound of bell (conditional stimulus).

   Thus, under classical conditioning, learning is a conditional response that requires building up an association between a conditional stimulus and an unconditional stimulus.

   These stages in classical conditioning are shown in Fig. 4.1.

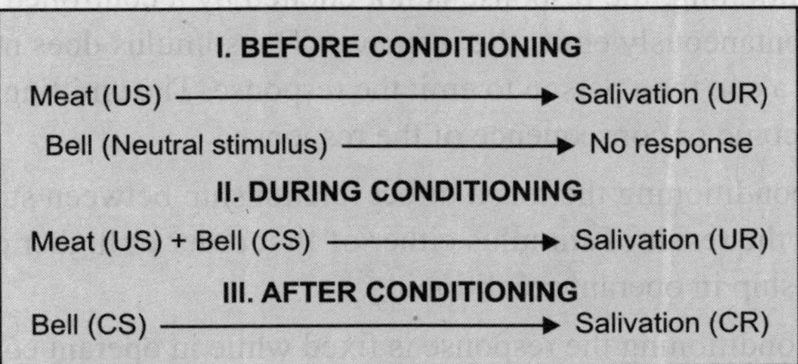

Fig. 4.1: Stages in Classical Conditioning

4 Ivan P. Pavlov, **The Work of the Digestive Glands** (translated by W.H. Thompson), Charles Griffin, London, 1902.

Classical conditioning has two important implications for understanding human behaviour. **First,** learning can be transferred to stimulus other than that used in the original conditioning. **Second,** reinforcement can be acquired as a conditioned stimulus becomes reinforcing under subsequent stages. This means secondary rewards are important in organisations. For example, a cleanliness drive was launched by a hospital to prepare for inspection by the top officials of the Health Ministry. As a result, nurses and other staff became utmost attentive to their duties. Such attention continued whenever there was a cleanliness drive even though there was no inspection.

Classical conditioning fails to explain total human behaviour. According to Robbins, "Classical conditioning is passive. Something happens and we react in a specific or particular way. It is elicited in response to a specific, identifiable event and as such, it explains simple and reflective behaviour. But behaviour of people in the organisations is emitted rather than elicited, and it is voluntary rather than reflective".[5] Skinner[6] suggests that the learning of complex behaviour can better be understood through operant conditioning.

2. **Operant Conditioning:** Operant refers to the behaviour that produces effects. Operant conditioning is based on the work of Skinner[7] who suggests that people emit responses that are rewarded, and will not emit responses that are either not rewarded or punished. Operant conditioning implies that behaviour is voluntary and it is determined, maintained and controlled by its consequences. This theory of learning is based upon the relationship between three elements: (*a*) stimulus situation, (*b*) behavioural response to situation, and (*c*) consequences of the response to the person. For example, employees in a company are required to undergo a training programme to become eligible for promotion. In this case, the possibility of losing promotion without training is stimulus situation. Attending the training programme is the behavioural response. Promotion is the consequence of the response. Thus, people learn the behaviours that are rewarded and engage in such behaviours. Managers can use the operant conditioning process to influence and control the behaviour of employees by designing a suitable rewards system.

Difference Between Classical Conditioning and Operant Conditioning: The main differences between the two types of conditioning are as follows :

(*i*) In classical conditioning, a specific stimulus is used to elicit a specific response. But in operant conditioning, the response is not elicited by a controlled stimulus. Rather the organism spontaneously emits the response. The stimulus does not elicit the response but serves as a cue for a person to emit the response. The emitting of response depends upon the outcome or consequence of the response.

(*ii*) In classical conditioning there is a direct relationship between stimulus and response. Behaviour is the result of stimulus either of first order or higher order. But there is no such relationship in operant conditioning.

(*iii*) In classical conditioning the response is fixed while in operant conditioning responses can vary in types and degrees.

5 Stephen P. Robbins, **Organisational Behaviour,** Prentice Hall, New Delhi, 1994, p. 112.
6 B.F. Skinner, **Science and Human Behaviour** Macmillan, New York, 1953.
7 B.F. Skinner, *op. cit.*

(*iv*) In classical conditioning response is involuntary. But in operant conditioning response is voluntary.

(*v*) In classical conditioning stimulus leads to response (S – R). On the other hand, in operant conditioning, response is instrumental in receiving the reward (R – S).

(*vi*) In classical conditioning, the individual does not choose the reinforcement. But in operant conditioning the individual can choose the reinforcement (reward) by giving the correct response.

Cognitive Learning

Cognition means an individual's ideas, thoughts, knowledge, interpretations, and understanding about himself and his environment. Cognitive theory of learning suggests that an organism learns the meaning of various objects and events and learned responses depend on the meaning assigned to stimuli. Cognitive theorists argue that the learner forms a cognitive structure in memory, preserves and organises information about the various events that occur in a learning situation. For example, in his place-learning experiments, Tolman[8] trained a rat to turn right in a "T" maze in order to get food. Then he started the rat from the opposite part of the maze. As per operant conditioning theory the rat should have turned right due to past conditioning. But the rat, instead, turned towards the food. After the experiment, Tolman concluded that the rat formed a cognitive map to decide how to get the food. Thus, the organism's action depends upon the cognitive structure retrieved from memory and reinforcement is not essential for learning.

The cognitive theory recognises the role of organism in the learning process. Learning is based on a relationship between cognitive cues and expectation and behaviour is goal directed. In this theory, one stimulus leads to another stimulus (S – S model) as compared to the classical conditioning (S – R) and operant conditioning (R – S).

The cognitive approach is used in several psychological processes like perception, learning attitude formation and motivation. Most of the early human relations training programmes were based upon this approach. Many expectancy theories of motivation centre around the cognitive model of human behaviour. Goal setting, expectations, attributions and locus of control are all cognitive concepts.

Social Learning

Social learning theory integrates the cognitive and operant conditioning approaches to learning. It suggests that people learn and acquire new behaviours by observing and imitating others[9]. Learning is neither a case of individual determinism (the cognitive view) nor of environmental determinism (classical and operant conditioning views). Rather it is a combination of both. Thus, social learning approach emphasizes the interactive nature of cognitive, behavioural and environmental determinants.

According to social learning theory, learning takes place in two steps :

(*a*) A person observes how others act and forms a mental picture of the act and its consequences (reward and punishment).

(*b*) The person acts out the formed image. If the consequences are positive, he repeats the act otherwise he does not repeat it.

---

8 Edward C. Tolman, **Purposive Behaviour in Animals and Men,** Century, New York, 1932.

9 Albert Bandura, **Social Learning Theory,** Prentice Hall, New Jersey, 1977.

For example, a person learns from others that 'fire burns the body'. There is no need for him to touch the fire. Thus, people learn through observation and direct experience.

Modelling: The modelling or vicarious processes essentially involve observational learning. A person learns many patterns of behaviour by watching his role models such as parents, teachers, superiors, film stars, etc. The influence that a model will have on an individual depends upon the following processes:[10]

1. **Attention Process:** A person will learn from a model only when he recognises the model and pays attention to his behaviour. One tends to be most influenced by models that are attractive, appear repeatedly and which one considers are important.
2. **Retention Process:** A model's influence depends on how well the person remembers the model's actions, even after the model is not available.
3. **Motor Reproduction Process:** The influence of a model will be strong if the person performs the model's actions or does what he has observed.
4. **Reinforcement Process:** A person will exhibit the model's behaviour if incentives or rewards are provided. Behaviours that are reinforced are given more attention, learned better and performed more often.

4.5 REINFORCEMENT

Reinforcement plays a vital role in the learning process. Reinforcement means anything that strengthens the response preceding it and induces repetitions of the response. Reinforcement is different from motivation. Reinforcement is an external explanation of behaviour whereas motivation is an internal explanation of behaviour. Motivation is based on needs which are cognitive and unobservable. On the other hand, reinforcement is based on environmental events and can be observed.

Reinforcement facilitates learning by conditioning the behavioural response. It may not be essential for learning but its presence increases the learning over a period of time, the learner may associate the behavioural response with the reinforcement. Fig. 4.2 shows the relationship between reinforcement and behaviour.

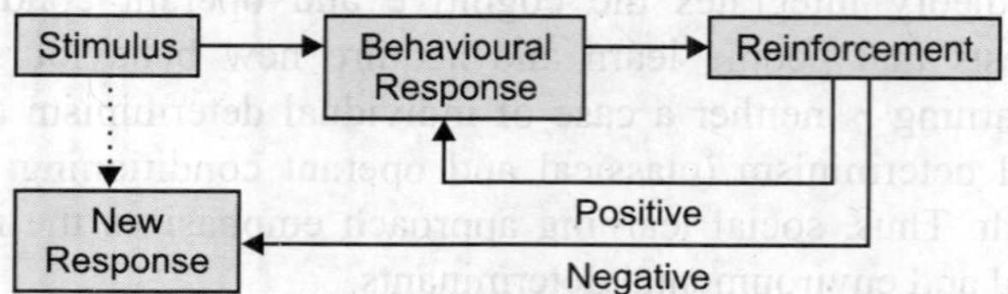

Fig. 4.2: Effect of Reinforcement on Learning

Types of Reinforcement

Various **types of reinforcement** that may be used in learning are given below :

1. **Positive Reinforcement:** When rewards are used to stimulate the desired behaviour and to strengthen the repetition of such behaviour in future, it is called positive

10 S.P. Robbins, *op. cit.,* p. 133.

reinforcement. For example, a manager may give a certificate of appreciation to a subordinate on the achievement of the specified sales target. An effective reinforcement is one that matches with the needs of the employee and that is contingent upon the desired performance.

Positive reinforcement may further be classified into primary and secondary reinforcement. **Primary or unconditioned reinforcers** are innately satisfying to an individual and directly satisfies his primary motives. It is independent of past experience and is an unlearned reward for the individual. Food, clothing, shelter and sex are examples of primary reinforcers. These are used in simple learning situations.

Secondary or conditioned reinforcers are learned cues and depend upon past experience. Praise, recognition, advancement, etc. are examples of such reinforcers.

Positive reinforcement may also be classified into intrinsic and extrinsic reinforcement. **Intrinsic** rewards are natural consequence of behaviour, *e.g.,* satisfaction arising out of a job well done. On the other hand, **extrinsic** have no direct relationship with behaviour, *e.g.,* payment of money for improving quality.

2. **Negative Reinforcement:** When a person learns to avoid or escape from unpleasant consequences, negative reinforcement takes place. For example, the factory supervisor may warn a worker who is not using safety device. In order to avoid warning (a negative consequence) the worker may start using the safety device (desirable behaviour). While positive reinforcement increases the probability of desirable behaviour for obtaining desirable consequence, negative reinforcement increases this probability to avoid undesirable consequence.

   Negative reinforcement is also known as **avoidance** because it is used to avoid negative consequence.

3. **Punishment:** When undesirable behaviour is reduced by providing negative consequences, it is called punishment. For example, an employee who frequently comes late for work is punished with a fine. In order to avoid similar punishment in future the employee starts coming in time. Both punishment and negative reinforcement are forms of negative control of behaviour. However, the two are different. While negative reinforcement strengthens and increases desirable behaviour in order to avoid undesirable consequence, punishment weakens and decreases undesirable behaviour.

   Punishment is a traditional method of reducing and eliminating undesirable behaviour. But it involves several possible dangers. **First,** punishment only tells a person what **should not** be done rather than what **should** be done. Therefore, the individual may commit one mistake after another as he seeks to find out through trial and error behaviour that will not be punished. **Second,** punishment causes resentment and frustrates the punished. It creates antagonism towards the punishing agent. As a result the effectiveness of punishment decreases over time. It becomes counterproductive in the work environment. Experts[11] have suggested the following guidelines for proper administration of punishment:

---

11 H.W. Babb and D.G. Kopp "Application of Behaviour Modification in Organisations : A Review and Critique", **Academy of Management Review,** 1978, pp 289-292 and R.D. Arvey and J.M. Ivancevich, "Punishment in Organisations : A Review, Propositions and Research Suggestions", **Academy of Management Review,** January, 1980, pp 123-132.

(*i*) Punish the undesirable behaviour rather than the person to avoid revenge.

(*ii*) The amount of punishment should be adequate enough to extinguish the specific undesired behaviour. Under-punishment may not eliminate the undesired behaviour while over-punishment may lead to undesirable consequences.

(*iii*) Administer the punishment in private. Punishing a person in front of others amounts to double punishment as the punished person loses face.

(*iv*) Punishment should be administered immediately after the undesired behaviour occurs. Every occurrence of the undesirable behaviour should be followed by punishment.

(*v*) Punishment must be used to make the person select the desired behaviour that is reinforced. Otherwise, the undesirable behaviour tends to reappear causing fear and anxiety in the person being punished.

(*vi*) Punishment must be so administered that it does not become a reward for undesirable behaviour.

4. **Extinction:** It refers to withdrawal of a positive reinforcement to eliminate behaviour that was considered desirable in the past but is no longer desirable. It is based on the principle that a response that is not reinforced will eventually disappear. When the reward for a behaviour is withdrawn, the behaviour will become less frequent and ultimately cease to occur. For example, a departmental head used to have informal discussion with his employees to know the reality of the situation. Now he starts avoiding such discussion. As a result employees will gradually stop having informal talks with him.

Schedules of Reinforcement

Research reveals that the timing of reinforcement determines the speed of learning and also how long lasting its effects will be. In other words, the effectiveness of reinforcement depends on the schedule of its administration. Skinner[12] and other psychologists have suggested the following schedules of reinforcement :

1. **Continuous Reinforcement Schedule:** Under this schedule, every positive behavioural response is followed by a reward. This type of reinforcement increases the desirable behaviour very rapidly. However, there is a rapid decline when the reinforcement is withdrawn. In organisational setting, it is not possible to reinforce behaviour every time it occurs.
2. **Partial Reinforcement Schedule:** Under this schedule, every correct behavioural response is not followed by reinforcement. This schedule is more lasting though it leads to slower learning as compared to continuous reinforcement. Partial reinforcement is more widely applied in organisations to change attitudes, values and norms. According to Ferster and Skinner there are four types of partial reinforcement schedules:

(***a***) **Fixed Ratio Schedule:** Under this schedule, reinforcement is given only **after a fixed number** of responses. For example, piece rate plan of wage payment is a fixed ratio schedule. This schedule tends to produce a high rate of response. Workers

12 C.B. Ferster and B.F. Skinner, **Schedules of Reinforcement**, Appleton, New York, 1957.

try to produce as many pieces as possible in order to earn maximum wages. An individual knows that reinforcement (reward) depends on the number of responses. Therefore, he shows the responses as quickly as he can.

(*b*) **Variable Ratio Schedule:** In this schedule, the reward is given only after a number of desired responses. But the number of responses differs from one reinforcer to another. For example, salespersons are given commission on successful sales calls. Sometimes a salesperson may be able to make a sale only after two calls on potential buyers. On other occasions, he may have to make ten calls to make a sale. Thus, the reward is variable in relation to the number of successful calls made by the salesperson. Research shows that this schedule is the most powerful in sustaining the desired behaviour.

3. **Fixed Interval Schedule:** Under this schedule, a reinforcement is administered only after a fixed time interval after the previous reinforcement. For example, employees are usually paid monthly wages for the time spent on the job. This time wage system provides the least motivation for hard work because reward is linked to time interval rather than work performance.

4. **Variable Interval Schedule:** In this schedule, the reward is given after a randomly varying length of time. This schedule generates a higher rate of responses and more consistent performance because the reinforcement is unpredictable. For example, when a factory supervisor visits workers at 12 a.m. everyday (fixed interval), performance tends to be high just prior to his visit and thereafter, it declines. If the supervisor visits at different points of time each day, performance is likely to be higher and more stable throughout the day.

4.6 ORGANISATION BEHAVIOUR MODIFICATION (OB MOD)

According to Robbins, "OB Mod is a programme where managers identify performance-related employee behaviours and then implement an intervention strategy to strengthen desirable behaviours and weaken undesirable behaviours."[13]

OB Mod is based on Skinner's operant conditioning technique of modifying behaviour so that behaviour becomes more conducive to goal accomplishment. It represents the application of reinforcement theory and relies on positive reinforcement. OB Mod provides managers a powerful means of changing the behaviour of employees. In the words of Schermerhorn, "OB Mod is the systematic reinforcement of desirable work behaviour and the non-reinforcement or punishment of unwanted work behaviour."[14]

4.6.1 Steps in OB Mod

The steps involved in OB Mod are as follows :

13 S.P. Robbins, *op. cit*, p. 253.

14 Schermerhorn, Hunt and Osborn, **Managing Organisational Behaviour,** John Wiley & Sons, New York, 1988, p 538.

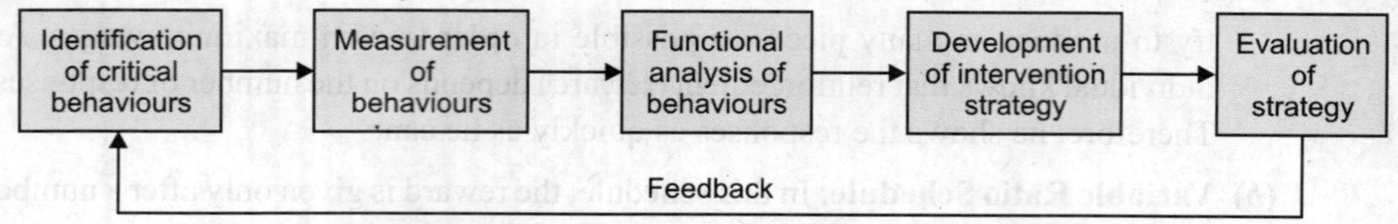

Fig. 4.3: Steps in OB Mod

1. **Identification of Critical Behaviours:** First of all, the behaviours that exercise significant influence on the organisation are identified. Employees may engage in several types of behaviour in the organisation. Behaviours that have significant impact on performance (*e.g.,* attendance, promptness, customer service, constructive criticism, discipline, etc.) are identified through mutual discussions between employees and their superiors. A behavioural audit may also be conducted to systematically analyse critical behaviours in each job.
2. **Measurement of Behaviours:** Once the critical behaviours are identified, actual behaviours are measured. The frequency with which critical behaviours occur over a period of time is recorded. If there is little or no discrepancy between desirable behaviour and measured behaviour, no further action is required. For example, if the rate of employee absenteeism is within the acceptable limit, no corrective action is necessary. Measurement of behaviour also reveals the circumstances asssociated with each critical behaviour.
3. **Functional Analysis of Behaviours:** A detailed analysis of present behaviour of employees is made to judge the consequences each of the behaviours produces and the conditions that cause such behaviour. It is necessary to identify the contingent consequences that have an impact on subsequent behaviour. There may be more than one competing contingency for every organisational behaviour. Therefore, functional analysis must not be deluded by the contingent consequences that on the surface appear to be affecting the critical behaviour.
4. **Development of Intervention Strategy:** An appropriate intervention strategy can be developed on the basis of critical behaviours that require change and the factors that cause such behaviours. Intervention strategies involve positive reinforcement, negative reinforcement, withdrawal of positive reinforcement, and punishment. The purpose of these strategies is to strengthen desirable behaviours and to weaken undesirable behaviours. The strategy must be appropriate to the situation and should produce the desired effect. It is not sufficient to develop intervention strategy. The strategy has to be implemented effectively.
5. **Systematic Evaluation of Strategy:** In the final stage of OB Mod, the success of intervention strategy is judged. Evaluation would reveal whether the undesirable behaviours have been converted into desirable behaviours or not. Changed behaviours can be compared with desired behaviours. If there is a positive change, the strategy has been successful. In case the change is insignificant, more appropriate strategies may have to be adopted.

4.6.2 Contributions (Utility) of OB Mod

OB Mod is a set of practical tools by which people can be made to learn new skills and behaviour. It has been applied successfully in several organisations to improve employee behaviour for organisational effectiveness. It helps managers to convert undesirable behaviour into desirable behaviour. The main strengths of OB Mod are as follows :

(*i*) OB Mod deals with observed behaviour. Therefore, it can be put to testing.

(*ii*) OB Mod can be used to make employees learn new behaviours thereby replacing undesirable behaviours.

(*iii*) Managers can use OB Mod to effectively control and regulate the behaviours of subordinates in the organisation.

(*iv*) It is comparatively easy to understand the techniques of OB Mod. Therefore, managers can use them without any difficulty.

OB Mod has been widely applied in the areas of human resource management, executive development, motivation, management of change and organisation development.

4.6.3 Criticism (Limitations) of OB Mod

The critics of OB Mod argue that it has been criticised on the following grounds :

(*i*) OB Mod tends to equate human beings with rats. Skinner's operant conditioning principles were developed after a series of experiments on white rats. But "organisations are more complex than Skinner's boxies" [15]

(*ii*) OB Mod techniques ignore the individuality of a person and constitute a threat to the concept of personal autonomy. These techniques are employed to manipulate and control human beings.

(*iii*) Behaviour modification restricts freedom of choice of behaviour. It works against the concepts of creativity and innovation which are necessary for the success of an organisation.

(*iv*) The idea of changing behaviour through reinforcement under OB Mod tantamounts to bribery because some reward is given when a person shows the behaviour as desired by the manager.

(*v*) OB Mod is based on the reinforcement theory of Skinner. It assumes that man is totally shaped by his environment. It doubts the intelligence of man and ignores the cognitive processes operating within him. The perception, beliefs, needs and expectations of people are not considered. Therefore, OB Mod is an over-simplified model.

(*vi*) Reinforcement under OB Mod appears to be in conformity with the traditional thinking that people need to be directed and controlled to get the work done. It challenges the integrity, wisdom and self-motivation of people. Many people today are enlightened and want self-actualisation.

(*vii*) OB Mod overemphasises external rewards and overlooks the internal causes of behaviour.

(*viii*) Some people argue that OB Mod is just like old wine in new bottle. It makes use of old techniques of behaviour modification. It is not a new technique of management.

(*ix*) OB Mod is said to be an impractical trial because organisational settings are different from experimental laboratories. It is too difficult to measure and analyse complex

---

15 Fred L. Fry, **"Operant Conditioning in Organisational Setting : of Mice or Men", Personnel,** July August, 1974, pp. 17-24.

behaviours most people engage in. Moreover, it is not easy to tie rewards to performance for reinforcement. OB Mod is basically a univariate method while organisations are multivariate.

Conclusion: Several ethical issues and practical problems are involved in OB Mod. There is need to reconcile need for control over behaviour with individual rights and human dignity. OB Mod is not a panacea for all problems of organisational behaviour. It cannot be applied indiscriminately to regulate and control employee behaviours. Rather it must be applied keeping in view its limitations and the characteristics of the organisation.

TEST QUESTIONS

1. What is learning? Distinguish between learning and maturation.
2. Explain the concept and nature of learning.
3. Explain the process of learning, pointing out clearly the elements involved in it
4. Discuss the factors that affect learning.
5. What is classical conditioning? How does it differ from operant conditioning?
6. "Classical conditioning connects stimulus with response while operant conditioning connects response with stimulus". Explain.
7. "Learning theory can be used to explain and control human behaviour". Comment.
8. "Any observable change in behaviour is *prima facie* evidence that learning has taken place". Do you agree? Give reasons.
9. "Most behaviours are learnt, some from the experience of self and some from the experience of others". Critically examine this statement.
10. Explain cognitive theory of learning.
11. Critically examine the social learning theory.
12. What do you mean by reinforcement in learning? How does it help in shaping the behaviour of people?
13. Explain the types of reinforcement which managers can employ to make employees learn new behaviours.
14. Explain with examples social learning. To what extent is it relevant in modern organisations?
15. Describe various schedules of reinforcement that may be used in learning.
16. Distinguish between positive and negative reinforcement. What precautions should be taken in administering punishment?
17. What is meant by Organisational Behaviour Modification (OB Mod)? Explain the steps involved in the process of OB Mod.
18. "Behaviour modification is based on operant conditioning". Explain
19. How is OB Mod useful to managers? What are its limitations?
20. Critically examine behaviour modification theory and its applications in work organisations.
21. Comment on the following statements :

(*a*) "Learning leads to change in behaviour".
(*b*) "Behaviour is a function of its consequences".
(*c*) "Classical conditioning is passive".
(*d*) "OB Mod is manipulative and unethical".
(*e*) "OB Mod is a powerful tool of motivation".

22. How do the processes of classical conditioning and operant conditioning shape our behaviour?
23. Why is OB Mod considered unethical?
24. Write a note on:
    Social learning theory
25. "Negative reinforcement is used for avoidance learning". Explain.
26. Discuss in detail the various theories of learning. Which theory is most relevant for a work organisation?
27. How are classical and operant conditioning theories different?
28. (*a*) "Reinforcement theory of learning is at the cost of behaviour modification". Examine this statement.
    (*b*) "Learning leads to change in human behaviour". Comment.

CASE STUDY

Hindustan Soaps Limited produces three soaps – Janata (for lower middle class), Lux (for middle class) and Supreme Lux (for upper middle class and rich). The company enjoys 50% market share for all the three categories of soap, with a clear-cut market leadership in the domestic market.

The company has got a strong workforce of 4,000 employees, working on automated plants with good system support. With traditional culture and organisation structure, each employee possesses super-specialisation in his/her job. This has brought up average productivity to 85% (which is highest in the industry).

Of late, the company has started facing competition from new entrants in the market (of which, three are foreign companies). These competitor companies are slim with limited workforce. It has been found that 20% of the company's workforce is extra, due to the concept of super-specialisation, causing non-mobility of the employees. It has also been observed that employee transfers, promotion to different newer jobs and acceptance of new job prescriptions are difficult. Too much of super-specialisation has also hampered the general awareness of the employees. It has created serious amount of monotony for them.

Thirty per cent of the company's employees are going to retire in the next two years. This retirement may be used for overall 'wage cost reduction', by avoiding fresh recruitment.

The company is seriously thinking of making its employees versatile, aggressive, innovative and receptive. New processes and products, fast decision making, flatness of the organisation etc., are the need of the hour. Therefore, an employee is not to be exposed to more than one area of activity and skill, so that better use of resources would be possible.

Discuss the pros and cons of multi-skilling of employees (in the light of overall resource leverage).

CHAPTER

5

ATTITUDES AND VALUES

CHAPTER OUTLINE

5.1 Concept of Attitudes
- Attitudes, Beliefs and Opinions

5.2 Components of Attitudes
5.3 Attitudes and Individual Behaviour
5.4 Theories of Attitude Formation
5.5 Factors Influencing Attitude Formation
5.6 Measurement of Attitudes
5.7 Effects of Employee Attitudes on Organisational Behaviour
5.8 Attitude Change
5.9 How to Develop Positive Attitudes
5.10 Concept of Values
5.11 Difference between Attitudes and Values
5.12 Types of Values
5.13 Factors Influencing Value Formation (Sources of Values)
5.14 Effect of Values on Behaviour
- **Test Questions**
- **Case Study**

Attitudes and values exercise a significant influence on human behaviour. They influence how one perceives objects, events and people in the context of organisations. Attitudes and value affect behaviour of employees and their performance. Therefore, managers must understand the attitudes and values of employees to manage them effectively.

5.1 CONCEPT OF ATTITUDES

The term "attitude" refers to the way a person feels about anything in his environment. It indicates a person's positive or negative feelings. According to Reitz[1], "Attitude is the persistent tendency to feel and behave in a favourable or unfavourable way towards some object, person

1 H.J. Reitz, **Behaviour in Organisations,** Richard D. Irwin, Illinois, 1977, p 250.

or idea". In the words of Schermerhorn and others[2], "Attitude is a predisposition to respond in a positive or negative way to someone or something in one's environment". Katz and Scotland have defined attitude as "a tendency or predisposition to evaluate an object or symbol of that object in certain way."[3]

On the basis of these definitions, the following **characteristics of attitudes** can be identified:

1. **Attitudes are Invisible :** Attitude is an internal state of a person or a psychological phenomenon. Therefore, it cannot be observed directly. However, it can be judged from the behaviour of a person. For example, if an employee is loyal, we may conclude that he has a positive attitude towards his organisation.
2. **Attitudes are Acquired:** Attitudes are gradually learnt over a period of time. The process of learning attitudes starts right from childhood and continues throughout the life of a person. For example, if a child's parents are highly optimistic, the child is likely to develop a similar attitude.
3. **Attitudes are Pervasive:** Every person has some kinds of attitudes. Attitudes are formed in the process of socialisation and may relate to anything in the environment.
4. **Attitudes Affect Behaviour:** An individual responds favourably or unfavourably to objects in his environemnt according to his attitudes.
5. **Attitudes Vary in Degree:** The intensity of attitudes may differ from person to person. One individual may have a more favourable attitude towards higher education while another individual is not so favourable.
6. **Attitudes are Evaluative:** Attitudes towards objects, events or people may be either positive (favourable) or negative (unfavourable).

Attitudes, Beliefs and Opinions

These three terms are very closely related but there is some difference between them. A belief is a hypothesis about something or someone. It reflects the manner in which something is perceived. What are supposed to be true is one's belief. For example, a manager may believe that chief executive of his company is honest which may or may not be true. On the other hand, the attitude of the manager towards the chief executive reveals whether he likes or does not like him. His belief will influence his attitude towards the chief executive.

An opinion reflects one's judgement. Attitudes are generally measured on the basis of expression of opinions. While attitudes are generalised predispositions, opinions tend to be more focussed. Opinions may be called expressions of attitudes. But according to Kolasa, "An opinion is response to a specifically limited stimulus, but the response is certainly influenced by the predisposition with which the individual is operating, that is, the attitude structure. Undoubtedly attitudes are basic to opinion as well as to many other aspects of behaviour."[4]

---

2 J.E. Schermerhorn *et.al.,* **Managing Organisational Behaviour,** John Wiley & Sons, New York, 1988, p. 80.

3 Daniel Katz and E. Scotland, "A Preliminary Statement to a Theory of Attitude Structure and Change" in S. Koch (ed.), **Psychology : A Study of a Science,** McGraw Hill, New York, 1956, p. G 425.

4 Blair J. Kolasa, **Introduction to Behavioural Science for Business;** Wiley Eastern, New Delhi, 1970, p 386.

5.2 COMPONENTS OF ATTITUDES

There are three basic components of an attitude which are given below:

1. **Cognitive or Informational Component:** It consists of an individual's perceptions, beliefs, ideas and values about an object. For example, an employee may believe that his boss is an autocrat. The cognitive component is sometimes called "opinion".

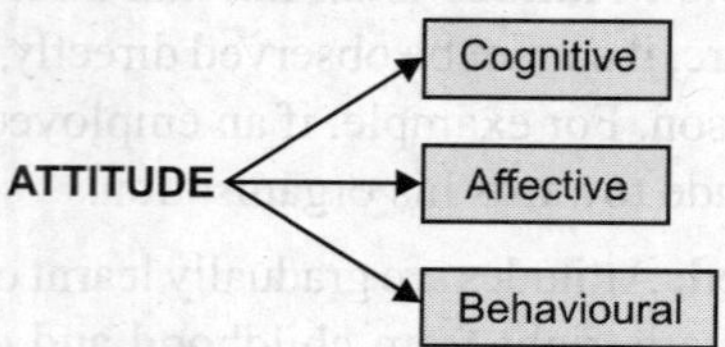

Fig. 5.1: Components of An Attitude

2. **Affective or Emotional Component:** It consists of an individual's emotions or feelings about an object. It is often expressed as like or dislike, good or bad, pleasing or displeasing, favourable or unfavourable. For example, an employee may dislike his boss on personal grounds.

3. **Behavioural or Overt Component:** It refers to the tendency of an individual to behave in a particular manner towards the attitude object. Both the cognitive and affective components influence the way a person intends to behave towards an attitude object.

5.3 ATTITUDES AND INDIVIDUAL BEHAVIOUR

How does an individual behave towards an object, idea or person depends primarily upon how does he interpret the total situation. Attitudes are one of the several factors that influence interpretation of the situation and the individual's response.

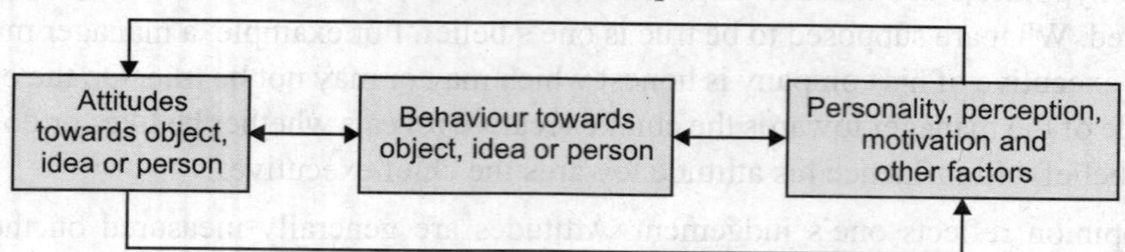

Fig. 5.2: Influence of Attitudes on Behaviour

According to Katz[5] attitudes serve four main functions as described below :

1. **Adjustment Function:** Attitudes are the means for reaching the desired goals or for avoiding undesirable results.

2. **Ego-Defensive Function:** Our attitudes serve the function of defending our self-image. For example, when an individual cannot admit his inferiority feelings he may bolster his ego by attitude of superiority over some minority groups.

5 D. Katz, "The Functional Approach to the Study of Attitudes", **Public Opinion Quarterly,** 1960, pp 163-204.

3. **Value-Expressive Function:** One's attitudes may express one's values or enhance one's self-identity. Value-expressive attitudes not only classify self-image but hold that self-image closer to the heart's desire.
4. **Knowledge Function:** This function is based on the need for understanding and making sense of the world. Attitudes that are inadequate for dealing with new and changing environment are thrown out. Attitudes provide consistency and stability to behaviour. With the help of knowledge about an employee's attitude, a manager can anticipate the employee's behaviour with a fair degree of accuracy.

5.4 THEORIES OF ATTITUDE FORMATION

Several theories have been developed to explain the processes underlying formation of attitudes. These theories may be classified into three categories as under :

1. **Cognitive Consistency Theories:** According to these theories, inconsistencies that arise between related beliefs create psychological tension. People attempt to reduce the inconsistency to avoid the tension. There are four such theories :

   (*a*) **Balance Theory:** This theory is concerned with consistency in the judgement of people and issues that are linked by some form of relationship[6]. Attitude formation consists of three elements – the person, other person, and impersonal entity. When the relationship between these elements is imbalanced, an individual has to restore balance cognitively in any of the four ways[7] — denial, bolstering, differentiation, and transcendence. **Denial** means denying a relationship whenever there is imbalance. **Bolstering** refers to adding another issue to the main issue. **Differentiation** involves splitting an element into two elements that are related in opposite ways to other elements in the situation and have a negative relation to each other. **Transcendence** involves combining elements into larger units to form a balanced structure.

   Balance theory is helpful in understanding the role of persuasive communication and interpersonal attractiveness in attitude formation. But it overlooks the degree of unit relationship and the relevance of other elements to the perceiver. Therefore, quantitative predictions about the degree of change in attitudes cannot be made.

   (*b*) **Congruity Theory:** This theory focusses on changes in the evaluation of a source and a concept which have an associative or disassociative linkage. Congruity means a stable state and incongruity is an unstable state. When a source and concept that are positively associated have exactly the same evaluations there is congruity.[8] Attitudes towards the source and the concept undergo change to resolve the incongruity.

   (*c*) **Consistency or Structural Theory:** The focus of this theory is on the consistency between a person's overall attitude and his beliefs about its relationship to his more

---

6 F. Heider, **The Psychology of International Relations,** John Wiley, New York, 1968

7 R.P. Abelson, "Modes of Resolution of Belief Dilemmas", **Journal of Conflict Resolution,** 1959 (3), pp. 343-352.

8 C.E. Osgood and P.H. Tannenbaum, "The Principle of Congruity in the Prediction of Attitude Change", **Psychological Review,** 1955 (62), pp. 42-55.

general value[9]. It suggests that when an attitude is altered, the relationship between the cognitive and affective components of the attitude changes. According to this theory persuasive communication can be used to change attitudes.

(*d*) **Cognitive Dissonance Theory:** According to this theory, whenever an individual's cognitions are incompatible (opposed to one's experience about the relationship of events) there is pressure to reduce or eliminate such dissonance. The dissonance can be reduced by (*i*) changing a behavioural element, (*ii*) changing an environmental element, and (*iii*) adding a new cognitive element.

An individual faces dissonance whenever his behaviour is contrary to his attitudes[10].

2. **Functional Theory:** This theory is based on the relationship of attitudes and efforts to the motivation of a person. According to Katz, an attitude that serves an adjustment function can be changed when either of the two conditions prevails : (*a*) the attitude and the activities related to it no longer provide the satisfaction they once did; or (*b*) the aspiration level of the individual has been raised. This theory has led to research in changing ego-defensive attitudes only.

   Kelman[11] has added another dimension to the functional theory. He has suggested three processes of attitude formation — compliance, identification and internalisation. **Compliance** means changing an attitude to gain a favourable reaction from other person or group. **Identification** refers to changing an attitude to maintain a positive self-defining relationship with the change agent. **Internalisation** implies adopting an attitude which is congruent with one's overall value system.

3. **Social Judgment Theory:** This theory tries to explain how existing attitudes mediate change in attitudes. An individual's initial attitude on an issue serves as a reference against which he evaluates other opinions. The range of opinions (known as the latitude of acceptance) which the individual finds acceptable encompasses the opinion that is characteristic of his own stand. The range of opinions which the individual finds objectionable (the latitude of rejection) encompasses the opinion he finds most objectionable.

5.5 FACTORS INFLUENCING ATTITUDE FORMATION

People are not born with specific attitudes. Rather they acquire attitudes through the process of learning. People learn from the environment in which they interact. The factors from which people learn or which influence the formation of attitudes are given below :

1. **Personality or Psychological Factors:** The psychological make-up of an individual consists of his perception, beliefs, ideas, values, etc. It plays a vital role in the formation of his attitudes. For example, persons having authoritarian personality tend to have ethnocentric attitudes. People with low level of intelligence and less education have

9 M.J. Rosenberg, "A Structural Theory of Attitude Dynamics", **Public Opinion Quarterly**, 1960 (24), pp 319-40.

10 L. Festinger, **A Theory of Cognitive Dissonance,** Harper & Row, New York, 1957.

11 H.C. Kelman, "Compliance, Identification and Internalisation : Three Processes of Attitude Change", **Journal of Conflict Resolution,** 1958 (2), pp. 51-60

conservative attitudes. However, personality itself is influenced by several hereditary and social factors.

2. **Family:** Family shapes the initial and core attitudes of a person. A newly-born child learns firstly from his mother and subsequently from other members of his family. This process is known as socialisation. Family is the primary group to which an individual belongs. Therefore, the attitudes of family members determine his early attitudes.

3. **Peer or Reference Groups:** A reference group is any group of people with which an individual associates himself. This group provides inputs to an individual for learning attitudes and makes him aware of alternative behaviours and life styles. An individual often seeks out others who share similar attitudes. He changes his attitudes to conform to the attitudes of the group whose approval is important for him. All the groups with which an individual interacts influence his attitudes. But the attitudes, norms and values of the primary group exercise the major impact on his attitudes.

4. **Social Factors:** Social class and religious affiliation also play an important role in forming the attitudes of an individual. At an early age an individual is taught that certain attitudes are acceptable and certain others are non-acceptable in the society. What is considered appropriate in one society and culture may be totally unacceptable in another culture and society. For example, extra-marital affairs common in the West are considered bad in India.

5. **Other Factors:** Organisational, economic and political factors also influence a person's attitudes. Nature of job, office layout, fellow employees, type of leadership and rewards associated with the job are examples of organisational factors. For example, an employee may form a negative attitude towards the management if the leadership style is autocratic. A person's economic status in society, rate of inflation in the country and the country's economic conditions may influence attitudes towards work, marriage, working women, etc. For example, attitudes towards working women have become more positive due to rising cost of living.

5.6 MEASUREMENT OF ATTITUDES

The most common measures of attitudes are the questionnaires. In a questionnaire the respondents are asked to evaluate and rate their attitude toward a particular object. Some of the scales used to measure attitudes are given below :

1. **Thurstone's Scale**[12] **:** In this scale a large number of statements, both favourable and unfavourable, are prepared. The statements may relate to any object, *e.g.,* religion, education, war, etc. Each of these statements is typed on a separate slip of paper. The statements are then placed in 11 piles. The most favourable statement is placed in pile 1 and the most unfavourable in pile 11. Other statements are placed in between depending on the degree of favourability or unfavourability. The scale is then presented to the respondents. Each respondent checks the statement with which he agrees. His attitude

12 L.L. Thurstone and E.J. Chave, **The Measurement of Attitude**, University of Chicago Press, Chicago, 1949.

score is then calculated as the average (arithmetic average or median) of the statements checked by him.

2. **Likert's Scale**[13] : This attitude scale consists of five degrees for each statement.

Strongly agree	Agree	Undecided (Neutral)	Disagree	Strongly disagree
5	4	3	2	1

Each respondent is asked to check one of the five degrees on the scale for every statement. The points show the degree of favourableness or unfavourableness with the given statements.

Likert's scale is considered better than Thurstone's scale because for every aspect only one statement is required which shows both positive and negative degrees. Likert's scale is easier, faster and more reliable.

In addition to scales, opinion surveys and interviews are also used to measure attitudes.

3. **Opinion Surveys:** Attitude scales are useful in indicating the relative level of employee morale. They do not reveal specific factors that may be sources of employee satisfaction. Opinion questionnaire can provide information about specific factors such as working conditions, pay, etc.

   In an opinion questionnaire a single response (yes or no) is obtained for each question. A questionnaire can be developed to judge opinions of employees as well as to measure their attitudes.

4. **Interviews:** In this method a consultant or an academician conducts interviews of employees to know their attitudes. In a guided interview the respondents are required to answer certain questions. In an unguided interview, they are asked to express their views on specified issues.

Map your attitude: Our emotional responses depend upon our thinking processes much more than we think they do. In crisis situations we might cry, laugh, be angry or be fearful depending upon what we THINK about the situation. Often we can change our unhappy responses just by changing our thinking about some situation. (This is the basis for the often-fast-acting, "thinking-style", therapies like rational emotive, option and cognitive)

Try answering the following quiz rapidly:

1. I sometimes think some other peoples' behaviour is wrong.
   - True • False
2. I have been known to say "that is the way I am."
   - True • False
3. Others often make me unhappy.
   - True • False
4. At times I worry about —
   - True • False
5. I tend to ruminate about the past.
   - True • False

13 Rensis Likert, "A Technique for Measurement of Attitudes", **Archives of Psychology,** 1952 (140).

6. I often have hurt feelings because of others' inconsiderateness.
   - True • False
7. Nasty names naturally hurt people.
   - True • False
8. Most impulses had best be squelched.
   - True • False
9. I have some flaws right now.
   - True • False
10. It is a healthy response to feel wounded by slander:
    - True • False
11. You hurt my feelings. Therefore, you were wrong and should change.
    - True • False
12. When I don't get what I want, I often become unhappy.
    - True • False
13. There is nothing miserable but what is thought so.
    - True • False
14. My judgements reflect my own unhappiness.
    - True • False
15. You get what you believe in.
    - True • False
16. My symptoms are the PERFECT result of my entire life.
    - True • False
17. Our 'right/wrong' judgements attract the 'wrong' people/actions/circumstances to us.
    - True • False

First, one must realize that one's thinking can be changed. Most of us never think that our thinking might be a cause of our distress. Each of the above questions can reveal an area in which you have unhappy thinking that can be changed either through your own personal growth processes or via more formal therapy.

Quiz answers: For maximum happiness the first twelve are false and the last five are true. Each statement you answered differently shows where your thinking may be causing you unhappiness. Changing your thinking about any such statement will make for more inner contentment for you.

5.7 EFFECTS OF EMPLOYEE ATTITUDES ON ORGANISATIONAL BEHAVIOUR

There is a tentative relationship between employee attitudes and organisational behaviour. Attitudes of employees provide clues to their behaviour and performance. Positive attitudes of employees help to improve performance of the organisation. In particular, employee attitudes influence the organisation in the following ways :

1. **Job Performance:** Employees with positive job related attitudes tend to perform better. The three main job related attitudes are as follows :
   (*a*) **Job Satisfaction:** The term 'job satisfaction' means the extent to which employees find fulfilment in their work. Employees with high level of job satisfaction hold positive attitudes towards their work and perform better on the job.
   (*b*) **Job Involvement:** It means the degree to which a person identifies with his job. Employees with high degree of job involvement are willing to work long hours and tend to be high performers.
   (*c*) **Organisational Commitment:** It refers to the degree to which an employee identifies himself with the organisation and wants to continue with it. Employees with high organisational commitment or loyalty are willing to extend efforts in the fulfilment of organisational goals.
2. **Employee Turnover:** Employee attitudes concerning job satisfaction, job involvement and organisational commitment also influence labour turnover. Generally employees having high levels of job satisfaction, job involvement, and commitment to the organisation stay longer.
3. **Absenteeism and Tardiness:** Employees with positive attitudes have lower rates of absence from work and tardiness than those with negative attitudes.
4. **Violence and Indiscipline:** Lack of job satisfaction and job involvement causes frustration which often manifests in the form of indiscipline and violence at workplace.

5.8 ATTITUDE CHANGE

Attitude changes are of two types — congruent and incongruent. The congruent change involves increasing the strength of an existing attitude to make it more favourable. For example, a less hardworking employee may be converted into a more hardworking one. Incongruent change involves changing the attitude in an opposite direction. For example, a non-punctual employee may be made a punctual one.

When the attitudes of employees hinder performance and effectiveness of the organisation, managers have to change attitudes of employees. While attempting to change attitudes, the following factors should be duly considered:

1. **Nature of Attitudes:** Several characteristics of attitudes are significant in attitude change. Simplicity, multiplexity, consistency, extremeness, interconnectedness of attitudes are these characteristics. The changeability of attitudes depends on these characteristics. For example, it is more difficult to change attitudes which are extreme and which are strongly supported by other attitudes. Similarly, attitudes which serve several strong needs or which reflect the core values of an individual are more resistant to change. It is more difficult to change the attitudes which are openly stated and to which an individual is highly committed.
2. **Personality of Attitude Holder:** Some persons can be persuaded more easily than others due to differences in their personality. For example, people with high self-esteem and

high degree of self-confidence do not accept change easily because they feel that their attitudes are more correct. Similarly, close minded persons cannot be persuaded easily to change their attitudes.

3. **Group Affiliation:** An individual often expresses his less extreme attitudes in terms of group. The group serves to preserve and protect attitudes of its members. When the affiliation of an individual to his group is strong, attitude change becomes difficult.

4. **Nature of Change Agent:** A manager with high status and enjoying great prestige is in a better position to change attitudes of employees. If the employees trust their boss, like him and have faith in him, they are more likely to accept change.

5. **Method of Attitude Change:** Another factor affecting attitude change is the way the message is communicated. Cohen[14] has suggested four methods of attitude change:

   (*a*) Communication of additional information.

   (*b*) Approval or disapproval of a particular attitude.

   (*c*) Group influence

   (*d*) Inducing engagement in discrepant behaviour.

   Communication that is easy, convincing and two-sided is more effective in attitude change. 'Fear appeals' can also be quite effective. For example, anti-smoking advertisements highlight the danger of cancer to smokers.

6. **Situational Factors:** The context within which attempts are made to change attitudes is also important. How one picks up the message, how cooperative the group is to the manager, under what conditions the message is delivered are all situational factors that affect attitude change.

5.9 HOW TO DEVELOP POSITIVE ATTITUDES

Development of positive attitudes among employees is in the interest of both the employees and the organisation. Some of the methods which managers use to develop positive attitudes in employees are given below :

1. **Setting Challenging Targets:** High achievers can derive satisfaction from the job if challenging targets are set before them. But such targets must not be just castles in the air. These must be based on reality keeping in view the strengths and weaknesses of the individual as well as the situation under which the work is performed.

2. **Building Positive Self-Esteem:** Developing positive self-esteem is helpful in inculcating positive attitudes. Givers generally have a higher self-esteem than takers. Therefore, the practice of helping others rather than merely serving self-interest can build positive self-esteem. People who consider themselves capable, successful and worthy individuals have better attitudes.

3. **Role Clarity:** A manager can develop positive attitudes among his employees by clearly defining each employee's role. Role clarity makes the employee sure about what is expected of him.

14 A.R. Cohen, **Attitude Change and Social Influence,** Basic Books, New York, 1984.

4. **Performance Feedback:** Another method for developing positive attitudes is to provide immediate feedback to employees about their performance.

5. **Participation:** Whenever possible, opportunities to participate in the decision-making process should be provided to employees.

6. **Reward System:** When rewards are closely tied with individual or group performance employee attitudes are likely to improve.

7. **Considerate Supervision:** A caring leader who shows concern for employee feelings can develop positive attitudes among them. He listens with empathy and refrains from attacking negative attitudes of employees. He avoids procrastination which means putting off work for future.

8. **Continuous Learning:** Learning is the process of acquiring new behaviours. One can learn by reading success stories of leading industrialists, sportspersons, politicians, etc. Learning also occurs through interactions with others. Managers can make learning an integral part of an employee's work both on the job and off the job.

5.10 CONCEPT OF VALUES

According to Milton Rokeach, a noted psychologist, values are "global beliefs that guide actions and judgements across a variety of situations". He further says, "Values represent basic convictions that a specific mode of conduct (or end-state of existence) is personally or socially preferable to an opposite mode of conduct (or end-state of existence)"[15]

The main characteristics of values are as follows :

1. **Part of Culture:** Values are a part of culture which consists of several other elements such as ideas, beliefs, attitudes, etc. Every society has its own culture and people in that society adhere to its cultural standards.

2. **Acquired:** Values are learned responses. An individual learns values through the process of socialisation. Values are inculcated and passed from one generation to another. Family, educational and other institutions shape the value system of an individual.

3. **Embedded:** Values cannot be known directly. They can be inferred from the behaviour of a person.

4. **Judgmental:** Values reflect a person's ideas as to what is right or wrong, good or bad, desirable or undesirable.

5. **Enduring:** Values are relatively stable and enduring. However, they vary in terms of their intensity. An individual does not give same importance to all his values. Ranking a person's values in terms of their intensity is known as **value system** or hierarchy of values.

6. **Core of Personality:** Values are an encompassing concept and are at the core of one's personality. Values exist to meet human needs.

---

15 Milton Rokeach, **The Nature of Human Values,** Free Press, New York, 1973, p. 5.

5.11 DIFFERENCE BETWEEN ATTITUDES AND VALUES

Basis of Difference	Attitudes	Values
1. Nature	Attitudes are specific and related to distinct objects, people or ideas	Values are general and are not related to any object, person or idea
2. Disposition	Attitudes are predispositional causing an individual to respond in a positive or negative manner	Values are judgmental and represent what ought to be. An individual responds on the basis of his judgment.
3. Representation	An attitude represents several beliefs that focus on a specific object or situation	A value represents a single belief that guides judgment and actions across objects and situations
4. Source	Attitudes are derived from personal experience	Values are derived from social and cultural norms
5. Stability	Attitudes are less enduring	Values are more enduring

5.12 TYPES OF VALUES

Different experts on human behaviour have classified values in different ways. A brief description of different classifications is given below :

Allport's Classification of Values

Allport and his associates[16] have classified values into six categories :

1. **Theoretic:** It implies interest in the discovery of truth through reasoning and systematic thinking.
2. **Economic:** It means interest in what is useful and practical affairs of the work.
3. **Aesthetic:** It refers to interest in art, beauty and harmony.
4. **Social:** It implies interest in people and human relationships.
5. **Political:** It denotes interest in gaining power and influencing others.
6. **Religious:** It represents interest in unity and understanding the cosmos as a whole.

Different individuals attach different importance to the above six values.

Graves' Classification of Values: Graves[17] has classified values into seven categories ranging from the lowest (reactive) to the highest (existential). These values are given below :

1. **Reactive:** It implies interest in basic physiological needs, and lack of awareness about self and others.
2. **Triabilistics:** It means desire for strong directive leadership and seeking safety by submitting to the power of authority figures.

16 G. Allport, P.E. Vernons and G. Lindzey, **A Study of Values,** Houghton Miffin, Boston, 1960.

17 C.W. Graves, "Levels of Existence : An Open System Theory of Values, **Journal of Humanistic Psychology,** 1970 (2), pp. 131-155.

3. **Egocentric:** It refers to desire for individual responsibility, selfishness and aggressiveness.
4. **Conformistic:** It means low tolerance for ambiguity, disregard for divergent values and desire that others accept their values.
5. **Manipulative:** It denotes achieving goals by manipulating things and people, desire for material things, status and recognition.
6. **Sociocentric:** It means desire to be liked and to build social relationships.
7. **Existential:** It means high tolerance for ambiguity, desire for self-expression and self-fulfilment.

England's Classification of Values

England[18], has classified values as follows:

1. **Pragmatic:** It means desire for whatever is practical and successful irrespective of good or bad.
2. **Moralistic:** It means interest in what is right, just and honest.

RoKeach's Classification of Values

Milton RoKeach[19] has classified values as under:

1. **Terminal Values:** These reflect what an individual ultimately strives to achieve, *e.g.*, comfortable life, family security, self-respect, freedom, sense of accomplishment, etc.
2. **Instrumental Values:** These reflect the means used to achieve the desired ends, *e.g.*, ambition, courage, honesty, imagination, etc.

According to RoKeach, there are 18 terminal values (ends) and 18 instrumental values (means). People hold these values in different degrees. These are given in the following table.

Types of Values

Terminal Values	Instrumental Values
1. A comfortable life (a prosperous life)	1. Ambitious (hardworking, aspiring)
2. An exciting life (a stimulating, active life)	2. Broad-minded (open-minded)
3. A sense of accomplishment (lasting contribution)	3. Capable (competence, effective)
4. A world at peace (free of war and conflict)	4. Cheerful (light-hearted, joyful)
5. A world of beauty (beauty of nature and the arts)	5. Clean (neat, tidy)
6. Equality (brotherhood, equal opportunity for all)	6. Courageous (standing up for belief)
7. Family security (taking care of loved ones)	7. Forgiving (willing to pardon others)
8. Freedom (independence, free choice)	8. Helpful (working for welfare of others)
9. Happiness (contentedness)	9. Imaginative (daring, creative)
10. Inner harmony (freedom from inner conflict)	10. Independent (self-reliant, self-sufficient)
11. Mature love (sexual and spiritual intimacy)	11. Intellectual (intelligent, reflective)
12. National security (protection from attack)	12. Logical (consistent, rational)
13. Pleasure (an enjoyable, leisurely life)	13. Loving (affectionable, tender)

18 George England, "Managers and Their Value Systems", **Economic Impact :** 1979 (27), pp. 23-27.
19 Milton RoKeach : **The Nature of Human Values,** Free Press, New York, 1973.

14. Salvation (saved eternal life)	14. Obedient (dutiful, respectful)
15. Self-respect (self-esteem)	15. Polite (courteous, well-mannered)
16. Social recognition (respect, admiration)	16. Responsible (dependable, reliable)
17. True friendship (close companionship)	17. Self-controlled (restrained, self-disciplined)
18. Wisdom (a mature understanding of life)	18. Honest (sincere, truthful)

Source: Milton RoKeach, *The Nature of Human Values,* Free Press, New York, 1973.

5.13 FACTORS INFLUENCING VALUE FORMATION (SOURCES OF VALUES)

A person's values develop as a result of learning and experience in the society and culture in which he lives and works. His parents, friends, teachers, and others with whom he interacts influence and shape his value system. The various factors that form values of an individual are described below :

1. **Family and Social Life:** The basic values of a person are shaped by his family members, friends, teachers and religion. These are called value-forming institutions. These institutions prescribe what is good or bad for a person. Good behaviour is rewarded and bad behaviour is punished. The values inculcated by one institution are reinforced by others.
2. **Work and Career:** Each work and career has its own values. Persons performing the work follow these values. For example, salespersons follow the value of 'customer satisfaction'. Work and career therefore create special values meant to ensure efficiency and unity among individuals and groups.
3. **Peers and Superiors:** A person learns and applies values from his colleagues and boss. He tends to follow the norms of his work group to earn the friendship and approval of his peers and superiors.
4. **Organisational Values:** Every organisation has its own value system or culture which represents the collective or shared values of its members. A person who works in an organisation subscribes to its values. Therefore, personal values of an individual may be modified by organisational values.
5. **Professional Codes:** Every profession has its own code of conduct and members of that profession are required to follow it. Many companies have formulated their own company codes or creeds. These codes lay down ethical norms to guide the behaviour of managers and workers. They exercise a significant influence on personal values of an individual.

5.14 EFFECT OF VALUES ON BEHAVIOUR

Values influence the behaviour of people in the following ways :

(*i*) Values influence a person's perception about the problems he faces and the steps he takes to tackle these problems. For example, the goals sought by an organisation and strategies adopted to achieve them largely depend upon the value system of its top management.

(*ii*) Values influence how an individual looks at other individuals and groups. Values shape interpersonal relationships.

(*iii*) Values determine the extent to which an individual accepts organisational goals and policies. When these are against the strongly held values of an individual, he may leave the organisation.

(*iv*) A person decides what is ethical or unethical behaviour on the basis of his value system.

(*v*) An individual judges success and achievement of himself and his organisation according to his core values. For one person high level of profitability may be success while for another success means reputation of the organisation.

TEST QUESTIONS

1. What is meant by attitudes? How do attitudes differ from beliefs and opinions?
2. Explain the components of an attitude.
3. Describe the concept and characteristics of attitudes.
4. How do attitudes influence individual behaviour?
5. Critically examine the theories of attitude formation.
6. Explain the factors that influence the formation of attitudes.
7. How can attitudes be measured?
8. "Job related attitudes are significant for understanding organisational behaviour". Explain.
9. What are the factors that a manager should consider while changing the attitudes of his employees.
10. Explain the steps that can be taken to develop positive attitudes among employees in an organisation.
11. What do you understand by the term 'values'? How values differ from attitudes?
12. Explain the types of values as suggested by RoKeach.
13. Discuss the factors that influence formation of values.
14. Explain how values influence behaviour.
15. (*a*) Distinguish between attitudes and values.

    (*b*) How does the Behavioural Intentions Model help explain that attitude-behaviour relationship sometimes may appear to be weak and at other times may appear to be strong?
16. Define attitudes. Discuss the methods by which attitudes of employees could be changed in organisations to facilitate its effective functioning.
17. "Attitude is not directly observable but inferred from what people say, feel or do". Explain with reference to the hierarchy of attitudes.

18. What sources influenced your attitude about M.Com. course before classes started for previous year? Has this initial assessment about your attitude changed since the course ended? How?
19. How are values different from attitudes?
20. "Job related attitudes are significant for understanding organisational behaviour." In the light of this statement explain the function and role of attitudes in the study of organisational behaviour.
21. What are the functions of attitudes? How are attitudes formed?
22. Do attitudes affect an individual's behaviour? Can the management change the attitude of its employees?
23. Explain job related attitudes.
24. Explain how the four structural models of attitudes (tri-component attitude model, multi-attribute attitude model, the trying-to-consume model, and attitude towards the ad model) capture various dimensions of attitude. Illustrate your answer with suitable examples.
25. What are attitudes? How are attitudes developed?

CASE STUDY

Read the case given below and answer the questions given at the end of the case study :

Ajay, doing MBA with a Management Institute, has taken up a summer job in a big factory at Faridabad. He has been assigned to small groups of men who are responsible for loading and unloading the boxcars that supply the materials and carry away the finished goods of the factory.

After two weeks of the job, Ajay was amazed at how little work the men in his crew accomplished. It seemed that they were found standing around and talking or in some cases, even going off to hide when there was work to be done.

Ajay often found himself unloading a boxcar while the other members of the crew were off messing around somewhere else. While Ajay complained to his co-workers, they made it very plain that if he did not like it he could quit, but if he complained to the supervisor, he would be sorry.

Ajay has been deliberately excluded from any of the crew's activities such as taking breaks together or having snacks at the popular restaurant across the street.

Yesterday, he went up to one of the older members of the crew and said, "I don't know why you people behave like this. I am just trying to do my job because I am here only for my summer assignment. I get a good salary which is all that I care about. I would have liked to know you all better, but frankly I am sure that I am not like you all."

The elder man replied : "Ajay, if you had been here as long as I have, you would have been just like us."

Questions

(*a*) Explain the group process involved in this case.

(*b*) Describe the degree and type of motivations of Ajay and other members.

(*c*) Do you think Ajay would change his attitude if he were to stay longer in the job? Explain the reason for your answer.

CHAPTER

6

MOTIVATION

CHAPTER OUTLINE

6.1. Concept of Motivation
6.2. Motivation and Behaviour
6.3. Motivation and Performance
6.4. Theories or Models of Motivation
    6.4.1 Maslow's Need Priority Model
    6.4.2 McGregor's Theory X and Theory Y
    6.4.3 Herzberg's Motivation Hygiene Theory
    6.4.4 McClelland's Achievement Theory
    6.4.5 Alderfer's ERG Theory
    6.4.6 Vroom's Expectancy Theory
    6.4.7 Adam's Equity Theory
    6.4.8 Porter-Lawler Model of Motivation
    6.4.9 Theory Z
    6.4.10 Contingency Approach to Motivation
- **Test Questions**
- **Case Study**

The job of management is to achieve organisational goals through the efforts of people. For this purpose management has to ensure that people are both able and willing to perform their jobs. Will to work can be created by motivating people. For this purpose managers must understand what people want from the organization and how to satisfy their wants.

6.1 CONCEPT OF MOTIVATION

The term 'motivation' has been derived from the word 'motive'. "A motive is an inner state that encourages, activates, or moves [hence motivation] and that directs behaviour towards goals"[1]. Motives are reflection of human needs. **Needs** are physiological and psychological drives. Those drives for which an individual has money and wants to spend it become **wants**.

The factors which are used to satisfy people and motivate them are called **incentives** or **motivators**.

---

1 Bernhard Berelson and Garry A. Steiner, **Human Behaviour** Harcourt, Brace and World, New York, 1964, p 240.

According to Dubin, "Motivation is the complex force starting and keeping a person at work in an organisation. Motivation is something that moves the person to action, and continues him in the course of action already initiated".[2]

McFarland has defined motivation as follows: "Motivation refers to the way in which urges, desires, aspirations, strivings, or needs direct control or explain the behaviour of human beings."[3]

On the basis of above definitions, the following characteristics of motivation can be identified:

1. **Motivation is an Internal Feeling:** Motivation refers to energetic forces within an individual that drive him to behave in a certain way. Environmental forces trigger these drives.
2. **Motivation is Based on Needs:** Motivation is based on human needs. The needs create a feeling that the individual lacks something. The individual attempts to overcome this feeling by engaging in some activity.
3. **Motivation Produces Goal Directed Behaviour:** Motivation leads the individual to behave in such a manner that his needs are satisfied. Motivation exercises profound influence on human behaviour. It harnesses human energy to the requirements of the organisation.
4. **Motivation is Related to Satisfaction:** Satisfaction means the contentment one experiences when one's want is satisfied. It is a consequence of rewards and punishments associated with past experiences. It is related to, but not synonymous with, motivation.
5. **Motivation is a Complex Process:** This complexity arises due to the following reasons:
   (*a*) Needs are internal feelings of an individual. Sometimes, the individual himself may not be aware of his needs and their priority. Human needs keep on changing and at times may be in conflict with each other. Therefore, it is quite difficult to understand human needs and to provide means for their satisfaction.
   (*b*) A particular need may lead to different behaviours in different individuals. For example, all employees in an organisation may want promotion. But they may adopt different means to achieve promotion.
   (*c*) A particular behaviour may emerge not due to the same need but because of different needs. For example, one employee may put a great deal of overtime to earn money while another employee may do it because he enjoys his work.

Fig. 6.1: The Motivation Process

2 Robert Dubin, **Human Relations in Administration,** Prentice Hall of India, New Delhi, 1974, p. 3.
3 Dalton E. McFarland, **Management Principles and Practices,** Macmillan, New York, 1974, p. 537

(*d*) Goal-directed behaviour does not always lead to need satisfaction. This may cause frustration in an individual.

(*e*) Gratification of a particular need may gradually lead to an increase in its intensity. For example, promotion of an employee to a more challenging job may intensify his drive to work harder in anticipation of the next promotion.

6.2 MOTIVATION AND BEHAVIOUR

Motivation and human behaviour are closely interrelated. Motivation explains how and why human behaviour is caused. As shown in Fig. 6.1, feeling of a need creates tension in the mind of a person. He tries to overcome this by engaging in behaviour that can satisfy his need. When the need is satisfied his tension disappears and a new need is felt. In case the need is not satisfied, the person feels frustrated and he modifies his behaviour. In case the person is unable to control the factors that cause frustration, he may react in any of the following ways:

1. **Flight or Resignation:** One way to deal with prolonged frustration is to leave the field or withdraw from the scene. For example, an employee may quit the job that is causing frustration.
2. **Apathy:** In this method the person shows indifference. For example, if an employee does not quit a frustrating job but remains absent psychologically by day-dreaming, thinking of something other than the job, reading on the job, etc.
3. **Aggression:** Aggression is an act or fact against someone or something. It may be verbal or physical. For example, an employee who has been denied promotion may verbally berate his boss. In an extreme case, the employee may damage some equipment or kick the door.
4. **Fixation:** Sometimes frustration may freeze old and habitual responses. A frustrating habit may eventually change into fixation due to too much punishment. For example, a child severely punished for sucking his thumb may continue to suck his thumb.
5. **Rationalisation:** A frustrated individual may blame someone for his failure. For example, a student who fails in an examination may blame the paper setter or the examiner.

6.3 MOTIVATION AND PERFORMANCE

An understanding of human needs and motives helps in explaining and predicting human behaviour. Such an understanding enables managers to take decisions and actions that can inspire employees to work hard for the success of the organisation. Motivation is essential for work performance. Employees will put necessary efforts to perform well only when they are willing to work. However, several factors other than motivation influence performance of an individual. All these factors are given below:

1. **Motivation:** High level of motivation drives a person to work. Motivated employees put their best efforts in the job. On the other hand, low level of motivation drives an

individual away from work. Motivation also helps to reduce employee absenteeism and turnover because motivated employees stay in the organisation. It becomes easy to introduce and implement changes in the organisation when the employees are motivated.

2. **Ability:** Ability consists of knowledge and skills. Able individuals perform better than those lacking in knowledge and skills required for the job.
3. **Sense of Competence:** An individual can perform better if he feels capable of doing the job. Similarly, those who believe that they can control and shape the course of events in their life [called internal locus of control) tend to perform better than those who believe that events in their life are beyond their control (known as external locus of control).
4. **Role Perception:** Role perception means how does a person really visualise his role in the organisation. If the role perception is based on reality and the role is clear, the individual can perform better. But in case an individual is not clear what is expected of him in the work situation (role ambiguity) performance suffers. Similarly, role conflict spoils individual performance. Role conflict means the individual engages in two or more roles simultaneously and these roles are mutually incompatible.
5. **Resources:** Resources of the organisation such as workplace layout, physical environment, reward system, leadership styles, training facilities, etc. exercise a significant influence on individual performance. Adequate and sound resources increase an individual's will to work and facilitate job performance.

6.4 THEORIES OR MODELS OF MOTIVATION

Various theories of motivation may be classified into two broad categories — cognitive and non-cognitive. **Cognitive models** focus on internal state and mental processes such as needs, desires, drives, values and expectations of the individual. On the other hand, **non-cognitive or reinforcement** models focus on external forces. These two approaches to motivation are not mutually exclusive but complementary. In real life, both internal and external forces influence work motivation. Cognitive models may further be divided into content theories and process theories. **Content theories** are based on the basic idea that individuals have certain needs and they engage in activities that will satisfy these needs. These theories attempt to answer the question: **what** motivates people? On the other hand, **process theories** seek answer to the question: **how** motivation occurs? These theories identify the variables that go into motivation and their interrelationships.

Let us discuss both types of theories.

6.4.1 Maslow's Need Priority Model

Abraham H. Maslow[4] has given a conceptual framework that explains human needs and their role in motivation. According to him human needs are arranged in a hierarchy as shown in Fig. 6.2.

4 A.H. Maslow, **Motivation and Personality,** Harper & Row, New York, 1954.

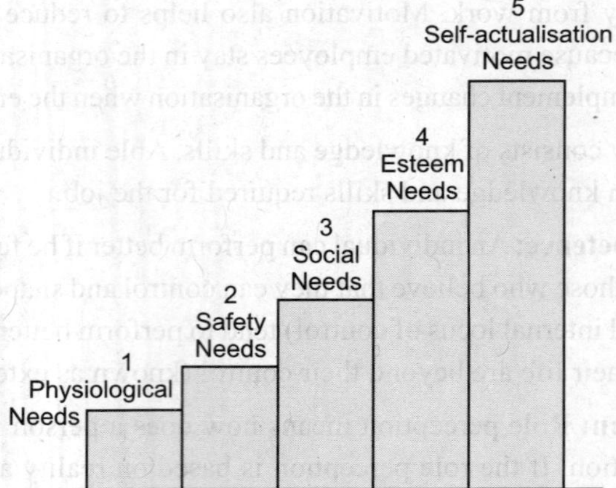

Fig. 6.2: Maslow's Need Hierarchy

1. **Physiological Needs:** These needs refer to the need for air, water, food, clothing and other necessaries of life. These needs relate to the survival and maintenance of human life. Therefore, these are also known as **survival needs.** "Man lives by bread alone so long as there is no bread".
2. **Safety or Security Needs:** Once the physiological needs are satisfied to a reasonable extent, a person seeks safety of life, job security, provision for old age and security against risks.
3. **Social Needs:** Man is a social being. He has a need for acceptance by others and a sense of belonging. Social needs include, companionship, conversation, belongingness, affiliation, etc.
4. **Esteem or Ego Needs:** These needs consist of self-confidence, self-respect, independence, power, feeling of personal worth, respect and recognition from others. These relate to prestige and status of a person.
5. **Self-Actualisation Needs:** These refer to self-fulfilment, maximisation of one's potential or fulfilment of one's mission in life. In Maslow's words it is "the desire to become more and more what one is, to become everything that one is capable of becoming."

These needs dominate human behaviour in a definite sequence. Second level needs do not dominate until the first level needs are reasonably satisfied and so on. According to Maslow man is a wanting animal and continues to want something or the other. He is never fully satisfied. When one need is satisfied, another need arises. Once a certain need is satisfied, it ceases to be a motivating force. In other words, unsatisfied needs motivate the individual.

The various need levels are interdependent and overlapping because each higher level need emerges before the lower level need is fully satisfied.

Critical Appraisal of Maslow's Theory

Maslow's need hierarchy theory is widely accepted but there is little empirical evidence to support it. The theory has been criticised on the following grounds:

1. **Superfluous Classification:** The need classification is somewhat artificial and arbitrary. Human needs cannot be put into neat water-tight five categories. Ordering of needs may

differ from one individual to another. For example, for some persons self-actualisation and esteem are more important than safety and social needs. There can be both reversal and discontinuity of need hierarchy. Need hierarchy is not rigid.

2. **Chain of Causation:** There is no concrete evidence that satisfaction of one need automatically activates the next level need in the hierarchy. It is also doubtful whether a satisfied need ceases to motivate behaviour.
3. **Multiple Motivation:** The proposition that at one time an individual seeks to satisfy only one need is doubtful. Several motives simultaneously influence a person's behaviour at any time. The theory does not explain this phenomenon of multiple motivation.
4. **Needs as Determinants:** The assumption that needs are the sole determinants of human behaviour is also doubtful. Innumerable factors rather than needs alone influence behaviour. Moreover, Maslow's theory presents a somewhat static picture of need structure. It overlooks the fact that the relative mix of needs changes during an individual's psychological development.
5. **No Cause-Effect Relationship:** There is often a lack of direct cause and effect relationship between needs and behaviour. A particular need may cause different behaviour in different people. For example, a hungry person may satisfy his hunger in different ways. Similarly, a particular behaviour may be the result of different needs. For instance, different individuals may seek money for different reasons.
6. **Individual Differences:** The relative intensity of needs and the manner of satisfying them differ among individuals. For example, for people in less developed countries physiological and safety needs may be more intense than for those in developed nations.
7. **Practical Difficulties:** It is very difficult to understand and categorise the needs of others. Sometimes, even the person concerned himself may not be aware of his own needs. There is another problem in applying Maslow's theory. An individual seeks to satisfy a higher level need when his lower level need is reasonably satisfied. This reasonable level may differ from person to person. It is very difficult to measure this subjective issue. Thus, Maslow's model is an oversimplified and incomplete description of motivation. However, the model is easy to understand and has a common sense appeal for managers. It is valid to some extent and has served as the basis for many other models of motivation.

6.4.2 McGregor's Theory X and Theory Y (Participation Model)

According to Douglas McGregor, while motivating employees managers make certain assumptions about human nature. There are two opposite sets of these assumptions which McGregor called Theory X and Theory Y.

Theory X: This theory is based on the following assumptions[5]:

1. Management is responsible for organising the elements of productive enterprises—money, materials, equipment, people—in the interest of economic ends.
2. With respect to people, this is a process of directing their efforts, motivating them, controlling their actions, modifying their behaviour to fit the needs of the organisation.

5 Douglas McGregor, **The Human Side of Enterprise,** McGraw Hill, New York, 1960.

3. Without this active intervention by management, people would be passive—even resistant—to organisational needs. They must be persuaded, rewarded, punished, controlled, and their activities must be directed. This is management's task. We often sum it up by saying that management consists of getting things done through other people.
4. The average man is by nature indolent—he works as little as possible.
5. He lacks ambition, dislikes responsibility, prefers to be led.
6. He is inherently self-centred, indifferent to organisational needs.
7. He is, by nature, resistant to change.
8. He is gullible, not very bright, the ready dupe of charlatan and the demagogue.

These assumptions about human nature represent the negative and traditional approach to motivation. Managers who believe in this approach attempt to structure, control and closely supervise employees. They feel that external control is the most suitable method of dealing with immature and irresponsible people. Workers have to be persuaded and pushed into performance through rewards and punishment. The classical organisation characterised by centralised decision making, highly specialised jobs, hierarchy, top down communications and external control is based on Theory X.

McGregor questioned the assumptions of Theory Y which suggests **carrot and stick approach** to motivation. He observed that this approach is inappropriate in today's work environment wherein most people seek satisfaction of esteem and self-actualisation needs. He suggested an opposite set of assumptions called Theory Y.

Theory Y: Theory Y is based on the following assumptions:

1. Theory X assumes human beings to be inherently distasteful towards work. Theory Y assumes that for human beings, work is as natural as play.
2. Theory X emphasises that people do not have ambitions and try to avoid responsibilities in jobs. The assumptions under Theory Y are just the reverse.
3. According to Theory X, most people have little capacity for creativity while according to Theory Y, the capacity for creativity is widely distributed in the population.
4. In Theory X, motivating factors are the lower needs. In Theory Y, higher-order needs are more important for motivation, though unsatisfied lower needs are also important.
5. In Theory X, people lack self-motivation and require to be externally controlled and closely supervised to get maximum output from them. In Theory Y, people are self-directed and creative and prefer self-control.
6. Theory X emphasises scalar chain system and centralisation of authority in the organisation while Theory Y emphasises decentralisation and greater participation in the decision-making process.
7. Theory X emphasises autocratic leadership while Theory Y emphasises democratic and supportive leadership.

Theory Y represents a modern approach to motivation. It suggests integration of individual goals with organisational goals by making the job the principal means of satisfying human needs. It stresses upon **job enrichment** which is the process of making the job interesting and challenging so that the person performing it can have a feeling of achievement, responsibility, autonomy, etc.

Comparison Between Theory X and Theory Y

Basis of Comparison	Theory X	Theory Y
1. Motivating factors	Lower level needs	Higher level needs.
2. Planning and decision making	(a) Superior sets objectives for subordinates (b) Little participation in decision making	(a) Superior and subordinates jointly set objectives (b) Active participation in decision making
3. Organisation structure	(a) Tall structure with narrow span of control (b) Centralisation of authority	(a) Flat structure with wide span of control (b) Decentralisation of authority
4. Directing	(a) Autocratic leadership (b) Top down communication (c) Carrot and stick approach to motivation (d) Close supervision	(a) Democratic leadership (b) Two-way communication (c) Job enrichment (d) Loose supervision
5. Controlling	(a) External and rigid control (b) Focus on past and fault finding (c) No participation in appraisal	(a) Internal or self control (b) Focus on future and problem solving (c) Participation in appraisal

Critical Appraisal of McGregor's Model

Theory X and Theory Y represent two extremes. No individual belongs completely to either of them. Each person is likely to possess the traits of both the theories in different degrees. Therefore, managers should apply an appropriate amalgam of both the theories to motivate different employees under different conditions.

Sometimes, a manager may have Theory Y assumptions but may behave in an autocratic manner to help employees in the short run to grow.

6.4.3 Herzberg's Two-Factor Theory (Motivation-Hygiene Model)

Frederick Herzberg[6] and his associates interviewed 200 engineers and accountants working in eleven firms in Pittsburg area of the USA. On the basis of their research, they classified all the factors affecting motivation into two categories —

(*i*) Hygiene or maintenance factors, and

(*ii*) Motivating factors.

Herzberg's Maintenance and Motivating Factors

Maintenance Factors	Motivating Factors
1. Company policy and Administration	1. Achievement
2. Technical Supervision	2. Recognition
3. Interpersonal relations with superior, peers and subordinates	3. Advancement
4. Salary	4. Work itself
5. Job security	5. Growth
6. Personal life	6. Responsibility
7. Working conditions	
8. Status	

6 Frederick Herzberg; Bernard Mausner and Barbara Synderman, **The Motivation to Work**, John Wiley, New York, 1959.

Maintenance factors when present at a satisfactory level prevent job dissatisfaction but do not increase motivation. The absence of these factors creates job dissatisfaction. Therefore, these factors are also known as **dissatisfiers.** These factors are external or **extrinsic** to the job. On the other hand, motivating factors are internal or **intrinsic** to the job. Their presence increases job satisfaction and motivation. Therefore, these are also known as **satisfiers**.

Herzberg observed that managers have hitherto been focussing on hygiene factors. They have been preoccupied with the environment of work rather than work itself. According to Herzberg the key to motivation lies in making job interesting and challenging that provides sense of achievement, recognition and responsibility.

Critical Appraisal of Herzberg's Theory

Herzberg's theory provides an insight into the problem of motivation. It highlights the role of job enrichment in motivation. The theory has, however, been criticised on the following grounds:

1. The two sets of factors are not mutually exclusive and do not operate in one direction only. What is a motivating factor depends upon the need level of the person concerned. For example, pay and status may be quite motivating for majority of blue collar employees particularly in a poor country like India.
2. Herzberg's theory is 'method' bound. Other methods used for similar study have shown different results. Interview is not a very reliable method because people tend to take credit for good things and blame others for bad events.
3. The two-factor theory is based on a very small sample. Two hundred accountants and engineers in one city of USA is not truly representative sample. Therefore, the validity of the theory is doubtful.

   Thus, Herzberg's model is an over-simplified portrayal of the factors that cause motivation. Satisfaction or dissatisfaction can arise from either the job itself or the conditions surrounding the job or from both.

Comparison Between Herzberg and Maslow Models

There is a great similarity between Herzberg's theory and Maslow's theory. Maslow's need hierarchy suggests how people try for the satisfaction of higher level needs. Any unsatisfied need becomes a motivator and governs human behaviour. Similarly, Herzberg's theory suggests that job content factors create motivation because lower level needs are reasonably satisfied. Maslow's physiological, security and social needs come under Herzberg's Maintenance factors. Motivating factors cover esteem and self-actualisation needs of Maslow's theory.

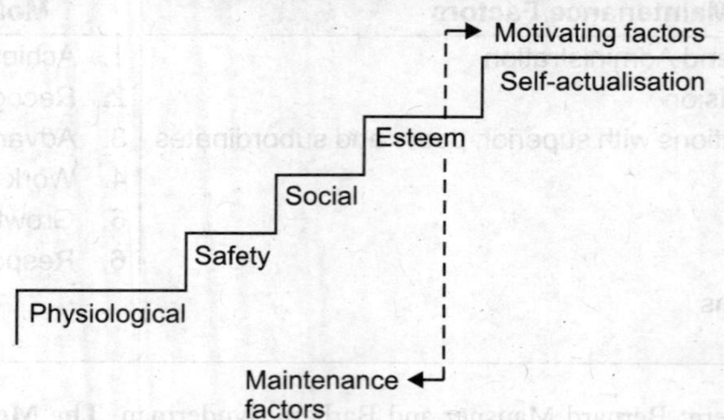

Fig. 6.3: Relationship between Maslow and Herzberg Models

There is some difference between the two theories. Maslow suggests that any unsatisfied need motivates people. It can, therefore, be applied to both blue collar employees and managers. On the other hand, Herzberg suggests that hygiene factors fail to motivate and, therefore, his theory is largely applicable to managers.

6.4.4 McClelland's Achievement Motivation Model

David McClelland[7] developed a theory of motivation which is based on three types of needs. These needs are described below :

1. **Need for Power (n Pow):** This is the need to dominate, control or influence people. Individuals with high need for power prefer to be put into leadership positions. They enjoy being "in charge" and seek influence over others. Power motivated persons wish to create an impact on the organisation by setting goals, taking decisions and directing people.
2. **Need for Affiliation (n Aff):** This is the need for companionship and meaningful relationships with others. It is the desire to be liked and accepted by others. People with a high affiliation motive strive for friendship and prefer cooperative situations. They are motivated by jobs that require frequent interactions with people.
3. **Need for Achievement (n Ach):** This is the need for success and personal accomplishment in competitive situations. People with high achievement motive take personal responsibility for finding solutions to problems. They like to take calculated risks and set moderate goals. They want concrete feedback on their performance.

   According to McClelland, managers have a high need for achievement and power and low need for affiliation. Therefore, they can better be motivated by challenge and potential of the job. McClelland suggested that need for achievement is essential for economic progress of a country. He gave the following achievement development course:

   (*a*) teach people how to think, talk and behave like a high achiever.

   (*b*) encourage people to set well planned and realistic work goals.

   (*c*) provide them concrete and frequent feedback on their performance.

   (*d*) train people how to talk to himself in positive terms and avoid day dreaming.

Critical Appraisal of McClelland's Theory

Achievement motivated people can no doubt be the backbone of any organisation or country. However, McClelland's model has been criticised on the following grounds:

(*i*) The evidence in support of this model is fragmented and doubtful.

(*ii*) Achievement motivation cannot be taught. A person acquires motives in childhood and it is very difficult to change them.

(*iii*) The model does not fully explain the process of motivation.

(*iv*) Achievement training is time consuming and expensive.

(*v*) The use of projective technique is objectionable.

---

7 David C. McClelland, **The Achievement Motive,** Appleton Century Crofts, New York, 1953.

6.4.5 Alderfer's ERG Theory

Alderfer[8] found some overlapping between the physiological, security and social needs. The lines of demarcation between social, esteem and self-actualisation needs are also not fully clear. Alderfer classified all human needs into three categories as follows:

1. **Existence (E) Needs:** These consist of Maslow's physiological and safety needs.
2. **Relatedness (R) Needs:** These include all those needs that involve relationships with other people whom the individual cares. These needs cover Maslow's social needs and that part of esteem needs which is derived from relationship with other people.
3. **Growth (G) Needs:** These needs involve persons making creative efforts to achieve full potential in the existing environment. These include Maslow's self-actualisation needs and that part of esteem needs which is internal to a person such as feeling of being unique.

ERG theory offers the following propositions regarding the satisfaction of these needs:

(*i*) The three need categories form a hierarchy only in the sense of decreasing concreteness. As an individual moves from a focus on existence to relatedness and to growth needs, the ways in which he can satisfy these needs become increasingly abstract.

(*ii*) Increase in the satisfaction level of any lower level need makes it less important. As an individual moves to a higher level need, he sets a higher goal for himself and becomes more productive and creative.

(*iii*) An individual is likely to satisfy his most concrete needs first and then move to the abstract needs. If the individual cannot satisfy his needs at a given level of abstraction, he drops back and again focusses on more concrete needs.

Critical Appraisal of ERG Theory

ERG model is an extension of Maslow's need priority model. Alderfer conceived ERG needs along a continuum which avoids the implication that the higher up an individual is in the need hierarchy, better it is. According to the ERG model different types of needs operate simultaneously. If the individual's particular path towards satisfaction is blocked, he may persist along that path. At the same time, he regresses towards more easily satisfiable needs. In this way, the model distinguishes between chronic needs which persist over a period of time and the episode needs which are situational and can change according to the environment.

6.4.6 Vroom's Expectancy Theory

Vroom[9] has presented a process theory of motivation. According to him, an individual's motivation towards an action depends upon his expectation that a certain action would lead to the preferred outcome. Vroom's theory is built around three concepts which are given below:

1. **Valence (V):** It means the strength of an individual's preference for a particular outcome. The valence is positive when the individual prefers attaining the outcome

---

8 Clayton P. Alderfer, Existence, Relatedness and Growth: **Human Needs in Organisational Settings,** Free Press, New York, 1972.

9 Victor H. Vroom, **Work and Motivation,** John Wiley & Sons, New York, 1964.

to not attaining it and *vice versa.* The valence is zero if the individual is indifferent towards the outcome.

2. **Instrumentality (I):** It means the probability that performance (first level outcome) will lead to the desired reward (second level outcome). For example, an individual who wants promotion will work hard if he feels that superior performance (first level outcome) will lead to promotion.

3. **Expectancy (E):** It means the probability that a particular action will lead to the desired performance. Expectancy denotes the relationship between effort and performance whereas instrumentality denotes the relationship between performance and outcome.

 Motivation is the product of valence, instrumentality and expectancy.

$$\text{Motivation} = \text{Valence} \times \text{Expectancy} \times \text{Instrumentality.}$$

 Motivation will be high when valence, expectancy and instrumentality are high and *vice versa.*

 Vroom's model has important **implications for managers. First**, a manager should offer rewards which have high valence for employees. **Second,** relationship between performance and reward (instrumentality) should be strengthened. Third, workers should be given training to increase their knowledge and skills so that they believe (expectancy) that extra efforts will lead to better performance [Fig. 6.4].

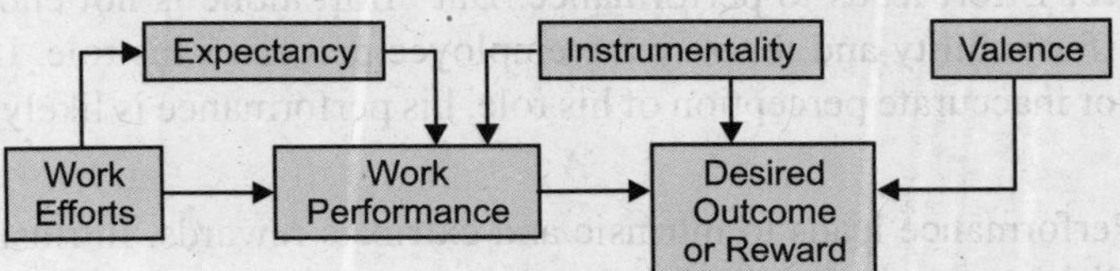

Fig. 6.4: Vroom's Expectancy Model

Critical Appraisal of Vroom's Theory

Vroom's theory recognises individual differences in work motivation. It also highlights the role of an individual's goals in influencing his behaviour and performance. The theory explains that individual behaviour is goal directed. The individual's perception about the consequence of a particular behaviour is quite significant. Vroom's theory is consistent with management by objectives. It is however difficult to apply the theory in practice. There is no way to measure valence, expectancy and instrumentality. The theory has not been fully tested empirically. The theory is overly rational. Everyone is neither willing nor able to calculate probabilities. Several factors other than those given in the theory affect the amount of efforts an individual is willing to put on the job.

In spite of these limitations the theory does not take an oversimplified and simplistic approach to motivation. It appears to be theoretically sound.

6.4.7 Porter and Lawler Model

Porter and Lawler have given a multivariate model to explain the complex relationship between job attitudes and job performance. The various elements of their model are shown in Fig. 6.5.

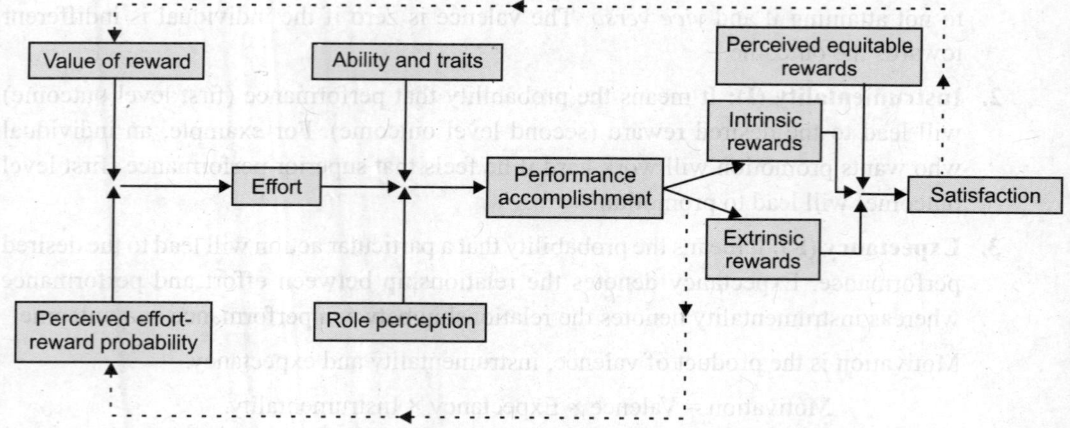

Fig. 6.5: Porter-Lawler Motivation Model

Effort: Effort means the amount of energy exerted by an individual on a given task. It is the result of the attractiveness of the reward and perception of effort-reward relationship. If an employee puts a high value on a reward and perceives that his effort will lead to this reward, he will exert great quantity of effort on the task. Motivation is the force that induces the employee to expend effort.

Performance: Effort leads to performance. But effort alone is not enough. Performance is the result of effort, ability and the way the employee perceives his role. If an employee has little ability and/or inaccurate perception of his role, his performance is likely to be poor despite great efforts.

Rewards: Performance leads to intrinsic and extrinsic rewards. Intrinsic rewards include sense of accomplishment and actualisation. Extrinsic rewards consist of pay, promotion, status, job security, etc. According to Porter and Lawler, intrinsic rewards are likely to be more directly related to performance. In addition, the perceived equity between rewards vitally affects the relationship between performance and satisfaction.

Satisfaction: Satisfaction depends upon the extent to which actual rewards fall short, meet or exceed the individual's perceived level of equitable rewards. If actual rewards meet or exceed perceived equitable rewards the individual will feel satisfied and *vice versa*.

Critical Appraisal of Porter-Lawler Theory

Porter and Lawler have refined and extended Vroom's model. They have given a more comprehensive and a more application-oriented model. Their model suggests that satisfaction is not fully determined by actual rewards. It also implies that satisfaction is more dependent on performance than performance is on satisfaction. This model explains fully the different variables influencing motivation. The model suggests that managers should clarify roles of employees and make the reward system more equitable.

Porter and Lawler model is, however, more complex than other models of motivation. It does not explain all motivated behaviour in all types of work organisations. The empirical support for the model is weak. The validity of the theory is mixed. However, the model provides a useful tool for understanding, predicting and influencing attitudes and behaviour in organisations.

6.4.8 Adam's Equity Theory

J. Stacy Adams[10] formulated a theory of motivation which is based on the social exchange process. Basically the theory points out that people are motivated to maintain fair relationship between their performance and reward in comparison to those of others. Equity theory is based on two assumptions about human behaviour.

1. Individuals make contributions (inputs) for which they expect certain outcomes (rewards).
2. Individuals decide whether or not a particular exchange is satisfactory by comparing their inputs and rewards with those of others in the form of a ratio. Equity exists when an individual believes that his own reward/input ratio is equal to that of others.

Examples of Inputs and Outcomes

Inputs	Outcomes
Time	Pay
Effort	Promotion
Education	Recognition
Experience	Security
Training	Personal development
Ability	Benefits
Ideas	Opportunity for friendship

There are two types of exchange relationship between an individual's inputs/outcomes in relation to those of others:

Overpaid Inequity: In this case, the individual perceives that his outcomes are more as compared to his inputs in relation to others. Schematically

$$\frac{\text{Person's outcomes}}{\text{Person's inputs}} > \frac{\text{Others' outcomes}}{\text{Others' inputs}}$$

This situation creates guilt feeling in the person.

Underpaid Inequity: In this case, the person perceives that his outcomes are less as compared to his inputs in relation to others. Schematically

$$\frac{\text{Person's outcomes}}{\text{Person's inputs}} < \frac{\text{Others' outcomes}}{\text{Others' inputs}}$$

This situation creates a sense of injustice in the person.

Equity: In this case, the person perceives that his outcomes in relation to his inputs are equal to those of others. Schematically

$$\frac{\text{Person's outcomes}}{\text{Person's inputs}} = \frac{\text{Others' outcomes}}{\text{Others' inputs}}$$

This situation creates satisfaction.

---

10 J. Stacy Adams, "Toward an Understanding of Inequity", **Journal of Abnormal and Social Psychology,** November 1963, pp. 422-436.

The major postulates of equity theory are as follows:

(*i*) Perceived inequity creates tension in the individual.

(*ii*) The amount of tension is proportional to the magnitude of inequity.

(*iii*) The tension created in the individual will motivate him to reduce it.

(*iv*) The strength of the motivation to reduce inequity is proportional to the perceived inequity.

An individual can re-establish equity in the following ways:

1. **Changing the Inputs:** The person may change his inputs to match his outcomes. He may increase his inputs in case of overpaid inequity and reduce his inputs in case of underpaid equity. Thus, he may work harder or work less hard as the case may be.
2. **Changing the Outcomes:** The person may try to change his outcomes by persuading or pressuring those who decide his outcomes.
3. **Changing Perception of Inputs and Outcomes:** The person may change his perception about inputs and outcomes. For example, he may start thinking that he deserves better outcomes as he works harder than anyone else.
4. **Changing Inputs and Outcomes of Others:** The person may persuade others to change their inputs. He may also change his perception of the inputs/outcomes relationships of others.
5. **Changing the Persons Compared:** The person may compare with someone whose inputs/outcomes relationship produces equity.
6. **Leaving the Situation:** In case the person is unable to adopt any of the methods given above, he may seek transfer to another department or location in the same organisation. He may even leave the organisation.

Critical Appraisal of Equity Theory

Equity theory has several implications for managers. **First,** the theory makes them realise that equity is one of the most important motives with employees. Therefore, motivation system in organisations needs to be equitable and fair. **Second,** feelings or perceptions of equity are as important as reality in work setting. Therefore, managers should attempt to improve perceptual skills of employees.

Equity theory is however difficult to apply due to the following reasons:

(*i*) It is very difficult to judge the perception about inputs/outcomes relationships.

(*ii*) Equity is a matter of comparison. The process by which an individual chooses the comparison person is unknown.

(*iii*) The theory does not specify the actions which an individual will take to re-establish equity.

6.4.9 Theory Z

William Ouchi[11] developed theory Z after making a comparative study of Japanese and American management practices and suggested that many Japanese practices can be adopted in American organisations. The main features of Theory Z are as follows:

---

11 William G. Ouchi, **Theory Z : How American Business Can Meet the Japanese Challenge,** Addison-Wesley, Reading Mass, 1981.

1. **Trust:** According to Ouchi, trust, integrity and openness are essential ingredients of every effective organisation. These three ingredients minimise the chances of conflict and help to win the maximum possible cooperation of employees. Trust means mutual faith and confidence between employer and employees.
2. **Strong Bond Between Organisation and Employees:** In order to create this bond, Ouchi suggests lifelong employment. When employees have job security they become loyal to the organisation. Slow evaluation and promotion also facilitates stability of employment.
3. **Employee Involvement:** Participation of employees in the decision-making process is an important feature of Theory Z. All decisions affecting employees should be taken jointly by management and employees. Joint decision-making increases employee commitment and gives due recognition to the employees.
4. **Informal Structure:** Theory Z suggests teamwork together with sharing of information, resources and plans. Ouchi gives the example of a basketball team which plays well together without formal reporting relationships. There should be minimum specialisation of positions and tasks so as to develop group spirit.
5. **Coordination Among People:** Ouchi suggests a less selfish and more cooperative approach to work. Complete openness and candour in human relationship are needed to develop a common culture. This requires an integrated organisation through coordination of people.

Evaluation of Theory Z

Theory Z has been lauded due to the following reasons:

(*i*) Theory Z offers a completely new approach to motivation.

(*ii*) It is not simply a theory of motivation but a comprehensive philosophy of management.

(*iii*) Some of the aspects of Theory Z (*e.g.,* a common canteen and similar uniform for everybody right from the managing director to the peon) have been applied in Maruti Suzuki and other companies having Japanese collaboration.

Theory Z, however, has been criticised on the following grounds:

(*i*) It is very difficult to provide lifetime employment to develop strong bond between organisation and employees. Employers do not like to retain inefficient workers. Employees also tend to change employers for better pay and other benefits.

(*ii*) In a highly diverse country like India, it is very difficult to develop a common culture in the organisation. Class feelings often develop on the basis of caste, religion, region, etc.

(*iii*) Employee involvement in the decision-making process has its limitations in Indian organisations.

(*iv*) In the absence of a formal structure a large organisation is likely to face chaos. Today specialisation is necessary and horizontal movement of employees may not always be possible.

Thus, Theory Z is not the last word on motivation. It does not offer a complete solution to the problems of management.

6.4.10 Contingency Approach to Motivation

The description and evaluation of various theories of motivation given above suggests that there is no single approach that is applicable in all situations. What motivates people is dependent on the situation. This is the basic theme of contingency approach to motivation. Human behaviour is very complex and cannot be predicted accurately. People differ greatly in many ways and no universal technique can motivate them all. Even the same individual cannot be motivated in the same way at different points of time.

The contingency approach suggests that before developing the motivational strategy, a manager must consider all the situational variables and the interrelationship among them. Guidelines offered by different theories of motivation should be appropriately used. Motivation at the micro (firm) level needs to be linked with motivation at macro (social) level. People who join an organisation have certain attitudes and values which are shaped by their families, ethnic groups and the society. These micro and macro variables must be taken into account while designing the system of motivation. Analysis of the needs, attitudes and values of employees offers clues about the factors which can motivate them.

A sound motivation system should be:

1. *Productive:* The motivation system should not only satisfy the individual needs of employees but it should also serve the interests of the organisation. This is possible when the motivational system reflects the objectives and philosophy of the organisation.
2. *Simple*: The system should be simple to understand by employees and easy to apply. Employees work towards the achievement of organisational goals only when they perceive a direct relationship between effort and reward. A complex and cumbersome system cannot be fully understood by employees.
3. *Competitive*: The cost of the system should be reasonable and there should be adequate attraction for employees to remain in the organisation. Motivation is not an end in itself. Therefore, the motivational system should be discarded whenever it fails to yield gains in excess of its cost. At the same time the system should not be inferior to the one adopted by the competitors.
4. *Comprehensive*: A sound motivational system must cater to the individual requirements of all employees and it should cover all types of activities. In the organisation, employees differ in terms of their needs and motives. It is, therefore, essential that a careful study of individual needs, degree of intensity and prospective consequences of satisfying or not satisfying them should be made and duly provided for in the motivational system. The system should consist of both financial and non-financial incentives.
5. *Flexible*: An effective motivational system must be flexible and not rigid. It should be capable of being adjusted easily and quickly to changes in the needs of employees. The incentives should be designed and applied according to individual differences among employees. This calls for a continuous review and appraisal of the system.
6. *Regular*: The system should be a permanent feature of the organisation. An *ad hoc* system fails to provide adequate motivation on a continuing basis.

TEST QUESTIONS

1. (*a*) Define 'Motivation' and explain its importance in the field of organisational behaviour.

   (*b*) Critically examine Porter Lawler's model of motivation. What previous assumptions about motivation theory does it contradict?

2. If someone asks you to explain why and how people are motivated to work in organisations, how would you respond? Outline your response.

3. What is job enrichment? Under what conditions is JE likely to be more successful? Discuss.

4. What happens when people are unable to satisfy their needs? Describe the patterns of behaviour associated with need dissatisfaction.

5. Think of the most highly motivated persons you know. What is it about them that makes you arrive at this judgement? Explain using your knowledge of theories of motivation.

6. Describe the interpersonal needs in terms of expressed behaviour and wanted behaviour. Give suitable examples.

7. "Hiring good people is still a relatively simpler task as compared to the task of retaining them. People may join a company because of its favourable image but will stay on only if they find appreciation for and satisfaction from their work." Critically evaluate the statement and discuss the underlying concepts.

8. Do you agree with the view that the incongruency between individual goals and organisational goals necessarily leads to frustration and conflict in the organisation? Give reasons for your answer.

9. Discuss the expectancy model of motivation. Explain the implications of this model for managers and organisations.

10. What are behaviour patterns of A and B as identified by Chris Argyris? How are they related to Theory X and Theory Y of Douglas McGregor?

11. Explain Herzberg's Two-Factor Theory. Differentiate it from Maslow's Theory of Need Hierarchy. Which of the two theories better explains the behaviour of people at work in India? Give reasons for your answer.

12. "Money holds the key to work motivation". Discuss. Also explain the role of non-financial incentives in motivation.

13. "Motivation is a product of values one seeks and one's estimation of the probability that a certain action will lead to those values". Discuss the motivation theory to which the above ideas apply.

14. What is the reason for lowered motivation of employees in the organisations in spite of taking care of all their basic requirements?

15. What steps can managers take to motivate such employees?

16. What is the basic concept in the expectancy theories of motivation? Which expectancy theory do you see as most relevant in the Indian context and why?

17. (*a*) Maslow's need hierarchy specifies several ways to satisfy people's needs on the jobs. Identify each of the five need categories specified by Maslow, and for each one describe something that can be done on the job to enhance need satisfaction.

    (*b*) According to equity theory, how might an individual who is overpaid feel and behave? What might such a person do to alleviate this inequity?

18. (*a*) Why are the Western explanatory models of work motivation considered inadequate in the Indian context? Analyse the historical and contemporary causes of work alienation in India.

    (*b*) What are the managerial applications of the expectancy and goal-setting theory of motivation?

19. What do you mean by Maslow's hierarchy of needs? Does financial incentives increase employee's commitment to organisation? Explain.

20. "Motivation is the product of values one seeks and one's estimation of the probability that a certain action will lead to those values". Discuss the idea contained in this statement, with suitable examples and the relevant model with diagram.

21. "To provide optimal incentives to the people at work to achieve desired results the management must understand prevailing level and nature of motives because without such information, it would not be possible to use suitable incentives, both tangible and intangible, to effectively mobilise and direct human efforts towards the attainment of organisational goals." Elucidate the statement with the help of motivational theories.

22. Distinguish between:

    (*a*) Theory X and Y.

    (*b*) Hygiene factors and motivational factors.

    (*c*) Content and process theories of motivation.

23. Different proposed motivation theories are too abstract and theoretical in nature, they do not have much relevance to the current business situations." Do you agree? Explain.

24. "Creating intrinsic motivation amongst the employees is the most challenging task being faced by managers today." Discuss.

25. What motivational techniques are relevant in the case of Indo Industrial Engineers?

26. Distinguish between:

    (*a*) Maslow's need hierarchy theory and Herzberg's two-factor theory.

    (*b*) ERG theory and Equity theory.

    (*c*) Equity theory and Expectancy theory.

    (*d*) ERG theory and McClelland's theory

    (*e*) Physical motives and psychological motives.

27. How are the behavioural patterns A and B of Chris Argyris related to Theories X and Y of Douglas McGregor?

28. Write a detailed note on Ken Thomas's model of intrinsic motivation.

29. "Motivation of each individual is very personal and general theories of motivation cannot apply to each individual." Critically evaluate the statement.
30. Compare and contrast motivation models given by Maslow and Herzberg. Do you find any similarity between the two models?
31. Distinguish between Theory X and Theory Y. Which one is more applicable to professionally qualified personnel and why?
32. Frederick Herzberg and his associates developed a need-based model of motivation. Compare his two-factor theory with Maslow's hierarchy of needs.
33. "Non-satisfaction of needs will always be negative". Comment on the statement. Justify your arguments with illustrations.
34. Write notes on:
    (*a*) Psychoanalytic Theory
    (*b*) Attribution Theory
    (*c*) Proximity Theory
35. "Money holds the key to work motivation in modern business organisations". Discuss.

CASE STUDY – 1

Ralph Henry had worked as a production chemist at Reorganisation Systems Diagnostics Corporation (SDC) for seven years. The last four of those years were with the MED group, during which he received two promotions to become the group's senior chemist. Conscientious and thorough in his work, Ralph was a stickler for details in the lab yet always willing to help others. Co-workers liked Ralph's pleasant, friendly manner and his lively conversations about sports and running (his major avocations). But beyond the immediate group. Ralph was rather private. He interacted with few people outside the MED group and rarely attended social functions and company parties.

Ralph had always enjoyed his career as a chemist. He was particularly pleased with the laboratory environment, which allowed him to work freely and independently, pursuing whatever challenge or idea that came along. It was no big surprise, then, when Ken Chang asked Ralph to become supervisor of the MED group and take over a role Chang had held for three years.

The Reorganization Systems Diagnostics Corporation makes diagnostic reagent kits and pharmaceutical instrumentation for hospitals, clinical laboratories and some government agencies. The firm was having difficulties containing costs and had recently announced the third consecutive decline in quarterly profits. Although sales were steady, with the latest announcement of profit erosion, senior management also announced a reorganization to consolidate product lines. As a result of the reorganization, Ken Chang was promoted to production manager of a newly created division, leaving vacant his former position as a supervisor of the MED group. While a supervisor, Ken spent much of his time outside the group and, in doing so, granted considerable autonomy to his chemists.

When offered the supervisor's position, Ralph initially balked, He explained to Ken his reluctance to leave the lab bench and his feelings of uneasiness about supervising a group of long time peers. All his education was in pure science; he had no management training or experience, Ken promised that Ralph could participate in management training seminars and expressed his confidence that Ralph would quickly master the art of management.

The promotion, after a week of contemplation, Ralph accepted. When his appointment was announced, members of the MED group were delighted and hosted a congratulatory luncheon for Ralph.

Six months into the supervisory job, Ralph's attitude was as conscientious and upbeat as ever. Much of his time was spent thoroughly checking each group member's work. Unlike Ken in the role of supervisor, Ralph required that all product tests be documented in detail and often requested that routine lab testing be repeated to confirm accuracy. Ralph took on most of these complex lab tasks himself and often worked late into the evening.

In mid-December a major crisis required Ralph's immediate attention, The deadline on a large U.S. Navy contract assigned to the MED group was moved from mid-February to mid-January, Management wanted very much to make good on this contract, as the Navy was a potential major customer. But because of technical difficulties, Ralph did not believe MED would meet the deadline, since SDC had a tradition of shutting down during the holidays. To respond to the pressure, Ralph called a meeting of all group members, something he rarely did. He spelled out the situation.

"As you're all aware, we are having a big technical problem with the Navy contract. To compound our troubles, I just got word from management that the deadline has been moved up one month to mid-January. This really puts us in a jam because the plant is scheduled to be shut down for 10 days over the holidays.

"Personally, I know the project is more important than my holiday plans, so I'm cancelling them. What I'd like to know is who will be willing to work with me, say a few of the 10 days? Of course, you'll get comp time-or overtime pay, if you prefer. How many of you will be willing to work with me?"

The group was silent. Not one of the 10 members raised a hand or spoke up.

Questions

1. What motivates Ralph Henry? How do these forces impact on his behaviour as a chemist? As a supervisor?
2. What likely motivates the other chemists in the MED group? How well does Ralph understand these motivational forces and adjust his supervisory behaviour to bring out their best? Compare the motivational impact on the chemists of Ken Chang's approach to supervision with that of Ralph Henry.
3. Why the "no hands" response to Ralph's request for help? What does it indicate about Ralph's development as a supervisor? Given no volunteers, what does Ralph do now?

CASE STUDY – 2

The newly appointed manager of the tool making department of a company has been reviewing the records of tool makers as a means of getting better acquainted with his men. He is using every possible means to get thoroughly acquainted because he has been told that the performance of this department has been on the decline and needs to be improved.

One day he paused at the record of Subhash Mohan because Subhash appeared to him as one of the below average men. The record surprised him because in education, psychological tests and previous ratings, Subhash was among the top ten per cent (10%). So he decided to have a meeting with Subhash in the afternoon.

The discussion between the two proceeded only a few minutes when Subhash invited the supervisor to stop at his house on way home to see some of his hobby work. There Subhash showed the supervisor some of the finest parts for miniature racing cars, kept in his workshop. And Mrs. Subhash pointed out that her husband can hardly be dragged out of his workshop to get a good night's sleep.

Questions

(*i*) Does Subhash have a motivational potential that could be exploited?

(*ii*) What are the reasons for Subhash's lack of motivation on the job?

(*iii*) What can the manager do to motivate Subhash ?

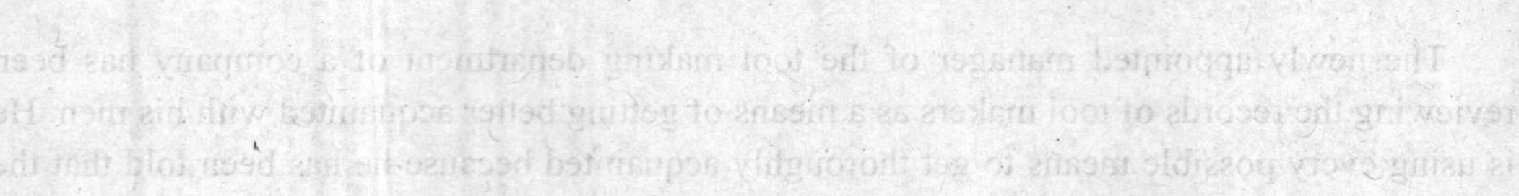

PART – II
GROUP BEHAVIOUR

7. Interpersonal Behaviour and Transactional Analysis
8. Group Dynamics
9. Power, Politics and Status
10. Leadership and Influence
11. Control
12. Morale and Job Satisfaction

CHAPTER

7

Interpersonal Behaviour and Transactional Analysis

CHAPTER OUTLINE

7.1. Concept and Nature of Interpersonal Behaviour
7.2. Transactional Analysis
- 7.2.1 Levels of Self-Awareness
- 7.2.2 Ego States
- 7.2.3 Life Positions
- 7.2.4 Complementary Transactions
- 7.2.5 Non-Complementary or Cross Transactions
- 7.2.6 Stroking
- 7.2.7 Uses and Benefits of Transactional Analysis
- **Test Questions**
- **Case Study**

We have discussed various aspects of individual behaviour in Part I of this book. In this part, different dimensions of group behaviour are described.

7.1 CONCEPT AND NATURE OF INTERPERSONAL BEHAVIOUR

While working in an organisation, people interact with one another. In these interactions, people affect each other's behaviour. For example, A affects B's behaviour and gets affected by B. Such interactions and their impact are collectively known as interpersonal behaviour. The main characteristics of interpersonal behaviour are as follows:

1. **Interactive:** Interpersonal behaviour involves interactions among people. These interactions are of several types.

   (*a*) One to one interactions, *e.g.,* an employee interacts with his/her peers, superior and subordinates.

   (*b*) One to group interactions, *e.g.,* a sales manager gives instructions, advice, etc. to all the branch managers in a meeting.

   (*c*) Group to one basis, *e.g.,* a group of office clerks makes a request or suggestion to their boss.

(*d*) Group to group basis, *e.g.*, a meeting between marketing department and production department.

2. **Coordination:** Interactions among people in an organization provide the clue that helps to maintain cooperation and teamwork between different parts of the organisation.
3. **Dyadic relationship:** Interactions among people are usually paired (two-person contacts) relationships.
4. **Cooperative or conflicting:** Interpersonal behaviour can be either cooperative or conflicting. When the interactions between people are mutually gratifying, it is cooperative behaviour. Such behaviour helps in achieving the goals of the organisation and provides satisfaction to the interacting parties. On the other hand, when the interactions among people cause dissatisfaction, it is conflicting behaviour. Such behaviour is also harmful for the organisation. Interpersonal behaviour becomes conflicting due to several causes like differences in value system, personality and interests, lack of interpersonal skills, etc.

Cooperative interpersonal behaviour is useful both for the organization and its members. Therefore, managers are always trying to ensure that interactions among the members are cooperative. This requires development of interpersonal or behavioural skills and their judicious application.

Some of these skills are described below:

1. **Positive Thinking:** In case individuals interact with a positive mindset, differences in interests and other minor causes of conflict can be sorted out easily. As a result interpersonal behaviour tends to be cooperative.
2. **Mutual Trust:** When two individuals have trust in each other, their interaction is likely to be gratifying for both. Therefore, trust everyone unless there is evidence to the contrary.
3. **Empathy:** If you try to look at things and events with others' viewpoint, you do not make false assumptions about others. Empathy creates mutual understanding which in turn leads to cooperative interpersonal behaviour.
4. **Courtesy:** Respect towards others creates a positive environment for interaction. Both the interacting persons can freely express their ideas and understand them in right perspective. Misgivings can be overcome easily and interpersonal behaviour tends to be cooperative.
5. **Shedding Ego:** Ego means focusing on self. A person with too much ego tends to be arrogant. Such an individual thinks and speaks too much of himself, his ideas and interest. Ego problem creates tension during interpersonal interaction. Therefore avoid ego problem to make interpersonal behaviour cooperative.

7.2 TRANSACTIONAL ANALYSIS

Transactional analysis (TA) is a technique used to help people better understand their own and others' behaviour, especially in interpersonal relationships. It is helpful in analyzing and understanding interpersonal behaviour. When two individuals interact, one of them responds to the other. This is called a social transaction and the study of these transactions is known as transactional analysis. Dr. Eric Berne developed TA for psychotherapy in 1950. Later on

Harris, James and Jongeward popularized TA. The main concepts involved in TA are levels of self-awareness, ego states, life positions, transactions and stroking.

7.2.1 Levels of Self-Awareness

Everyone interacts with others with an image of self and others. The image is both conscious and unconscious. The two images may be called interself which forms the basis of dyadic relationship. Joseph Luft and Harrington Ingham have developed a diagram for understanding different levels of self-awareness. This diagram is known as Johari Window (a combination of the first few letters of their names).

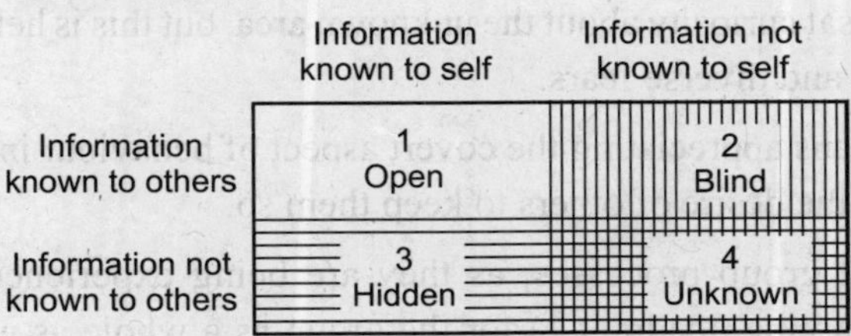

Fig. 7.1: Johari Window

Johari Window consists of four quadrants which collectively represent the total person in relation to others. These four quadrants are described below:

1. **The open self:** This quadrant implies those motives, feelings, etc. of one person which are known to him and which he is willing to share with others. In this state the person is straightforward and sharing. The individual as well as others know his motives, feelings and behaviour.
2. **The blind self:** This quadrant implies those motives, feelings, etc. of a person which are known to others but not known to him. The individual is not aware of what is happening to him but the people know it. A person often copies such blind behaviour unconsciously from important people.
3. **The hidden self:** This quadrant implies what an individual knows about himself but others do not know. This is private and hidden within a person because he does not share it with others. We learn to hide many motives and feelings right from our childhood.
4. **The unknown self:** This quadrant implies what is unknown to both the individual and to others. This part is mysterious and one may experience it in dreams. Some motives and feelings are so deep-rooted and vague that no one, including the individual, knows them.

Self-awareness is not static but keeps on changing. With change in awareness, the quadrant in which a person's psychological state is classified also changes. Jongeward[1] has developed the following principles of change in self-awareness:

(*i*) A change in any one quadrant will affect all other quadrants.

(*ii*) It takes energy to hide, deny, or be blind to behaviour which is involved in interaction.

---

1 Dorothy Jongeward: **Everybody Wins –Transactional Analysis Applied to Organizations,** Addison-Wesley, Reading Mass, pp. 62–63.

(*iii*) Threats tend to decrease awareness; mutual trust tends to increase awareness.

(*iv*) Forced awareness (exposure) is undesirable and usually ineffective.

(*v*) Interpersonal learning means a change has taken place so that the quadrant I is larger, and one more of the quadrants has grown smaller.

(*vi*) Waking with others is facilitated by a large enough area of free activity. It means more of the resources and skills of the persons involved can be applied to the task at hand.

(*vii*) The smaller is the first quadrant, the poorer is the communication.

(*viii*) There is universal curiosity about the unknown area, but this is held in check by custom, social training, and diverse fears.

(*ix*) Sensitivity means appreciating the covert aspect of behaviour in quadrants 2,3, and 4, and respecting the desire of others to keep them so.

(*x*) Learning about group processes, as they are being experienced, helps to increase awareness (enlarging quadrant 1) for the group as a whole as well as for individual members.

(*xi*) The value system of a group and its members may be observed in the way the group deals with unknowns in the life of the group itself.

7.2.2 EGO States

Everyone interacts with others in terms of three psychological positions which are known as ego states. An ego state is a behavioural pattern or a person's way of thinking, feeling and behaving.

There are three ego states: Parent, adult and child. These have no relationship with a person's age. A person of any age may have these ego states in different degrees. Moreover, a person can move from one ego state to another at anytime.

1. **Parent (P) Ego:** This ego state comprises the judgmental, value-laden, moralising and rule-making part of personality. An individual acting with the parent ego tends to be dogmatic, upright and overprotective. Physical and verbal cues such as wagging finger to show displeasure and reference to rules and regulations indicate that a person is acting with the parent ego.
2. **Adult (A) Ego:** This ego state is rational, information seeking and problem solving. A person interacting with adult ego views others as equal, worthy and respectable. Logical thinking and reason are the main characteristics of adult ego state. Physical and verbal cues such as thoughtful conversation and factual discussion indicate adult ego state.
3. **Child (C) Ego:** This ego state is characterised by emotional, spontaneous, impulsive behaviour. Anxiety, dependence, fear, hate and conformity are other characteristics of child ego. Physical and verbal cues such as giggling, tantrums, compliance, seeking attraction and coyness indicate child ego state.

Behavioural patterns of each of the these ego states are given in Table 7.1.

Table 7.1: Behavioural Patterns at Three Ego States

Parent EGO	Adult EGO	Child EGO
1. Teaching	1. Rationality	1. Spontaneous
2. Demonstrating	2. Testing	2. Impulsive
3. Rules and laws	3. Exploring	3. Wishing/fantasising
4. Do's and dont's	4. Estimating	4. Creating
5. Truths	5. Evaluating	5. Experiencing joy/frustration
6. How to	6. Storing data	6. Feeling internally
7. Tradition	7. Figuring out	7. Seeing, hearing, touching

Three points about the ego states are significant:

(*i*) While interacting with others, an individual tends to display all the three ego states.

(*ii*) Each ego state has both positive and negative features — it can increase or decrease a person's feeling of satisfaction.

(*iii*) A person's ego state can be observed not only from his word but also from his body language.

7.2.3 Life Positions

A person's behaviour towards others is largely based on the person's assumptions about self worth and worth of others. These assumptions are formed through experience since childhood.

Thomas Harris has called these assumptions life positions which tend to be more stable than ego states. These life positions are shown in Fig. 7.2.

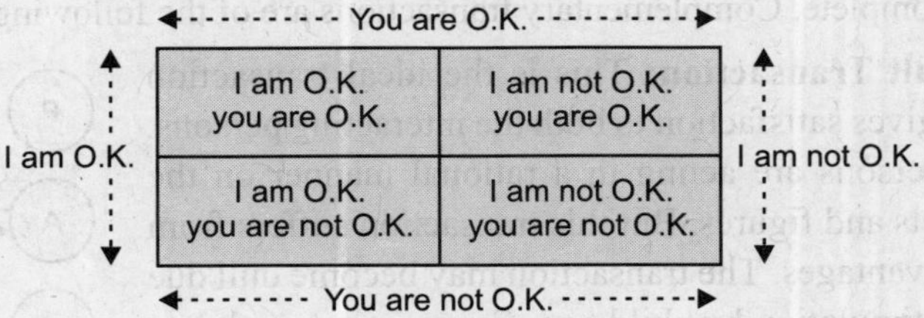

Fig. 7.2: Life Positions

1. **I am O.K. you are O.K.:** This is the ideal life position. People with this life position have a positive outlook. They feel that life is worth living and show a high level of mutual give and take. Such people can freely express their views and solve their problems easily. Managers working from this life position feel comfortable with delegation of authority as they have confidence in themselves as well as in their subordinates. This life position is based on adult ego state.
2. **I am O.K. you are not O.K:** This life position is adopted by people who were too much ignored or victimised during their childhood. Such people feel whatever they do is right and blame others for their miseries. Managers working with this life position consider delegation of authority a threat because they do not trust others. This life position is based on parent ego state.

3. **I am not O.K. you are O.K.:** People with this life position feel powerless and always keep on grumbling. They feel others are more competent and have fewer problems. Managers working with this life position are unpredictable and erratic in behaviour. They use their bad feelings as an excuse to act out against others.
4. **I am not O.K. you are not O.K.:** People with this life position lack confidence in themselves as well as in others. They feel the whole world is miserable and life is not worth living. This is a desperate life position and may lead to suicide in extreme cases. Children completely neglected by their parents and brought up by servants tend to adopt this life position. Managers working with this life position neither take decisions in time nor delegate authority in proper manner.

One of these four positions dominates each individual's life. The most desirable position is 'I am O.K. you are O.K'. This position leads to adult-adult transactions. It shows healthy acceptance of self and others. It can be learnt through education, counselling and conscious choice. The other three life positions are less mature and less efficient.

7.2.4 Complementary Transactions

A transaction is the basic unit of social interaction. It consists of a stimulus (S) from one person and the response (R) from another person. The study and analysis of transactions is the heart of transactional analysis. On the basis of ego states of persons involved, transactions can be complementary or non-complementary.

A transaction is complementary when a stimulus from one person gets the predicted response from the other person. The transaction is said to be complementary because both the interacting individuals are acting in the perceived and expected ego state. When the stimulus and response pattern is charted, the lines are parallel. In such a transaction, both persons are satisfied and communication is complete. Complementary transactions are of the following types:

1. **Adult-Adult Transaction:** This is the ideal transaction because it gives satisfaction to both the interacting persons. Both the persons are acting in a rational manner on the basis of facts and figures. But this transaction suffers from some disadvantages. The transaction may become dull due to lack of stimulation by child ego. Focus on rational data procedures may cause deadlock. In such a situation, the superior may have to adopt the parent ego state to take the decision. Fig. 7.3 shows an adult-adult transaction.

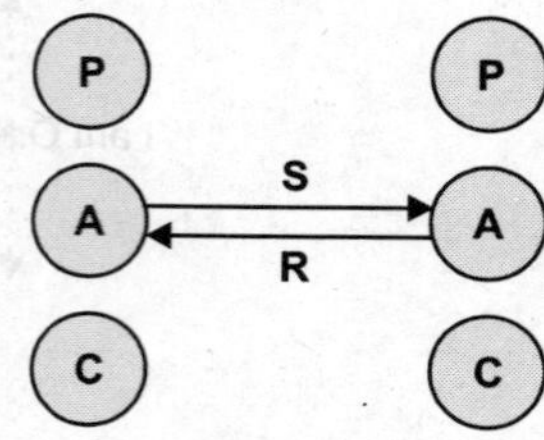

Fig. 7.3: Adult-Adult Transaction

2. **Adult-Parent Transaction:** In this transaction, the manager acts with the adult ego state and tries to use facts and figures. But the subordinate acts with the parent ego state and tries to dominate the superior. Adult-parent transaction may help a new manager understand the rules and procedures of the past. But the subordinates may develop hostile feelings towards their boss. Fig. 7.4 shows an adult-parent transaction.

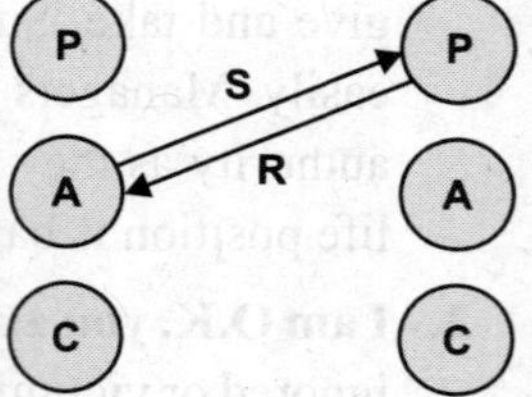

Fig. 7.4: Adult-Parent Transaction

3. **Adult-Child Transaction:** In this transaction, the manager is rational but the employee is emotional. The manager can allow the employee to be

creative provided the former knows the ego state of the latter. The employee may act in an irrational manner due to his child ego. In case the manager wrongly assumes that the employee will respond with adult ego state both the superior and the subordinate may feel frustrated. Fig. 7.5 shows an adult-child transaction.

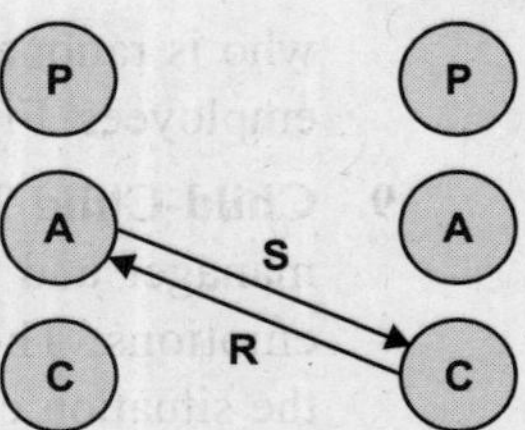

Fig. 7.5: Adult-Child Transaction

4. **Parent-Parent Transaction:** In this type of transaction, the manager uses rewards, criticism, rules and admonitions. The transaction can be beneficial if the employee supports him. Otherwise there may be needless competition between the two as the employee tries to push his own ideas. Fig. 7.6 shows a parent-parent transaction.
5. **Parent-Adult Transaction:** In this transaction the manager tends to be upright, dogmatic and over-protective. But the employee does not respond in the expected manner. Therefore, both of them feel frustration and the relationship may be temporary. Fig. 7.7 shows a parent-adult transaction.

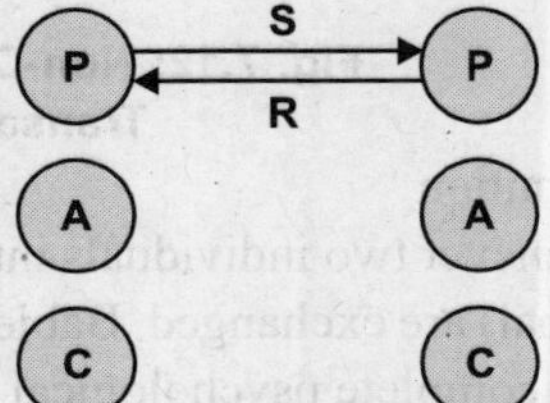

Fig. 7.6: Parent-Parent Transaction

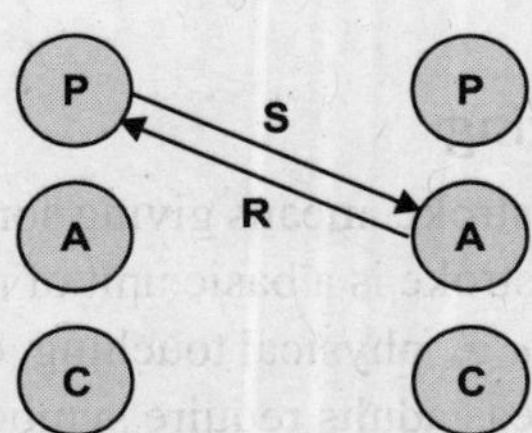

Fig. 7.7: Parent-Adult Transaction

6. **Parent-Child Transaction:** When the manager interacts with parent ego and the employee responds with child ego, there can be satisfaction for both. Conflict and pressure are eliminated. But in the long run personality of the employee may remain underdeveloped which may create a feeling of frustration. Fig. 7.8. shows a parent-child transaction.

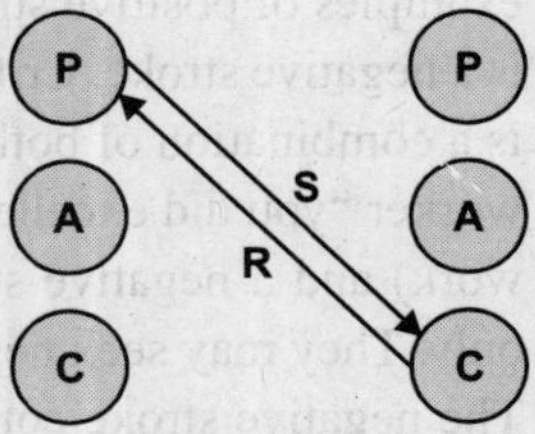

Fig. 7.8: Parent-Child Transaction

7. **Child-Parent Transaction:** In this type of transaction, the employee dominates the manager. A strong and overbearing subordinate may use ridicule and other forms of punishment to make the boss to surrender. Fig 7.9 shows a child-parent transaction.
8. **Child-Adult Transaction:** The manager makes decisions on the basis of whims, fancies and emotions due to his child ego state. This causes frustration to the employee

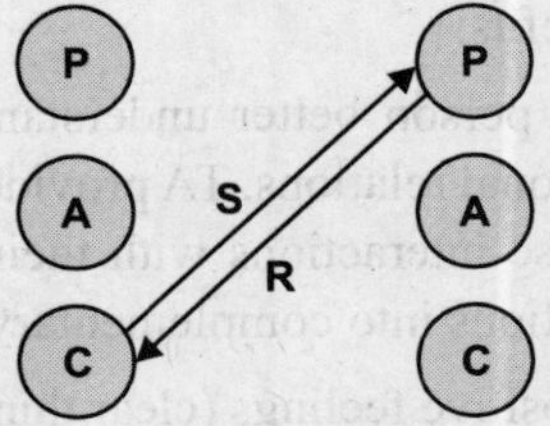

Fig. 7.9: Child-Parent Transaction

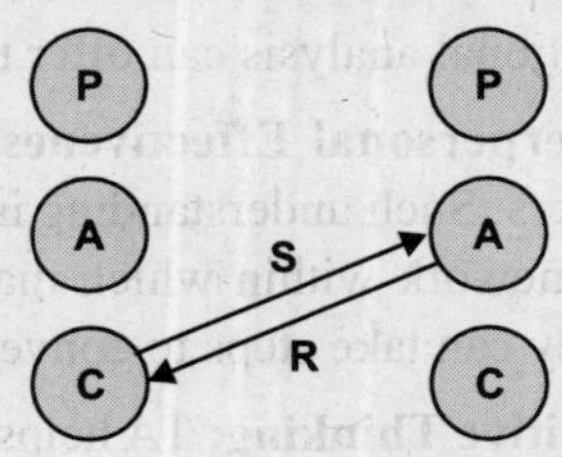

Fig. 7.10: Child-Adult Transaction

who is rational. As a result the organisation may lose good employees. Fig. 7.10 shows a child-adult transaction.

9. **Child-Child Transaction:** In this type of transaction, both manager and employee are acting on whims, fancies and emotions. Therefore, the organisation suffers badly and the situation cannot last long. Fig. 7.11 shows a child-child transaction.

Fig. 7.11: Child-Child Transaction

7.2.5 Non-Complementary or Cross Transactions

A non-complementary or cross transaction occurs when the person who initiates the transaction does not get the expected response. In such a transaction the stimulus-response lines are not parallel. For example, a superior tries to deal with the worker on adult-to-adult basis but the worker responds on a child-to-parent basis. The situation is shown in Fig. 7.12.

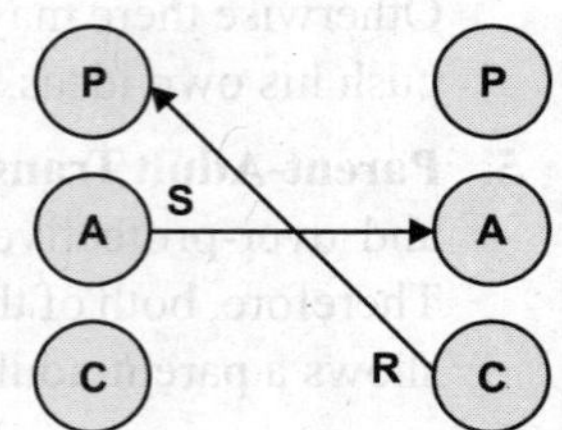

Fig. 7.12: Non-Complementary Transaction

7.2.6 Stroking

The term 'stroke' means giving some kind of recognition to the other. A stroke is a basic unit of motivation. Whenever two individuals interact with each other, strokes (*e.g.*, physical touching, eye contact, verbal) are exchanged. Babies need physical affection whereas adults require symbolic stroking for complete psychological development.

Strokes are of three types — positive, negative and mixed. The stroke that makes one feel good or O.K. is a positive stroke. Praise, affection, pat on the back (*e.g.*, 'excellent work') are examples of positive strokes. On the other hand, the stroke that makes one feel bad or not O.K. is a negative stroke. Criticism, scolding, hating are examples of negative strokes. A mixed stroke is a combination of both positive and negative strokes. For example, a superior's comment to a worker "you did excellent despite your limited experience" includes a positive stroke (excellent work) and a negative stroke (limited experience). People do not always seek positive strokes only. They may seek negative strokes also to relieve themselves of their guilt or low self-image. The negative stroke completes a social transaction and provides a social equilibrium for them. But negative strokes rarely change the undesirable behaviour. A manager can secure positive behaviour by avoiding the punishing parent-to-child approach and initiating an adult-to-adult interaction. For example, the supervisor might say "Good morning, Ali, did you have some problem?" This is likely to reduce the probability of tardy work in future.

7.2.7 Uses and Benefits of Transactional Analysis

Transactional analysis can offer the following benefits:

1. **Interpersonal Effectiveness:** TA can help a person better understand himself and others. Such understanding improves interpersonal relations. TA provides a theoretical framework within which managers can analyse interactions with their subordinates. They can take steps to convert crossed transactions into complementary transactions.

2. **Positive Thinking:** TA helps in developing positive feelings (clear thinking, courage, conviction, optimism, gratification, etc). Such positive feelings can enhance mutual

trust and credibility leading to good employer-employee relations. Stroking, positive reinforcement and inner dialogue through TA can be used to develop positive thinking.

3. **Motivation:** Under TA, positive strokes and complementary transactions can be used to satisfy human needs and thereby motivate employees. Managers can enrich jobs so that employees get positive strokes by performing their jobs.

4. **Effective Leadership:** TA helps managers in adopting leadership styles more suitable to the situation. When a manager interacts with a single ego state, his choice of leadership style is limited. By changing his ego state from parent to adult, a manager can change from authoritarian to democratic style.

5. **Organization Development:** TA can be helpful in the process of organisation development. According to Jongeward[2] TA is useful in six areas of organisation development:

   (*a*) to maintain adult-adult transactions,

   (*b*) to give an OK to the natural child,

   (*c*) to identify and untangle crossed transactions,

   (*d*) to minimize destructive game playing,

   (*e*) to maximise encounters, and

   (*f*) to develop supportive policies, systems and work environment.

Jongeward points out that transactional analysis is useful due to the following reasons:

(*i*) It is easy to learn.

(*ii*) It is practical and usable tool of positive communication.

(*iii*) It provides better insight into self and others thereby increasing a person's on-the-job effectiveness.

(*iv*) It can be helpful in solving personal and family problems.

(*v*) It provides a common language with the help of which people working together can solve communication problems.

(*vi*) It is a non-threatening approach to self evaluation.

(*vii*) It provides a method for analysing both people and organisations.

TEST QUESTIONS

1. What do you understand by interpersonal behaviour? Describe the skills required for cooperative interpersonal behaviour.
2. What is transactional analysis (TA)? How does it help in understanding human behaviour?
3. "Interpersonal behaviour is poor due to lack of self-awareness". How does Johari Window help in improving awareness of self?
4. What are the different ego states involved in transactional analysis? Explain the behavioural patterns that emerge from each ego state.

---

2 Dorothy Jongeward and Philip Seyer : **Choosing Success — Transactional Analysis on the Job,** John Wiley, New York, 1978.

5. What is meant by life positions? Explain various types of life positions involved in transactional analysis.
6. Describe various complementary transactions, pointing out the situations in which each transaction is useful.
7. What is stroking? How does it influence the behaviour of people?
8. Explain the benefits of transactional analysis.
9. Explain the concepts of life positions and Johari Window. Critically examine their relevance for Indian organisations.
10. What are the various ego states? State their functions.
11. (*a*) Explain a non-complementary transaction between a supervisor and a worker.
    (*b*) Give a few examples of positive strokes.
    (*c*) What is "I am O K, you are not O.K."?
12. Discuss the concept of the positions. How can strokes be used to change the behaviour of people in organisations?
13. A supervisor was annoyed with one of his workers. He went to the shop floor and gave a bit of his mind to the worker and returned. The worker felt hurt and made a complaint to the manager. The manager called the supervisor and advised him : 'Criticism should always be offered in private while praises in public'. The supervisor did not agree with this view and argued that if criticism is offered in private, only the worker will know about it and since others will not know, they may think that the misdeed has gone unpunished. Therefore, unless admonition is given in public, it will not have a moral effect on others, which is the maximum of discipline and punishment in an industry. The manager said that a criticism, if offered in public, would demoralize the employee and demotivate him. Also, a controversy may arise about the quantum of admonition given to the worker and a comparison may be made between other persons. With whom do you agree and why?
14. What is TA? What are the functions of the three basic ego states in TA? How can an understanding of TA be of value to the modern manager? Explain.
15. On the basis of your experience in the IPGP session, discuss how the ratios of panes in one's Johari Window varies as the level of mutual trust and exchange of feedback varies in the group in which one is interacting.
16. What are some of the key ingredients of meaningful feedback? What guidelines will you follow in giving feedback in order to effect desired changes in the other person? On the basis of your experiences also identify the situations where feedback failed to create desired response.
17. In what way your knowledge about your 'Type' in MBTI will help you in work situation? How would it help another person if she knew about your preferences?
18. What are the basic tenets of a helping relationship? What purpose will be served by adopting a non-directive approach in helping another person?
19. What do you understand by assertive behaviour ? How would you distinguish it from aggressive or passive behaviour ? Give suitable example from your group sessions.

20. Discuss the role of 'feedback' and 'self disclosure' in facilitating the effectiveness of interpersonal relationship.

    Give examples:

21. What is ulterior transaction ? Discuss the dynamics of 'Games people play' in an organisation with suitable examples.
22. Write notes on any three of the following:

    (*a*) Thinking and feeling

    (*b*) Role efficacy

    (*c*) Dealing with anger

    (*d*) Social styles

23. Illustrate how the knowledge of ego states, nature of transaction and life positions can help a manager to understand Superior-Subordinate relationship.
24. Write brief notes on the following:

    (*a*) Johari Window and its implications.

    (*b*) Principles of giving effective interpersonal feedback.

25. Examine the concepts of 'Ego States', 'Strokes' and 'Games' in the context of social interaction among people.

    Contrast and compare 'Transactional Analysis', 'Behaviour Modification' and 'Gestalt Approach' as tools of organisation development.

26. Explain three ego states in transactional analysis and significance of these for human behaviour.
27. What is Transactional Analysis? Briefly discuss the four life positions which an individual may hold with respect to himself/herself and others.
28. Johari Windows is a popular model for understanding the dynamics of interpersonal relations. Explain.
29. Distinguish between classical conditioning and operant conditioning.
30. Suppose Ms. Krithi Nair, a senior manager, is an ENFP, while her key subordinate Ms. Shefali Sharma is an ISTJ. What would you envisage to be the effect of their types in the work situation?
31. How does the knowledge of MBTI help you to communicate with someone who is not your type? How might you work with the other type better or differently in a team-building session than you might have before attending the MBTI workshop? Give suitable examples.
32. What are the factors which may assist us in making better use of feedback both as the giver and receiver of feedback?
33. Distinguish between supportive and corrective feedback with suitable examples.
34. Explain three ego states and various types of transactions between two persons with the help of suitable diagram and examples of real life situations.

35. Distinguish between:
   (*a*) Parent Ego State and Child Ego State.
   (*b*) Arena and Blind Spot in Johari Window.
   (*c*) Complementary and Non-complementary transactions
36. "The 'flow' experience arises more often at work than during leisure and is sometimes called being 'in the zone'. It is characterized by intense concentration and motivation that centers on the process more than on the goal." Elucidate the statement with suitable examples.
37. Briefly explain various types of ego states in Transactional Analysis. Give examples to explain complementary and crossed transactions along with lessons for managers in business organisations.
38. Discuss the relevance of Johari Window in decision making by managers in the corporate world. Give suitable examples in support of your answer.
49. "There can be only one way in which transactions can take place between the boss and the subordinate." Comment. Explain with the help of the concepts of Transactional Analysis.
40. "There is no need to study Johari Window as it is not important to know what you don't know about yourself." Comment. Also make the diagram to explain the Johari Window along with examples.
41. How can an understanding of Transactional Analysis be of value to a modern manager? Explain with the help of suitable illustrations.
42. Do you agree that human beings have some parts in them known to others but unknown to themselves? Discuss the importance of Johari Window and its relevance for developing people in an organisation.
43. What is transactional analysis? How can its knowledge lead to better interpersonal behaviour?
44. How is Johari Window useful in analysing the causes of interpersonal conflict?
45. Explain ego states and various types of transactions between two persons.

CASE STUDY

R.K. Nair, formerly a Regional Manager of Premier Soap Co., had recently been promoted as General Manager (Sales). Rajesh Puri, Nair's immediate superior, had told him that his primary duty is to bring up all four sales regions to a set sales quota so as to take early advantage of the emerging regional market trends. But Nair anticipated problems with one Regional Sales Manager, Mahesh Anand. Although he liked the man personally, he felt that Anand exerted excessive control over operations in his region and that the result was a lack of initiative on the part of district sales managers who reported to Anand and the salesmen themselves.

While he was Regional Manager, Nair had often pointed out to Anand that if a Regional Manager insists on approving all key decisions by his District Managers, and countermanding decisions made without his consent, his subordinates would be inclined to protect themselves by taking no risks and deferring even minor decisions; the result would be a less flexible response to market pressure and a reduced share of the market. However, Anand had not taken Nair's advice seriously. Anand believed in making sure that every subordinate knew that he was under his control, "I have learned the hard way", Anand would say. "That if you do not make sure that every salesperson was doing the job right, some of them won't do their job right".

At the time of his promotion, Nair resolved to put his bias aside and give Anand a fair chance. During his visit to Anand's region, however, Nair was distressed to find that many of his fears seemed to have come true Salesmen were reluctant to make decisions that might have improved the market position of the company's products without the approval of their district manager, who in turn was often reluctant to grant that approval without checking with Anand. The result was a conservative and mostly uniform approach to an increasingly volatile and segmented market. Thus, Anand's region was falling behind the others in meeting the new sales quotas.

Even then, Nair clung to his resolve. He felt that differences in exercise of authority were to some degree a matter of taste, and it would be unfair that all his managers operate the same way. He was also aware of the informal grapevine between the four Regional Managers, and he feared that if he made an issue of the matter which was essentially a philosophical difference between him and one of his subordinates, others might hear of it and lose their respect for him.

At a monthly meeting with Rajesh Puri, his superior, Nair confessed that the deviations between forecasted and actual sales were due almost entirely to the inability of one region, that of Anand, to keep pace with the record of the other three. In fact, sales had even begun to decline in Anand's region.

Puri observed that Nair's initial reluctance to interfere with Anand's way of functioning was understandable but a year had passed since Nair took over, and his continued inaction could hardly be justified. "You should not have waited till sales started declining in that region", Puri remarked. He further accused Nair of inaction in order to preserve his own image as a fair and judicious person. However, Puri did not specify the action he wanted Nair to take.

Nair then called- Anand for a private meeting. Anand interpreted the situation as a matter of bad luck and attributed it to the ineptness of a particular District Manager whom he proposed to discharge. Nair noted that the decline in sales was roughly uniform in all districts of Anand's region, and whatever the particular District Manager's faults may be, he could not be blamed for the region's poor performance. He then asked Anand to attempt a sharp and sustained change of approach. Although Anand was sceptical; he agreed to try.

During the next several weeks, the sales decline was arrested in this region, although the lost market share could not be recovered. Anand went to some length to assure Nair that he had allowed his subordinates greater freedom to take decisions on their own. But he also reported that the policy was working no batter than he thought it would, because the district managers continued to seek his advice.

Nair's problem was to decide whether he could accept the position as it was or whether he would have to take more drastic action.

Questions

1. Compare Nair's and Anand's attitude towards exercise of authority.
2. Was Puri right in not giving Nair specific instructions for dealing with Anand? Why or why not?
3. What should Nair do now ?

CHAPTER

8

GROUP DYNAMICS

CHAPTER OUTLINE

8.1. Concept of Group Dynamics
8.2. Concept and Nature of Group
8.3. Types of Groups and Cliques
8.4. Stages in Group Development
8.5. Theories of Group Formation
8.6. Reasons for Emergence of Informal Groups (Benefits to Employees)
8.7. Functions of Informal Groups (Benefits to Management)
8.8. Dysfunctions (Demerits) of Informal Groups
8.9. How to Deal with Informal Groups
8.10. Factors Influencing Group Behaviour
8.11. Group Norms
8.12. Group Cohesiveness
8.13. Relationship between Group Cohesiveness and Productivity
- **Test Questions**
- **Case Study**

An organisation consists of several groups. These groups exercise tremendous influence on the behaviour and performance of their members. It is necessary to understand the nature, structure, formation and working of these groups for effective management of an organisation.

8.1 CONCEPT OF GROUP DYNAMICS

Group dynamics is the study of interactions between members of a group. It involves the study of the formation, structure, processes and working of groups and their influence on individuals. Kurt Lewin, a social psychologist at the University of Iowa, USA, developed group dynamics as an academic and research discipline in 1930. According to Lewin, group dynamics refers to the interactions and forces among group members in a social situation. In the words of Newstrom and Davis, "The social process by which people interact face to face in small groups is called group dynamics".[1]

1 John W. Newstrom and Keith Davis: **Organisational Behaviour — Human Behaviour at Work,** McGraw Hill, New York, 1997, p. 340.

Group dynamics provides answers to the following questions:

(*i*) Why are groups formed?

(*ii*) How are groups formed?

(*iii*) What forces operate in groups?

(*iv*) How groups make decisions and solve problems?

(*v*) How groups change and adapt themselves?

(*vi*) How groups achieve unity and handle conflicts?

(*vii*) How groups influence the behaviour and working of their members.

8.2 CONCEPT AND NATURE OF GROUP

A group consists of "two or more persons who are interacting with one another in such a manner that each person influences and is influenced by the other."[2] According to Edgar Schein, "A group is any number of people who interact with one another, are psychologically aware of one another and perceive themselves to be a group". Members of a group interact with one another to achieve a common goal. Thus, a group is a collection of two or more persons who have a common goal, interact with one another to achieve the goal, are aware of one another and perceive themselves to be a group. A group is different from a mere aggregation of people, *e.g.,* people sitting in a cinema hall, people travelling in a bus, people standing on a railway platform, etc.

The essential features of a group are as follows:

1. **Two or More Persons:** There must be at least two persons to form a group because a single person cannot interact.
2. **Interaction:** Members of a group interact with one another. They share their ideas and feelings through face-to-face talk or other means of communication.
3. **Common Goal:** Members of a group share some common objectives. The common goal or interest binds the members together. For example, lawyers practising in the High Court may form a Bar Association to protect and promote their common objectives and interests.
4. **Awareness:** Members of a group must be psychologically aware of one another. Persons working in close proximity are likely to form a group.
5. **Collective Identity:** People must perceive themselves to be a group.

An aggregation of persons can be called a group only when it satisfies the conditions given above.

8.3 TYPES OF GROUPS AND CLIQUES

Groups may be classified into several categories as follows:

1. **Primary and Secondary Groups:** A primary group consists of a few persons who share a common goal, a sense of common identity and common interest. There is a

2 Marvin E. Shaw : **Group Dynamics — The Psychology of Small Group Behaviour,** McGraw Hill, New York, 1971, p. 10.

close face-to-face interaction among its members. A family, a friendship group, a play group and a work group are examples of primary groups.

A secondary group, on the other hand, consists of comparatively a large number of persons. Interactions among its members are loose and the group is less cohesive. A municipality, a university, a village are some examples of secondary groups.

2. **Membership Groups and Reference Groups:** A membership group consists of persons who actually belong to the group. They may or may not be satisfied with being members of the group. For example, students of the same class and section in a college constitute a membership group. A reference group is a group with which a person identifies himself or to which he would like to belong. For example, a student of a particular college may like to belong to some other more prestigious college. There may be a conflict between the norms and values of membership group and reference group.
3. **In-Groups and Out-Groups:** An in-group consists of persons who religiously abide by the prevailing values and norms of the society. These members command influence because their behaviour patterns are considered desirable or the "in-thing". An out-group, on the other hand, consists of persons whose values and norms differ from those prevailing in the society. Such a group may be large but it is considered an "out-thing" and commands little influence.
4. **Small and Large Groups:** A small group comprises a few persons who have close interactions and interpersonal relations. A family is a small group. On the other hand, a large group comprises a large number of persons who have loose interactions and interpersonal relations. A country is an example of a large group.
5. **Formal and Informal Groups:** A formal group is a work group deliberately created by management to achieve the goals of the organisation. Authority-responsibility relationships among its members are clearly defined. The group is required to perform the prescribed roles. The activities of its members are governed by rules, regulations and procedures. Formal groups may be relatively permanent (Board of Directors) or temporary (task force). Formal groups are of two types — (*i*) command group, and (*ii*) task group.

   A **command group** consists of a manager and the subordinates who directly report to him. A division or department is, for example, a command group. On the other hand, a **task group** consists of people of similar rank and it is constituted to perform the assigned task. A committee, a project team and a task force are examples of a task group.

   An informal group is a small group of persons who voluntarily join together to share some common interest, need or background. It emerges spontaneously when some people regularly interact due to personal or social reasons. A club, a chess group in an office are examples of informal groups. Informal groups are of two types — (*a*) friendship group, and (*b*) interest group. A **friendship group** emerges to satisfy the needs for belonging, affection and acceptance. An **interest group** arises to pursue some common interest such as to play cards during lunch break.

Distinction Between Formal and Informal Groups

Basis of Distinction	Formal Group	Informal Group
1. Size	Large in size	Relatively small
2. Stability	More stable	Less stable
3. Formation or origin	Formed by higher authority — planned and deliberate	Formed by members themselves — spontaneous
4. Purpose	To achieve organisational goals	To satisfy the needs and interests of members
5. Authority	Members get authority through the process of delegation	Some members command more authority due to their personal qualities
6. Communication	Prescribed — through the chain of command	Grapevine — can flow in any direction
7. Behaviour of members	Governed by the prescribed rules and regulations	Governed by the group's norms, beliefs and values
8. Structure	Well structured	Unstructured
9. Nature	Official	Unofficial
10. Focus	On positions	On persons
11. Leadership	Superior	Any member
12. Source of control	Rewards and punishment	Social sanctions

8.3.1 Sayles' Classification of Groups

On the basis of pressure tactics adopted by small groups, Sayles[3] identified the following kinds of groups in organisations :

(*i*) **Apathetic Groups:** An apathetic group is composed of relatively low paid and low skilled assembly line workers. They hardly use any pressure tactics due to lack of unity and power. Such a group is indifferent to the formal organisation and has no acceptable leader.

(*ii*) **Erratic Groups:** This type of group comprises semi-skilled workers who work together in performing jobs that require interaction. They display considerable unity but their behaviour towards management is inconsistent. Sometimes, they are cooperative and on some occasions antagonistic towards management.

(*iii*) **Strategic Groups:** A strategic group formulates a strategy to put pressure on other groups and the management. The group members perform jobs that require special skills and judgement. Such a group is very active in the activities of the trade union.

(*iv*) **Conservative Groups:** A conservative group consists of professionals and other highly skilled employees. They work on their own at higher levels of the organisation. This type of group is very strong and stable.

8.3.2 Cliques

A clique is formed to gain and control power. It consists of a few persons (five or six) who interact regularly and observe certain norms or standards. Dalton[4] has identified the following types of cliques.

---

3 L.R. Sayles: **Behaviour of Industrial Work-Groups, Prediction and Control,** John Wiley & Sons, New York, 1958.

4 Dalton M; **Men Who Manage,** John Wiley & Sons, 1959.

1. **Horizontal Clique:** It consists of persons of more or less the same rank and working in the same unit. Its members work for some common interest and follow certain norms or standards. It is the most common type of clique.
2. **Vertical Clique:** It consists of persons of different ranks. For example, a manager may be a member in a clique consisting mainly of workers. Such a clique is formed either because the superior is dependent on the subordinates for some purpose or because they are familiar with each other.
3. **Mixed or Random Clique:** This type of clique consists of people of different ranks and departments. They may be residing in the same locality or travelling by the same bus or may be members of the same club.

8.4 STAGES IN GROUP DEVELOPMENT

The typical stages in the development of a group are as follows:

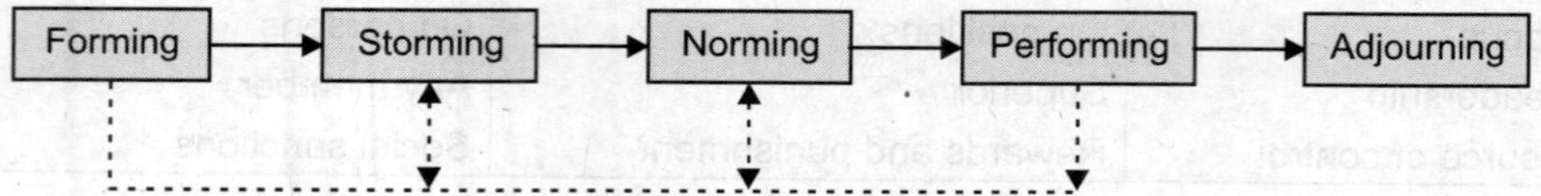

Fig. 8.1: Five-Stage Model of Group Development

1. **Forming:** At the first stage, people get introduced to each other. They share personal information, begin to accept each other and start turning their attention towards the tasks of the group. At this stage, interaction among group members is cautious particularly when they are not familiar with one another.
2. **Storming:** While in the first stage group members perceive and assess each other, in this stage they compete for status and argue for appropriate strategies to be used for achieving the group's goals. Such interaction may create anxiety and tension due to individual differences.
3. **Norming:** At this stage, group members begin to settle. The group starts moving towards cooperation. A tentative balance among competing forces is struck. Group norms are developed to guide the behaviour of members.
4. **Performing:** With the help of group norms, the members learn to handle complex problems. Group members perform their functional roles and accomplish their tasks efficiently.
5. **Adjourning:** This is the last stage in the development of a group. Sooner or later a group has to be adjourned. Groups formed for special purposes, *e.g.*, committee, task force are adjourned after the purpose is achieved. Other types of groups undergo some changes. Interaction among members comes to an end after the group is adjourned.

8.5 THEORIES OF GROUP FORMATION

In order to explain the logic behind the formation of groups, the following theories have been formulated:

1. **Propinquity Theory:** Propinquity means nearness. According to this theory, people affiliate with one another due to spatial or geographical proximity. In an organisation, employees who work in the same part of the factory or office are more likely to form a group than those who are not located near one another. The propinquity theory explains group formation on the basis of physical nearness. However, the theory does not explain more important issues in group formation. Nearness is only a facilitating factor. It is not essential that nearness will lead to group formation.

2. **Homans' Theory:** According to Homans, "The more activities persons share, the more numerous will be their interactions and the stronger will be their shared activities and sentiments; and the more sentiments persons have for one another, the more be their shared activities and interactions".[5] This theory is thus based on three interrelated concepts, namely, activities, interactions and sentiments. The members of a group share activities and interact with one another not just because of physical proximity, but also to accomplish goals. The key element is interaction which leads to development of common sentiments (Fig. 8.2).

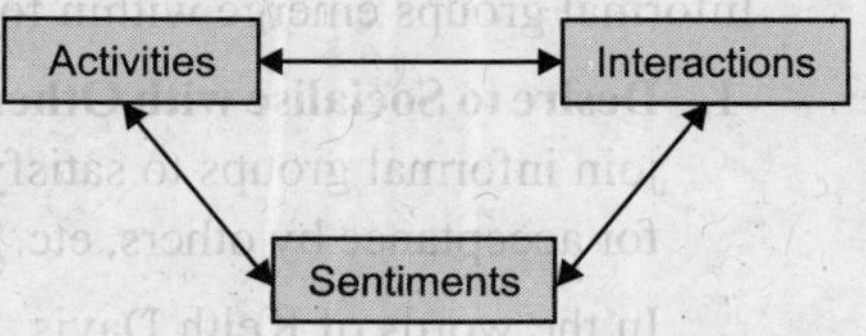

Fig. 8.2: Interaction Theory of Group Formation

Homans' theory provides a better explanation of group formation. Interactions not only help in goal accomplishment but also in problem solving and coordination. People who interact continuously and closely tend to form a powerful group.

3. **Balance Theory:** According to Newcomb, "Persons are attracted to one another on the basis of similar attitudes towards commonly relevant objects and goals. Once a relationship is formed, it strives to maintain a symmetrical balance between the attention and the common attitudes. If an imbalance occurs, attempts are made to restore the balance. If the balance cannot be restored, the relationship dissolves".[6] Thus, the balance theory adds the factor of balance to proximity and interaction. Fig. 8.3 shows that A interacts with B and they form a group due to their common attitudes, values, religion, life style, etc. They will strive to maintain a balance and if they fail the group will get dissolved.

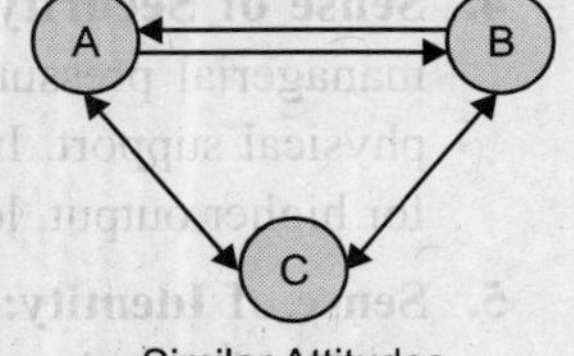

Fig. 8.3: Balance Theory of Group Formation

The balance theory does not provide a complete view of group formation. Similar attitudes do not necessarily lead to group formation. There are many other reasons behind formation of groups.

4. **Exchange Theory:** According to this theory, an individual will join a group when he expects the reward will be more than the cost. There is an exchange relationship in terms of rewards and costs of associating with a group. Rewards from interactions gratify needs whereas costs incur anxiety, frustration, embarrassment or fatigue.[7] A person is

---

5 Gorge C. Homans : **The Human Group,** Hartcourt Brace, New York, 1950.

6 Theodore Newcomb : **The Acquaintance Process,** Holt Rinehart & Winson, New York, 1961.

7 John W. Thibaut and Harold H. Kelly: **The Social Psychology of Groups,** John Wiley, New York, 1959.

likely to join the group only when the reward is equal to or more than the cost. Thus, propinquity, interaction and balance, all have a role in exchange theory.

Each of the above theories attempts to explain the reasons for group formation. But no theory explains the total situation. Therefore, it is necessary to discuss the various factors that lead to formation of groups.

8.6 REASONS FOR EMERGENCE OF INFORMAL GROUPS [BENEFITS TO EMPLOYEES]

Informal groups emerge within formal organisation due to the following causes :

1. **Desire to Socialise with Others:** Human beings want to associate with one another. They join informal groups to satisfy their social needs such as the need for belonging, need for acceptance by others, etc. These groups provide warmth and support to employees.

   In the words of Keith Davis, "Man is a social being. He wants to belong, to associate with others rather than to work in isolated loneliness. Out of this drive of man, the informal organisation arises". Informal groups provide companionship.

2. **Job Specialisation:** In large organisations, jobs are specialised. An employee concentrates on a single task which causes boredom and monotony. People lack a sense of achievement and pride in their work. They develop informal relationship to release their tension and frustration. Informal groups help them.

3. **Hierarchical Control and Communication:** In a large organisation, there is a long chain of command. A large gap exists between superiors and subordinates. Workers form informal groups which are free from social distance and repressive controls.

4. **Sense of Security:** Employees form small groups to protect their interests from managerial pressure and external threats. The group provides them emotional and physical support. Informal groups protect their members from management pressure for higher output, longer working hours and better quality of work.

5. **Sense of Identity:** Workers get more identified in small informal groups. They get recognition and status which is not available in the formal groups.

6. **Source of Information:** Members of an informal group get information which may not be available to them in the formal organisation. Informal communication is very fast as there are no barriers of chain of command, status, etc.

7. **Outlet for Frustration:** An employee may be facing several problems relating to his family life and work life. These problems cause severe stress and frustration. He can release such frustration and tension by sharing his feelings and anxieties with other members of an informal group.

8. **Job Satisfaction:** Small informal groups may improve job satisfaction of their members by helping them to adjust to the job environment.

9. **Perpetuation of Cultural Values:** A person can preserve his cultural identity by associating with those having similar cultural background. He gets psychological satisfaction by maintaining his cultural values.

8.7 FUNCTIONS OF INFORMAL GROUPS [BENEFITS TO MANAGEMENT]

Informal groups are important not only to their members. These groups can help the management in achieving organisational goals in several ways :

1. **Restraint on Managers:** Informal groups act as a check on high-handedness of managers. They restrict managers from abusing their power or crossing their limits. They help to make the organisation more democratic.
2. **Filling up Gaps in Manager's Abilities:** Members of an informal group can make up for lack of some skill on the part of a manager. For example, they may help their boss informally in case he is weak in planning.
3. **Generation of New Ideas:** Informal groups provide a supportive environment wherein members can engage in creative thinking. They can provide new ideas to management for improving the quality and quantity of work performance.
4. **Higher Motivation and Morale:** Cohesive informal groups provide satisfaction to employees. It serves as a safety valve for releasing tension and frustration. As a result the motivation and morale of workforce improve and absenteeism and labour turnover are reduced.
5. **Solving Work Related Problems:** Informal groups help in solving work problems of their members. Through it employees can share job knowledge and help one another in doing their jobs.
6. **Channel of Communication:** Informal communication cuts across hierarchical and departmental boundaries and transmits information very fast. Management can use it to share information with employees and to judge their reaction to its proposals.
7. **Executive Development:** In informal groups more talented members are accepted as informal leaders. Management can pick up such leaders to fill vacancies at junior executive level in the future.
8. **Coordination:** A manager can develop better relations with employees through informal contacts. He can consult the leaders of informal groups and can seek their cooperation in getting things done from employees.
9. **Order and Discipline:** Informal groups develop some norms of behaviour. These norms define good and bad conduct, legitimate and illegitimate activities. These therefore, help to bring order and discipline among workers.

8.8 DYSFUNCTIONS (DEMERITS) OF INFORMAL GROUPS

Informal groups can create the following problems for management:

1. **Resistance to Change:** Informal groups often resist changes which they perceive as a threat to their structure and culture. They exert strong pressure on their members for conformity and loyalty to groups.
2. **Role Conflict:** Every member of an informal group is also a member of some formal group. He faces a role conflict when the behaviour expected from him is opposite to

the behaviour required in a formal group. For example, a superior who has informal relationship with workers may face difficulty in enforcing work standards laid down by management.

3. **Rumour:** Informal groups may become the source of rumours. Ambiguity in the formal organisation, anxiety and insecurity and desire to put pressure on management are the main causes of rumour. An outbreak of rumour can be very harmful to the organisation and its management.

4. **Negative Attitude of Informal Leaders:** The leader of an informal group may manipulate the behaviour of his subordinates in order to increase his influence. He may induce and even instigate the workers to work against the interests of the organisation. He may create conflict between management and workers.

8.9 HOW TO DEAL WITH INFORMAL GROUPS

Management does not create informal groups and cannot dissolve them. Therefore, managers should take appropriate steps to make constructive use of informal groups for the benefit of the organisation. The following steps may be taken for this purpose:

(*i*) Recognise and accept the existence and inevitability of informal groups. Remember "formal and informal organisations are complementary to each other just as two blades are essential to make a pair of scissors workable". Therefore, let the employees feel that management accepts and understands informal groups.

(*ii*) While taking any decision consider its possible impact upon informal groups.

(*iii*) Wherever possible integrate interests of informal groups with the interests of the organisation.

(*iv*) Ensure that activities of the formal organisation do not unnecessarily threaten the informal groups.

(*v*) Norms and relationships of informal groups which are favourable for the organisation should be incorporated into the formal structure.

(*vi*) Use informal communication to fill gaps in formal communication.

(*vii*) Establish rapport with informal leaders and seek their cooperation in making employees work for organisational goals.

8.10 FACTORS INFLUENCING GROUP BEHAVIOUR

The behaviour and performance of informal groups depends on several factors such as the following :

1. **Group Size:** A large group has more resources and can generate more ideas. It can perform more complex tasks. But it inhibits free interaction and communication among the members. Social loafing is more common in large groups.

2. **Group Composition:** A homogeneous group enjoys greater unity among its members. A group is homogeneous when its members are similar in age, education and other personal characteristics. But a heterogeneous group may be more creative.

3. **Roles:** Every member of the group behaves according to his own perception and the expectations of other members.
4. **Leadership:** The leader exercises a great influence on the functioning of the group. He may channelise the resources and energy of the group in constructive or destructive manner.
5. **Group Norms:** Every group lays down some norms or standards and its members tend to behave in accordance with these rules of behaviour.
6. **Group Cohesiveness:** The degree of attachment of members to their group is called group cohesiveness. A more cohesive group tends to be more powerful.
7. **External Conditions:** An informal group works within the framework of the formal organisation. The strategy, structure, resources, culture, rules and regulations of the formal organisation affect the functioning of informal groups existing within it.

8.11 GROUP NORMS

Informal groups establish standards which indicate their members what they ought or ought not to do. These standards of acceptable behaviour are known as group norms. Members of a group tend to conform to these norms. These norms differ from group to group. For example, norms of a group in a factory may be totally different from the norms of a club. Group norms may be strong or weak. The strength of norms depends on the status and stability of the group and members' affiliation with the group. When the group is powerful and stable, its members are closely affiliated and discipline is high, group norms tend to be strong. For example, a school requires its students to wear uniforms, remain quiet in the classroom and cooperate with their teachers.

Hackman[8] has identified the following characteristics of group norms:

(*i*) Norms summarise and simplify group influence processes. They summarise and highlight those things that the group feels important to control.

(*ii*) Norms apply only to behaviours, and not to private thoughts and feelings. Behavioural compliance from the members is sufficient and private acceptance of norms is not necessary.

(*iii*) Norms are generally developed only for behaviours which are considered as important by most group members.

(*iv*) Norms usually develop gradually, but the process can be shortened if members so desire. If, for some reasons, group members decide that a particular norm is now desired, they may simply agree to institute such a norm suddenly by declaring that 'from now on' the norm exists.

(*v*) Not all norms apply to everyone in the group in the same manner. High-status members enjoy more freedom to deviate from the 'letter of the law' than do other members.

Group norms perform two important functions. **First,** norms help the group to accomplish its goals. All methods and procedures which facilitate achievement of group goals are considered

8 J.R. Hackman : "Group Influence on Members" in M.D. Dunnetti (ed.), **Handbook of Industrial and Organisational Psychology,** Rand McNaily, 1986.

legitimate and members follow them. **Second,** norms help the group to maintain itself as a group. These ensure that group unity is maintained by resisting external pressure and behaviour that threaten the existence of the group.

The extent to which members conform to group norms depends upon the following factors:

(*i*) A more stable and cohesive group tends to exercise more conformity to its norms.

(*ii*) When group goals and individual goals mesh, members are more likely to adhere to group norms.

(*iii*) If the group faces external threats, there is greater conformity to group norms.

(*iv*) Less intelligent, more authoritarian and high-status members conform more to group norms than more intelligent, less authoritarian and low-status members.

8.11.1 Methods of Enforcing Group Norms

A group may take the following actions to enforce its norms:

1. **Education:** Members may be educated about how the group norms contribute to the accomplishment of group goals. Adherence to group norms can also be increased by involving the members in the activities of the group.
2. **Surveillance:** Regular monitoring helps to judge the degree to which members adhere to group norms. Then the group leader can take appropriate actions to ensure conformity to group norms.
3. **Warning:** Members who do not adhere to group norms can be warned of the consequences. Such warning can increase adherence on the part of group members.
4. **Sanctions:** Appropriate actions may be taken to ensure conformity to group norms. But sanctions can lead to negative consequences. Therefore, sanctions should be used only when other methods fail. Rewards are a better method than sanctions.

8.12 GROUP COHESIVENESS

Group cohesiveness means the degree of attachment of the members to their group. In a highly cohesive group, members conform strictly to the group norms and the group leader represents the feelings of all members. Such a group is powerful and can face any external threat.

The basic features of a cohesive group are as follows :

(*i*) The members share the group goals and norms and have common interests and background.

(*ii*) The number of members is relatively small.

(*iii*) The members interact among themselves quite frequently and have very effective interpersonal communication.

(*iv*) Members have high loyalty to the group because the group enjoys high status.

(*v*) The members stand united against any perceived external threats to the group.

(*vi*) The members keep themselves glued to the group as they feel that the group will satisfy their needs.

(*vii*) The group has a history of success in the past.

8.12.1 Factors Influencing Group Cohesiveness

The main factors which determine the degree of group cohesiveness are as follows :

1. **Nature of the Group:** A group whose members are similar in age, education, status, background, etc. tends to be more cohesive. In other words, a homogeneous group is more cohesive than a heterogeneous group. Similarly, stable relationships among members increase group cohesiveness.
2. **Size of the Group:** A small group is likely to be more cohesive than a large group. This is so because interaction among a few persons can be more frequent and close than among a large number of persons. It is easier to have close relationship among the members of a small group than among the members of a large group.[9]
3. **Location of the Group:** When the members of a group are located close to each other, they interact among themselves frequently and freely. Such interaction increases group cohesiveness. If the group is isolated from other group it can be more cohesive. Where there is no dividing line between one group and another, cohesion becomes difficult because a chain of interactions develops among members of various groups.
4. **Status of the Group:** A high-status group enjoys greater loyalty from its members and group cohesion tends to be high. On the other hand, a low-status group tends to be less cohesive because members are less loyal to it.
5. **Group Leadership:** A dynamic and energetic leader can motivate the group members to work with zeal for the attainment of common goals. He can build and maintain high degree of loyalty to the group. As a result the group becomes very cohesive.
6. **Dependence on the Group:** A group is more attractive when its members are more dependent on it for satisfying their needs. Such a group is more cohesive. Similarly, cohesiveness increases when group members are mutually dependent on each other in their activities.
7. **Competition:** High degree of competition among the members of a group reduces group cohesiveness. On the other hand, competition between two or more groups makes them more cohesive. Management can increase competition between groups and reward cooperative behaviour to increase group cohesiveness for achieving organisational goals.
8. **Outside Pressures:** When a group faces pressures from other groups, its members forget their personal differences and solidarity among themselves increases. However, it may also happen that the group is unable to bear the excessive pressure and group cohesiveness cannot be created to withstand the pressure from outside.[10]

8.13 RELATIONSHIP BETWEEN GROUP COHESIVENESS AND PRODUCTIVITY

Hawthorne Experiments revealed that informal groups have their own norms of production and employees stick to these norms due to group pressures. The common perception is that

9 L. Libo : **Measuring Group Cohesiveness,** Institute of Social Research, Ann Arbor. Michigan, 1953.

10 Alvin Zander : "The Psychology of Group Processes", **Annual Review of Psychology** Vol. 30, 1979, p 436.

highly cohesive groups are more effective. But the relationship is much more complex than what it appears to be. **First,** high cohesiveness is both a cause and outcome of high productivity. **Second,** the relationship is moderated by the degree to which the group's attitude is aligned with its own goals or those of the larger organisation of which it is a part.

The relationship between group cohesiveness and productivity is shown in Fig. 8.4.

Performance Norms	Cohesiveness: High	Cohesiveness: Low
High	High productivity	Moderate productivity
Low	Low productivity	Moderate to low productivity

Fig. 8.4: Group Cohesiveness and Productivity

When group cohesiveness and performance norms are high productivity tends to be high. But productivity will be low despite high group cohesiveness if the performance norms are low. In case of high performance norms moderate productivity can be expected even from less cohesive groups.

These findings have important implications for managers. They should not focus merely on increasing group cohesiveness. They must attempt to align group norms with organisational goals to increase productivity.

Cartwright[11] has laid down the following guidelines for making constructive use of groups:

1. If the group is to be used effectively as a medium of change, those people who are to be changed and those who are to exert influence for change must have a strong sense of belongingness to the same group.
2. The more attractive the group is to its members, the greater is the influence that the group can exert on its members.
3. In attempts to change attitudes, values or behaviour, the more relevant they are to the basis of attraction to the group, the greater will be the influence that the group can exert upon its members.
4. The greater the prestige of a group member in the eyes of the other members, the greater the influence it can exert.
5. Efforts to change individuals or sub-groups of a group, which if successful, would have the effect of making them deviate from the norms of the group will encounter strong resistance.
6. Strong pressure for change in the group can be established by creating a shared perception by the members of the need for change, thus making the source of pressure for change lie within the group.

11 Dorwin Cartwright; "Achieving Change in People : Some Applications of Group Dynamics" in Keith Davis and William G. Scott (eds.), **Readings in Human Relations,** McGraw Hill Book Co; New York 1956, pp. 219–230.

7. Information relating to the need for change, plans for change and consequences of change must be shared by all relevant people in the group.
8. Changes, in one part of a group, produce strains in related parts which can be reduced only by eliminating the change or by bringing about readjustment in related parts.

TEST QUESTIONS

1. What is Group Dynamics? Explain the main issues involved in the study of groups.
2. What is group dynamics? How is it important in understanding human behaviour in work organisations?
3. "High cohesiveness in a group leads to higher productivity". Do you agree? Give reasons.
4. Explain the concept of Group Dynamics. How can you make use of group dynamics for the benefit of the organisation?
5. Why should organisations be concerned about the functions of groups?
6. What do you mean by 'Apathetic Group'?
7. Why people join groups?
8. Discuss the theories of group formation.
9. Why is a thorough understanding of the dynamics of work groups vital to a supervisor?
10. What is intergroup relation? How does it help employees in an organisation?
11. Explain the factors that influence group effectiveness.
12. Discuss different methods of group decision making, pointing out their merits and demerits.
13. What are conditions related to decision making? How it affects decision making?
14. Discuss the nature of group dynamics which prevail in informal organisation and its impact on the effectiveness of the organisation as a whole.
15. What are the factors that induce and sustain group cohesiveness? What are the effects of group cohesiveness on group members and the organisation?
16. "Organisations don't function strictly according to official prescriptions." In the light of this statement, discuss the dysfunctions of informal organisation and suggest guidelines for the constructive use of informal relations.
17. What is group cohesiveness? How does the process of group think affect the effectiveness of the group? Discuss steps to reduce the impact of group think.
18. (*a*) Why all groups are not teams?
    (*b*) Discuss the essential elements of teams with suitable examples.
19. (*a*) As a Manager what are the various group process factors that you can observe to be more effective in a work group?
    (*b*) Identify the various stages of group development and apply them to any group to which you belong. Do all the stages apply?
20. Review a film dealing with group dynamics that you have seen and discuss the following:
    (*a*) What factors hinder and facilitate consensus? What are group building skills?
    (*b*) How can decision by consensus create synergy in the group?

21. Write short notes on :
    (*a*) Stages of group development
    (*b*) Group member roles
    (*c*) Group cohesiveness
    (*d*) Group norms
22. One of your employees takes offence when none is intended. He overreacts to anything that sounds like criticism. He is difficult to communicate with, because you have to watch every word. He seems perpetually on the defence and is considered by everybody as thin-skinned. He is a very good worker, but when he feels offended or hurt, he does not work as well. You can hardly protect him from reality. Sometimes he must be corrected or criticized. Then you have a problem—a demoralized, possibly demotivated employee. How do you deal with him?
23. He is a highly valuable employee but is sometimes a pain in the neck. He is temperamental. Schedules usually must be constructed around him. He does not conform easily to conditions imposed on him by others. His standards of performance are high, because he—not you—insists on it. He may from time to time throw his weight and temper around. His loyalty is plainly to himself and his skills or professional field rather than to you and the organisation. There are many times when you feel you need him, and yet you wonder how you can live with him. Should you meet his need for special treatment?
24. Explain the stages of group development with suitable examples.
25. Discuss the nature of group dynamics which prevails in informal organisation and its impact on the effectiveness of the organisation as a whole.

CASE STUDY – 1

Quite recently, Mr. George has jointed Marketing Group of a large industrial concern having an annual turnover of Rs. 70 crore. In their anxiety to cope with the external and internal environment the concern has decided to design its products to suit the needs of the target customer, both in India and abroad. It is also to offer an acceptable level of service to the customer and their value for money. Accordingly, various changes in the organisational structure were done and the product concept was introduced.

The demand of the Marketing Group was very heavy. Based on his past experience and professional competency. Mr. George was specifically chosen to head the Marketing Group.

In the initial stages, Mr. George had to take stock of the working of this group and he was soon able to observe that many of its members were adopting the group norms, were very nice and polite to each other, were quite free to probe each other about their feelings, and a sort of friendly, cooperative and congenial atmosphere prevailed in this group. There was harmonious working relationship among its members which facilitated maximum contribution of everybody and high degree of acceptance of Mr. George for its inclusion in the group.

On a six-monthly review it was found that because of concerted efforts of each and every member of this Marketing Group the overall performance of the concern in terms of booking of orders, growth, profitability, etc., improved considerably. The concern received high recognition and various awards for its emergence as a successful marketeer as also in building of high degree of customer confidence by sustaining international standards of excellence in product quality, performance and service, particularly in regard to supply of spares and after-sales service.

The management issued appreciation letters to its employees and the members of the Marketing Group, in particular, were suitably rewarded for their grand performance.

Encouraged by the six-monthly operating results, the management decided to go in for further expansion of its business in order to retain market leadership in the manufacture of sophisticated industrial machinery and for this purpose they decided to have excellent collaboration with leading companies abroad, of course, by adopting requisite formaliteis. Need was accordingly felt to induct Managerial specialists and that was how Mr. Thomas, along with a few professionals, joined this group. Mr. Thomas, though equally capable like Mr. George, was placed as number two. After one month it was noticed that this Marketing Group was having an entirely different atmosphere. There were signs of very few high participators and the number of low participators went up. The highs became quiet, the lows suddenly became talkative.

A sort of rivalry started planning in this group resulting in withdrawing tendency of most of its members and prevalence of mounting tensions. Different patterns of interactions started developing in the group and sub-grouping were noticed – one sub-group was supporting Mr. George and other one was under Mr. Thomas who was busy in constant disagreement and creating negative feelings and adopting undesirable group norms. All this ultimately resulted in hindrance to the smooth working of the Marketing Group. The very purpose of the management for developing/strengthening this group had been defeated and the management had to suffer a great setback. All its hopes were shattered. The overall performance of the concern during this period showed downward trend and the management could hardly afford to be a silent spectator to this odd situation. Therefore, immediate corrective steps had to be undertaken by the management and Mr. Thomas, along with a few trouble-makers (who were found responsible for vitiating group atmosphere), were transferred to other groups with a note of warning about their conduct.

At the end of the year, on reviewing the performance of the concern in general and that of the Marketing Group in particular, it transpired that the Marketing Group under Mr. George was coming up smoothly and there was a very effective teamwork within the small group who was trying hard to make up the deficiency for the earlier period. The ultimate result was that, by virtue of sincere efforts of this group along with other group, the concern was able to keep its image and was also able to fulfil national expectations.

Questions

1. Identify the issues involved in the above case.
2. "Group dynamics constitute items such as morale, atmosphere, influence, participation, cooperation, etc." Comment.
3. "Clever marketing strategy is the *sine qua non* of existence amidst the fierce competition for survival." Examine.

CASE STUDY – 2

P.I. Technologies (India) Ltd. is a firm in Hyderabad, which has gained much with its clients in Europe and N. America and thus has secured several new projects. Its sudden growth and growing competition compelled it to make necessary changes in the internal organisation structure with the help of outside consultants. The company decided to tackle its problems through newer commitments and developing understanding among its employees. The high tech workforce had to be geared and improve the effectiveness of lower level supervisor.

What the company did was to establish a collateral organisation of managers from different departments which would report to the stering committee of the collateral structure. This structure was sufficient to permit experimentations and development of new ideas and methods that might later be incorporated into the formal organisation. This was aimed at redesign of an assembly line for higher performance and employee satisfaction. A similar system which the company introduced in its office in Bangalore started giving results. However, Mr. Goverdhan Reddy, the newly appointed CEO, thought that a collateral organisation is redundant and hence, decided to do away with the new system.

Questions

1. Do you find any theoretical reasons for the existence of a collateral organisation within an organisation?
2. When similar attempts started giving results in its other office, why should not the CEO give time to experiment the same in Hyderabad office also?
3. Had you been in the place of Mr. Reddy, what would you have done and why? Explain.

CHAPTER

9

POWER, POLITICS AND STATUS

CHAPTER OUTLINE

9.1. Concept and Nature of Power
9.2. Difference between Power and Authority
9.3. Sources of Power
9.4. Traits of Successful Power Users
9.5. Guidelines for Effective Use of Power
9.6. Mulder's Theory of Power Distance
9.7. Tactics Used to Gain Power
9.8. Concept and Nature of Organisational Politics
9.9. Causes of Politics in Organisations
9.10. Dysfunctions of Organisational Politics
9.11. Handling Organisational Politics
9.12. Concept of Status
9.13. Sources or Determinants of Status
9.14. Functions of Status System
9.15. Status Symbols
9.16. Problems Caused by Status System
- **Test Questions**
- **Case Study**

9.1 CONCEPT AND NATURE OF POWER

The term 'power' may be defined as "the ability to get things done the way one wants them to be done". It is the ability to control the actions of others. In the organisational context, power means "the capacity to influence the behaviour of others." If a person has power, it means he has influence on the behaviour of other individuals. The essence is control over the behaviour of others[1]. A manager's power is his ability to cause subordinates to do what he wants them to do.

The main characteristics of power are as follows:

(*i*) Power represents the capacity or ability to influence the behaviour of others.

1. John K. Galbraith: **The Anatomy of Power,** Houghton Miffin Co., New York, 1983.

(*ii*) Power is exercised to accomplish certain goals.

(*iii*) Power is specific as it can be exercised by someone in some situation. All people cannot exercise power at all times or in all situations.

(*iv*) Another fundamental feature of power is dependence. The more a person is dependent on you, the more power you have over him.

(*v*) Power denotes reciprocal relationship between two or more persons. It is based on the two-way concept of influencing others and being influenced.

(*vi*) Power is neither completely formal nor informal. It is rather a mixture of two.

(*vii*) A person has only as much power as others allow him to do.

9.2 DIFFERENCE BETWEEN POWER AND AUTHORITY

The term 'authority' means the right of a superior to decide and command the subordinates. For example, a manager has the right to assign tasks to subordinates and require them to perform these tasks. A person may have the right (authority) but may lack the ability (power) to enforce his rights. Similarly, a person may have the power to do something but lacks authority to do it.

There are several differences between power and authority [Table 9.1].

Table 9.1: Distinction Between Power and Authority

Basis of Distinction	Power	Authority
1. Meaning	Ability to influence the behaviour of others	Right to decide and command others
2. Scope	Wide concept — authority is institutionalised power	Narrow concept — can be a type of power.
3. Nature	Personal quality	Attached to a position.
4. Delegation	Cannot be delegated	Can be delegated.
5. Flow	Can flow in all directions	Flows downwards.

9.3 SOURCES OF POWER

French and Raven[2] have identified the following sources of power.

1. **Reward Power:** The ability to reward is an important source of power. Managers have reward power because they decide the increments, promotions and other rewards of subordinates. Subordinates also have the power to reward or punish their superiors by doing or not doing the assigned tasks. They may accept or reject the authority of superiors.
2. **Coercive Power:** It means the ability to punish for not carrying out orders or for not achieving results. Managers can exercise coercive power over subordinates by threats of withholding promotions, transfers, demotion, dismissal, reprimands, and other punishments. Subordinates obey their superiors due to fear of punishment.

2 J.R.P. French and B.H. Raven: "The Bases of Social Power" in Darwin Cartright (ed.), **Studies in Social Power,** University of Michigan Press, Ann Arbor, 1959, pp. 150-167

3. **Legitimate Power:** It refers to the formal rights attached to the position held by a person in the organisation. The power is inherent in the formal position and may, therefore, be called 'positional power'. Society accepts the rights of the position holder and, therefore, the rights are known as legitimate power. Subordinates have an obligation to accept the power of their superiors.
4. **Expert Power:** The source of expert power is the expertise or special skills of a person. For example, a doctor has expert power on his patients and a lawyer has expert power over his clients. Expert power may be lost when the expertise becomes obsolete. For example, an excellent typist may no longer have power due to the invention of computers.
5. **Referent Power:** A person has referent power when others admire him and want to imitate his attitudes and behaviour. For example, young persons try to emulate the visible behaviour of film stars and sports stars.

Social scientists have identified two more sources of power — (*a*) **information power**, and (*b*) **connection power**. People who possess or have easy access to valuable information have power over those who are in need of such information. Anybody having connections or links with powerful people has connection power.

The various sources of power given above are interrelated and interdependent in the following ways :

(*i*) Use of reward power can increase referent power because people like those who reward them.

(*ii*) With increase in legitimate power, reward power, coercive power and referent power also increase. Legitimate power is a mark of high status and honour and people are attracted to high-status individuals. Similarly, people associate high position holders with expertise.

(*iii*) Frequent use of coercive power reduces referent power because people start disliking the person who exercises coercive power.

(*iv*) Expert power can give rise to legitimate power because the organisation promotes the competent and with higher position legitimate power increases.

(*v*) Referent power can increase legitimate power and expert power. People attribute legitimacy and expertise to attractive individuals.

9.4 TRAITS OF SUCCESSFUL POWER USERS

According to Kotter[3], managers who use their power successfully possess the following traits:

1. They are sensitive to the source of their power and take actions that are consistent with the expectations of people. For example, an expert in one field might lose credibility if he attempts to influence people in a different field.

3. John P. Kotter: "Power Dependence and Effective Management", **Harvard Business Review,** (July-August 1977), pp. 135-136.

2. They are aware of the costs, benefits and risks of using each source of power. They understand which source of power to use in different situations and with different people.
3. They recognise that each source of power is useful in a particular situation. They try to develop their skills and expertise so that they can use what source of power is needed.
4. They have career goals which allow them to acquire and use power. They seek jobs that build skills and require the type of power which they can comfortably use.
5. They temper their power with maturity and self-control. They avoid impulsive or egoistic display of their power and avoid tactics which are unnecessarily harsh on people around them.
6. They know that power is necessary to get things done. They feel comfortable in the use of power. They accept the fact that it is necessary to influence the behaviour of others to achieve goals.

9.5 GUIDELINES FOR EFFECTIVE USE OF POWER

Research or empirical work provides several guidelines concerning the use of power.

(*i*) The purpose of power is to influence others for getting things done.

(*ii*) There is no evidence of power unless it is exercised.

(*iii*) The effect of power is reduced when it is exercised outside its perceived limits.

(*iv*) The stronger the power base, the greater is the power. Formal position is the strongest power base and coercion is weakest.

(*v*) Managers who use their power in a positive manner (*i.e.,* for the benefit of the organisation) will be more effective than those who use it in a negative manner (*i.e.,* for self-aggrandisement or domination).

(*vi*) Users of reward power are liked more than users of coercive power.

(*vii*) Expert power is positively and consistently correlated with satisfaction and performance.

9.6 MULDER'S THEORY OF POWER DISTANCE

Different individuals have different power. The degree of inequality in power is known as "power distance". Mulder's theory of power distance holds that[4] :

(*i*) The high-power individual attempts to maintain and if possible to expand power distance with low-power individual.

(*ii*) The low-power individual attempts to reduce the power distance with high-power individual.

Mulder's theory is based on the proposition "the more exercise of power will give satisfaction". The theory has some appeal to the behavioural scientists but has not been tested empirically.

4 M. Mulder : **The Daily Power Game,** Leiden the Netherlands, Mennen Asto. 1977.

9.7 TACTICS USED TO GAIN POWER

Individuals and groups use several tactics to gain power in an organisation. Some of these tactics involve cooperation while others are competitive in nature. These are given below:

1. **Bargaining or Trade-Off:** It means negotiation of ***quid pro quo*** agreement between two parties. Each party offers some benefits or concession to the other party to resolve the conflict. Collective bargaining agreement between management and labour union is an example of such negotiation. The party having greater bargaining power is able to obtain more benefits than the sacrifices made.
2. **Cooptation:** In this tactic, a group takes a member of another group in its policy-making committee to blunt criticism or threat from the latter. For example, the representative of financial institutions or trade union may be taken in the board of directors of the company.
3. **Coalition:** It refers to a temporary alliance of two or more individuals or groups. The coalition members are able to increase their power over non-members. In a coalition, the members pool their efforts and energy to achieve common goals. In organisations, coalitions are formed to influence goal setting and distribution of benefits. Coalition is an interesting mix of cooperation and competition.
4. **Competition:** An organisation has limited resources in the form of funds, space, support staff, etc. Therefore, different groups in the organisation compete with each other to secure a greater share of such resources. Each group tries to push through that criteria or basis for distribution of resources which will fetch it more.
5. **Pressure:** This method of gaining power is hostile. For example, trade union might hold threat of a slowdown or strike to pressurise the management to accept its demands. Similarly, management may use threats of lockout, suspension, dismissal to make labour accept its terms. Threats may provoke counter-threats. Yet pressure is a common feature of power struggle in work organisations.

In addition to the above, the following strategies are used to acquire position power in organisations :

(*i*) **Centrality:** The individual or group controlling activities that are central to the organisation has more positional power. For example, the finance department has extra power because it approves expenses and payments of all other departments.

(*ii*) **Scarcity:** The individual or group that can acquire more scarce resources enjoys more power. For example, the ability to obtain more funds from Government and non-government sources may be more important determinant of power in an academic institution than the number of graduates created by it.

(*iii*) **Substitutability:** The more indispensable is an individual or group to an organisation, greater is its power. The expertise or speciality of the individual or group may make it indispensable.

(*iv*) **Uncertainty:** Heads of those functional departments which can better cope with uncertainty in the environment enjoy more power. For example, marketing people become more powerful when markets are highly competitive, production experts are powerful when materials are scarce and demand is high, labour experts are powerful when labour is scarce and public relations or lobbyists enjoy power when government regulations impinge on the organisation.

9.8 CONCEPT AND NATURE OF ORGANISATIONAL POLITICS

Organisational politics is the process whereby power is acquired and exercised over others to satisfy one's desires. According to Farrell and Peterson, "Politics in an organisation refers to those activities that are not required as a part of one's formal role in the organisation, but that influence or attempt to influence the distribution of advantages and disadvantages within the organisation."[5]

In the words of Tushman, "Politics refers to the structure and process of the use of authority and power to effect definition of goals, direction and the other parameters of the organisation. Decisions are not made in a rational or formal way but rather through compromise, accommodation and bargaining."[6]

The definitions given above reveal the following **features of organisational politics:**

(*i*) Politics and politicking are an inevitable part of organisation. It is a reality of organisational life. Politics occurs at all levels though it is more common at higher levels of authority. When everybody plays politics, an organisation may become a political battlefield. To ignore politics is to ignore an important part of organisational life. "Politicking is endemic to every organisation regardless of size, function or character of ownership".[7] However, the degree of politics may differ from organisation to organisation.

(*ii*) Politics involves the use of some kind of power or pressure over others to achieve certain goals. In fact, politics and power are inextricably interwoven with the fabric of organisational life.

(*iii*) Political behaviour is self-serving in nature. Under it, attempts are made to use the organisations's resources for giving benefits to self or to others.

(*iv*) Political behaviour is outside the specified job requirements of an individual or group. The practices and procedures used in it are not formally recognised.

(*v*) Political decisions may not be rational from the organisation's point of view as these are taken for self-interest.

(*vi*) There are several forms of political behaviour such as lobbying for or against someone, horse trading, exchanging favours, making coalitions, spreading rumours, leaking confidential information, withholding key information from decision-makers, compromises, eliminating adversaries.

---

5 D. Farrell and J.C. Peterson: "Pattern of Political Behaviour in Organisations", **Academy of Managment Review,** July 1982, p. 405.

6 M.L., Tushman, "A Political Approach to Organisation", **Academy of Management Review,** 1977, p. 217.

7 John M. Pfiffner and Frank P. Sherwood: **Administrative Behaviour**, Practice Hall of India, New Delhi, 1968, p. 331.

(*vii*) All behaviour is not political. For example, an employee asking for promotion is not political behaviour. But using the threat of labour union strike is a political act.

(*viii*) Political behaviour is intentional as the person involved knowingly influences others to advance self-interest. It is essentially concerned with who gets what, when and how.

(*ix*) An organisation is a political entity in the sense that it consists of people who pursue their self-interests.

9.9 CAUSES OF POLITICS IN ORGANISATIONS

Individuals adopt political behaviour in an organisation due to the following reasons :

1. **Desire for Power:** Members of an organisation play politics to gain power and control. Everybody wants power to influence others in the organisation. Conflict between line managers and staff experts is a typical example of power struggle.
2. **Competition for Resources:** Resources in an organisation are scarce. People indulge in politics to obtain a greater share of these resources. For example, executives fight over roomsize, support staff, private parking space, funds, etc.
3. **Subjective Performance Appraisal:** It is very difficult to evaluate performance in a fully objective manner. Whenever employees feel there is some bias in evaluation, they play politics against their boss.
4. **Saturation in Career:** People work hard to gain promotions. But when a person cannot rise above a certain level due to lack of competence or vacancy at the higher level, he may resort to politics. In other words, everyone tries to rise to his level of incompetence. This is known as the **Peter Principle**[8]. Sometimes, an individual may also indulge in politics because he is prevented beyond his capacity to perform.
5. **Discretionary Powers:** Some positions in an organisations are vested with discretionary powers to be used in exceptional situations. People resort to politics to grab such positions or to be close to such a position holder.
6. **Joint Decision Making:** There are certain issues which can be decided jointly by two or more groups. One group cannot achieve its goals without the cooperation of another group. These groups may play politics to further their interests. Parleys between production department and marketing department is one such example.
7. **Unwillingness to Share Power:** Power hungry managers do not want to share their power with subordinates. They engage in maneuvering and manipulation to deny active say to employees in decision making.

Political Tactics
• Attacking and blaming others • Instrumental use of information • Image building and impression management • Support building of ideas

8 Lawrence J. Peter and Raymond Hall, **The Peter Principle,** Pan Books, London, 1969.

- Praising others, ingratiation
- Power coalitions, strong allies
- Associating with influential people
- Creating obligations/reciprocity

Source: R.W. Allen, et.al, "Organisational Politics : Tactics and Characteristics of Actors," **California Management Review,** Fall, 1979, pp. 77-83.

9.10 DYSFUNCTIONS OF ORGANISATIONAL POLITICS

Any action or behaviour that hinders the achievement of organisational goals is dysfunctional. Organisational politics is guided by self-interest or self-aggrandizement. Whenever individual and organisational goals are incongruent or non-complementary, political behaviour is dysfunctional (Fig. 9.1)

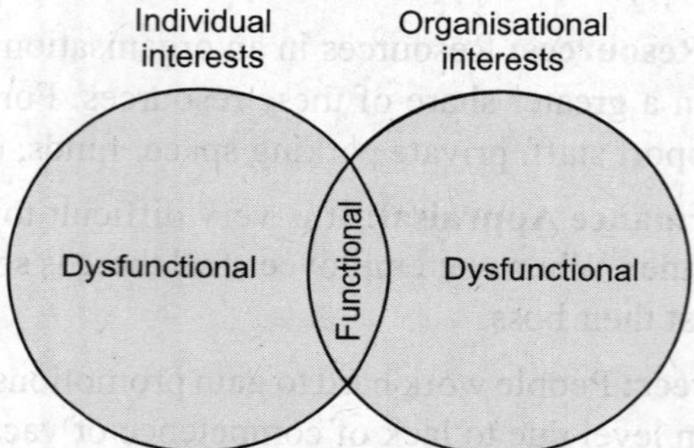

Fig. 9.1: Impact of Politics on the Organisation

Politics can have the following negative consequences for the organisation:

(*i*) Efficiency and effectiveness of the organisation may suffer due to poor job performance. For example, a senior manager may manipulate the selection process to ensure that his daughter who is not fully competent is appointed on the post. As a result job performance will be poor.

(*ii*) Politics in the organisation may create conflicts between individuals or groups. Much time, effort and energy are wasted in such conflicts on planning attacks and counter-attacks. People are not able to concentrate on task accomplishment. This will obstruct the achievement of organisational goals.

(*iii*) Power politics may weaken the motivation and morale of employees. Bitterness arises between victors and victims and the latter get frustrated.

(*iv*) Some persons who are experts in political behaviour may acquire too much power. They may misuse their power to further self-interest or to exploit others. "Power corrupts and absolute power corrupts absolutely" is a popular saying.

(*v*) Empirical work[9] suggests that the managers who are more adept in political activities are comparatively more successful in getting promotion despite being less effective in work performance and satisfaction of subordinates.

9 R. Wayne Mondy and Shane R. Premeaux, "Power, Politics, and the First Line Supervisor," **Supervisory Management,** January 1986, pp 37-38.

According to Robbins,[10] dysfunctional political behaviour can occur in the following forms:

(*i*) Scapegoating

(*ii*) Passing the buck

(*iii*) Red-herring tactics

(*iv*) Sabotage

(*v*) Falsification or hiding important information

(*vi*) Discrediting others

(*vii*) Indulging in deliberate bad ballyhoo techniques, etc.

9.11 HANDLING ORGANISATIONAL POLITICS

Organisational politics is primarily harmful for the organisation. Some of the steps that can be taken to check it are as follows :

1. **Well Defined Tasks:** Top management should clearly define the jobs and duties of people. This will help employees to know what is expected of them and serve as an objective criteria for performance evaluation. Therefore, they will be less tempted to engage in politics to gain recognition. Moreover, if jobs are challenging, employees will have to work hard to complete them and will have little time and energy for engaging in politics.

2. **Proper Allocation of Resources:** When scarce resources are distributed among individuals and work units, there will be less competition for these resources. Appropriate policies should be formulated and consistently applied for this purpose.

3. **Fair Appraisal System:** An objective performance evaluation system can reduce bias. Pay increases, promotions and other rewards should be based purely on performance. This will minimise political activity for gaining rewards.

4. **Effective Communication:** A two-way communication can keep top management aware of the perception of employees on different issues. Management can reduce undesirable political behaviour by responding quickly to the genuine needs and aspirations of employees.

5. **Responsible Leadership:** Subordiantes tend to imitate their supervisors. Therefore, managers must behave properly otherwise they may unintentionally encourage undesirable political activity in the organisation. If employees perceive their bosses to be incapable, insecure or irresponsible, they try to bully or manipulate for undue favours, etc.

9.12 CONCEPT OF STATUS

Status is an important feature of every group whether it is a work-group, an organisation or a society. Status means the relative ranking that a person holds in a group, organisation or society.

10 Stephen P. Robbins, **Organisational Behaviour: Concepts and Controversies,** Englewood Cliffs, New Jersey, Prentice Hall, 1979, p. 404.

According to Barnard[11] status is "that condition of the individual that is defined by a statement of his rights, privileges, immunities, duties and obligations in the organisation and, obversely by a statement of restrictions, limitations, and prohibitions governing behaviour, both determining the expectations of others in reference thereto". Status refers to some visible markings that systematically rank individuals and groups in relation to each other. For example, in a university, the difference between Assistant Professor, Associate Professor and Professor is status.

Status may be formal or informal. The former is derived from a hierarchical position or rank in the organisation whereas the latter is earned by a person through personal qualities such as education and experience. Social status means the relative ranking of an individual in the society.

9.13 SOURCES OR DETERMINANTS OF STATUS

1. **Ascribed-Achieved:** The prestige which a person derives due to birth in a prominent family is ascribed status. For example, the status which a family member or relative of a chairman, president, prime minister, chief minister, etc. enjoys is ascribed. On the other hand, the prestige earned by a person by virtue of his education, skills, etc. is achieved status. For instance, Narayan Murthy achieved status by creating Infosys Technology, a world class company.
2. **Scalar-Functional:** In a formal organisation, status is related to the position of an individual in the hierarchy. For example, Managing Director has a higher scalar status than Director, Marketing, in a company. Status attached to the function performed by an individual is functional status. For example, white collar workers (clerks) are viewed as superior to blue collar workers (factory workers).
3. **Positional-Personal:** The prestige attached to the position occupied by a person is positional status. For example, a Supreme Court Judge enjoys a higher status than a High Court Judge. Anybody occupying the 'chair' will have the same status irrespective of personal qualities. Personal status refers to the prestige earned due to connections, attractiveness, sociability, etc. The status of film stars is personal.
4. **Active-Latent:** A person performing several roles may have different status in each role. For example, a clerk is lowly placed in the organisation. But he may enjoy considerable prestige in his locality due to active role in the Residents Welfare Association.

9.14 FUNCTIONS OF STATUS SYSTEM

Every organisation has some kind of status system which performs the following functions:

1. **Facilitates Communication:** An effective communication system is essential for the proper functioning of every organisation. Status system facilitates communication in several ways :

   (*a*) Status system makes communication authentic. The letterhead contains the name, position and title of the communicator.

---

11 Chester I. Barnard : "The Functions of Status Systems", in Robert K. Merton et.al. (eds.), **Readings in Bureaucracy**, Free Press, New York, 1952, p. 242.

(*b*) Status system makes communication authoritative. Both scalar and functional systems of status indicate that the message has come from an authoritative source.

(*c*) Status system makes communication intelligible because both the sender and the receiver use clear and understandable language.

The status system also provides understanding concerning who is to lead and who is to follow.

2. **Provides Motivation:** Status serves as an incentive. The prestige associated with status satisfies ego. As ego is an important psychological need, employees are motivated to work hard to attain status. Moreover, status is an important means to gain other benefits. It supplements monetary incentives. The motivational value of status is increasing because people now-a-days are not satisfied with *status quo*. More and more individuals strive for higher positions, prestigious residence, right type of car and other symbols of status.

3. **Fixes Responsibility:** Status system creates a sense of responsibility among members of the organisation. They avoid any such conduct that results in loss of status, because reduction in status is a humiliating experience. The desire to improve and maintain status in the organisation makes them feel responsible towards the job. When people act with responsibility their behaviour becomes more stable and reliable.

4. **Protects Personal Integrity:** Status system helps to protect the personality and integrity of people. More competent individuals need the distinctions of status system. Otherwise they may feel that their intelligence and superior skills are not recognised. Subordinates feel that accepting orders from a superior is much better than accepting orders from nobody. Therefore, status system preserves the integrity of both superior and subordinate members of the organisation.

9.15 STATUS SYMBOLS

Status symbols refer to a set of externally visible markings that systematically rank individuals and groups in relation to each other. They are indicators on the basis of which a higher status person can be distinguished from a lower status person. Various types of status symbols are as follows :

1. **Titles and Designations:** The title or designation attached to the position held by a person is one of the most obvious symbols of status. The title 'President' indicates that he is the most important person in the organisation. The next important person is 'vice-president'. Similarly, 'Vice Chancellor' enjoys a higher status than "Pro Vice Chancellor' in a university. In order to motivate senior executives, an organisation may change the designations of heads of departments. For example, 'Marketing Manager' may be redesignated as 'Director-Marketing'.

2. **Insignia:** Several identification marks are used to differentiate higher status people and places from lower status people and places. For example, a minister's car bears a flag. Similarly, hotels are classified on the basis of stars, *e.g.,* five star hotel, three star hotel, etc.

3. **Clothing:** The dress is often used to indicate the status of an individual. Clothing reveals the occupation and social standing of employees. The office staff wear white colour dress, whereas factory workers wear blue colour dress, Executives wear suits. Clothing of a person influences the attitudes and behaviour of others towards him.
4. **Pay and Perquisites:** Every organisation designs a salary structure. Employees are placed in various grades. An employee placed in higher grade has higher status. Persons with higher status are given special perquisites such as fully furnished bungalow, chauffeur driven car, club membership, fully-paid foreign travel for family, etc.
5. **Physical Facilities:** Status of employees can be distinguished on the basis of various facilities provided to them at the workplace. For example, senior executives are provided well-furnished rooms, private parking space, etc. Roomsize, type of furniture, and even nameplates indicate status of an individual in the organisation. A private dining room may be provided to executives whereas workers take their lunch in a common canteen.

9.16 PROBLEMS CAUSED BY STATUS SYSTEM

Status system may cause the following problems:

1. **Social Distance:** Status system may increase the social distance between superiors and subordinates. The top executive might feel lonely in isolation. When status distinctions are great mutual cooperation between managers and workers is reduced. Overemphasis on status distinctions may also hamper authoritative communication among members of the organisation. The high offices become insulated and do not remain in touch with workplace realities.
2. **Inequity:** Overemphasis on status may create a sense of inequality or inferiority among those who have low status. Those denied status may be dissatisfied and become jealous of those having status. The status holders may be preoccupied too much with maintenance of their status and its symbols.
3. **Ignoring Competence:** The status accorded to the position may undermine individual competence. For example, the vice-president may be the chairman's son-in-law, the chief engineer may be a mechanic and a doctor may be less capable than the nurse. Incompetent individuals may hold higher status and more power than competent individuals.
4. **Friction:** Status system may cause conflicts among employees. There may be a tussle among them to acquire more status. Status considerations may affect working relationships. For example, an employee may resist transfer to a smaller office or branch due to the feeling that it affects his status.
5. **Financial Burden:** Several physical facilities provided to high status holders involve a heavy expenditure. The contribution of these position holders may not be commensurate with the expenditure involved in maintaining their status symbols.
6. **Anxiety and Frustration:** Some may feel that they are entitled to higher status but are powerless to get it. Such a feeling of **status deficiency** creates anxiety and frustration in their minds. Status inconsistency leads to unhappiness. Status inconsistency means status symbols are not in harmony. For example, the title of the position is right but the title-holder is not given the appropriate private office.

When there is **lack of congruency** between the perceived ranking of an individual and the facilities provided to him, order and motivation are disturbed. For example, two employees of equal rank are given different types of accommodation. When the gross earnings of a supervisor are lower than those of a worker, workers may reject the supervisor's authority.

When the behaviour of a person is inconsistent with the expected behaviour, there is **status discrepancy.** For example, a factory manager may take lunch with the workers. Such discrepancy may undermine the manager's authority and influence over workers. Similarly, a professor may lose respect from students by asking for advice from an assistant professor. Efficiency and effectiveness may suffer.

7. **Deviation from Group Norms:** Conformity to group norms may suffer due to status system. High-status members of a group are often given power discretion to deviate from group norms. Other members value such high-status members and accept their behaviour.

TEST QUESTIONS

1. What is meant by the term 'Power'? Distinguish between Power and Authority.
2. Define Power. How are Power and Politics related?
3. Enumerate the factors which contribute to political activity in an organisation.
4. How do some people in an organisation require and exercise greater power than others? Explain the nature and significance of power relations in a large manufacturing concern. Relate your answer to game theory and Fiedler's contingency theory.
5. What are the implications of tall and flat organisation structures which result from narrow and wide spans of management respectively?
6. How does power structure influence the effectiveness of an organisation? Briefly explain.
7. Explain various sources of power.
8. Describe certain power strategies used in your organisation.
9. What are the factors that influence political behaviour in organisations? Illustrate your answer with examples from your own organisation.
10. Describe the traits of successful power users.
11. Discuss the guidelines for effective use of power.
12. Explain the tactics used by individuals and groups to gain power in an organisation.
13. What is organisational politics? Why do organisational members resort to political behaviour?
14. Explain organisational politics with particular reference to Satyam Computer Services Ltd.
15. Politics is inevitable in an organisation. Explain. How can politics be constructive and positive?
16. What is meant by the term 'status'?
17. Explain the functions of status system in an organisation.

18. Discuss various types of status symbols.
19. Explain the problems that status system can create in work organisations.

CASE STUDY – 1

One of the areas in which .organizations are finding power to be an extremely important consideration in today's knowledge management is the protection of intellectual property, specifically patent protection. When a firm secures a patent, it gains knowledge power over the marketplace. However, if this patent cannot be defended against violators, it has little value. A good example of a patent protection battle is that of Fusion Systems, a small, high-tech American firm, and Mitsubishi, the giant Japanese conglomerate.

Several years ago, Fusion developed a core technology that allowed it to manufacture high-intensity ultraviolet lamps powered by 500 to 6,000 watts of microwave energy. The company obtained patents in the United States, Europe, and Japan. One of its first big orders came from the Adolph Coors Company for lamp systems to dry the printed decoration on beer cans. Other customers included Hitachi, IBM, 3M, Motorola, Sumitoms, Toshiba, NEC, and Mitsubishi. The last purchased Fusion's lamp system and immediately sent it to the research and development lab to be reverse engineered. Once Mitsubishi had stripped down the product, it began filing patent applications that copied and surrounded Fusion's high-intensity microwave lamp technology. Fusion was unaware of what was going on until it began investigating and found that Mitsubishi had filed nearly 300 patent applications directly related to its own lamp technology. When Fusion tried to settle the matter through direct negotiations, the firm was unsuccessful. In addition, Mitsubishi hired the Stanford Research Institute to study the matter and the Institute concluded that the Japanese company's position was solid. However, the chairman of the applied physics department at Columbia University, who was hired by Fusion, disagreed and—after reviewing the patent materials from both companies—concluded that Mitsubishi had relied heavily on technology developed at Fusion and that Mitsubishi's lamp represented no significant additional breakthrough.

Mitsubishi then offered Fusion a deal : Mitsubishi would not sue Fusion for patent, infringement if Fusion would pay Mitsubishi a royalty for the privilege of using "its" patents in Japan. Mitsubishi would then get a royalty-free, worldwide cross-licence of all of Fusion's technology. Fusion responded by going to the Office of the U.S. Trade Representative and getting help. The company also found a sympathetic ear from the Senate Finance Committee and the House Republican Task Force on. Technology Transfer, as well as from the secretary of commerce and the American ambassador to Japan. As the dispute was dragged through the courts, Mitsubishi began to give ground in the face of political pressure. At the same time, Fusion continued to develop innovations in its core field of expertise and remains the leader in both Japanese and worldwide markets. The company believes that as long as it maintains the exclusive rights to this technology, competitors will not be able to erode its market power.

Questions

1. What type of power does a patent provide to a company? Is this the same kind of power that people within a firm attempt to gain ?
2. What types of political strategies has Mitsubishi used to try to gain power over Fusion? Identify and describe any three.

3. How has Fusion managed to retaliate successfully? Identify and describe three tactics it has employed.

CASE STUDY – 2

Ice Cool Private Limited was an ice cream manufacturing company employing about 100 persons including persons at various levels of management. Because of increasing business, the company needed to strengthen its accounting procedure particularly through computerisation. For this purpose, the company decided to hire a new manager, designated as assistant business manager. The company invited applications through press advertisement. After receiving the applications, it appointed a selection committee consisting of members of top management including business manager Rakesh Mohan. The committee interviewed several candidates and finally selected Bishwash as new assistant business manager. Bishwash was neat, well dressed and quite articulate.

Bishwash joined the company immediately and started working very hard. He used to put extra efforts and even worked during holidays as he did not have any family responsibility. He gained the reputation of being a dedicated and competent employee, his strong point being his knowledge of accounting and computer system. He was reporting to Rakesh Mohan, the business manager who was quite impressed with his working.

At that time, the company had no computer system, and its accounting procedures were in need of considerable improvement. Anil Kumar, the managing director of the company, directed Rakesh Mohan to get the needful done. Since most of accounting work related to scales, no separate accounting department existed and the work was performed under the direction of business manager. Bishwash was mainly appointed to strengthen the accounting aspects of the business. He was asked to prepare a project so that necessary changes can be made. In order to get the first hand information about the problem, Bishwash began meeting regularly with Anil Kumar without the knowledge of Rakesh Mohan. There was no attempt to have secret meeting; Anil Kumar would just call Bishwash in for a report without bothering to tell Rakesh Mohan. The management team, whose members were with the company for a quite long period, had formed a tight-kait group and appeared satisfied with the company. They all worked together and the company prospered in spite of fierce competition.

The meetings between Anil Kumar and Bishwash continued and Rakesh Mohan was gradually losing contact with the project and its progress. In fact, Bishwash was almost reporting directly to the managing director though he was placed under business manager and retained his title of assistant business manager. Rakesh Mohan was now visibly upset over the development and was also concerned about Bishwash's spreading share of influence. He started feeling down in the company.

Questions

1. What is the nature of problem in this case?
2. Could Rakesh Mohan have prevented Bishwash's assumption of power? If so, how specifically could it have been done?
3. Suggest the courses of action now available to Anil Kumar, Rakesh Mohan, and Bishwash.

CHAPTER

10

LEADERSHIP AND INFLUENCE

CHAPTER OUTLINE

10.1. Concept and Nature of Leadership
10.2. Difference between Leadership and Management
10.3. Formal and Informal Leaders
10.4. Importance of Leadership
10.5. Styles of Leadership
10.6. Continuum of Leadership Behaviour
10.7. Trait Theories of Leadership
- Great Man Theory
- Trait Theory

10.8. Behavioural Theories of Leadership
- Michigan University Studies
- Ohio State University Studies
- Managerial Grid
- Likert's Management Systems

10.9. Situational Theories of Leadership
- Fiedler's Contingency Model
- House's Path-Goal Theory
- Life Cycle (Maturity-Immaturity) Theory
- Reddin's Tridimensional Model
- Hersey-Blanchard Model

10.10. Transactional Leadership
10.11. Transformational Leadership
- **Test Questions**
- **Case Studies**

Every organisation is an aggregation of people for some common goals. These goals can be achieved only when the people behave in accordance with the rules, policies and procedures of the organisation. An organisation depends upon leadership to influence the behaviour of its members in the right direction.

10.1 CONCEPT AND NATURE OF LEADERSHIP

Leadership is essentially a continuous process of influencing the behaviour of others to work willingly for the achievement of predetermined goals. According to Tannenbaum *et al,* "Leadership is interpersonal influence exercised in a situation and directed through communication process, towards the attainment of a specified goal or goals."[1]

In the words of James Gibbin, leadership is "a process of influence on a group in a particular situation at a given point of time and in a specific set of circumstances that stimulates people to strive willingly to attain organisational objectives, giving them the experience of helping to attain the common objectives and satisfaction with the type of leadership provided".

On the basis of the definitions given above, the following **features of leadership** can be identified :

1. **Leadership is a Process of Influence:** Leadership is a process whereby a person (leader) exercises influence over the behaviour of a group of people (called followers). A person is said to have an influence over others when they are willing to accept his advice, guidance and direction and to carry out his wishes.
2. **Leadership is a Continuous Process:** Leadership is an ongoing process rather than a one-time activity. The essence of leadership lies in followership.
3. **Leadership is Goal-Oriented:** Leadership is a relationship between a leader and his followers. This relationship arises out of their functioning for common goals.
4. **Leadership is Situational:** Leadership is a function of the leader, the followers and the situation. It is always related to a particular situation at a given point of time. Therefore, the type or style of leadership can vary from situation to situation.
5. **Leadership Involves Stimulation:** Leadership is a function of creating the willingness to work enthusiastically to attain organisational goals. A leader is considered successful when he is able to convince people to subordinate their personal interests to the common interests.
6. **Leadership Provides an Experience of Contribution:** Leadership gives everybody the feeling of helping in attaining the common objectives. It happens when the leader feels the importance of individuals, gives them recognition and informs them about the importance of activities performed by them.

10.2 DIFFERENCE BETWEEN LEADERSHIP AND MANAGEMENT

Leadership and management are interrelated and both involve influencing the behaviour of others. But there are several differences between the two :

1. **Relationship:** Manager-subordinate relationship arises within the context of a formal organisation. On the other hand, leader-follower relationship can occur even outside an organisation. For example, a mob and an informal group have leaders but not managers.

1 Robert Tannenbaum *et.al.,* **Leadership and Organisation : A Behavioural Science Approach**, McGraw-Hill, New York, 1961.

2. **Source of Influence:** Managers influence the behaviour of their subordinates with the help of authority attached to their positions in the organisational hierarchy. On the contrary, leaders influence the behaviour of their followers with the help of power derived from their personal qualities. Followers accept their leaders' direction because they have faith in them.
3. **Focus:** The focus of leadership is on the vision and purpose of the group. Management, on the other hand, focuses mainly on operating results, *e.g.,* efficiency, profits, etc. by establishing appropriate structures and systems. In other words, leadership focuses on top line whereas management focuses on bottom line.
4. **Approach:** The approach of management is largely transactional, *i.e.,* obtaining results in exchange for rewards and penalties. On the other hand, the approach of leadership is primarily transformational.
5. **Process:** Leadership is a proactive and collective process for inspiring people to willingly work for accomplishment of common goals. But management is mainly a reactive and individualistic process of controlling people to behave in the desired manner.

10.3 FORMAL AND INFORMAL LEADERS

As stated earlier, leaders exist in both formal and informal groups. Managers are formal leaders because they hold positions in the formal organisation. When a person is appointed or elected for a superior position, he gets formal authority attached to that position in the organisation. He also becomes responsible for achieving the organisational objectives. Managers and other office-bearers (*e.g.,* prime minister, minister, secretary, etc.) are formal leaders. A formal leader is one who possesses formal authority to direct and control his subordinates.

Informal leaders do not hold a formal position. They emerge when group members willingly accept their orders and guidance. When a manager fails to provide the kind of leadership desired by his subordinates, an informal leader emerges to fill the void. Sometimes, an informal leader is more acceptable to employees than their formal leader or boss. In such a situation, the formal leader is only a position holder as he cannot win the voluntary cooperation of his people.

A leader need not be a manager but a good manager must have many qualities of a leader. A leader derives his influence from his followers who feel that he can satisfy their needs and desires. Therefore, a successful leader does not require appointment or election on a formal position. But a manager needs the qualities of a good leader. He cannot rely solely upon the use of authority for getting the desired results. Subordinates seldom put maximum efforts under the pressure of authority. In order to obtain the desired results the manager must win their trust. This can be done with the help of leadership qualities.

10.4 IMPORTANCE OF LEADERSHIP

History reveals that good leadership is equally essential for success in a war, a freedom movement, a business, or a team game. A leader performs several important functions :

1. **Creating the Vision:** The leader sets up the vision and mission to be achieved. He lays down the goals for his followers and interprets them to guide them.
2. **Motivating People:** Good leadership is a source of inspiration for the group. According to Terry, "A leader breathes life into the group and motivates it towards goals. The lukewarm desires for achievement are transformed into a burning passion for accomplishment."[2]
3. **Providing Guidance:** A leader guides his people towards the achievement of predetermined goals. He provides advice, assistance and support to his followers.
4. **Building Morale:** The leader shapes the thinking and attitudes of employees. He creates self-confidence among them and makes them recognise their hidden potential. High morale leads to higher productivity and growth of the organisation.
5. **Creating Teamwork:** Leadership is essential for developing mutual cooperation and unity among the followers. A well-knit team of people can overcome obstacles and accomplish extraordinary results.
6. **Facilitating Change:** Dynamic leadership is the best mechanism for organisational change. An effective leader can overcome resistance to change by convincing people of the need for change.
7. **Representation of People:** A leader is the representative of his people. He takes initiative in all issues that influence the interests of his group. He serves as the spokesman to outsiders and attempts to fulfil the needs of his followers. The leader acts as the linking pin between the people, the organisation and the external forces.

10.5 STYLES OF LEADERSHIP

The pattern of behaviour adopted by a leader to influence the behaviour of his followers or subordinates is called leadership style. On the basis of the degree of power which a leader shares with his people (known as power orientation), there are three leadership styles:

1. **Autocratic or Authoritarian or Directive Leadership:** Under this style, all decision-making power is centralised in the leader. The leader takes all important decisions and expects the subordinates to obey his orders without any question. He does not give the subordinates any freedom to influence his behaviour. He exercises tight control and supervision over them. There are three types of autocratic leaders. **First, exploitative autocrat** uses criticism and penalties to influence the subordinates. **Second, benevolent autocrat** uses **praise and rewards** to motivate people. **Third, incompetent autocrat** adopts autocratic style to hide his incompetence.

   The main ***advantages*** of autocratic leadership are as follows :

   (*i*) It permits quick decision-making because only one person (the leader) takes decisions.

   (*ii*) It makes full use of the leader's qualities and potential.

---

2 George R. Terry, **Principles of Management,** Richard D. Irwin, Homewood Illinois, 1988, p. 412.

(*iii*) It satisfies subordinates who do not want to take initiative and prefer to work under a centralised authority and strict discipline.

(*iv*) It requires less competent subordinates. The organisation can function even when the subordinates are inexperienced.

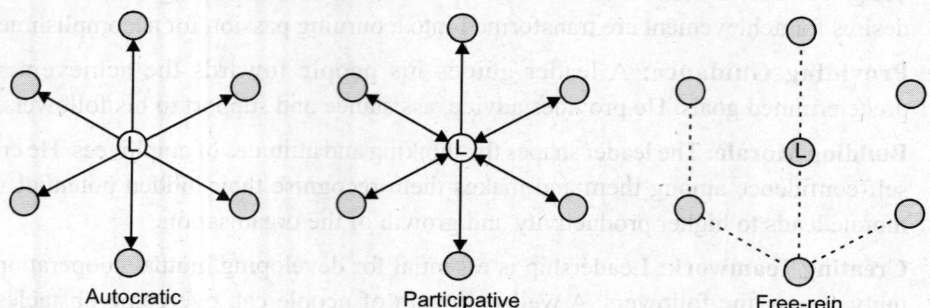

Fig. 10.1: Leadership styles.

Autocratic leadership suffers from the following **disadvantages :**

(*i*) It causes frustration, lower morale and conflict which are harmful to efficient functioning of the organisation.

(*ii*) As the subordinates are given no freedom to exercise initiative and judgement, they remain uninformed, insecure and underdeveloped.

(*iii*) Autocratic leadership is becoming unacceptable as the new generation has greater social awareness and do not like to work under rigid direction and control.

2. **Participative or Democratic or Consultative Leadership:** In this style, the leader takes decisions in consultation with his followers. He shares power by allowing the group to participate in the decision-making process. The subordinates become aware of the goals to be achieved and the conditions affecting them and their jobs.

The main **advantages** of participative leadership are as follows :

(*i*) It improves the motivation and morale of subordinates. Their attitudes towards their jobs, the leader and the organisation improve due to their mental and emotional involvement.

(*ii*) It increases the acceptance of management ideas. They are a party to the decisions and, therefore, implement them whole-heartedly.

(*iii*) It increases cooperation between management and employees. As a result, conflict, absenteeism and labour turnover are reduced.

(*iv*) It helps to develop a sense of responsibility among employees.

(*v*) It increases stability and growth of the organisation by developing future leaders.

Participative leadership suffers from the following ***disadvantages*:**

(*i*) It is time-consuming and may cause delay in decision-making.

(*ii*) It requires knowledgeable and experienced subordinates who can share power and contribute to decision-making.

(*iii*) Over a period of time subordinates may develop a habit of expecting to be consulted on every issue. When they are not consulted they feel slighted, insulted and become resentful and uncooperative.

(*iv*) Some employees want minimum interaction with their superiors. For them participation is discouraging and frustrating.

(*v*) A manager may use participation covertly to manipulate employees.

3. **Free-Rein or Laissez-Faire Leadership:** Under this style, there is almost complete delegation of authority to subordinates. They have complete freedom to make and execute decisions within the broad policy framework set up by management. The leader maintains contacts with outsiders to bring the information and materials the group needs. Free-rein leadership involves abdication of authority by the leader and gives all responsibility to the group. It ignores the leader's contribution just as autocratic leadership ignores the group's contribution.

   Free-rein leadership may be appropriate under the following conditions :

   (*i*) When the subordinates are highly knowledgeable, experienced and well-trained.

   (*ii*) When the subordinates are highly motivated and have a full sense of their responsibility to the organisation.

   (*ii*) When the organisational goals are full clear and acceptable to the subordinates.

   Free-rein leadership tends to allow different units of the organisation to work at cross-purposes which can degenerate into chaos.

4. **Paternalistic Style:** Under this style, the leader treats his subordinates like family. As the head of family he helps, guides and protects them. He takes most of the decisions and shares little power. But he provides good working conditions, welfare facilities and fringe benefits. This style has been popular in Japan, India and Korea due to their cultural backgrounds.

Comparison Between Leadership Styles

Point of Comparison	Autocratic Style	Consultative Style	Free-Rein Style
1. Decision-making	Leader sole decision-maker	Leader makes decision in consultation with subordinates	Subordinates themselves make decision
2. Communication	One-way (downward) communication	Two-way communication	Free flow of communication
3. Motivation techniques	Fear and punishment (negative incentives)	Rewards and involvement (positive incentives)	Self-direction and self-control
4. Nature of discipline	Implicit obedience of order and instructions	Interchange of ideas and recognition of human values.	Self-discipline or control
5. Authority delegation	Strict supervision and control. No delegation	Delegation of authority	Complete delegation of authority
6. Orientation	Task-oriented style	People-oriented style	People-oriented style

7. Needs	Physiological and safety	Ego needs	Self-actualisation needs
8. Opportunity to subordinates	No scope for initiative and creativity 'I' style	Scope for initiative and creativity 'We' style	Full scope for initiative and creativity 'You' style
9. Focus	Leader-centred	Group-centred	Individual-centred
10. Role of leader	Provides direction	Maintains teamwork	Provides support and resources

10.6 CONTINUUM OF LEADERSHIP BEHAVIOUR

In reality there can be several leadership styles between the two extremes of autocratic and free rein. Tannenbaum and Schmidt have described a range of possible leadership behaviour available to a manager. Each style is a combination of the degree of authority used by the boss and the area of freedom available to subordinates [Fig. 10.2]. The left extreme shows **boss-centred leadership** wherein the manager exercises a high degree of control. The right extreme shows **employee-centred leadership** wherein the manager exercises very little control. In between there are varying degrees of control.

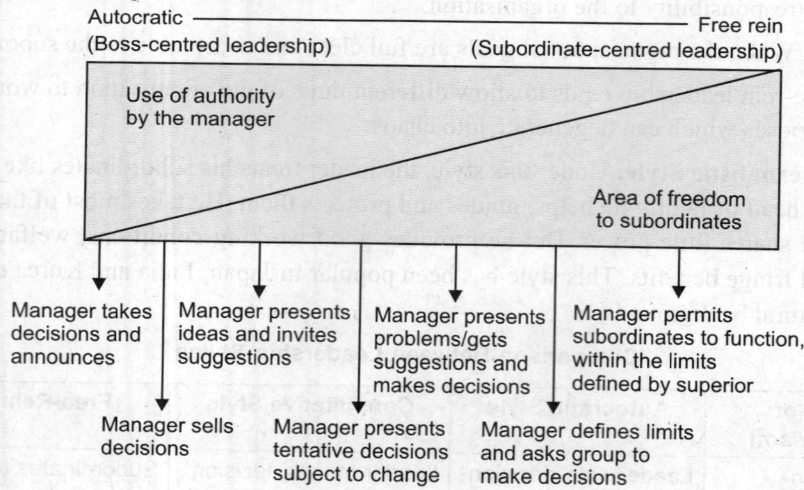

Fig. 10.2: Leadership Continuum

Leadership continuum is a more realistic picture of leadership behaviour. It shows that a wide choice is available to the manager. The style which a manager should adopt depends upon the following forces :

(*i*) **Forces in the Manager:** These include the value system of the leader (authoritarian or democratic), his confidence in subordinates, his tolerance of ambiguity.

(*ii*) **Forces in the Subordinates:** These consist of subordinates' need for independence, their readiness to assume responsibility for decision-making, their understanding of organisational goals and problems, their tolerance for ambiguity, and their experience with and expectations of leadership.

(iii) Forces in the Situation: These comprise the type of organisation, nature of tasks, group effectiveness, time pressure, etc.

The main weakness of the continuum approach is that it presents uni-dimensional view of leadership. An increase in one type of behaviour is automatically seen as a decrease in the opposite type. Research[3] reveals that the two are not opposite ends on a continuum. A manager can have both the orientations in varying degrees.

10.7 TRAIT THEORIES OF LEADERSHIP

Experts on leadership have developed several theories or models to explain leadership. These theories may be classified into three broad categories — trait-based theories, behavioural theories, and situational theories.

According to trait-based theories, leadership is mainly a function of personality. In other words, a leader has certain traits or qualities which followers do not have. Trait theories are as follows :

10.7.1 Great Man Theory

According to this theory 'leaders are born, not made'. A person is born with or without the traits required for leadership. Leaders in general and great leaders in particular are born and not made. Therefore, ordinary people cannot aspire to become leaders or to attain greatness. The leadership qualities are bestowed by the divine power and cannot be acquired through education and training. For example, Napoleon is said to have natural 'qualities to be a leader'.

10.7.2 Trait Theory

Modern theorists argue that **leaders are made, not born**. There is nothing inborn or divine and leadership qualities can be learnt through training and experience. There is no unanimous list of qualities which successful leaders require. Some of these qualities are as follows :

(i) **Commanding Personality:** Good physique (height, weight, etc.), sound health, appearance, stamina, charm and other physical features are to some extent important for leadership. These at least create a good impression because these are the most visible traits.

(ii) **Intelligence:** A leader needs a higher level of intelligence than his followers. He requires the ability to think logically, analyse correctly and interpret clearly different aspects of an issue. He has sound judgment.

(iii) **Self-Confidence:** A good leader has confidence in himself. Self-confidence is essential to boost the morale and motivation of followers. Courage and persistence are not possible without self-confidence.

(iv) **Maturity:** A successful leader is emotionally mature and has balanced temperament. He has high tolerance for ambiguity and frustration. A leader needs the ability to convert adversity into opportunity and despondency into hope.

(v) **Inner Drive:** A good leader has the inner urge to keep achieving. He takes initiative and does not lose hope during adversity. His attitude is positive.

---

3 Keith Davis : *op. cit.*, p. 112.

(*vi*) **Vision and Foresight:** The ability to visualise the future and imagination are essential for success in leadership. He is alert to what is happening around. He has good insight into environment. Leadership is also about transforming vision into reality.

(*vii*) **Sense of Responsibility:** A leader takes personal responsibility for the consequences of his actions. Only a responsible leader can win the trust and faith of people. A leader is dependable.

(*viii*) **Open-minded:** A leader is willing to adopt new ideas and views of others. He has adaptability and modifies his behaviour as per the situation. A leader must be the change he wants to see in his people.

(*ix*) **Fairness and Objectivity:** A successful leader is free from bias and prejudice. Honesty, justice and integrity are the hallmarks of such a leader.

(*x*) **Sociability:** A good leader is sociable and cooperative. He understands human nature and can win the voluntary cooperation of people. A leader is as good as his team. A leader must instil trust and energy in the team and empower them to deliver results.

There is some truth in both great-man theory and trait theory. Some leadership qualities are inborn and some can be acquired through education, training and experience. It is also true that traits help an individual in becoming a leader. But trait approach to leadership suffers from several **drawbacks:**

(*i*) There is no common list of traits found in all successful leaders. Hundred years of study and research has failed to produce a set of traits that can be used to differentiate leaders and non-leaders. For example, good personality is desirable but there have been many successful leaders without good personality.

(*ii*) Trait approach fails to identify the traits which are necessary to acquire or maintain leadership.

(*iii*) It is very difficult to measure traits. How much of a particular trait a leader should have to make it effective is not clear. Measurement of a trait usually takes place after a person becomes a leader. Leadership traits vary according to the type of work performed.

(*iv*) Trait approach does not consider the total situation. Personal traits are only one of the several elements. The same person may prove a successful leader in one situation but may fail in another situation. There is no definite connection between traits and success in leadership because leadership is always situational. According to Merton, "The trait theory failed because it is the leadership situation — the nature of the subordinates and task — that determines what leader traits are essential for effective leadership. Such traits differ somewhat from situation to situation."[4]

10.8 BEHAVIOURAL THEORIES OF LEADERSHIP

The behavioural approach is based on the assumption that effective leadership is the result of effective role behaviour. Success in leadership depends on what leaders do rather than what

4 Charles R. Merton, **Human Behaviour in Organisations: Three Levels of Behaviour,** Prentice Hall, New Jersey, 1981, p 286.

they are. Behavioural scientists have tried to identify effective behavioural patterns for leaders. Four such studies are given below :

10.8.1 Michigan University Studies

The Institute for Social Research at the University of Michigan conducted empirical studies to identify leadership styles that lead to higher performance and satisfaction of a group. These studies identified two distinct styles of leadership[5] :

(*i*) **Employee-Centred (Relation-Oriented) Leadership:** This style considers every employee important and shows concern for needs of employees. Employee-centred leaders concentrate on human relations.

(*ii*) **Production-Centred (Task-Oriented) Leadership:** This style concentrates on the technical aspect of work and treats employees as tools to achieve organisational goals. The focus is on productivity, close supervision of employees, rules and procedures.

Comparison Between Leadership Orientations

Employee-Centred Leader	Production-Centred Leader
1. Treats employees as human beings.	1. Treats employees as tools in the production process.
2. Shows concern for the well-being of employees.	2. Emphasises production targets and technical aspects of the job.
3. Encourages and involves employees in decision-making.	3. Exercises close supervision and control.

Michigan Studies contended that employee-centred leadership led to higher employee satisfaction and productivity. On the other hand, production-centred leadership caused frustration, absenteeism and turnover thereby reducing productivity and satisfaction.

The Michigan Studies became popular as these were compatible with the prevailing system in 'post-Hawthorne America'. These findings led to the widespread belief that the employee-centred leadership was superior. But these studies were criticised due to the following reasons:

(*i*) The studies failed to suggest whether leader behaviour is a cause or effect. They did not clarify whether employee-centred leadership increased productivity or highly productive group induced employee-centred leadership.

(*ii*) The studies did not consider the personal characteristics and tasks of employees. They also ignored situational variables.

(*iii*) In practice, leaders may adopt both employee orientation and task orientation in different degrees to suit the particular situation. But the Michigan Studies are static.

10.8.2 Ohio State University Studies

The Bureau of Research at Ohio State University analysed actual leadership behaviour in a wide variety of situations. These studies identified two dimensions of leadership behaviour[6] :

---

5 Daniel Katz, *et.al.*, **Productivity, Supervision and Morale in Office Situation,** Survey Research Centre, University of Michigan, Ann Arbor, 1950.

6 Roger M. Stogdill and Alvin E. Coons, **Leader Behaviour : Its Description and Measurement,** The Ohio State University, Ohio, 1957.

(*i*) **Initiating Structure (IS):** It refers to the extent to which the leader defines the patterns of organisation, channels of communication, and work methods or procedures to accomplish organisational goals.

(*ii*) **Consideration (C):** It refers to the extent to which the leader establishes rapport, mutual respect and two-way communication with his subordinates.

The studies suggested that IS and C are two independent and distinct dimensions and are not mutually exclusive. A high score on one dimension does not require a low score on the other. Thus, leadership behaviour can be plotted on two separate axes rather than on a single continuum. The four quadrants in Fig. 10.3 show different combinations of IS and C.

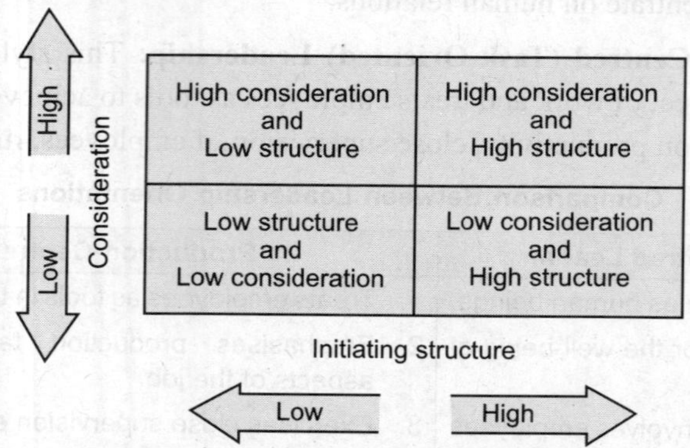

Fig. 10.3: Ohio State University Leadership Quadrants

Ohio studies caught the imagination of managers due to their simple but powerful reasoning. These studies have a high intuitive appeal for practising managers. Several training programmes made use of them. But these studies were criticised on the following grounds :

(*i*) It is extremely difficult for a leader to adopt both the dimensions. According to Fiedler the two dimensions are not distinct and independent.

(*ii*) The belief that high IS and C mix leads to better performance is questionable. There is no significant relationship between leader behaviour and productivity.[7]

(*iii*) Ohio studies present an oversimplified model of reality. The model completely ignores the impact of environmental variables or the situation on leader behaviour.

10.8.3 Managerial Grid

Blake and Mouton[8] developed and identified five leadership styles by combining two dimensions — concern for people and concern for production [Fig. 10.4].

1. **The 9,1 Style (Task):** This style puts maximum emphasis on the job and treats employees as instruments of production. Human interactions are minimised. The boss exercises authority and subordinates are expected to obey him without any question.

7 Korman, "Consideration and Initiating Structure. A Review", **Personal Psychology,** 19 Winter 1966, pp. 349-362.

8 Robert R. Blake and Jane S. Mouton, **The Managerial Grid,** Gulf Publishing Co., Houston, 1964.

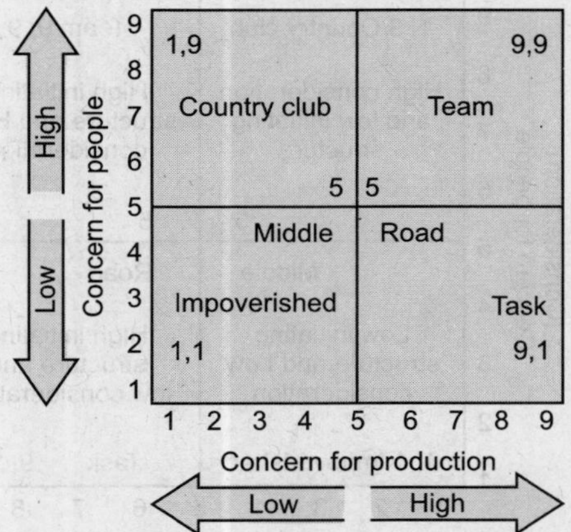

Fig. 10.4: Managerial Grid

2. **The 1, 1 Style (Impoverished):** Under this style, the boss exerts minimum influence with group members. He shows little concern for both production and people. He passes on blame on others for failure yet criticises only for self-defence. There is minimum involvement required to sustain relationship with the organisation. Subordinates are left to do the job in their own ways.
3. **The 5, 5 Style (Middle Road):** In this orientation, the leader attempts to maintain a balance between work and satisfaction of subordinates. He listens to their suggestions and uses informal relationships for the organisation. This style is based on the assumption that people work willingly if the reasons for working are explained to them.
4. **The 1, 9 Style (Country Club):** Under this style, the leader pays thoughtful attention to the needs of people to create a comfortable and friendly work environment. The focus is on the group not on individuals. Subordinates are expected to perform reasonably to avoid action against them.
5. **The 9, 9 Style (Team):** This style seeks to integrate employees with the organisation through their participation in decision-making. A common stake in the organisation or interdependence is created to develop relationships of mutual trust and respect. Work is sought to be accomplished through committed employees. Blake and Mouton suggest this is the best leadership style.

Managerial Grid has been widely used as a technique for training managers. It is said to be effective in improving attitudes and behaviour of executives. It has a commonsense appeal and helps managers to identify their leadership styles. It serves as a useful framework for practising managers. But the suggestion that 9, 9 style is always the best is questionable.

There is one basic difference between Managerial Grid and Ohio studies. The former is an **attitudinal model** that measures the predispositions of a manager. On the other hand, Ohio studies are a **behavioural model** that indicates how others perceive the leader's actions. These two models can be combined as shown in Fig. 10.5.

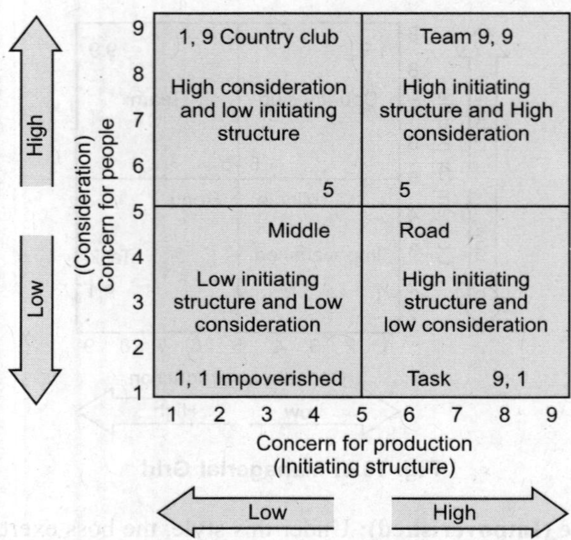

Fig. 10.5: Merger of Managerial Grid and Ohio State Structure

10.8.4 Likert's Management Systems

Rensis Likert and his associates at the University of Michigan (USA) conducted an extensive study of management styles and patterns in a large number of organisations. Likert developed four systems of management as shown in Table 10.1. These systems indicate the stages of evolution in the patterns of management. A brief description of these four management systems is given below :

Table 10.1: Likert's Systems of Leadership

Organisational Variable	System 1 (Exploitative-Autocratic)	System 2 (Benevolent-Autocratic)	System 3 (Consultative)	System 4 (Democratic)
1. Extent to which superiors have confidence and trust in subordinates.	Has no trust and confidence in subordinates.	Has condescending confidence and trust such as master has on servant.	Substantial but not complete confidence and trust, still wishes to keep control over decisions.	Complete confidence and trust in all matters.
2. Extent to which superiors behave so that subordinates feel free to discuss important things about their jobs with their immediate superior.	Subordinates do not feel at all free to discuss things about the job with their superior.	Subordinates do not feel very free to discuss things about the job with their superior.	Subordinates feel rather very free to discuss things about the job with their superior.	Subordinates feel completely free to discuss things about the job with their superior.

3. Extent to which immediate superior generally tries to get subordinates' ideas and opinions and make constructive use of them.	Seldom gets ideas and opinions of subordinates in solving problems.	Sometimes gets ideas and opinions of subordinates in solving problems.	Usually gets ideas and opinions and usually tries to make constructive use of them.	Always gets ideas and opinions and always tries to make constructive use of them.

Source: Rensis Likert, *The Human Organisation,* McGraw-Hill, New York, *1967.*

A brief description of Likert's management systems is given below:

System 1—Exploitative-Autocratic: The managers under this system make all work-related decisions and order their subordinates to carry out the decisions. The manager also defines standards and methods of performance. The subordinates have absolutely no say in the decision-making process. The communication between the manager and his subordinates is highly formal in nature and downward in direction. Such managers believe in threats and punishments to get things done. They exercise strict supervision and control over the subordinates.

System 2—Benevolent-Autocratic: System 2 managers are also autocratic but they are not exploitative. They adopt a paternalistic approach towards the subordinates. They allow some freedom to subordinates to carry out their tasks within the prescribed limits. The manager adopts patronising attitudes towards the obedient and faithful subordinates. They are rewarded for accomplishment of goals. But the subordinates who do not carry out their tasks are treated harshly. Thus 'carrot and stick' approach of motivation is adopted under this system.

System 3—Consultative: Managers under this system set goals and issue order after discussing them with the subordinates. They take major decisions themselves and allow subordinates to take the routine decisions. Subordinates are free to discuss the work-related matters with the managers. Thus, there is two-way communication in the organisation. Managers trust subordinates to carry out their tasks. Greater emphasis is placed on rewards than on penalties to motivate the subordinates. The control system tends to be goal-oriented and flexible.

System 4—Democratic: Under this system, goals are set and work-related decisions are taken by the subordinates. Supervision and control are group-oriented. Managers are friendly and supportive in their attitudes towards the subordinates. Subordinates are permitted self-appraisal on the basis of mutually set goals. In addition to economic rewards, subordinates are given a sense of purpose and feeling of worth. The communication system is completely open. (See Table 10.1).

Likert suggested that System 4 is the ideal system towards which organisations should work. On the basis of intensive research in a wide range of organisations, Likert found that organisations with System 4 outperformed those with the other systems. He advocated System 4 as the best way to develop and utilise human resources. He suggested leadership training at all levels of management so as to move managers to System 4 management. He found that democratic or participative management develops supportive relationships leading to higher productivity and workers' satisfaction. A System 4 manager enjoys full trust and confidence of his subordinates. He manages with the full consent and cooperation of the followers. Likert states that leadership and other processes of the organisation must be such as to ensure that in all interactions and in all relationships within the organisation, each member in the light of his values, desires and expectations will view the experience as supportive and one which builds and maintains a sense of his personal worth and importance[9].

10.9 SITUATIONAL THEORIES OF LEADERSHIP

Behavioural theories suggest one particular leadership style ignoring the situational factors. Leadership is a complex social and interpersonal process. An effective leader is one who can adapt his style according to the requirements of the particular situation. Situational theories suggest that leadership can best be understood as an interaction between the leader, the group members, and the situation. Four situational theories of leadership are given here.

10.9.1 Fiedler's Contingency Model

According to the situational approach, there is no one best leadership style universally applicable in all situations. The same style may be very effective in one situation but a failure in another situation. Fiedler theory is called 'contingency model' because the leader's effectiveness is contingent or dependent on three variables which are as follows[10]:

1. **Leader-Member Relations:** These refer to the degree of confidence and trust followers have in their leader. If employees respect the manager and willingly accept him, formal authority is not essential for getting the work done.
2. **Task Structure:** It means the degree to which job requirements are clearly defined. If the tasks are highly structured, employees are at ease with a directive leadership style.
3. **Leader Position Power:** It refers to the power inherent in the leader's position in the organisation. A leader has more power over group members if he can use several rewards and sanctions and enjoys the support of his organisation.

Each of these variables can be 'high' or 'low'. Fiedler developed eight possible combinations of these variables which range from favourable to unfavourable situations.

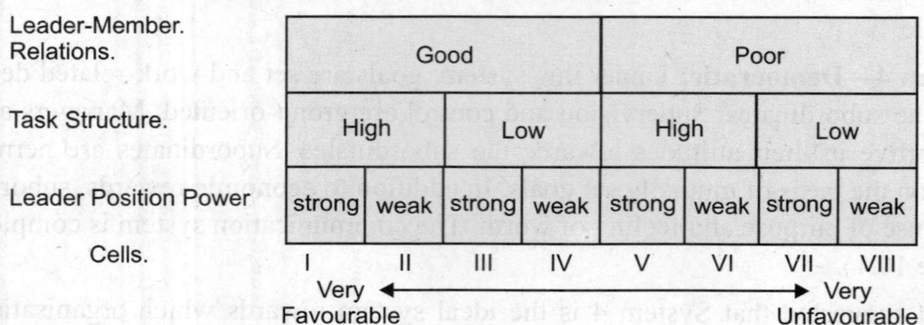

Fig. 10.6: Fiedler's Classification of Leadership Situations

9 Rensis Likert, **The Human Organisation,** p. 47.

10 Fred E. Fiedler, **A Theory of Leadership Effectiveness,** McGraw-Hill Book Co., New York, 1967.

The favourableness of a given situation means "the degree to which the situation enables the leader to exert his influence over his group".[11]

In order to identify the leadership style suitable for a given situation, Fiedler developed **Least Preferred Co-worker (LPC) scale**. In developing this scale, Fiedler asked his respondents to identify the traits of an individual with whom they would least like to work. These traits and their degrees are as follows :

Friendly	8	7	6	5	4	3	2	1	Unfriendly
Enthusiastic	8	7	6	5	4	3	2	1	Unenthusiastic
Cooperative	8	7	6	5	4	3	2	1	Uncooperative
Helpful	8	7	6	5	4	3	2	1	Frustrating
Interesting	8	7	6	5	4	3	2	1	Boring
Distant	8	7	6	5	4	3	2	1	Close

High LPC score indicates good interpersonal relations and high consideration. On the other hand, low LPC score reflects focus on task accomplishment and low interpersonal relationships. Fiedler suggested that **task-oriented** leadership is suitable under very favourable (cell I) and very unfavourable (cell VIII) situations because those situations require the leader to take charge. In moderately favourable situations (cells IV, V and VI), **relationship oriented** style is appropriate as the leader must win the cooperation of his subordinates. On the basis of his contingency model Fiedler developed the leader match training programme to improve leader effectiveness. This programme is based on the assumption that it is much easier to change the situation than leader's personality and style. This programme involves three steps :

(*a*) determine whether the leaders are task or relationship oriented;

(*b*) classify the situational factors; and

(*c*) select appropriate strategy to change the situation.

For example, if a relationship-oriented leader faces a highly favourable situation, the leader should be trained to modify it so that it fits his style.

Fiedler's model is considered significant as it suggests that leader effectiveness is the result of interaction between leadership style and the situation. It also points out that a leader cannot switch over from one style to another to match the situation. The model has been criticised on the following grounds :

(*i*) LPC is confusing and not fully reliable. The same person may get different LPC scores on different days.[12]

(*ii*) The model is unidimensional. It suggests that leaders can be either task-oriented or relationship-oriented.

(*iii*) The model has predictive power but lacks explanatory power. It does not explain why the same style is appropriate in both very favourable and very unfavourable situations.

---

11 *Ibid.*

12 Woe E. Stinson and Lane Tracy, "Some Disturbing Characteristics of the LPC Score", **Personnel Psychology,** 27 (1974), pp 477-485.

(*iv*) According to Fiedler, leader-member relations is the most important situational factor. But further research[13] revealed that task structure is the only important variable. Fiedler overlooked some situational variables such as subordinates' expectations of leader behaviour and the ability of the leader to influence his superior.

(*v*) The model is highly complex. It does not explain how situational factors affect leadership style. Fiedler suggested changing the situation to fit the leader's style. But it is very difficult to change the situation.

Despite these limitations, Fiedler's theory is significant because it points out the situational nature of leadership. It suggests actions that can be taken to improve a leader's effectiveness. Fiedler's model has become a forerunner to several situational models of leadership.

10.9.2 House's Path-Goal Theory

Robert House[14] developed a situational model of leadership. Like other situational models, the path-goal theory attempts to predict leadership effectiveness in different situations. It suggests that leaders can optimise effectiveness by influencing the path-goal perceptions and need satisfaction of subordinates. The theory states that a leader's job is to clarify goals and to clear path to these goals by providing guidance, support and rewards. The term path-goal is used because the leader smoothens the path to work goal and provides rewards for achieving them. The theory focuses on how leader influences subordinates' perceptions of the valence, instrumentality and expectancy. Subordinates arc motivated by the leadership style to the extent it influences expectancy (goal paths) and valence (goal attractiveness). Thus, path-goal theory is. in fact, an extension of Vroom's expectancy theory of motivation.

The main propositions of the path-goal model are as follows:

1. Leader behaviour is acceptable and satisfying to the extent that the subordinates perceive such behaviour as an immediate source of satisfaction and as instrumental to future satisfaction.
2. Leader behaviour is motivational or successful if it results in the satisfaction of subordinates' needs and complements their environments by providing support, guidance and rewards necessary for effective performance.

The leader should motivate the subordinates by clarifying paths to work goals. The paths to goals should be clarified by eliminating confusion or conflicting ideas which the subordinates may hold. Employees make their optimum contribution to the organisational goals where they perceive that their personal satisfaction is dependent on their effective performance. He should provide guidance and support to remove bottlenecks in achieving the goals. He should also increase the number and kind of rewards available to the subordinates.

The path-goal model visualises four types of leader behaviour which arc given below:

(*i*) Instrumental or Directive: Leader focuses on planning, organising and coordinating the activities of the subordinates. This style is similar to the initiating structure in the Ohio State Studies.

---

13 J.C. Campbell, *et.al.,* **Management Behaviour, Performance and Effectiveness,** McGraw-Hill, New York, 1970.

14 Robert J. House, "A Path-Goal Theory of Leader Effectiveness", **Administrative Sciences Quarterly,** Sept. 1971, pp. 321-328.

(*ii*) **Supportive:** Leader is friendly and approachable to the subordinates. He shows concern for their needs and welfare. The style is similar to the consideration in the Ohio State Studies.

(iii) Participative: Leader consults the subordinates and shares information with them. He incorporates their suggestions in his decisions.

(*iv*) **Achievement-oriented** leader sets challenging goals for the subordinates and displays confidence in their abilities.

According to House, the appropriate leadership style is determined by two types of situational variables—(*i*) Personal characteristics of subordinates, and (*ii*) Environmental pressures and demands.

Characteristics of Subordinates: The style selected by the leader should be compatible with the needs, abilities and personalities of the subordinates. For instance. a subordinate with high ability to perform the task effectively will prefer supportive leadership style while an incompetent subordinate may like directive style. Similarly, subordinates with strong affiliation motive may prefer a supportive leader but directive style may be acceptable to those with safety and security needs. The personality of the subordinates is also an important variable in path-goal model. Internally-motivated subordinates who believe that they can control their own behaviours prefer a supportive leader. But externally-motivated subordinates who believe that fate controls their behaviour prefer a directive leader.

Work Environment: Work environment includes the variables that are outside the control of subordinates but influence their job satisfaction. These variables are :

(*i*) Subordinates' task—structured or unstructured; (*ii*) formal authority system—rules, policies, procedures, etc.; and (*iii*) primary work group—its characteristics and stage of development. House asserted that if the subordinates are working on highly unstructured tasks characterised by high degree of role ambiguity, they require leader directive behaviour to clarify paths to goal achievement. But if the tasks are structured and well-defined, leader directiveness is redundant and supportive leader is preferred. The relationship between leader directiveness and subordinates' satisfaction with the task structure is shown in Fig. 10.7.

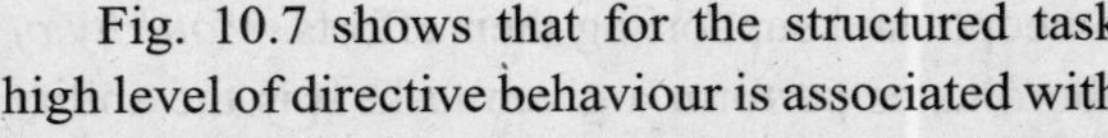

Fig. 10.7: Hypothetical Relation between Directive Leadership and Subordinates' Job Satisfaction

Fig. 10.7 shows that for the structured task high level of directive behaviour is associated with low job satisfaction. On the other hand, a high level of directiveness is associated with high job satisfaction for the unstructured task. In short, the path-goal model proposes that leader behaviour will be effective to the extent it assists the subordinates cope with environmental uncertainties.

A leader who is able to reduce the uncertainties of the job is considered to be satisfying because he increases the expectations of the subordinates that their efforts will lead to desired rewards.

Evaluation: The path-goal model is more elaborate than Fiedler's contingency model because it takes into account both the personality characteristics of subordinates as well as situational variables. It not only suggests what type of leader may be effective in a given situation but also explains why the leader is effective. The model also provides a heuristic framework for the new researchers in the field of leadership effectiveness. But the model has been criticised for the following reasons:

(*i*) It is a complicated model and its empirical testing is difficult due to methodological complexities.

(*ii*) The model is sketchy in nature requiring further refinement. It is in its infancy and there is relatively little research to support it. Some research studies report findings contrary to the model.

(*iii*) The model is *post hoc* in the sense that some of the research evidence supporting it was also used to construct it.

(*iv*) The theory is incomplete and provides a tentative explanation of the leadership style. It does not consider the effects of personal traits that may constrain the selection of leader behaviour. It does not explain the effects of leader behaviour on factors other than subordinates' expectations and satisfaction. It is also based on the assumption that a leader can change his behaviour to suit various situations.

In spite of these limitations, House's theory is appreciated because it not only suggests the type of leader behaviour that may be effective in a given situation but also explains why it is effective. The path-goal theory is somewhat more elaborate than Fiedler's intuitive model. Moreover, House's theory provides a heuristic framework for further research in leadership.

10.9.3 Life Cycle (Maturity-Immaturity) Theory

Paul Hersey and Kenneth Blanchard have made a systematic conceptualisation of situational factors as related to leadership behaviour. It is based on a curvilinear relationship between task behaviour, relationship behaviour and the maturity level that followers exhibit in performing the task. The focus is on followers. Followers in any situation are vital not only because individually they accept or reject the leader but because as a group they actually determine whatever personal power the leader may have. *Task behaviour* is the extent to which a leader provides direction, telling them what to do, when to do it, where to do it and how to do it. It means setting goals for subordinates and defining their roles. *Relationship behaviour* is the extent to which a leader engages in two-way communication providing support and encouragement. It means actively listening to people and supporting their efforts. *Maturity of followers* means the readiness with which subordinates perform a given task. It is the ability and willingness of people to take responsibility for directing their own behaviour. It is a relative concept, and therefore, is a question of degree.

The life cycle theory suggests that the leader behaviour must change as subordinates become mature. As followers' maturity level increases, less task behaviour and less support is required. Hersey and Blanchard suggest four styles of leadership that match different maturity levels of subordinates. The appropriate leadership style for a given level of maturity is portrayed by the prescriptive curve passing through the four leadership quadrants as given in Fig. 10.8.

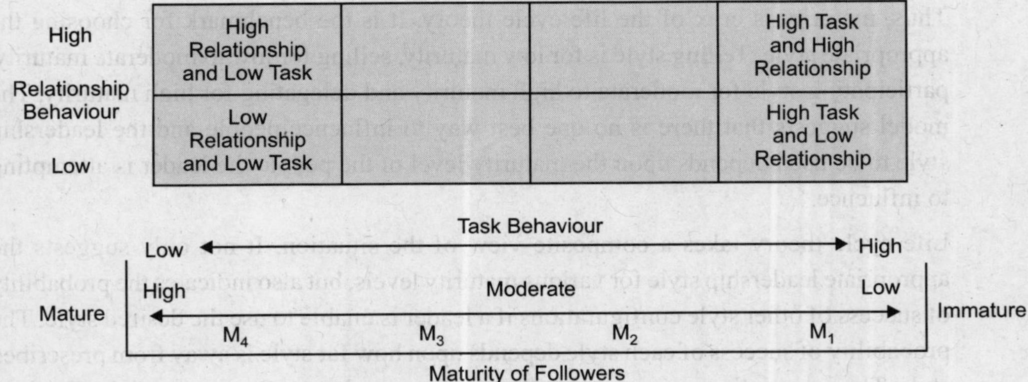

Fig. 10.8: Life Cycle Theory

Source: Adapted from Paul Hersey and Kenneth Blanchard, *Management of Organisational Behaviour: Utilising Human Resources*, Prentice-Hall of India, New Delhi, 1982, p. 152.

Each of the four leadership styles is a combination of task and relationship behaviour. The appropriate leadership style for each of the four maturity levels includes the right combination of direction (task behaviour) and support (relationship behaviour).

1. **Telling (S_1):** When subordinates are both unable and unwilling (M_1) to take responsibility, they require clear and specific directions. Therefore, high-task behaviour and low-relationship behaviour is the most appropriate style at this level of maturity. Subordinates lack both competence and confidence. Leader should, therefore, tell them what, how. when and where to do the various tasks. That is why this style is called 'telling'.
2. **Selling (S_2):** When subordinates are unable but willing (M_2) to take responsibility, leader behaviour should be both directive and supportive. Followers are confident but lack skills. Directive behaviour is needed due to lack of ability while supportive behaviour is required to reinforce willingness and enthusiasm of subordinates. At this maturity level followers will accept a decision if they understand the reason for the decision and if their leader provides help and direction. The leader explains the decision and persuades the followers to accept it. This style involves high-task behaviour and high-relationship behaviour.
3. **Participating (S_3):** At this level, subordinates are able but unwilling (M_3) to do what the leader wants. Therefore, they require motivational force. The leader needs to open the door to support the followers through active listening and participation. Thus, a supportive and non-directive style is the most appropriate. The leader plays facilitation and communicating role sharing decision-making with subordinates. This style involves high-relationship behaviour and low-task behaviour.
4. **Delegating (S_4):** At this level subordinates are both able and willing (M_4) to take responsibility. They require very little guidance, support and direction. Therefore, they should be permitted to decide on what, how, when and where to perform the task. They are assigned responsibility for carrying out the plans, This style involves low-relationship behaviour and low-task behaviour.

Thus, maturity is crux of the life cycle theory. It is the benchmark for choosing the appropriate style. Telling style is for low maturity, selling for low to moderate maturity, participating style for moderate to high maturity and delegating for high maturity, The model suggests that there is no one best way to influence people and the leadership style to be used depends upon the maturity level of the people the leader is attempting to influence.

Life cycle theory takes a composite view of the situation. It not only suggests the appropriate leadership style for various maturity levels, but also indicates the probability of success of other style configurations if a leader is unable to use the desired style. The probability of success of each style depends upon how far style is away from prescribed style. The prescriptive curve suggests that the four quadrants are not watertight divisions but each one tapers off and merges into the next as the mix of task and relations undergoes a change. The theory helps the practising managers to determine what to do in a given situation. Another implication of the theory is that subordinates' maturity level should be increased through training. The theory has been a major component in the training programmes of leading companies like Bank of America, IBM, Carter Pillar, Mobil Oil, Xerox. The theory also has intuitive appeal.

Life cycle theory clarifies some conceptual issues. It suggests that maturity level of followers has an important influence on leader behaviour. It also points out that as maturity level changes, the leader must change his style to remain effective.

The theory suffers from the following limitations:

(*i*) The model has not been properly tested and refined through scientific analysis. It lacks empirical support.

(*ii*) The model is based on the assumption that the leader is able to judge the actual maturity level of subordinates. This may not always be possible. If the subordinates disagree with the leader's assessment of their maturity level, conflicts may arise.

(*iii*) The theory also assumes that as the maturity level changes, the leader has adequate style flexibility to move from high task to relationship behaviour. But the leader may be unable to change his style.

10.9.4 Reddin's Tridimensional Model

William J. Reddin developed a three-dimensional model of leadership. The three dimensions are: task orientation, relationship orientation and effectiveness. By adding the effectiveness dimension, Reddin has integrated the concepts of leadership style with the situational demands of a specific environment. Task orientation is the extent to which a manager directs his subordinates towards goal accomplishment. Relationship orientation is the extent to which a manager has interpersonal relationships. It is characterised by mutual trust, respect for subordinates' ideas. Effectiveness is defined as the extent to which a manager is successful in his position. When the style is appropriate to a given situation, it is called effective. When the style is inappropriate to a given situation, it is termed as ineffective. Thus, the difference between effective and ineffective style is often not the actual behaviour but the appropriateness of the behaviour to the environment in which it is used.

Reddin suggested four basic styles. Each of these styles has an effective as well as an ineffective equivalent. Thus, the four basic styles result into eight styles. These eight styles represent eight possible combinations of task orientation, relationship orientation and effectiveness as shown in Fig. 10.9.

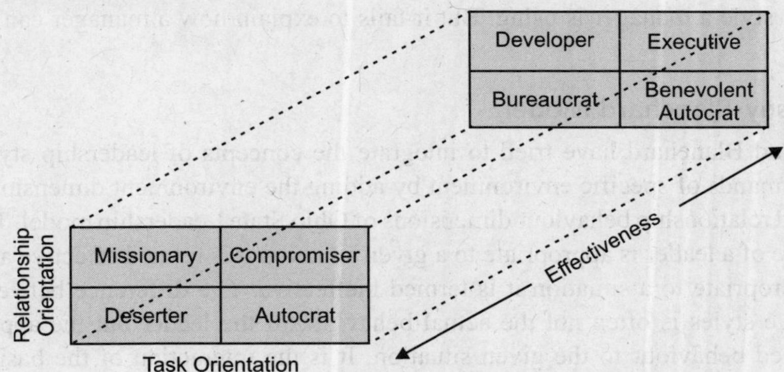

Fig. 10.9: Tridimensional Model of Leadership Effectiveness

Table 10.2: Reddin's Leadership Styles

Ineffective Styles		Basic Styles		Effective Styles
Missionary	⟵	Relegated	⟶	Developer
Deserter	⟵	Separated	⟶	Bureaucrat
Autocrat	⟵	Dedicated	⟶	Benevolent Autocrat
Compromiser	⟵	Integrated	⟶	Executive

These eight styles in Table 10.2 show different degrees of effectiveness of the basic styles.

Missionary: He seeks harmony and avoids conflicts. His objective is to keep his subordinates happy. He is basically do-gooder.

Deserter: He avoids involvement and responsibility. He works to rule and has low commitment. He is passive and escapist.

Autocrat: He is interested only in the immediate job and has no concern for others. He takes unilateral decisions and centralises authority. He relies more on negative motivation and has no confidence in others. He is task-oriented.

Compromiser: He has high concern for both task and people. He is a poor decision-maker and avoids decisions. He allows various pressures to influence him.

Developer: He has high concern for people and low concern for task. He trusts people and believes in commitment to work. He provides freedom of self-expression and freedom of action.

Bureaucrat: He has high concern for rules and regulations. He is impersonal and does not take initiative. He has low concern for both people and work.

Benevolent Autocrat: He has high concern for task and low concern for people. He relies on positive motivation for getting things done.

Executive: He has high concern for both people and task. He uses team management and sets high standards. This is a democratic leadership style.

The three-dimensional model suggests that no single style is appropriate in all situations. It provides a clearer picture of the managerial world than the two-dimensional managerial grid. Reddin's model is also useful for integrating the leader behaviour with the situation. It suggests that a manager should have an adequate style that leads to effectiveness. It helps in identifying the particular style a manager is using. But it fails to explain how a manager can improve his style.

10.9.5 Hersey-Blanchard Model

Hersey and Blanchard have tried to integrate the concepts of leadership styles with the situational demands of specific environment by adding the environment dimension to the task behaviour and relationship behaviour dimensions of Ohio State Leadership model. They suggest when the style of a leader is appropriate to a given situation it is termed effective and when the style is inappropriate to a situation it is termed ineffective. The difference between effective and ineffective styles is often not the actual behaviour of the leader but the appropriateness of the observed behaviour to the given situation. It is the interaction of the basic style with the environment that results in a degree of effectiveness or ineffectiveness. In reality the third dimension is the environment in which the leader is operating. "Although effectiveness appears to be an either/or situation in this model, in reality it should be represented as a continuum. Any given style in a particular situation could fall somewhere on this continuum from extremely effective to extremely ineffective. Effectiveness, therefore, is a matter of degree, and there could be an infinite number of faces on the effectiveness dimension rather than only three. To illustrate, the effectiveness dimension has been divided into qualities ranging on the effective side from + 1 to +4 and on the ineffective side from –1 to –4."[15]

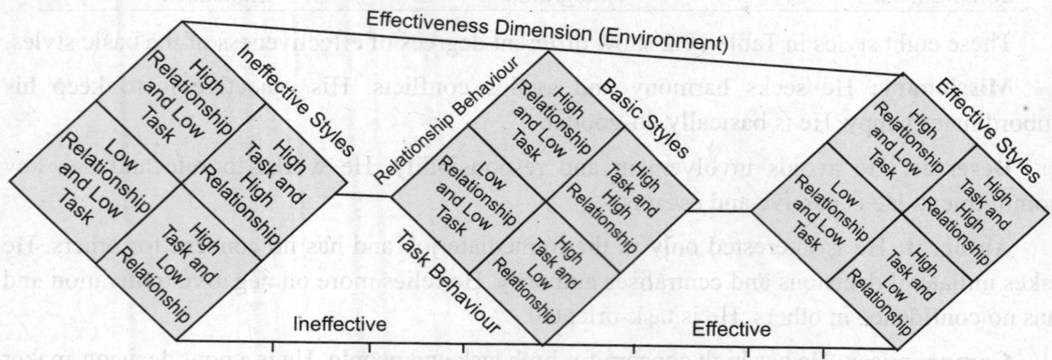

Fig. 10.10: Tridimensional Leader Effectiveness Model

Source: Paul Hersey and Kenneth Blanchard, *op. cit.*, p. 98.

Hersey-Blanchard's model is different from Reddin's model in two respects: (*i*) using environment as an effectiveness dimension and (*ii*) using the behavioural notions in place of attitudinal concepts of Reddin.

The four effective and the four ineffective styles are, in essence, how appropriate a leader's basic style is to a given situation as seen by his or her followers, superior or associates. Table 10.3 describes briefly one of many different ways each style might be perceived as effective or ineffective by others.

15 Paul Hersey and Kenneth Blanchard, *op. cit.*, p. 97.

Table 10.3: How the Basic Leader Behaviour Styles may be seen by others when they are Effective or Ineffective.

Basic	Effective	Ineffective
High Task and Low Relationship Behaviour	Seen as having well-defined methods for accomplishing goals that are helpful to the followers.	Seen as imposing methods on others; sometimes seen as unpleasant and interested only in short-run output.
High Task and High Relationship Behaviour.	Seen as satisfying the needs of the group for setting goals and organising work, but also providing high levels of socio-emotional support.	Seen as initiating more structure than is needed by the group and often appears not to be genuine in interpersonal relationships.
High Relationship and Low Task Behaviour	Seen as having implicit trust in people and as being primarily concerned with facilitating their goal accomplishment.	Seen as primarily interested in harmony; sometimes seen as unwilling to accomplish a task if it risks disrupting a relationship or losing "good person" image.
Low Relationship and Low Task Behaviour	Seen as appropriately delegating to subordinates decisions about how the work should be done and providing little socio-emotional support where little is needed by the group.	Seen as providing little structure or socio-emotional support when needed by members of the group.

Source: Paul Hersey and Kenneth Blanchard, *op. cit.*, p 99.

"A model such as the Tridimensional Leader Electiveness Model is distinctive because it does not depict a single ideal leader behaviour style that is suggested as being appropriate in all situations. For example, the high task and high relationship style is appropriate only in certain situations. In basically crisis-oriented organisations such as the military or the fire department, there is considerable evidence that the most appropriate style would be high task and low relationship, since under combat, fire, or emergency conditions success often depends on immediate response to orders. Time demands do not permit talking things over or explaining decisions. But once the crisis is over, other styles might become appropriate for the chief to engage in other styles while his staff are participating in an ancillary function, such as maintaining the equipment or studying new fire-fighting techniques."[16]

10.10 TRANSACTIONAL LEADERSHIP

James Burns has identified two types of leaders—transactional and transformational. In transactional leadership, the leader determines what subordinates need to do to achieve objectives, clarifies the task requirements and helps subordinates become confident that they can achieve their objectives. The leader offers rewards to the subordinates who accomplish the tasks assigned to them. The focus is on achieving current objectives and clarifying the role of subordinates. The transactional leader has a sense of commitment to the organisation and conforms to its norms and values. He engages in a bargaining relationship with his followers. He tells employees what they need to do to obtain rewards. Transactional leadership involves exchange relationship between the leader and the followers.

16 Hersey and Blanchard : *Op. cit.*, p. 98.

A transactional leader directs the efforts of others through tasks, rewards and structures. Transactional leadership is inadequate to meet fully the challenges and demands of today's dynamic work environment. A transformational leader arouses extraordinary effort and performance.

10.11 TRANSFORMATIONAL LEADERSHIP

Transformational leaders are those who through personal vision and energy inspire followers and exercise a major impact on their organisations. Such leaders are also known as charismatic leaders. Occasionally, a leader emerges whose personal charisma catches public attention and support. Mahatma Gandhi, Winston Churchill, Martin Luther King. Lee Iacocca are recognised as charismatic leaders. Charismatic leaders have very high levels of self-confidence, moral conviction, vision, referent power and other personal qualities which capture the commitment, sacrifice and energy of followers. They communicate high expectations from followers and confidence that followers will perform up to their expectations. They stir followers to look beyond their own interests for the good of others.

A transactional leader improves performance within a given context but does not try to change the organisation's course. On the other hand, a transformational leader changes the organisation's context altering its culture and strategy to fit better with the environment. Transformational leaders are change agents and they develop a new set of values and behaviours.

How to keep your leaders happy:

- Match profiles of people you recruit to future needs. As the company grows, an employee grows too – and he or she can become an asset to the company in a few years down the line.
- Set goals for people you hire. They will have something to work for and look forward to.
- Make the job profile very clear to the person you are recruiting. There should be absolutely no scope for any kind of confusion.
- If you are introducing a team in your organisation to the new leader, make sure their apprehensions are allayed and all questions answered. Ensure a trust-based relationship is built between the boss and his team.
- Help ease leaders in their new role. Explain things, introduce them to buddies.

TEST QUESTIONS

1. (*a*) What traits do you think characterise a successful leader? Do you agree with Blake and Mouton that there is one best style of leadership?

   (*b*) Identify and describe the three situational variables presented in Fiedler's contingency theory of leadership.
2. Think of some leadership situations and indicate how a leader should change his or her style to match those situations for improving his or her effectiveness.

3. Bring out the similarities and dissimilarities between Fiedler's contingency model and path-goal theory of leadership.
4. Is the manager of a group always its leader? What does the existence of leadership substitutes tell us about the role of leadership? Discuss.
5. What can managers learn for managing their organisations from the leadership models derived from the Ohio State and Michigan studies on leadership?
6. How would you differentiate between a successful and an effective leader? Enumerating various leadership theories, briefly discuss various aspects of the Managerial Grid Theory.
7. Explain, according to Fred Fiedler's Contingency Model, how leadership style interacts with situational variables.
8. What implication could be drawn for organisations from Path-Goal Theory of Leadership? Discuss.
9. "Behavioural theories of leadership are static". Do you agree? Discuss.
10. Suggest appropriate leadership styles if —
    (*a*) the tasks are unstructured and the subordinates have lower needs to satisfy; and
    (*b*) the subordinates possess moderate levels of maturity.
11. Critically examine Fiedler's contingency model of leadership effectiveness.
12. "To be an effective leader, one should use all the styles to some extent rather than relying on one style exclusively." Discuss the validity of this statement with respect to the application of different styles of leadership in work environment.
13. Which of the theories of or approaches to leadership is most appropriate for the society you live in? Why?
14. Describe the conditions under which different types of leadership are most and least effective, noting the various theories that make these claims.
15. (*a*) Distinguish between successful and effective leadership.
    (*b*) Compare Fiedler's Contingency Model of Leadership with Life Cycle Theory,
16. Explain the role of leadership in increasing the productivity of organisation. Discuss two theories of leadership.
17. Briefly identify the major styles from Blake and Mouton's grid, from Hersey and Blanchard's situational model, and from Likert's four systems. Which are more effective or less effective? Comment.
18. (*a*) Describe the Five Components of Emotional Intelligence at work.
    (*b*) Why is empathy particularly important today as a component of leadership?
19. (*a*) "Leaders are born not made." Comment.
    (*b*) "Leader effectiveness is contingent upon whether the style used is appropriate to the demand of the situation." Critically examine the leadership theory that advocates this view.
20. Distinguish between charismatic leader and non-charismatic leader.

21. Write notes on:
    (*a*) Trait theory of leadership.
    (*b*) Situational approach to leadership.
22. Assume that you are the CEO of a manufacturing company facing stiff competition from the Chinese manufacturers. You may make suitable assumptions about the product line and other things about the company. What leadership styles you would adopt to face this competition and ensure that your company maintains the profits which it was maintaining till date as you are aware that if you continue on the same path, then it is a potentially sick company?
23. Distinguish between:
    (*a*) Transactional leader and
    (*b*) Transformational leader.
24. "A good leader is not necessarily a good manager". Do you agree? Give reasons for your answer.
25. "The leader influences and is influenced by followers". Comment.
26. "Leadership is situational". Comment.
27. "Trust and integrity is the foundation for Leadership to be effective". Comment. Also discuss key characteristics of Charismatic Leadership.
28. Discuss the guidelines for becoming a transformational leader.
29. Critically examine Path-Goal Theory of leadership. What are its implications?
30. "Effective leadership is a function of three variables — the leader, the led, and the situation". Explain
31. Explain the characteristics of various leadership styles, describing the situations under which each style is useful.
32. Is participative style of leadership preferable to other styles? Give reasons in support of your answer.
33. "Most effective leaders show great concern both for the task and for the people". Explain.
34. Explain the path-goal theory of leadership. Is the theory relevant in today's environment in India?
35. Identify and describe "substitutes for" or "neutralisers of" leadership.
36. List and explain the contingency variables in leadership participation model.
37. "A good leader is one who understands his subordinates, their needs and their sources of satisfaction". Comment.
38. "The most effective leaders show high concern both for people and task". Comment.
39. "Hersey-Blanchard's situational model is based on a limited number of variables but these variables are quite significant". Comment.

CASE STUDY – 1

Among other labels and titles, Norman Brinker has been called entrepreneur, pioneer, visionary and mentor. These titles and labels were acquired through the 40+ years of his legendary career in the restaurant industry.

Always looking for a challenge, Brinker started his restaurant career in the late 1950s as a partner in the Jack-in-the-Box restaurant chain. This initial experience forged a love for the restaurant business. In 1966, he developed Steak and Ale, the forerunner of what is now referred to as casual dining. In 1971, he sought out another challenge in the restaurant industry, developing the Bennigan's chains. In 1976, he sold the Steak and Ale and Bennigan's chains to the Pillsbury Corporation, becoming a vice-president for Pillsbury. He quickly ascended to the presidency of Pillsbury, but he left in 1983 to buy a 40 per cent interest in the Chili's restaurant chain. In 1984, Brinker International was formed, and Norman Brinker pursued an aggressive growth strategy for the company.

Since it was formed, Brinker International has developed into "the premier casual dining restaurant company in the world and has received numerous accolades through the years for its outstanding performance." As of the end of fiscal year 2003, Brinker International had 1,402 company operated, jointly developed, and franchised units in 49 states and 22 nations. The Brinker International brands include Chili's Grill and Bar, Ramano's Macaroni Grill, On the Border Mexican Grill and Cantina, Maggiano's Little Italy, Bog Bowl Asian Kitchen, Corner Bakery Cafe, and Rockfish Seafood Grill. Brinker International had annual revenues of approximately $3.8 billion in the fiscal year 2003. Each year from 2000 to 2003, Brinker International was listed among the "400 Best Companies in America" by Forbes magazine.

Norman Brinker has been recognized on numerous occasions for his leadership capabilities. He is "widely regarded as one of the most influential chain builders in food service history." Brinker's leadership philosophy is that "winners attract winners." Brinker clearly has confidence in himself, and justifiably so. He has successfully led several companies in a highly competitive industry in which many fail. Moreover, Brinker likes to surround himself with people who believe in themselves and are (or can be) successful. He says: "The people I've been able to attract over the years are terrific individuals. They want to do better. And the success is contagious."

Under his leadership, Brinker International developed a culture "driven by integrity, teamwork, passion, and an unwavering commitment to making sure each and every guest has an enjoyable dining experience." Through example and personal involvement, Norman Brinker promoted an ethical organisational culture where people respect one another and work collaboratively in seeking to provide excellent meals and excellent service.

Norman Brinker has ended his formal leadership within the restaurant industry, but his influential reach will continue. In retiring from Brinker International in 2000 but remaining as Chairman emeritus, Norman Brinker formally turned over the leadership reins of the company to Ron McDougall, a protègè whom he had groomed since the two began working together in 1974 at Steak and Ale. In passing the leadership torch to McDougall, Brinker observed that his successor "is one of the strongest, most visionary individuals that I've ever been associated with. He is a born leader, an adept team builder, and the best strategist in business."

McDougall has served as Brinker's Chief Executive Officer since 1995 and as Chairman since Norman Brinker became chairman emeritus in 2000. According to Brinker's 2003 Annual Report, McDougall will hand over the CEO duties to Doug Brooks while remaining as chairman of the board. Brooks is a 25-year Brinker employee and president and chief operating officer since 1999. Todd Diener, a member of the Brinker management team since 1981, will succeed Brooks. The top management transitioning and continued success of Brinker International is due in no small part to the mentoring provided by Norman Brinker. As chairman emeritus, Norman Brinker is not involved in the day-to-day operations of Brinker International. However, he will "travel and address franchisee groups, spreading his casual dining gospel of good management, great food and fun that was his hallmark throughout his career." He most assuredly will be listening to customers, trying to find out what they are thinking. "He even visits competitors' restaurants, walking around as if he runs the place, stopping to inquire about the food and service." As Richie Jackson, executive vice-president of the Texas Restaurant Association, observes: "Norman will still be building leadership and mentoring in his capacity as chairman emeritus."

Questions

(*a*) In what ways was Norman Brinker a manager? In what ways was he a leader?

(*b*) Describe the nature of followership that Norman Brinker has sought to develop at Brinker International.

(*c*) What skills would you personally need to develop to become a leader like Norman Brinker? What could you do to develop or refine those skills?

(*d*) What do you think is the most important leadership lesson in this case? Explain your answer.

CASE STUDY – 2

Inderjit is about 40 and for the last one year has been the Chief Executive of a manufacturing company, that operates autonomously, but belongs to a large group. He has firm ideas on how best to manage people. In general terms, he believes that people respond best when the pressure is on them.

Inderjit has tremendous energy. He comes to work at 7.00 o'clock and stays late each evening. He works very hard and expects others to do the same. He is a stickler for details and often sends his managers running back from meetings to collect more facts. Face to face meetings with him are something like inquisitions. He has a very aggressive questioning style and bowls people out when he notices mistakes. He is proud that he can move heaven and earth to 'fix' problems. Since he is good both in technical and financial matters, he tends to intervene as soon as he suspects a deficiency. He almost 'pounces' to sort out himself.

When there is a problem to be solved, Inderjit likes to call all those involved together in committee room, irrespective of rank or reporting relationships and forces the facts out on the table. In order to bring out the truth, he adopts a very challenging style. What is more, he will even keep the group at it all night, if necessary, keeping aside other commitments. Eventually, he succeeds in solving the problem and also gets advance warning about other likely problems.

Raghunath, the personnel manager, is one who reports to Inderjit and particularly resents this treatment. He finds it degrading for a man in his position and also feels that, as personnel manager, he must do something to change Inderjit's style. Raghunath is seriously concerned about the effects of Inderjit's behaviour. He notices that his colleagues are showing signs of stress, they are putting in enormously long hours. They have become more competitive towards each other and less cooperative. They spend lots of precious time talking about Inderjit in his absence and trying to anticipate "his next move".

Another alarming effect of Inderjit's behaviour is that senior managers spend long hours getting the details right, so that Inderjit's probing will not catch them out. Managers who were previously willing to delegate, are now less inclined to do so. They feel the only right way is to do things themselves. The managers thus spend all their time on day-to-day issues, and are not inclined to do any forward planning.

Ironically, Inderjit has complained to Raghunath that too many managers are "fire fighting" instead of doing what they are paid to do, that is, "to think" and "to act". He told Raghunath that he could not understand why people "don't realise that conflict management is nothing but stimulating alternative courses of action? What I really want is for them to go back, think again and tell me about it."

Questions

(*a*) What would be your analysis of Inderjit's style of leading his people?

(*b*) What problems have evolved or may evolve due to Inderjit's behaviour?

(*c*) Suggest some remedial measures to resolve the situation.

CASE STUDY – 3

Mr. Krishnan has recently joined as the Managing Director of a car manufacturing company which at present is incurring heavy losses. Mr. Krishnan has been entrusted with the formidable task of rejuvenating the company. He faces many challenges to achieve this task, such as controlling costs and expenses, increasing the productivity and boosting the morale of the employees so that they unhesitatingly cooperate to achieve the set standards of output.

Mr. Krishnan, in his previous company, also a car manufacturing company, as the Deputy Managing Director, had proved to be a proficient manager and a talented leader who had successfully inspired his employees to increase the productivity. He was commended for his maximum concern for both people and production and also for bringing about integration and harmony between the needs of employees and of production.

In the new company also, Mr. Krishnan has pursued his policy of participative management and has shown high concern for production and people. With a view to revising the company back to health, he initiated some major changes. First of all, he decentralised the organisation so that the subordinates could exercise their discretion and initiative in decision-making and their imagination and creativity in performing their other functions. Furthermore, he empowered the junior managers to sanction expenditure up to a specified limit without seeking prior approval of the higher level. Communication system was also improved to facilitate free flow of upward and downward communication.

Mr. Krishnan also adopted several measures to cut cost and wasteful expenditure. He banned donations to charitable institutions but increased the amount being spent on the welfare activities meant for the employees.

Will Mr. Krishnan's leadership style prove effective in ensuring bright future of the company? Some employees are of the view that lot of things are being done but they might not be effective in the long run. Others disagreed with them and said, 'Okay, we will give it a try.'

Questions

(*a*) In view of the behavioural theories of Leadership, which style is Mr. Krishnan pursuing in the company?

(*b*) Identify the changes introduced by Mr. Krishnan in the company. What in your view could be their likely impact?

(*c*) Can money be an effective motivator in the context of the above case?

CHAPTER

11

CONTROL

CHAPTER OUTLINE

11.1 Concept of Control
11.2 Nature of Control
11.3 Relationship between Control and Planning
11.4 Need and Significance of Control
11.5 Limitations or Dysfunctions of Control
11.6 Steps in the Process of Control
11.7 Kinds or Types of Control
11.8 Control of Human Element
11.9 Reactions of People to Controls
11.10 Behavioural Implications of Control
11.11 Reasons for Human Resistance to Controls
11.12 Overcoming Resistance to Controls
11.13 Management by Exception (MBE)
- Test Questions
- Case Studies

Control is an essential part of every organisation. The process of management is incomplete without control. Controls keep the activities of an organisation on the right track and in alignment with its goals and plans.

11.1 CONCEPT OF CONTROL

Control is the process of ensuring that activities are producing the desired results. It involves monitoring the outcome of activities, reviewing the feedback and if necessary taking corrective action. "The managerial function of controlling is the measurement and correction of performance in order to make sure that enterprise objectives and the plans devised to attain them are accomplished."[1] According to Hicks and Gullet, "Controlling is the process by which management sees if what did happen was what was supposed to happen. If not, necessary adjustments are made."[2]

1 Harold Koontz and Henri Weihrich, **Essentials of Management,** McGraw-Hill, New York, 1990, p. 393.

2 Herbert G. Hicks and C.R. Gullet, **Management of Organisations,** McGraw-Hill, New York, p. 497.

11.2 NATURE OF CONTROL

The main characteristics of control are as follows :

1. **Pervasive Function:** Control is essential in all types of organisations and at all levels of management. It is a function of every manager — from chief executive to supervisor.
2. **Continuous Function:** Control is a never-ending and ongoing process. It continues so long as an organisation exists.
3. **Looking Back:** Control involves review of past activities and results. It analyses actual performance and identifies reasons of deviations from planned performance.
4. **Looking Ahead:** Control aims at future as past cannot be controlled. It suggests guidelines for future standards and actions. Thus, control is forward-looking.
5. **Dynamic Process:** Control is a flexible and not a rigid process. It is a positive and normative force.
6. **Action-oriented:** The essence of control lies in the corrective action taken to keep the organization on the right track. An effective control system suggests timely action to prevent wastage of resources.
7. **Maintains Freedom:** Contrary to popular opinion, control does not curtail the freedom of people. Rather it guides their behaviour towards the achievement of organisational goals.

Thus, planning is the basis, action is the essence and information is the guide to control.

11.3 RELATIONSHIP BETWEEN CONTROL AND PLANNING

There is close interrelationship between control and planning functions of management. Planning serves as the basis of control by laying down the standards against which actual performance is to be judged. Control is blind without planning as one does not know where to go. At the same time planning is meaningless without control because control ensures that operations proceed according to plans. In the words of Koontz and Weihrich, "Planning and control are the inseparable (siamese) twins of management. Unplanned actions cannot be controlled for control involves keeping activities on course by correcting deviations from plans. Any attempt to control without plan would be meaningless since there is no way anyone can tell whither he is going — the task of control, unless first he knows where he wants to go — the task of planning."[3] Thus, there is a reciprocal relationship between planning and control as shown in Fig. 11.1.

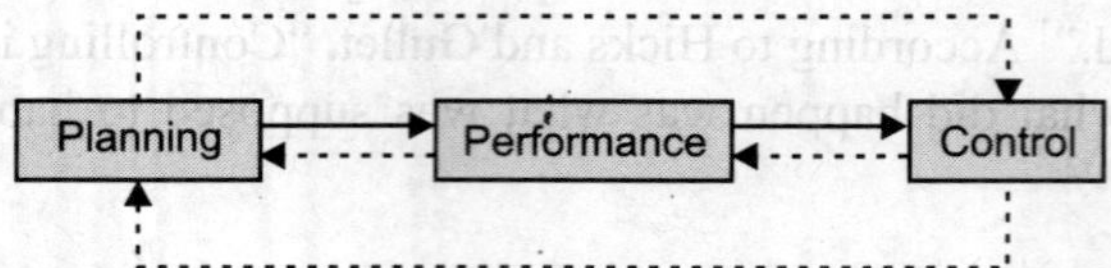

Fig. 11.1: Relationship between Planning and Control

3 Koontz and Weihrich, *op. cit.*, p. 113.

According to Geotz, "Managerial planning seeks consistent, integrated and articulated programmes, while management control seeks to compel events conform to plans".

11.4 NEED AND SIGNIFICANCE OF CONTROL

Organisations are deliberate and purposive and are not self-regulating. Therefore, every organisation needs a control system to ensure that its activities are leading to the desired results. A sound control system helps organisations in achieving their objectives in the following ways:

1. **Guides Operations:** Just as road signals are essential to ensure smooth traffic, control is necessary to keep the activities of an organisation on the right track. It indicates what should be achieved, what is being actually achieved and what should be done to match the two.
2. **Improves Planning:** Control systems reveal shortcomings, if any, in planning. Necessary steps can be taken to improve plans and standards in future
3. **Facilitates Decision-Making:** A control system serves as the framework of rational decision-making. "Control is needed both to simplify the making of subsequent decisions and to ensure the realisation of the objectives implicit in the original long-range policy decisions".[4]
4. **Helps in Decentralisation:** There is an increasing trend towards decentralisation of authority in modern organisations. But decentralisation may result in misuse of authority in the absence of adequate controls.
5. **Simplifies Supervision:** Effective control simplifies supervision by ensuring order and discipline among employees. It identifies weak points and helps supervisors in checking performance. It helps to expand the span of control particularly at the operating level.
6. **Ensures Coordination:** Modern organisations are large and complex. Maintaining unity and teamwork among different work groups in the organisation is very difficult. An effective control system helps in this task.

11.5 LIMITATIONS OR DYSFUNCTIONS OF CONTROL

Control suffers from the following drawbacks:

(*i*) Control is an expensive and time-consuming process. Considerable time and effort is involved in exercising control over day-to-day operations.

(*ii*) It is very difficult to set standards of performance in exact quantitative terms. Similarly, it is very difficult to measure performance in certain areas such as human resource management.

(*iii*) Employees often resist controls due to the feeling that controls reduce their freedom and initiative.

(*iv*) Excessive and rigid controls hurt employee morale and creativity. Superior-subordinate relationships may deteriorate.

4 W.T. Jerome, **Executive Control — The Catalyst,** John Wiley & Sons, New York, 1961, p. 81.

(*v*) Information system in an organisation may not be sound enough to indicate causes of resistance and poor performance. Control system becomes ineffective when responsibility for failure cannot be fixed.

(*vi*) An organisation cannot control external forces such as government policies, social changes, technological changes and changes in fashion.

Some of the steps that may be taken to make control effective are as follows:

1. Standards of performance must be established in consultation with employees. These standards must be fully explained to them.
2. Standards of performance must be attainable but challenging.
3. Measurement of performance must be objective and impartial.
4. Corrective action must be clearly related to the cause of deviation and it must be timely.
5. Control system should be flexible. The focus should be on improvement rather than on finding faults.

11.6 STEPS IN THE PROCESS OF CONTROL

1. **Establishment of Standards:** The control process begins with the setting up of standards which serve as the criteria for measuring results. Performance standards may be set up in terms of quantity, quality, cost and time. These can be both quantitative (tangible) and qualitative (intangible). Standards may be:

   (*a*) **Physical standards,** *e.g.,* quantity of output, number of customers, sales volume, etc.

   (*b*) **Monetary standards,** *e.g.,* cost of production, selling costs, sales revenue, net profit, etc.

   (*c*) **Time standard,** *e.g.,* dates by which particular jobs must be completed.

   Standards depend on the nature of work. But these must be reasonably flexible. Strategic control points should be established for all operations so that controls are economical and there is focus on the key areas.

2. **Measurement of Performance:** After standards are established, the next step is to measure actual performance of individuals and work groups. Several questions are decided before measuring performance, *e.g.,* what to measure, how to measure, when to measure. Performance must be measured in the same units in which standards were set up so that the two are comparable. Personal observations, sampling, accounting computers, etc. can be used to measure performance. Measurement or appraisal should be by results. Performance may be measured after the completion of the job or during the performance. For example, in assembling task, each part is checked before assembling. Effective appraisal requires focus on three key aspects[5] :

5 Edward E. Lawler III and John G. Rhode, **Information and Control in Organisations,** Goodyear Publishing Co., California, 1976.

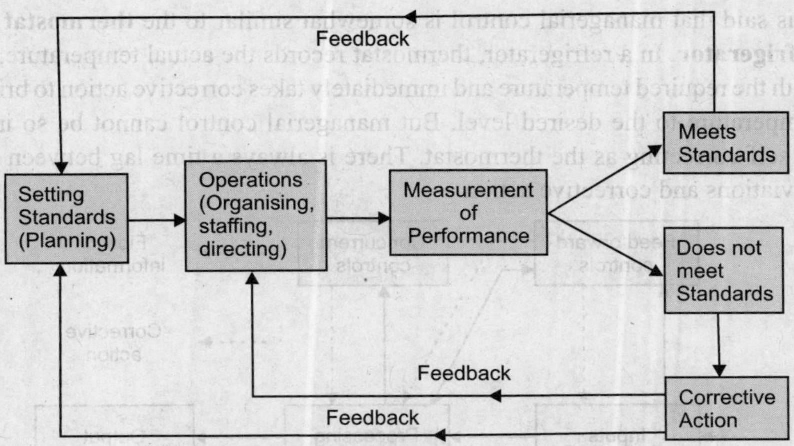

Fig. 11.2: The Process of Control

(*a*) **Completeness:** Take into account both measurable and non-measurable aspects of performance.

(*b*) **Objectivity:** Assess performance without any bias or subjective judgement.

(*c*) **Responsiveness:** Believe that effort and performance lead to improvement.

3. **Comparison of Performance with Standards:** Actual performance is compared with the standard performance. The difference between the two is known as **deviation.** Deviation may be positive or negative. It is neither necessary nor desirable to report all deviations to the top management. Only exceptional deviations which have serious negative impact require corrective action. This is called **management by exception**. The causes of such deviations should be identified after thorough investigation.
4. **Taking Corrective Action:** The last step in the control process is taking corrective action to prevent recurrence of deviation in future. Corrective action may require change in standards, reassignment of tasks, training of workers, motivation, etc. It should be noted that a positive or favourable deviation is not always bad. Favourable deviation may be due to low standards and in such a case standards must be raised. Similarly, negative deviation may be caused by too high standards which require correction.

Corrective action must be **immediate** so that the position can be rectified speedily. It must be **basic** so as to permanently cure the cause of deviation. If deviation is intolerable, the remedial action should be **disciplinary** so as to radically improve behaviour. But disciplinary action need not be punishment. Positive action tends to be more acceptable to employees.

11.7 KINDS OR TYPES OF CONTROL

On the basis of the 'time' at which control is exercised, controls are of three kinds — feedback, concurrent and feedforward.

1. **Feedback Control:** It is also known as **post-action or historical control**. Under it results are measured after the action is completed. Information about past performance (feedback) serves as the basis for corrective action. Income statement, balance sheet, disciplinary action for poor performance are examples of feedback control.

It is said that managerial control is somewhat similar to the **thermostat system in a refrigerator**. In a refrigerator, thermostat records the actual temperature, compares it with the required temperature and immediately takes corrective action to bring the actual temperature to the desired level. But managerial control cannot be so instantaneous or self-correcting as the thermostat. There is always a time lag between recording of deviations and corrective action.

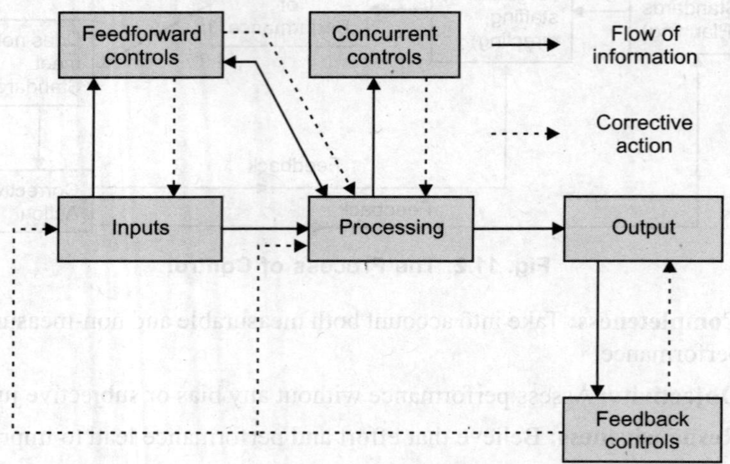

Fig. 11.3: Types of Control

2. **Concurrent Control:** It is also known as **steering or real time control**. It involves taking corrective action while the activity is being performed and before any major damage is done. For example, when you drive a car, you must adjust your steering continuously depending upon the turns on the road, obstacles and other factors. In a factory, control chart and safety check are examples of concurrent control.
3. **Feedforward Control:** It is also known as **predictive or preventive control**. It involves anticipating the problems and taking corrective action before starting the activity. Preventive maintenance is an example of feedforward control. Under it, each machine is checked at regular intervals to prevent breakdown. Another example is cash budget which is prepared to estimate flow of cash in next year. Steps are taken to meet any anticipated shortage of cash. Feedforward control is timely and prevents possible damage. But there are difficulties in applying it :

(*a*) It is relatively more costly.

(*b*) Many activities are not amenable to continuous monitoring.

(*c*) It requires thorough planning and analysis and careful discrimination in selecting the control points.

11.8 CONTROL OF HUMAN ELEMENT

Every organisation needs controls to regulate the behaviour of its members and to increase its effectiveness. In the absence of controls, individuals tend to pursue their own interests at the cost of organisational goals. Controls are essential to ensure that the employees work as per standards, procedures and rules of the organisation. But the type of control to be exercised depends on the work environment. If the work is repetitive and routine, managers depend mainly on mechanical controls. When the work is highly varied and creative, control should be cooperative. Open work environment increases productivity and creativity of employees. If the work cannot be specified in advance, cannot be measured precisely or strict supervision is not possible, self-control is desirable.

Though controls are indispensable, the human element must be recognised in designing them. People are the key element in the workplace. Therefore, management must know the reactions of employees for various types of controls imposed on them. Employees usually resist controls which restrict their freedom and obstruct the achievement of their personal goals. In his study on the impact of controls on human beings, Tannenbaum[6] comes to the following conclusions :

(*i*) Control has both rational and symbolic implications. It tells what an individual must or must not do. It also indicates the individual's importance and freedom in the organisation.

(*ii*) Most persons prefer to exercise control over themselves and their surroundings. They usually experience greater satisfaction when they are able to exercise self-control.

(*iii*) When one can exercise some control, one is more likely to identify with and support the organisation's objectives.

(*iv*) Persons who are unable to exercise control tend to be less satisfied with their work. They tend to be apathetic and alienated and lack personal involvement.

(*v*) Those who exercise control may more willingly accept controls upon themselves.

11.9 REACTIONS OF PEOPLE TO CONTROLS

Subordinates react to controls in the following ways[7] :

(*i*) **Compliance:** Employees comply willingly because they are accustomed to imposition of controls.

(*ii*) **Purposeful Deviation:** Subordinates devise innovative ways to deviate from controls and keep the deviations from being discovered.

(*iii*) **Aggression:** Employees sabotage controls and shift their accountability to others.

(*iv*) **Absenteeism:** Some employees remain absent from the workplace to escape controls for a temporary period.

(*v*) **Resignation:** Some employees may leave the organisation permanently.

(*vi*) **Apathy:** Subordinates may develop an attitude of indifference towards controls.

(*vii*) **Transfer:** Some employees seek transfer to other departments where controls are less stringent.

6 Arnold S. Tannenbaum, "Control in Organisations : Individual Adjustment and Organisation Performance" in Arnold S. Tannenbaum (ed.), **Control in Organisations,** McGraw-Hill, New York, 1968, pp. 307-309.

7 Thierauf KleKamp and Geeding, **Management : Principles and Practices,** John Wiley & Sons, Santa Barbara, 1977, p. 668.

(*viii*) **Join Informal Groups:** Employees may join informal groups to resist the pressures generated by controls.

(*ix*) **Join Labour Unions:** Workers join trade unions to nullify the adverse effects of controls.

11.10 BEHAVIOURAL IMPLICATIONS OF CONTROL

Behavioural opposition to control may be in the form of disagreement with standards, reporting procedures, cost allocation pertaining to control systems, and, in some cases, the need for control itself.[8]

1. **Impact of Standards on Behaviour:** Standards of performance are usually set by the management. Employees view them negatively due to two reasons.[9] **First,** subordinates do not understand the standards because these are imposed on them without explaining their need and significance. **Second,** employees may find it difficult or impossible to accomplish the standards due to unexpected conditions. In order to make standards acceptable to employees, management can adopt the following guidelines:[10]

   (*i*) Subordinates should be involved in the establishment of standards. Participation of employees leads to legitimacy in the standards.

   (*ii*) Standards must be well defined so that employees can easily understand them.

   (*iii*) Standards must be set in such a way that they convey 'freedom to fail'. Employees should be assured that they will not be unfairly censured for an occasional mistake or for deviation which are outside their control.

2. **Impact of Measurement on Behaviour:** Human beings by nature resist evaluation of performance. Employees oppose performance appraisal when they feel it is not objective and proper. Dissatisfaction with appraisal also arises when:

   (*i*) measurement is not timely,

   (*ii*) measurement does not measure all that is being done and gets only at the surface, and

   (*iii*) measurement concentrates on deviation and does not account for effort.[11]

   In order to overcome opposition to measurement of performance, management should allow employees to participate in measuring their performance. In addition, the appraisal system should highlight the efforts and achievements rather than deviations.

3. **Impact of Corrective Action on Behaviour:** Control process is incomplete without corrective action taken to avoid recurrence of deviations in future. But employees usually dislike correction because their ego is hurt. They blame the control system itself because it exposes their limitations before their peers, superiors and subordinates.

---

8 Dan Voich, Jr. and Daniel A. Wren, **Principles of Management,** The Ronald Press, New York, 1968, p. 263.

9 Henri L. Sisk, **Principles of Management,** South-West Publishing, Cincinnati, 1973, p. 690.

10 Raymond E. Miles and Roger C. Virgin, "Behavioural Properties of Variance Control," **California Management Review,** Spring, 1966, p. 59.

11 Henri L. Sisk, *op. cit.,* pp. 691-692.

Management can avoid such negative reactions by enforcing positive control through learning, behaviour modification, etc. Threat, punishment and other forms of negative control should be avoided.

11.11 REASONS FOR HUMAN RESISTANCE TO CONTROLS

People dislike and resist control due to several reasons such as the following:

(*i*) Individuals perceive controls as curbs to their freedom and as instruments of oppression.

(*ii*) Employees feel controls suppress their creative urges and innovative skills.

(*iii*) The standards of performance are imposed from the top without consulting the employees. Subordinates feel the standards are unrealistic and rigid.

(*iv*) Performance evaluation focusses on finding faults rather than on the efforts and contribution of employees.

(*v*) Controls are administered in an arbitrary and discriminatory manner.

(*vi*) Even intelligent and responsible employees are not allowed to exercise self-control.

11.12 OVERCOMING RESISTANCE TO CONTROLS

Controls are essential for the smooth functioning of an organisation. But controls are effective only when people accept them. People often try to reap the rewards of good performance and shift tactfully the blame for poor results to others. Cooperation from employees can be expected only when they feel control is a positive force and desirable. Both control and freedom are essential but too much of either can be detrimental to the organisation. An optimum mix of freedom and control is essential for the organisational effectiveness. Therefore, due consideration to the human element should be given while setting up and executing controls. Management must identify causes of any resistance to controls and then take appropriate steps to overcome the resistance. Some of these steps are given below:

(*i*) The persons whose behaviour and performance are to be controlled must be involved in designing and implementing the controls.

(*ii*) The control system should be flexible and realistic. It must allow variations in human behaviour.

(*iii*) The control system must permit self-control and allow people to be creative. It must not suppress the genuine aspirations of people for self-expression and self-development.

(*iv*) There should be positive reinforcement in the form of rewards for acceptable behaviour and performance.

(*v*) The principle of 'control by exception' should be followed. It involves selective control and reflects faith in the ability and character of employees.

(*vi*) The control system should be objective and consistent. It should not allow discrimination on any basis other than performance.

(*vii*) Employees should be convinced that controls are meant to achieve the common goals rather than to curb their freedom. Their reactions and suggestions must be heard and if relevant implemented.

11.13 MANAGEMENT BY EXCEPTION (MBE)

Management by exception is a key principle of control in organisations. It means "a system of identification and communication that signals the manager when his attention is needed; conversely it remains silent when his attention is not required".[12] The essence of management by exception is that only exceptional deviations in performance should be brought to the notice of management. For example, the head of quality control in a factory sets up a standard that two defects per 100 units of output are acceptable. Under MBE management is informed only when there are more than two defects in a lot of 100 units of output.

Management by exception is based on the maxim that **an attempt to control everything may end up controlling nothing.** A manager who tries to check each and every minor deviation may fail to pay adequate attention to critical problems. Management by exception has the following **benefits**:

(*i*) It saves time of busy managers.
(*ii*) It identifies critical problem areas.
(*iii*) It reduces frequency of decision-making.
(*iv*) It focusses attention and efforts on more important matters.
(*v*) It stimulates communication.
(*vi*) It makes use of more knowledge and data.
(*vii*) It is necessary in big organisations.

Management by exception should not be mistaken as management by crisis. Otherwise, there can be disastrous results such as breakdown in control and planning.

TEST QUESTIONS

1. Define control and explain its need and importance in modern organisations.
2. "Planning is the basis of control, action its essence, delegation its key and information its guide". In the light of this statement, explain the nature of control.
3. "Planning is meaningless without control and control is aimless without planning". Explain in this context the relationship between planning and control.
4. "Control is best aimed at results, not at people as such". Comment
5. Explain the main steps involved in the process of control.
6. "The existence of control system implies that all is not well with the organisation". Do you agree? Give reasons.
7. Distinguish clearly between feedback control, concurrent control and feedforward control.

---

12 Lester R. Bittle, **Management by Exception,** McGraw-Hill, New York, 1964, p. 5.

8. How do people react to controls?
9. Explain the behavioural implications of different stages in control process.
10. Why do people resist controls? Suggest measures to overcome such resistance.
11. Write short notes on :
    (*a*) Dysfunctions of control.
    (*b*) Management by Exception.

CASE STUDY – 1

Patel Mills manufactures woollen clothes. Over the years it has earned an envious reputation in the market. People associate Patel Mills with high quality, woollen garments. Most of the existing employees have joined the company long back and are nearing retirement stage. The process of replacing these old employees with younger ones, drawn from the nearby areas, has already begun.

Recently, the quality of the garments has deteriorated considerably. Though the company employs the best material that is available, the workmanship has gone down. Consequently, the company has lost its customers in the surrounding areas to a great extent. The company stands in the eyes of general public, depreciated and devalued. The production manager, in a frantic bid to recover lost ground, held several meetings with his staff but all in vain. The problem, of course, has its roots in the production department itself. The young workers have started resisting the bureaucratic rules and regulations vehemently. The hatred against regimentation and tight control is total. The old workers, on the verge of retirement, say that conditions have changed considerably in recent years. In the days gone by, they say, they were guided by a process of self-control in place of bureaucratic control. Each worker did his work diligently and honestly under old set-up. In an attempt to restructure the organisational set-up, the managers who have been appointed afterwards brought about radical changes. Workers under new contract had very little freedom in the workplace. They are expected to bend their will to rules and regulations. Witnessing the difference between the two cultures, the young workers, naturally, began to oppose the regulatory mechanism devised by top management. The pent up feelings of frustration and resentment against management, like a gathering storm, have resulted in volcanic eruptions leading to violent arguments between young workers and foremen on the shop floor. In the process, production has suffered, both quantitatively and qualitatively. The production manager, in an attempt to weather out the storm, is seriously thinking of bringing about a radical change in the control process that is prevailing now in the organisation.

Questions

1. Analyse the problems leading to the deterioration in the quality of the manufacture in the company.
2. Critically evaluate the finding that old supervisors complain and new workers too resist any type of control.
3. What type of control system would you suggest to the company to improve the production?

CASE STUDY – 2

The Connair Company is considered to be a leader in the design and production of industrial and commercial air-conditioning equipment. While most of the products were standard items, a considerable number involving large sales volume were specially designed for installation in big office buildings and factories. Besides being an innovator in product design and having an exceptionally good customer service department, the company is well known for its high-quality products and its ability to satisfy the customer requirements promptly.

Because of its rapid growth, the company had to be careful with its cash requirements, especially for accounts receivable and for inventories. For many years, the company had kept inventories under close control at a level equal to 1.7 times the monthly sales, or a turnover of nearly 6 times per year. But, all of a sudden, inventories soared to triple monthly sales, and the company found itself with ₹ 30 crore of inventories above a normal level. Calculating a cost of carrying inventory at 30 per cent of the value of inventories (including the cost of money, storage and handling, and obsolescence), it was estimated that this excess inventory was costing the company ₹ 9 crore per year in profits before taxes. In addition, it forced the company to call on its bank for more loans than had been expected.

Mr. Deepak Mehra, president of Connair, was understandably worried and intense when this matter came to his attention. He was told that the primary reasons for this rise in inventory were excessive buying of raw materials in advance because of anticipated shortages and the failure of a new computer software, with the result the people in the production and purchasing departments were not having complete information as to what was happening to inventory for several months.

Mr. Mehra, taking the stand that no company should let something like this surplus inventory occur without advance notice and that no manager can be expected to control a business on the basis of history, instructed his vice-president for finance to come up with the programme to get better control of inventories in the future.

Questions

1. What do you find wrong with Connair's controls? Elucidate.
2. Would a feedforward system of control help? How? How would you try to apply it to Connair?
3. Are there any other techniques or approatches to control that you would suggest? Explain.

CHAPTER

12

MORALE AND JOB SATISFACTION

CHAPTER OUTLINE

12.1. Concept of Morale
12.2. Nature (Characteristics) of Morale
12.3. Measurement of Morale
12.4. Factors Influencing Morale
12.5. Morale and Productivity
12.6. Building High Morale
12.7. Concept of Job Satisfaction
12.8. Importance of Job Satisfaction
12.9. Consequences of Job Dissatisfaction
12.10. Determinants of Job Satisfaction
- **Test Questions**
- **Case Study**

Morale and job satisfaction are important psychological concepts in the field of organisational behaviour.

12.1 CONCEPT OF MORALE

Morale refers to "a composite of feelings, attitudes and sentiments that contribute to general feelings of satisfaction".[1] It indicates the willingness of a group of persons to pull together persistently in pursuit of common purpose. "It is a state of mind and spirit affecting willingness to work which, in turn, affects organisational and individual objectives".[2] Morale is the degree of enthusiasm with which the members of a group work together to achieve group goals.

1 Jack Halloran, **Applied Human Relations : An Organisational Approach,** Prentice Hall, New Jersey, 1978, p. 129.

2 Robert M. Guion, "Industrial Morale — The Problem of Terminology", **Personnel Psychology,** 1958, pp. 59-61.

12.2 NATURE (CHARACTERISTICS) OF MORALE

The main features of morale are as follows :

(*i*) Morale is **psychological concept.** It represents the state of mind and spirit.

(*ii*) Morale is a **multidimensional concept** because it is a complex mixture of several elements. It recognises the influence of job situation on attitudes of individuals and also includes the role of human needs as motivational forces.[3]

(*iii*) Morale is a **group phenomenon**. It represents the collective attitudes of members of a group.

(*iv*) Morale like health is a **relative term.** By itself it does not convey any meaning unless it is specified in terms of degree.

(*v*) Morale is **contagious** as both favourable and unfavourable attitudes can spread among people. It can deteriorate rapidly when seriously unfavourable events take place.

(*vi*) Morale is **different from teamwork.** Morale is a state of mind whereas teamwork is a condition. Good morale is helpful in achieving teamwork but it is possible that teamwork is high but morale is low.

(*vii*) Morale is a **long-term phenomenon.** Building high morale is a long-term and continuous process. It cannot be achieved through one short action or short-term tactics such as contents or peptalks.

(*viii*) Morale is **different from motivation** though both are cognitive concepts and are interrelated.

Distinction Between Morale and Motivation

Basis of Distinction	Morale	Motivation
1. Meaning	Overall attitudes of people towards the organisation	Willingness to work
2. Nature	Group phenomenon	Individual phenomenon
3. Function	A function of freedom or restraint	A function of needs and drives
4. Mobilisation	Mobilisation of sentiments	Mobilisation of energy
5. Relationship with productivity	Not directly linked with productivity	Directly related to productivity

12.3 MEASUREMENT OF MORALE

It is difficult to measure morale because it is intangible in nature. The methods used to measure morale are as follows :

1. **Observation Method:** Managers try to measure the morale of employees by observing their actions and behaviour. Performance or productivity is not a reliable measure

3 Dale S. Beach, **Personnel : The Management of People at Work,** MacMillan, New York, 1980, p. 443.

of morale because correlation between morale and productivity is low. "The serious shortcoming of observation as a yardstick to measure current morale is that the activities and events indicate a change to a lowered morale which has already occurred. The manager, therefore, should be extremely keen in his observation in order to do as much as possible to prevent such changes".[4]

2. **Attitude Survey:** An opinion survey is a good measure of morale. It indicates how employees feel about their jobs, superiors and the organisation. Such a survey is conducted through a questionnaire. Employees are requested to fill in the questionnaire. The answers given by the employees are compiled and inferences are drawn about their morale.
3. **Morale Indicators:** The factors which indicate employee attitudes towards their jobs, superiors and the organisation are called morale indicators. Absenteeism, labour turnover, waste and scraps, grievances, accidents, indiscipline, defective output are such indicators. When these are high, morale is said to be low and *vice versa*.

Indicators of Low Morale	Indicators of High Morale
• High rates of absenteeism and labour turnover	• Low rates of absenteeism and labour turnover
• Excessive grievances and complaints	• Minimum grievances and complaints
• Lack of discipline	• High degree of discipline
• Friction among employees	• Cooperation among employees
• Antagonism towards management	• Pride in the organisation
• Lack of commitment to the organisation	• Loyalty and commitment to the organisation
• Frustration among employees.	• Willing cooperation towards organisational goals.

12.4 FACTORS INFLUENCING MORALE

Several internal and external factors influence employee morale. These factors are given below:

1. **External Factors:** These include the personality, psychological state, physical health, family background, friends and relatives, intelligence level, etc. of the employee. Every human being is unique and these factors influence his perception and attitudes. External factors are largely beyond the control of management. However, these factors can be considered while selecting employees.
2. **Internal Factors:** These consist of the following:

   (*i*) Organisational Goals: When the goals of the organisation are worthwhile and realistic, employees develop positive feelings towards the organisation.

   (*ii*) Organisation Structure: When lines of authority and responsibility are well-defined, and there is decentralisation of authority, employee morale tends to be high.

---

4 Theo Haimann, **Professional Management — Theory and Practice,** Eurasia Publishing House, New Delhi, 1969, p. 453.

(iii) **Nature of Work:** Dull, monotonous and repetitive jobs tend to bring down morale. On the other hand, interesting and challenging jobs that suit the skills and competence of employees tend to improve their morale.

(iv) **Working Conditions:** A clean, safe, comfortable, and pleasant work environment creates positive attitudes among employees. Good working conditions are, in fact, essential for high morale.

(v) **Management Philosophy:** Superior's behaviour and temperament towards subordinates is an important determinant of morale.

(vi) **Work Group:** An individual's attitudes and feelings are shaped by his co-workers and the work group to which he belongs.

(vii) **Compensation:** Wage, salary, allowances, fringe benefits and incentives exercise a significant influence on employee morale.

12.5 MORALE AND PRODUCTIVITY

Generally, it is assumed that high morale and high productivity always go together. The argument of human relations experts is that workers with high morale put their time and efforts on jobs and, therefore, productivity goes up. But in reality, there is no such direct and positive correlation between morale and productivity. Several factors other than morale (*e.g.*, technology, training, supervisory style, rewards and penalties, etc.) influence productivity [Fig. 12.1].

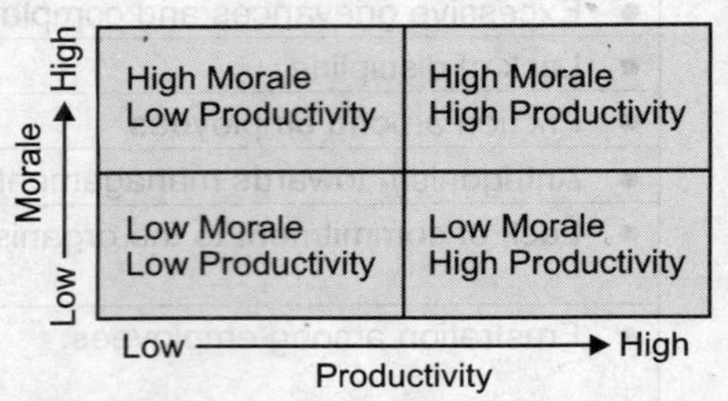

Fig. 12.1: Relationship between Morale and Productivity

1. **High Morale and High Productivity:** When employees are highly motivated and trained and the supervision is considerate, high morale may lead to high productivity. But the two may not increase in the same proportion. This is an ideal situation because it leads to best possible use of human resources.

2. **High Morale and Low Productivity:** When employees are merely happy but not motivated to work hard, productivity may be low despite high morale. Defective materials, outdated technology, lack of training and inefficient supervision may cause low productivity.

3. **Low Morale and High Productivity:** In the short run, close supervision, high technology, punishment for poor performance may raise productivity in spite of low morale. But this combination cannot be sustained for long.

4. **Low Morale and Low Productivity:** This is a normal situation. When employee attitudes towards jobs, management and organisation are negative, productivity tends to be low.

Thus, the relationship between morale and productivity can vary from organisation to organisation and from time to time. Employees may get social satisfaction through affiliation and belonging to a group. But their productivity may be low because they conform to group norms which are much lower than official standards of performance.

12.6 BUILDING HIGH MORALE

Morale building takes time and requires sustained efforts. Managers can use the following techniques to improve the morale of their employees:

1. **Workers' Participation:** Active participation of employees in managing the organisation is a very effective method of building high morale. It creates a sense of belonging and 'wanted' among employees. Therefore, employees must be consulted and taken into confidence while taking decisions and introducing change affecting them. Management should encourage workers to freely express their opinions, suggestions and grievances.
2. **Considerate Leadership:** The leadership style of managers should match the expectations and preferences of employees. Leaders of informal groups exercise a major influence on employee morale. Therefore, managers can work with informal leaders to improve morale.
3. **Two-Way Communication:** Open communication between the management and workers helps to build mutual understanding and trust. Workers should be allowed to ask questions and seek clarifications.
4. **Employee Training:** Training helps to improve the competence and confidence of employees. They feel that management takes interest in them and their fear of the job is eliminated.
5. **Incentives and Rewards:** A well designed system of financial and non-financial incentives can improve the motivation and morale of employees.
6. **Welfare Measures:** Employee welfare facilities such as canteen, sports, housing loans, company vehicles, etc. should be provided.

12.7 CONCEPT OF JOB SATISFACTION

Job satisfaction is the degree of contentment or pleasure which a person feels by performing a job. "It is a person's emotional reaction to the job itself. If you like your job intensely, you will experience high job satisfaction. If you dislike your job intensely, you will experience job dissatisfaction".[5] Thus, "job satisfaction is the amount of overall positive effect or feelings that individuals have towards their jobs".[6]

Job satisfaction, like morale, is an intangible concept as it indicates emotional feelings.

---

5 Andrew J. DuBrins, **The Practice of Supervision,** Universal Book Stall, New Delhi, 1988, p. 58.

6 D.C. Feldman and H.J. Arnold; **Managing Individual and Group Behaviour in Organisations,** McGraw-Hill, New York, 1983, p. 192.

12.8 IMPORTANCE OF JOB SATISFACTION

Job satisfaction is important due to the following reasons :

1. **Job Satisfaction Improves Physical and Mental Health of Employees:** People who like and enjoy their jobs are likely to live longer. Job satisfaction is important for psychological adjustment and happy life of a person. In fact job satisfaction and life satisfaction are inextricably bound. Lack of satisfaction on the job creates maladjustment and personality problems. A chronologically upset person makes life vexatious for others.
2. **Job Satisfaction Reduces Absenteeism and Labour Turnover:** Employees who are happy with their jobs do not remain absent from work. They also stay with the organisation longer.
3. **Job Satisfaction Creates Good Public Image:** People who feel satisfied with their work-life speak favourably about their oganisation. Goodwill of the organisation increases and as a result the organisation can attract well-qualified people.
4. **Job Satisfaction and Productivity:** It is said that 'a satisfied worker is a productive worker'. But in practice there may be no direct cause and effect relationship between job satisfaction and productivity. According to Porter and Lawler it is productivity that leads to satisfaction. If a job holds little potential for intrinsic rewards, and if extrinsic rewards bear a very little relationship to the performance level of the individual, the resultant connection between satisfaction and performance tends to be weak and tenuous. In such a situation management can strengthen the link between performance and satisfaction in two ways :
   (*i*) Modify the task so that it becomes capable of yielding intrinsic rewards for performance.
   (*ii*) Correct the reward system so that it acts as an incentive for higher performance, *i.e.,* higher performances receive proportionally higher extrinsic rewards.

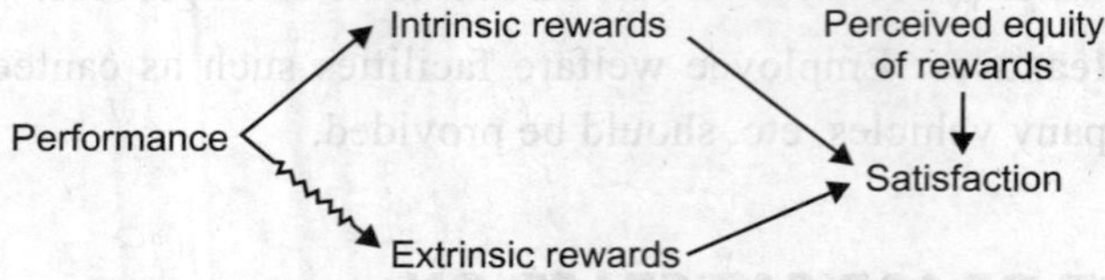

Fig. 12.2: Porter and Lawler's Model

12.9 CONSEQUENCES OF JOB DISSATISFACTION

Dissatisfaction with the job can lead to several harmful consequences such as the following:

1. **Absenteeism:** Employees who are dissatisfied with their job tend to be frequently absent from work for minor excuses. Job dissatisfaction creates a lack of will to work and alienates the employee from work.
2. **Labour Turnover:** A dissatisfied employee tends to leave the organisation and seek satisfaction elsewhere. High labour turnover increases the cost of recruitment and training of new employees.

3. **Negative Publicity:** Dissatisfied employees express their discontent to others both inside and outside the organisation. Such "bad mouthing" makes the organisation unpopular. As a result the organisation faces difficulty in recruiting new employees. It may also lead to loss of some business.

12.10 DETERMINANTS OF JOB SATISFACTION

Several factors contribute to job satisfaction. These are described below :

1. **Nature of Job:** When an employee is asked to perform the job that matches his aptitude, job satisfaction tends to be high. Job content factors such as recognition, responsibility, advancement, achievement influence job satisfaction. Repetitive jobs tend to be dissatisfying.
2. **Type of Supervision:** Authoritarian subordinates are likely to be more satisfied under close supervision. On the other hand, employee-centred supervision enhances job satisfaction for other employees who want respect, friendship, warmth, etc.
3. **Work Group:** Employees who have enough opportunity for social interaction with their colleagues tend to be more satisfied. The degree of satisfaction depends on the relationship with the group members and the employee's own need for affiliation.
4. **Occupation Level:** Higher level employees tend to have higher levels of job satisfaction. Higher level jobs carry more prestige and enhance self-esteem. These jobs also provide more power, autonomy, pay and diversity of work. However, greater variety of tasks may not increase the satisfaction of employees unless the tasks form a unified and meaningful whole.
5. **Age:** Job satisfaction usually tends to be high when people enter the workforce. It decreases and then stabilises for several years. After the age of roughly thirty years, there is gradual increase in job satisfaction. Finally, there may be a slight dip due to pre-retirement apprehension. When people begin their work with unrealistic expectations, they may experience low job satisfaction. Similarly, a retiring employee may feel obsolete and useless. These feelings make him dissatisfied at work.
6. **Race and Sex:** Harrick[7] argues that females are less dissatisfied than males because females have less job and pay opportunities than males.
7. **Education Level:** Highly educated people tend to have higher expectations from their jobs. Such people experience more job dissatisfaction when they are employed on lower levels.

TEST QUESTIONS

1. What do you understand by morale? Distinguish between morale and motivation.
2. How can morale be measured? Suggest measures for building high morale in an organisation.

---

7 Neal Q. Harrick, "Who is Unhappy at Work and Why", **Manpower,** US Department of Labour, Vol. 4, 1972.

3. "Morale is perhaps the most important factor affecting the productivity of employees". Explain the relationship between morale and productivity in the light of this statement.
4. "Morale and productivity are related to each other for organisational success". Do you agree? Give reasons for your answer.
5. Explain the factors that influence employee morale.
6. What is job satisfaction? What is its significance for organisational effectiveness?
7. Discuss the consequences of job dissatisfaction.
8. Explain the factors that determine the degree of job satisfaction.

CASE STUDY

Pradip was a Senior Programme Officer in a medium-size IT company. He had joined the company as a Junior Programme Officer and after four years he was promoted as Senior Programme Officer. Pradip was very hard working and sincere in his work and expected others to put in their best efforts. Both his superiors and subordinates generally appreciated his work and behaviour. He was quiet by nature and did not believe in loose talk.

A vacancy for the post of Assistant Manager-Systems came up in the organisation and Pradip was confident that he would be promoted to the vacant position. However, one of his colleagues, who had joined the company later than he had, was promoted. Pradip approached Senior Manager and HOD and expressed his concern that he had been discriminated and that he should have been promoted. Both of them told him that the management knew who was to be promoted and on what basis, and that he should not interfere in such matters. Since then Pradip became extraordinarily quiet and withdrawn.

Later one day, a team from a consultancy firm came to the company and spent the day observing Pradip and others at work. They came on the next two days also. During these days Pradip felt a strained and tense atmosphere in the office. There was a feeling among the employees that something was brewing.

In the following week rumours circulated among the employees that the company was likely to be sold to an NRI group which was interested in establishing operations in India. During this period, a number of employees approached Pradip and wanted to know from him the reasons for the consulting team visiting the company. Another employee asked Pradip. "Is there going to be layoff?" Rumours led to an apprehension of retrenchment. But Pradip had little to say, and had not heard anything from his superiors; nor did he have any knowledge as to why the consultancy firm had come to observe their work.

Questions

1. What specific changes do you notice in Pradip's behaviour and in what way will his behaviour affect the performance of the company and why?
2. If you were Pradip's manager and have noticed the change in his behaviour, what immediate steps you would have taken and why?

PART – III
OVERALL BEHAVIOUR

13. Nature and Types of Organisations
14. Organisation and Environment
15. Nature and Scope of Organisational Behaviour
16. Organisational Goals
17. Organisational Change
18. Organisational Development
19. Organisational Climate and Culture
20. Organisational Conflicts
21. Organisational Effectiveness

CHAPTER

13

NATURE AND TYPES OF ORGANISATIONS

CHAPTER OUTLINE

13.1. Need for Study of Organisations
13.2. Concept of Organisation
13.3. Characteristics of Organisations
13.4. Organisation as a System
13.5. Organisations and Biological Systems
13.6. Importance of Organisations
13.7. Typologies (Types) of Organisations
- **Test Questions**
- **Case Study**

People are by nature social and want to live and work together. Moreover, an individual cannot fulfil all his needs and desires alone. Therefore, people cooperate and join together to fulfil their needs and desires. Whenever two or more persons combine their efforts and resources for some common purpose, an organisation comes into existence.

13.1 NEED FOR STUDY OF ORGANISATIONS

It is necessary to study the nature, types, structure and working of organisations because we are all surrounded by organisations. Modern society is a society of organisations. "We are born in organisations, educated by organisations, and most of us spend much of our lives working for organisations. We spend much of our leisure time paying, playing and praying in organisations. Most of us will die in an organisation, and when the time comes for burial, the largest organisation of all — the state—must grant official permission".[1] What we eat, drink, wear, read, play, rest and sleep, all are influenced by organisations. In fact, organisations affect every aspect of our life and shape our destiny.

We may study organisations from two perspectives — micro and macro. In the micro perspective the focus is on human beings. Under it, we study an individual's psychological make-up, his interaction with other individuals and groups, factors influencing his behaviour

1 Amitai Etzioni, **Modern Organisations,** Prentice Hall, New Delhi, 1965, p. 24.

in the organisation, and the strategies that may be used to secure desirable behaviour in the organisation. This micro study of organisations is a well-developed discipline and is known as **organisational behaviour**. The macro perspective considers organisation as the unit of analysis. It involves the study of the goals, structure and technology of an organisation and its interaction with the environment. This macro study of organisations is a discipline called **organisation theory.** The two disciplines taken together provide a complete picture of organisations.

13.2 CONCEPT OF ORGANISATION

According to Parsons[2], an organisation is **a social unit which is deliberately constructed and reconstructed to seek specific goals.** However, all social units are not oragnisations. Corporations, armies, schools, hospitals, churches and prisons are included but tribes, classes, ethnic groups and families are excluded.[3]

Scott defines organisations in a more elaborate manner as follows : "Organisations are defined as collectivities … that have been established for the pursuit of relatively specific objectives on a more or less continuous basis".[4] According to this definition, organisations have relatively fixed boundaries, a normative order, authority rank, a communication system, and an incentive system which enables various types of participants to work together in the pursuit of common goals.

In the words of Barnard, organisation is "a system of consciously coordinated activities or forces of two or more persons".[5] This definition assigns more importance to the members of the organisation than the organisation because individuals bring the organisation into existence. "An organisation comes into existence when there are a number of persons in communication and relationship to each other and are willing to contribute to a common endeavour."[6]

13.3 CHARACTERISTICS OF ORGANISATIONS

The distinguishing features of modern organisations are as follows :

(i) **Aggregation of People:** An organisation is an identifiable collection of human beings. It is not merely a number of persons collected at random. Rather it is a group of persons who are interrelated and interdependent. This identifiable group separates it from other elements in its environment. It determines the boundary of the organisation.

(ii) **Goal Orientation:** Each and every organisation is designed for some objective. It is a purposeful creation. Objectives indicate the desired state of affairs which the

---

2 Talcott Parsons, **Structure and Process in Modern Societies,** The Free Press, New York, 1960.

3 Amitai Etzioni, *op. cit.,* p. 3.

4 W.R. Scott, "Theory of Organisations" in Robert E.R. Farris (ed.), **Handbook of Modern Sociology,** Random McNally, Chicago, 1964, p. 488.

5 Chester I. Barnard, **The Functions of the Executive,** Harvard University Press, Cambridge, Mass., 1938, p. 73.

6 *Ibid.,* p. 72.

organisation attempts to achieve over a time period. Objectives legitimise the existence of the organisation. The success of the organisation is measured in terms of attainment of its objectives.

(*iii*) **Deliberate and Conscious Creation:** An organisation is the outcome of deliberate and conscious actions. There is a contractual relationship between the organisation and its members. It can be terminated by either side. An organisation is a social entity but it is different from casual gathering of people having temporary relationships.

(*iv*) **Relatively Permanent:** An organisation is a relatively permanent social entity. It is created to last for a long time. But this does not mean an organisation is static or fixed. Its membership, structure, objectives and activities keep on changing.

(*v*) **Coordination of Activities:** The tasks are divided and subdivided into departments and sections. Due to this division of labour or specialisation, there is need to coordinate or integrate the work performed by different work units. Coordination is necessary because all the work units contribute to the common goals.

(*vi*) **Structure:** An organisation has a structure into which various individuals are fitted. The role of every member in the structure is defined. There is a hierarchy of authority which helps to coordinate and control.

(*vii*) **Rationality:** Every organisation has certain rules, regulations and procedures. All members of the organisation are expected to behave according to these norms or standards. The desirable behaviour is rewarded and the undesirable behaviour is penalised. An organisation also provides for substitution of its members to ensure rationality in behaviour.

13.4 ORGANISATION AS A SYSTEM

We can better analyse and understand an organisation if we consider it as a system. A system is a set of interacting and interdependent parts arranged according to some plan. It has been defined as "an organised or complex whole, an assemblage or combination of things or parts forming a complex unitary whole".[7]

A system may be either closed or open. A closed system does not interact with the external environment whereas an open system is in constant interaction with the environment. All living beings (human beings, animals, birds, insects, etc.) are open systems. Non-living things such as bricks, metals, wood, etc. are closed systems. In reality, no system is completely open or closed. Organistions are selectively open.

Open System versus Close System

Open Systems	Closed Systems
1. Continuously interact with their environment.	1. Have no interaction with the environment.
2. Dynamic and flexible.	2. Rigid and static.
3. Neither self-contained nor self-maintaining require restructuring.	3. Self-contained and self-maintaining.

7 Richard A. Johnson, Fremont E. Kast and James E. Rosenzweig, **The Theory and Management of Systems,** McGraw-Hill, New York, 1989, p. 4.

4. Biological.	4. Mechanical *e.g.* an automatic watch.
5. Negative entropy — import more energy than is expended, can grow or decline.	5. Close loop — do not grow over time.
6. Feedback mechanism that helps them to maintain equilibrium	6. No such feedback mechanism

As an open system, an organisation has the following characteristics[8] :

1. **Importation of Energy (Inputs):** An organisation takes certain inputs from its environment. These inputs include human resources, capital, materials, technology information, etc. No organisation can survive and function without these inputs.
2. **Transformation or Throughput:** An organisation converts the inputs into some kind of outputs. This conversion process is known as transformation or throughput. A business organisation may convert its inputs into products and services.
3. **Outputs:** An organisation exports its outputs to the environment. The outputs may be intended or unintended. The outputs and manner of exporting them determine the viability and existence, survival and growth of the organisation.
4. **System as a Cycle of Events:** The input-throughput-output sequence is cyclical in nature. The outputs serve as a source of inputs which in turn determines the outputs. The cycle continues so long as the organisation operates. An organisation operates in its **environment** which influences it and gets influenced by it.
5. **Negative Entropy:** Entropy is a law of nature which suggests that all organisations tend to disorganise and die. An organisation must reverse this process in order to survive. It must import more energy from the environment than what it spends. For example, a business organisation must earn profits so as to survive in the long run.
6. **Information Feedback:** Information (response to outputs) from the environment helps the organisation to correct itself so as to remain on the right track. Therefore, an organisation must allow the entry of negative information or feedback from the environment.
7. **The Steady State (Homoeostasis):** The importation of energy from the environment to check negative entropy results in some sort of 'steady state'. However this steady state is not a true equilibrium or motionless. As importation of inputs and exportation of outputs is a continuous process, the equilibrium keeps on changing or is dynamic. The term homoeostasis implies 'steady state'. It is used in Biology to refer to the process by which a living being regulates itself around a stable state. For example, a human being maintains his/her body temperature despite variations in the environmental temperature.
8. **Differentiation:** An organisation, like other open systems, moves towards differentiation and specialisation of roles and functions. As conditions permit, it brings more specialists and creates specialised departments to have better control over the environment.
9. **Integration and Coordination:** With increasing differentiation, an organisation requires more integration and coordination between specialised parts. Mechanisms like priorities, standard operating procedures and rules are used for this purpose.

---

8 Daniel Katz and Robert L. Kahn, **The Social Psychology of Organisations,** John Wiley, New York, 1978, pp. 23-30.

10. **Equifinality:** This characteristic of open systems suggests that an organisation can reach the same final state through any of several routes. It is not necessary that every organisation chooses the same course of action or strategy to become successful.

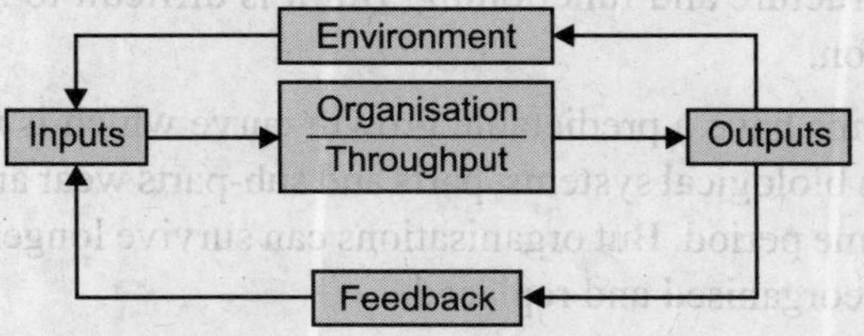

Fig. 13.1: Organisation as an open system

Implications of Open System View of Organisations: Considering an organisation as an open system has the following implications :

(*i*) An organisation continuously interacts with its environment. It is dependent on the environment both for inflow of inputs and outflow of outputs. Therefore, management must keep the organisation in tune with the demands of the environment.

(*ii*) While designing the structure, systems and processes of an organisation, managers must keep in mind the requirements of the environment.

(*iii*) There is no one best way to attain goals of the organisation. It all depends on the needs of the target market and other factors in the internal and external environment.

13.5 ORGANISATIONS AND BIOLOGICAL SYSTEMS

Katz and Kahn[9] have made a comparison between biological systems and social systems. Their comparison reveals both similarities and differences between organisations and biological systems.

Similarities: Both organisations and biological systems have the following attributes :

(*i*) Like biological systems, an organisation has interrelated and interdependent parts. What happens to one part (subsystem) influences other parts. Therefore, change in one part cannot be introduced without understanding its implications to other parts.

(*ii*) Both the systems are open systems and continually interact with their environment. They try to adapt themselves to the changing conditions and cannot survive without such adaptation.

(*iii*) Both the systems have a tendency to grow provided they survive in the process of adaptation.

Differences: Organisations differ from biological systems in the following ways:

(*i*) Biological systems are natural whereas organisations are man-made systems. Therefore, organisations are not as perfect as biological systems. For example, the parts of an organisation are less stable and fixed and their interrelationships are less definite and precise.

9 Katz and Kahn, *op. cit.*, pp. 23-30.

(*ii*) Biological systems are small and their physical boundaries are visible. But organisations may be very large and their boundaries are not always visible. A biological system has both physical features (anatomy) and physiological processes. It can be studied in terms of both structure and functioning. But it is difficult to identify the functioning of an organisation.

(*iii*) Biological systems have a predictable growth curve which is not found in the case of organisations. In biological systems, parts and sub-parts wear and tear out and can work up to a certain time period. But organisations can survive longer because their parts can be more easily reorganised and replaced.

(*iv*) Organisations are more flexible than biological systems. The former can be adapted to a wide range of objectives. Organisations can be designed and redesigned to effectively deal with the environmental challenges.

(*v*) The various elements of a biological system are held together by physical ties. But in case of organisations these ties are only psychological and social. Therefore, organisations require an external mechanism for control and balance.

13.6 IMPORTANCE OF ORGANISATIONS

Organisations are formed and they grow due to the following reasons :

1. **Limitations of Individuals:** Organisations are usually formed to achieve objectives due to the limitations of individuals. The biological capacity of an individual is limited and he/she cannot do everything alone. For example, an individual cannot move a large stone or any other very heavy object. Individuals overcome their biological limitations and increase their capabilities by forming organisations. Through an organisation the physical and mental abilities of several individuals can be pooled to perform any task.
2. **Material Reasons:** Hicks and Gullett[10] have identified three material reasons for organisations. These reasons are as follows :

   (*a*) Enlarge abilities: Organisations help individuals enhance their capacities in two ways. **First,** an individual can do what he could not do alone. For example, launching a spacecraft or building a warship are possible only through organised efforts. **Second,** organisations enable individuals to specialise in jobs most suitable to them. Such division of labour and specialisation helps to increase efficiency through better utilisation of resources.

   (*b*) Compress time: An organisation reduces the time needed to accomplish an objective. In many situations time is more important than efficiency. For example, a group of firefighters can extinguish a big fire and save lives more quickly than an individual.

   (*c*) Accumulated Knowledge: In the absence of organisations, an individual must learn everything from scratch. An organisation allows individuals to take advantage of the knowledge and experience of their predecessors.

---

10 Herbert G. Hicks and C.R. Gullett, **The Management of Organisations,** McGraw-Hill, New York, 1975, pp. 8-12.

3. **Social Reasons:** Human beings always want relationship with others to satisfy their social and psychological needs. An individual cannot satisfy these needs without associating with others. For example, a person joins a work organisation not only for economic benefits but also to get social satisfaction. Social organisations like clubs are formed only for social reasons.

13.7 TYPOLOGIES (TYPES) OF ORGANISATIONS

Organisation typology means a scheme of categories into which organisations can be classified. It helps us to analyse and understand different types of organisation. It is a multi-dimensional tool for differentiation and classification of organisations. There is no single correct typology of organisations. According to Litterer an effective typology should satisfy the following criteria[11] :

(*i*) The typology must be developed along some important general variable or property of organisations which allows a clear differentiation of organisations.

(*ii*) The variable must be one of a set of important organisational variables.

(*iii*) The variable chosen must lead to information or understanding important to the users.

A simple classification of organisations is on the basis of **size** — small, medium, large and giant. Another classifications is on the basis of **legal form** — sole trader, partnership firm, joint stock company and cooperative society. Another one is **ownership** — public, private and joint. According to the **area of operations** — local, regional, national and international. These classifications do not provide an analytical framework for the study of organisations. Three useful typologies of organisations are given below :

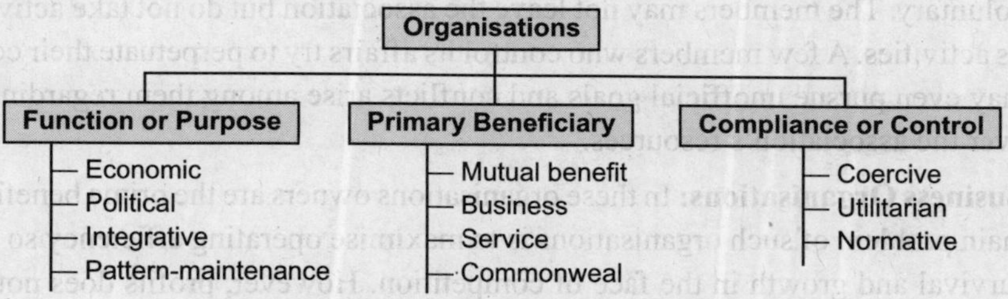

Fig. 13.2: Typology of organisations

13.7.1 Typology Based on Function or Purpose

Parsons[12] has classified organisations into the following categories on the basis of functions or purposes which they perform in society :

1. **Economic Organisations:** These organisations are engaged in producing goods and services for the society. They are run primarily for the purpose of earning profits. These include industrial, commercial and trading concerns.

---

11 Joseph A. Litterer, **The Analysis of Organisations,** John Wiley & Sons, 1973, p. 9.

12 Talcott Parsons, **Structure and Process of Modern Societies,** Free Press, New York, 1960, pp. 45-46.

2. **Political Organisations:** These organisations are created to achieve the basic values such as peace and stability in the society. They collect resources from various sources and spend them judiciously to provide service to the society. Government agencies and departments, legislature, etc. are examples of such organisations.

3. **Integrative Organisations:** These organisations are concerned with social control. They maintain law and justice in the society. Police force, courts and other protective organisations are included in this category. They attempt to check disturbing elements in the society to ensure that society functions in the desired manner.

4. **Pattern-Maintenance Organisations:** These organisations are concerned with knowledge, culture and other long-term issues in the society. Educational institutions, research institutions, religious institutions, clubs, etc. are included in this category.

Typology Based on Primary Beneficiary

On the basis of primary beneficiary (*cui bono*), organisations have been classified as follows[13]:

1. **Mutual Benefit Associations:** The associations like trade unions, political parties and professional bodies are created to serve the interests of their members. These associations are supposed to function in a democratic manner through control by their members. But it is difficult to maintain internal democracy due to two reasons — membership apathy and oligarchical control. Initially, there is excitement and dedication on the part of members. But over time, members lose interest and do not participate actively in the activities of the association. As a result, power and control passes in the hands of a selected few.

   In mutual benefit associations, organisation structure is loose and membership is usually voluntary. The members may not leave the association but do not take active interest in its activities. A few members who control its affairs try to perpetuate their control. They may even pursue unofficial goals and conflicts arise among them regarding command over the association's resources.

2. **Business Organisations:** In these organisations owners are the prime beneficiaries. The main problem of such organisations is to maximise operating efficiency so as to ensure survival and growth in the face of competition. However, profits does not remain the main consideration. Several interest groups like customers, employees, government, etc. contribute directly or indirectly and have their own claims. In addition to these pressures, the organisation may pursue certain social goals to improve its public image. But ultimately the survival of business organisations depends on adequate return on investment for the risks undertaken by the owners.

3. **Service Organisations:** In case of hospitals, educational institutions, social welfare agencies, legal aid societies and other service organisations, clients are the prime beneficiaries. For example, in case of a university, its students are the beneficiaries. But the beneficiaries do not have control over service organisations. They do not know

---

13 Peter M. Blau and Richard W. Scott, **Modern Organisations,** Routledge & Kegan Paul, London, 1966, pp. 42-58.

the means that will best serve their interest. Therefore, the administrators of such organisations must keep the interest of clients in mind rather than their self-interest. The professionals who run service organisations must emphasise two things. **First,** service is more important than observing procedures. **Second,** they rather than clients should decide the nature of service. They should neither overlook the clients nor become captive of them while rendering services. However, in practice, a clash between the professional ethics and personal goals of the professional can arise.

4. **Commonweal Organisations:** In case of army, police force, fire service, post office and other commonweal organisations, public at large is the prime beneficiary. They provide security and certain common services to the society as a whole. The internal structure of these organisations tends to be bureaucratic because efficiency rather than democracy is the main criterion. But the connection between their ultimate control and benefits to the recipients is remote.

13.7.2 Typology Based on Compliance or Control

Compliance means obeying somebody who has power. In an organisation, subordinates are expected to comply with the orders and instructions of their superiors. However, the degree of compliance may vary from individual to individual depending upon the authority and power (personal influence) of the superior, and the expected benefits to the subordinate from compliance with the superior's orders.

According to Etzioni, the following types of power is commonly used in organisations[14] :

(*i*) **Coercive Power:** It involves application or threat of application of physical sanctions or punishments. In case a subordinate does not comply with the authority, the superior may withdraw certain benefits or punish him with fine. In organisations like prisons where coercive power is frequently used, managerial style is autocratic.

(*ii*) **Utilitarian Power:** It involves use of material rewards for good performance. Subordinates comply with the orders of their superior due to expectation of rewards. Use of utilitarian power leads to positive leadership style.

(*iii*) **Normative Power:** It involves use of symbolic rewards like prestige and esteem. Subordinates who want these rewards obey their superior. Besides power, the involvement also influences a subordinate's behaviour. The degree of involvement indicates how strongly a person is interested in the organisation. For any organisation, an individual may be strongly attracted, indifferent, or strongly repelled and thus be placed on the continuum of involvement. For the purpose of analysis, this continuum may be broken into three parts : alternative involvement, calculative involvement, and moral involvement. In **alternative involvement,** the individual would prefer not to be connected with the organisation. In **calculative involvement**, the individual may be attracted to the organisation due to certain benefits. In **moral involvement,** the organisation is important to the individual and to be a member of it is valuable to him.

According to Etzioni, the three bases of power and three kinds of involvement taken together give nine types of compliance relationships as shown below :

14 Amitai Etzioni, **A Comparative Analysis of Complex Organisations,** Free Press, New York, 1961.

Basis of Power	Kind of Involvement		
	Alienative	Calculative	Moral
Coercive	1	2	3
Utilitarian	4	5	6
Normative	7	8	9

Out of these nine relationships, some are more workable than others. The most workable positions are 1, 5, 9 and the least workable positions are 3 and 7. This is so because in various organisations, some characteristics of power and involvement, which are opposite to each other, seldom exist. The relationships along the diagonal (1, 5, 9) have been labelled **congruent types** because the type of involvement and the effect of the type of power used tend to converge.[15] The other six positions represent non-congruent types of relationships.

13.7.3 Typology Based on Degree of Formality

According to the degree of formality, organisations have been classified into two categories — formal and informal.

1. **Formal Organisation:** It is the structure of well-defined jobs, each having a definite measure of authority, responsibility and accountability. The formal organisation is created by management to achieve organisational goals. Therefore, it is called official. It lays down the pattern of relationships between individuals and the rules and regulations to guide and control their behaviour.[16]
2. **Informal Organisation:** It emerges spontaneously out of interaction between individuals in a formal organisation. Whenever people work together informal groups bound together by some common interests emerge. Such groups collectively constitute informal organisation. The emphasis in these groups is on status, power and politics. Informal organisation is a natural grouping of people at work. It comes into existence due to the limitations of formal organisation. Management does not create informal groups nor can management eliminate them. Therefore, managers should use these groups to support and supplement the organisation.

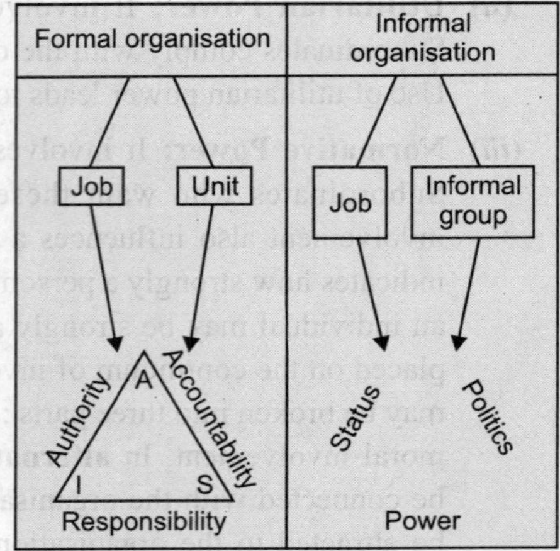

Fig. 13.3: Formal and Informal Organisations

Homans[17] has suggested a model for an integrated study of formal and informal relationships. This model is based on three concepts — activities, interactions and sentiments. Activities (A) refer to what a person actually does, Interactions (I) are the interpersonal contacts, and Sentiments (S) represent the emotional reactions of organisational members.

In the formal organisation, management establishes the activities and interactions of members.

---

15 Amitai Etzioni, *op.cit.,* pp. 12-13.

16 Samuel Deep, **Human Relations in Management,** Glencoe Publications, California, 1978, p. 120.

17 George C. Homans, **The Human Group,** Harcourt Brace, New York, 1950.

They are expected to show certain sentiments about the work and the organisation. In case of informal organisation, 'role' refers to the actual behaviour of an individual.

Table 13.1: Comparison between Formal and Informal Organisations

Point of analysis	Formal organisation	Informal organisation
1. Structure	Planned, rational and stable	Spontaneous, emotional and dynamic
2. Goals	Profit/service to society	Member satisfaction
3. Focus	Job	Role
4. Authority	Positional, flow top down	Depends on persons, flows bottom up
5. Communication	Well defined formal routes and flow of information one way and often slow	Grapevine; channels unspecified and information flow two way and very fast.
6. Control system	Promotions or demotions based on performance	Norms regulate behaviour
7. Behaviour	Rules and regulations govern behaviour	Work group norms, values govern behaviour.

Source: Adapted from J.L. Gray and F.A. Starke: **Organisational Behaviours** (Columbus, Ohio, Charles E. Merrill Publishing Co., 1977), p. 138.

TEST QUESTIONS

1. Define the term 'organisation' and explain the need for studying organisations.
2. Explain the characteristics of modern organisations.
3. Describe the characteristics of organisation as a system. What are the implications of system view of organisation?
4. "Organisation is an open adaptive system". Explain the interaction between technical subsystems and social subsystems.
5. Distinguish between organisations and biological systems. What are the similarities between them?
6. Discuss the importance of organisations in modern society.
7. What do you mean by typology of organisations? Discuss the typology of organisations based on primary beneficiary.
8. "Organisations are pervasive in modern society". Explain why.
9. Explain the typology of organisations based on function or purpose.
10. Discuss the typology of organisation on the basis of compliance.
11. Explain Etzioni's classification of organisations, giving suitable examples.
12. Distinguish between formal and informal organisations.
13. "Typology is a useful tool for organisational analysis". Comment and explain *cui bono* typology of organisation.
14. Write short notes on:
    (*a*) Homoeostasis
    (*b*) Homans' Model.

15. "Organisations don't function strictly according to official prescriptions". In the light of this statement, discuss the dysfunctions of informal organisation and suggest guidelines for the constructive use of informal relations.

CASE STUDY

Sunder Chemicals was established in the year 1965 with 400 workers and was manufacturing a couple of pharmaceutical products. After three years of initial crisis, the company found itself in a very prosperous situation. In 1985, the company employed about 25,000 employees working in 15 different departments.

Mr. Parikh was incharge of the Tablet Department having 30 workers. In the day shift, Parikh was assisted by Mr. Patel for the general supervision of the department.

Mr. Joshi was one of the workers in the Tablet Department about whom Patel did not have a good opinion as Joshi was in the habit of remaining absent without leave. Patel often found him taking leave under false pretexts. Patel did not have any other complaint about Joshi.

One day Joshi approached Patel with a request to grant him leave for a week, as he wanted to go on a pilgrimage with his family. Patel this time flatly refused to grant leave to him saying that he was not prepared to believe him considering his past record. Joshi felt very sorry about this and seemed to be disturbed.

During the lunch break, he was not in a mood to talk with his co-workers with whom he otherwise talked very cheerfully. On observing this, Mr. Solanki, a very old worker who was with the company from its inception, asked Joshi if there was something wrong with him. Joshi narrated the matter and broke into tears saying that his old parents would be unable to go on a pilgrimage.

Solanki was very popular among the group and always helped his co-workers by representing their case to the management. He was in general very hostile towards the officers and they in turn did not have good opinion about him. Solanki assured Joshi that he would certainly get his leave granted.

Solanki went to see Patel on the same day and found him giving instructions to some workers. Throwing the leave application on Patel's table, Solanki very arrogantly asked him why he was not sanctioning leave to Joshi. Patel felt very bad about the manner in which Solanki asked this and that too in front of his subordinates. But, controlling his emotions, he simply told him to ask Joshi to discuss the same with him. Solanki said that Joshi had authorised him to discuss this matter. He further accused Patel by saying that he unnecessarily harassed workers and that he will have to give up this habit, or he should be prepared to face the consequences. Patel, feeling very much insulted, asked him (Solanki) to get out of the department. On hearing this Solanki reacted very furiously and pushing Patel physically, told him, "I will now straighten you." After saying this, he himself left the department. Immediately, Patel saw Parikh and briefed him about the incident. Parikh regarded this as a very serious matter, and informed the Personnel Officer, Mr. Amin, to take appropriate action in the matter. Considering this as a gross misconduct, Mr. Amin served Solanki with a charge-sheet. The company had a consistent policy for disciplinary action and in such cases the punishment would be that of discharge.

Solanki was a very active member of the representative union which had very good relations with the management. Management always supported this union against another union which was very aggressive and protested against all actions of the management. When workers of the department came to know that Solanki had been charge-sheeted, they all approached the Secretary (of the recognised union) and strongly requested him to see that Solanki did not lose his job. They all agreed that Solanki was, to some extent, at fault. The Secretary, after hearing the full story, remarked that Solanki should have rather taken the constitutional course to deal with the matter. The workers said that in any case Solanki should not lose the job, as he had fought for his co-worker and not for himself. Considering the insistence of the workers, the Secretary decided to see Amin. In the meantime, a written petition was also handed over to Amin by the workers.

The Secretary met Amin and conveyed to him the feeling of the workers. He pointed out that this was the first time when workers had expressed their desire so forcefully. The Secretary further requested Amin to reconsider the case for the following reasons :

(*i*) All the workers were insistent and felt involved in the matter and if they were dissatisfied, the popularity of the union may decline, thus paving way for the other obstinate union.

(*ii*) The Secretary assured that he would see to it that Solanki does not misbehave like this in future.

Amin had been until now very consistent with the policy and he thought that this may become a very significant deviation from the rules. On the other hand, he thought that it would be rather difficult for him to observe consistency in this case, as otherwise he will have to displease the workers and perhaps the other union might take up the opportunity to establish a footing in the company. In the meanwhile, Parikh telephoned Amin and said that his workers had approached him and requested him to consider the case sympathetically. He insisted that he considered this as a very serious thing and that no mercy may be shown in Solanki's case.

Questions

1. What is the problem in the case?
2. Indicate the individual, managerial and organisational causes that have led to the problem.
3. What other realistic alternatives did Patel, Parikh and Amin have which could have avoided the problem? How can you explain Patel's behaviour?
4. Discuss the alternatives now available to Parikh and Amin. Discuss the consequences of these alternatives for the organisation and the feasibility of enforcing these alternatives.

CHAPTER

14

ORGANISATION AND ENVIRONMENT

CHAPTER OUTLINE

14.1. Concept of Environment
14.2. Nature of Environment
14.3. Emery and Trist Typology of Environment
14.4. Dimensions of Environment
14.5. Organisation-Environment Interface
14.6. Strategies to Deal with Environment
- **Test Questions**
- **Case Study**

The environment of an organisation is of two types — internal and external. The internal environment consists of the structure, management, culture, resources, etc. which affect the various subsystems of the organisation. The external environment includes all those conditions and forces that lie outside the organisation and affect its performance. In this chapter we are concerned only with external environment.

The classical theory treated an organisation as a closed system and, therefore, the focus was on the internal environment. On the other hand, the modern theory considers an organisation as an open system which has continuous interaction with its external environment. The external environment is quite complex and dynamic. Therefore, the open system perspective is much more difficult than the closed system viewpoint.

As an open system, an organisation imports inputs from the environment, transforms them into outputs and exports the outputs to the environment which is known as the **supra system**. However, in real life, an organisation is partially open and partially closed. Therefore, organisations are called **selectively open** systems. In order to be effective, managers must understand the interface between organisation and environment and design appropriate strategies to deal with environmental forces.

14.1 CONCEPT OF ENVIRONMENT

Environment means all those institutions, factors and forces that influence the performance of an organisation but over which the organisation has little control. In the words of Robbins, "An organisation's environment represents anything outside the organisation itself."[1]

Environment of an organisation consists of all the elements which lie outside it but which have an impact on its functioning and performance. Environmental forces are largely beyond the control of an organisation and its management. Environment is the framework within which an organisation operates. If organisation is considered a system, environment is the **supra system.** As stated in the previous chapter, environment provides inputs to an organisation and gets outputs from the organisation. In other words, there is a 'give-take' relationship between an organisation and its environment.

14.2 NATURE OF ENVIRONMENT

The environment of an organisation is characterised by the following features :

1. **Complexity:** The more diverse the activities in the environment, the greater is the complexity of environment. A wide range of heterogeneous elements increase the complexity. But environmental complexity is also a matter of perception. One organisation may perceive the same environment complex while another organisation may see it as simple.

   Organisations which operate in a simple environment have an advantage in decision-making over those working in complex environment. Decision-making in a complex environment requires a large volume and a large variety of information. Human memory has limitations. Therefore, a sound system is needed for monitoring the environment and processing the information.
2. **Variability:** When the degree or rate of change in environment is high, the environment is called **volatile**, otherwise it is **static** or **stable**. Modern organisations function in highly dynamic environment because the changes are fast and sudden. Environmental variability depends on the frequency of change, the degree of difference involved in each change, and the degree of irregularity in the overall pattern of change. There are four types of environmental variability — low stable change, high stable change, low unstable change, and high unstable change.

When the degree of variability in the environment is very high, uncertainty in task performance is high. Uncertainty reduces the ability of the organisation to preplan its activities.

Table 14.1: Factors Affecting Environmental Uncertainty and Dependence.

The environment is more uncertain and less predictable when :
1. it is more differentiated.
2. it is changing quickly.
3. there are numerous interconnections between its various components.
4. required resources are not widely available.
5. these resources are not evenly distributed.
6. increasing relatedness disturbs the environmental components and the linkages between them.

Source: M.T. Hannan and J.H. Freeman—"The Population Ecology of Organisations", *American Journal of Sociology,* 1977, Vol. 82, pp. 929-964.

1 Stephen P. Robbins, **Organisational Behaviour,** Prentice Hall, New Delhi, 1994, p. 523.

The complexity and volatility of environment may be combined to determine environmental uncertainty. Such a combination yields four quadrants (Fig. 14.1).

Degree of Complexity	Degree of Change: Stable	Degree of Change: Dynamic
Simple	Stable, predictable environment. Few products and services. Limited number of customers, suppliers and competitors. Minimal need for sophisticated knowledge.	Dynamic, unpredictable environment. Few products and services. Limited number of customers, suppliers and competitors. Minimal need for sophisticated knowledge.
Complex	Stable, predictable environment. Many products and services. Many customers, suppliers and competitors. High need for sophisticated knowledge.	Dynamic, unpredictable environment. Many products and services. Many customers, suppliers and competitors. High need for sophisticated knowledge.

uncertainty

Fig. 14.1: Environmental Dimensions.

(*i*) **Stable and Simple:** Organisations operating in such an environment generally provide few products with a limited number of customers, suppliers and competitors. In addition, the sources of raw materials are few and easily identifiable. Both the degree of change and the degree of complexity are low. Decisions can, therefore, be made with some certainty about the end results.

(*ii*) **Stable-Complex:** In this quadrant the degree of change is low but the degree of complexity is high. In other words, the number of customers, competitors and suppliers has increased. The degree of knowledge associated with serving these customers is high.

(*iii*) **Dynamic-Simple:** An organisation operating in this environment faces high degree of change. But the number of customers, competitors and suppliers is limited. For example, a clothing manufacturer selling to retail outlets faces rapidly changing styles of clothing.

(*iv*) **Dynamic-Complex:** Here the environment is highly unpredictable. The number of customers, competitors and suppliers is also large. Electronics and computer software firms face such an environment.

As the environment moves from stable-simple to dynamic-complex, information about the environment decreases and the effects or specific organisational actions become increasingly unknown.

14.3 EMERY AND TRIST TYPOLOGY OF ENVIRONMENT

Case studies made by Emery and Trist illustrate how environments evolve from simplicity and stability to complexity and change. They have developed a typology of organisational environment which is ordered on a continuum from static or routine to dynamic or turbulent[2]. The four kinds of environment that organisations may confront are : placid-randomised, placid-

2 E.E. Emery and E.L. Trist, "The Causal Texture of Organisational Environment", **Human Relations,** February 1965, pp. 21-32.

clustered, disturbed-reactive, and turbulent-field. Each type of environment is increasingly more complex than the previous one. These environments are described below :

1. **Placid-Randomised Environment:** In this type of environment, the environmental forces are randomly distributed and change occurs slowly. The environment is relatively simple and no single force can have a significant impact on the organisation. The environmental changes are slow and easier to predict. Even small firms can exist in this type of environment.
2. **Placid-Clustered Environment:** In this type of environment change occurs slowly, but threat occurs in clusters. It is more complex than the first type. It is possible to predict this environment by analysing cause-effect relationship of probable events. Organisations can perform well through proper planning. Such organisations are comparatively larger and more hierarchical. They have mechanistic structures but there is comparatively more decentralisation of authority.
3. **Disturbed-Reactive Environment:** In this environment, there are many similar organisations which seek similar end results on the basis of similar inputs. The focal organisation must predict the actions of competing organisations. But the actions of competing organisations cannot be predicted on the basis of simple cause-effect relationship. The focal organisation must adopt a more flexible approach and an organic structure.
4. **Turbulent-Field Environment:** This is the most complex and dynamic environment. The complexity arises as a result of : (*a*) inter-connectedness of organisations, (*b*) greater inter-dependence between society and organisations, (*c*) the increased use of research and development to meet competition. In order to deal with such environment, the organisation must adopt organic structure and dynamic functioning.

Thus, the typology of Emery and Trist is based on the level and degree of change in the environment.

14.4 DIMENSIONS OF ENVIRONMENT

1. **General Environment:** General or **indirect action** environment consists of economic, socio-cultural, politico-legal, technological and international forces. These forces provide the general framework within which organisations operate. General or remote environment influences organisations through the task environment [Fig. 14.2].

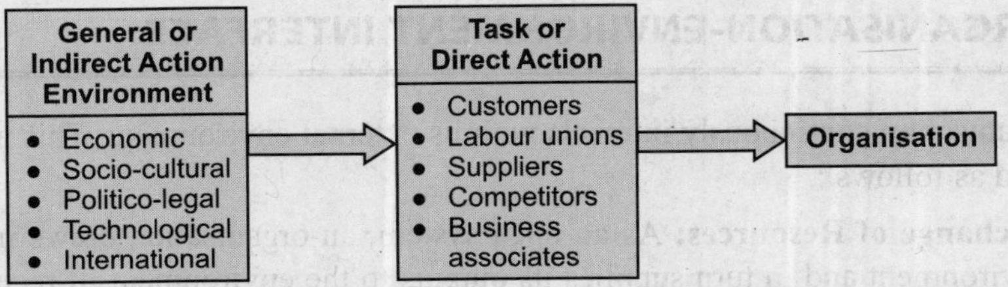

Fig. 14.2: General and Task Environment of Organisation.

(*i*) **Economic Environment:** It consists of the national economic system (nature of property rights, ownership of means of production, role of price mechanism, etc., economic planning, national income and its distribution, economic policies (monetary policy, fiscal policy, trade policy) and markets, etc. Economic conditions influence the functioning and performance of business organisations. For example, when excise duty on cars is reduced, the sales of car manufacturing firms increase. Factor markets affect the availability and cost of inputs. For instance, rise in the prices of sugarcane increases the cost of production of sugar mills. Similarly, adverse conditions in the capital market make it difficult to raise capital by issue of shares and debentures to the public.

(*ii*) **Socio-Cultural Environment:** It consists of population trends, level of urbanisation, education system, mobility of labour and cultural forces. All these exercise influence on business organisations. For example, level of education determines the quality of manpower. Changes in the attitudes and habits of people have increased the demand of fast food, readymade garments, healthcare facilities, etc.

(*iii*) **Politico-Legal Environment:** It includes the country's political system, political parties, political stability, foreign policy, laws and judiciary, etc. These forces have a significant impact on business. For example, since 1991 Government of India adopted the policy of economic liberalisation, privatisation and globalisation (LPG). As a result, a large number of multinational corporations have set up business in India leading to cut-throat competition for Indian companies.

(*iv*) **Technological Environment:** It consists of the state of technology, rate of technological change, etc. State of technology determines the cost, life and quality of products and services. Business firms now have to undertake research and development (R&D) in order to face the challenge caused by rapid changes in technology. Advancements in information technology have reduced the time and cost involved in transportation and communication.

(*v*) **International Environment:** International forces are exercising increasing influence on business firms in India due to globalisation. For example, inflows and outflows of investment by Foreign Institutional Investors (FIIs) cause significant changes in Sensex.

2. **Task Environment:** Task or direct action environment is specific for each organisation whereas general environment is the same for all organisations. Moreover, task environment exercises a direct influence on an organisation. For example, **customers** in India are now more aware of their rights and satisfying them is becoming more difficult. Similarly, **labour unions,** suppliers etc. put pressures on a business firm.

14.5 ORGANISATION-ENVIRONMENT INTERFACE

An organisation continuously interacts with its external environment. This interaction can be described as follows :

1. **Exchange of Resources:** As an open system, an organisation draws inputs from its environment and in turn supplies its outputs to the environment. It receives inputs in the form of raw material, labour, finance, energy, technology, etc. It converts these inputs into outputs and supplies the outputs to the environment. Outputs are in the form of goods and services to customers, wages and salaries to employees, dividends and interest to investors, taxes to the Government, etc. Business has to perceive and

meet the needs and expectations of different groups in the environment. It may have to modify its goals and priorities for this purpose.

2. **Exchange of Information:** An organisation must exchange information with its environment. It scans changes in the environment and collects relevant information for decision-making and control. The organisation also transmits information to shareholders, customers, suppliers, Government and the general public. These groups are interested in the working and performance of the organisation. The organisation is also legally bound to provide some information to shareholders, government agencies, etc. Thus, exchange of information is an important form of interaction between an organisation and its environment.
3. **Exchange of Influence:** The external environment holds considerable power over an organisation by virtue of its command over information and other inputs. It offers both opportunities and threats to the organisation. For example, Government, trade unions, investors, customers and suppliers exert considerable influence on the structure and functioning of an organisation. The organisation is also dependent on the environment for disposal of its outputs. In turn, a large organisation can influence its environment. Thus, there is a reciprocal interdependence between an organisation and its environment.

Interaction between the organisation and environment has the following implications:

1. The interaction is both wide and varied. The environmental forces may affect different organisations in different ways. For example, the technological environment is of key importance to the computer industry but of lesser importance to the furniture industry.
2. The environmental forces may affect different parts of an organisation in different ways. For example, technological environment may affect the research and development department more significantly than it does the production department. Similarly, fiscal policy of the Government exercises a direct influence on the finance department and indirect influence on other departments.
3. At any point of time changes in certain environmental components may have a more significant effect on the organisation than changes in other components. For example, change in demand for automobiles may lead to revision of production schedules. Change in government excise rates on automobiles may have no such immediate effect.
4. Environmental influence process is very complex because different components of the environment interact. The impact of these forces may not be quite deterministic due to counteracting factors. There is no direct cause-effect relationship between an organisation and its environment.
5. The environment is quite dynamic and the rate of change may not be uniform over a period of time.
6. Different organisations may respond to the environmental changes differently.
7. Environment does not have a unilateral influence on organisations. Organisations also affect the environment both individually and collectively.
8. It is the responsibility of management to perceive, understand and manage the environment. Managerial response to environment determines the success of organisations. Greater awareness of and improvement of environment will help both organisations and the environment in the long run.

While analysing and understanding the interface between the organisation and its environment, the diversity of both these entities must be considered. On the one hand, the nature of interface depends on the size of the organisations, its age, the nature of its business, the nature of ownership, nature of management, *i.e.,* its uncertainty or predictability, stability or dynamism, complexity or simplicity.

14.6 STRATEGIES TO DEAL WITH ENVIRONMENT

In order to survive and grow, an organisation must devise and execute appropriate strategies to deal with its environment. These strategies may be classified into two broad categories — (*i*) strategies for insulating the organisation from environmental forces, and (*ii*) strategies for gaining control over certain aspects of the environment.

1. **Insulation of the Organisation:** These strategies aim at minimising the negative impact of environmental forces on the organisation. This can be done partly by not allowing the environmental forces to penetrate freely into the organisation and affect its routine operations. But this can be done only on a selective basis because an organisation is an open system. Another alternative to avoid the negative influence of external forces is **boundary spanning.**[3] Under this strategy, the organisation uses boundary spanners like marketing research to anticipate environment changes. The following strategies can be adopted to minimise the impact of these changes :

   (*i*) **Buffering:** Under this strategy, an organisation stockpiles inputs and/or outputs to absorb fluctuations in the environment. For example, a cloth manufacturer may maintain a stock of cottons to meet their shortages. Similarly, it may keep a large stock of cloth to face fluctuations in demand for cloth. In this way, the organisation can maintain its operations.

   (*ii*) **Smoothing or Levelling:** This strategy is adopted to smoothen the sales throughout the year. During periods of low demand inducements like discount and free gifts are offered to increase demand. For example, air conditioners, air coolers and fans are sold at discounts during the winter season.

   (*iii*) **Rationing:** When demand exceeds the supply, priority is given to more needy users. For example, during the summer season, demand for electricity is in excess of its supply. Therefore, electricity supply to commercial users is reduced (rationed) so that domestic users can get regular supply throughout the summer.

   (*iv*) **Adaptation:** The structure, systems and processes of the organisation are adapted to environmental conditions. This strategy can be adopted when its is possible to forecast or anticipate changes in the environment. For example, Indian Railways increases the number of trains during holidays and festivals to meet the expected rush of passengers.

2. **Gaining Control over Environment:** An organisation can reduce its dependence on the environment by gaining control over some aspects of the environment. This can be done in the following ways :

3 James D. Thompson, **Organisation in Action,** McGraw-Hill, New York, 1967.

(*i*) **Creation of Prestige:** An organisation can increase its influence on customers and suppliers by building reputation in public. A favourable public image can be created through advertising, publicity, etc. Such an image enables the organisation to increase its sales and to procure inputs at lower costs.

(*ii*) **Agreements:** The organisation may enter into agreements with suppliers of raw materials, labour unions, financial institutions, competitors, etc. to gain control over its environment. This is a cooperative strategy[4] which reduces uncertainty for both the parties.

(*iii*) **Cooptation:** It is the process of absorbing new elements into the policy-making structure of an organisation as a means of averting threats or maintaining its stability in the changed circumstances. That is why business organisations appoint outside directors representing financial institutions, labour unions, etc. By appointing such directors the organisation can make them aware of its problems and create a common understanding with them. It also helps the organisation to gain support for its goals and policies.

(*iv*) **Coalescing:** Under this strategy two or more interdependent organisations create a joint venture or merger. These organisations become allies to pursue some common objectives. Coalescing may be for procurement of inputs, disposal of outputs or meeting competition. The organisations can have better control over the environment by pooling together their resources.

(*v*) **Procurement of Key Personnel:** An organisation can appoint senior executives, technical experts and key personnel to enhance its capacity to face competition and other environmental pressures. For example, family business houses in India are appointing qualified professionals to meet competition from multinational corporations.

(*vi*) **Lobbying:** It means the process of convincing powerful groups in the environment to act in favour of the organisation. An organisation may lobby on its own or through liaison with some members of the ruling party and political donations. Big corporations indulge in political lobbying to increase their influence on the environment. In addition, apex associations of business firms like Federation of Indian Chambers of Commerce and Industry (FICCI) and Confederation of Indian Industries (CII) lobby with Government agencies to safeguard the interests of their member organisations.

TEST QUESTIONS

1. Define the term 'environment'. Explain the nature of environment in terms of complexity and variability.
2. Critically examine Emery and Trist's typology of environment.
3. "Modern organisations are selectively open." Comment on this statement and explain the nature of interface between an organisation and its environment.
4. Explain the General Environment and Task Environment of organisations.

---

4 James D. Thompson and William J. McEwen, "Organisational Goals and Environment : Goal Setting as an Interaction Process", **American Sociological Review,** February, 1958, pp. 23-31.

5. "The external environment of modern organisations is complex and volatile." Explain
6. "Environmental forces exercise a significant influence on an organisation." Discuss.
7. "Organisations respond to their environment by adopting many alternative strategies." Explain.
8. "An organisation is not a fully open system." Elaborate.
9. "An organisation can insulate itself from the negative impact of environment without being a closed system." Explain.
10. "Organisations are sub-systems of a broader supra system — the environment". Elucidate the statement.
11. Explain Emery and Trist's model for understanding linkages between organisation and environment with the help of examples of organisations you are familiar with.

CASE STUDY

Mr. Vaibhav Chhabria, the founder and chief executive of a growing company with the staff strength of 20 executives, 40 supervisors and 250 operative personnel, remarked in one of the meetings of his executives, "I will have no organisation charts and position descriptions of any kind in our company ... You know organisation charts and position descriptions have a tendency of making people feel that they own a position and so they want to keep it to themselves. I will have none of these."

Mr. Ashish Chopra, the Finance Manager, who heard all this at the meeting got puzzled and kept thinking if it was really possible to do away with organisation chart and job descriptions in actual practice. One day, in an informal chat with Mr. Rajesh Jain, Marketing Manager, Mr. Chopra remarked, "Mr. Chhabria's approach is highly impractical. We have been using organisation chart and position descriptions over the past seven years in one form or the other. I don't think we can function effectively without these. Of course, the organisation structure must be flexible enough to meet the challenges likely to be posed by the environment in future."

Questions

(*i*) What is the key issue in this case?

(*ii*) What solution would you offer and why?

CHAPTER

15

NATURE AND SCOPE OF ORGANISATIONAL BEHAVIOUR

CHAPTER OUTLINE

15.1 Concept of Organisational Behaviour
15.2 Nature of Organisational Behaviour
15.3 Role of Organisational Behaviour
15.4 Foundations of Organisational Behaviour
15.5 Contribution of Behavioural Sciences
15.6 Models of Organisational Behaviour
15.7 Difference between Organisation Theory and Organisational Behaviour
15.8 Determinants of Organisational Behaviour

- **Test Questions**
- **Case Study**

An organisation is an association of people. The major problem of modern organisations is to maximize the efforts and contributions of people towards the achievement of organisational goals. These efforts and contributions depend upon the behaviour of individuals and groups in the organisation. Therefore, managers must understand the factors which influence human behaviour at work and mould such behaviour in the desired manner.

The study of organisational behaviour (OB) helps to serve three purposes. **First,** it assists in understanding the human behaviour in work organisations and causes of behaviour. **Second,** it is useful in developing a workable set of assumptions for predicting human behaviour in organisations. **Third,** it reveals which determinants of behaviour can be controlled and which are beyond controls. Managers can learn about normal and abnormal range of behaviour. The study of OB inculcates creative thinking for solving human problems in organisations. OB is a human tool for human benefit.[1] It helps predicting human behaviour and in developing generalisations for anticipating the effects of certain actions on human behaviour. It provides a rational thinking about people and their behaviour.

The field of OB, however, is complex and does not provide a simple answer to problems of organisations. OB does not substitute managerial judgement but helps in formulating an informed judgement.

1 Keith Davis and J.W. Newstrom, **Human Behaviour at Work,** *op. cit.,* p. 5.

15.1 CONCEPT OF ORGANISATIONAL BEHAVIOUR

Some of the popular definitions of OB are given below:

"Organisational behaviour is an academic discipline concerned with understanding and describing human behaviour in an organisational environment. It seeks to shed light on the whole complex human factor in organisations by identifying causes and effects of that behaviour."[2]

— Keith Davis

"Organisational behaviour is a branch of the social sciences that seeks to build theories that can be applied to predicting, understanding and controlling behaviour in work organisationas."[3]

— Aldag and Brief

"Organisational behaviour is a subset of management activities concerned with understanding, predicting and influencing individual behaviour in organisational settings."[4]

— Callahan

"Organisational behaviour is the systematic study of the nature of organisations, how they begin, grow, develop, and their effect on individual members, constituent groups, other organisations and larger institutions."[5]

"Organisational Behaviour is a field of study that investigates the impact that individuals, groups and structure have on behaviour within organisations, for the purpose of applying such knowledge toward improving an organisation's effectiveness."[6] *— Robbins*

Thus, organisational behaviour is the study and application of knowledge about how people act within organisations. Its focus is on individuals, groups and the organisation and interrelationships between them. It is concerned with the behaviour of individuals and groups and the impact of structural design on their behaviour.

15.2 NATURE OF ORGANISATIONAL BEHAVIOUR

An analysis of the definitions given above reveals the following features:

1. **A Field of Study:** Organisational behaviour is a separate field of study. It has emerged as a distinct field of study due to the significance of human behaviour in organisations. It contains a body of theory, research and application.
2. **Part of General Management:** OB is a part of general management and not the whole of management[7]. It is a behavioural approach to the study of organisations and their management. It is a relatively new discipline.

2 Keith Davis, **Human Behaviour at Work,** Tata McGraw-Hill, New Delhi, 1975.

3 Ramon J. Aldag and Arthur P. Brief, **Managing Organisational Behaviour,** West Publishing, St. Paul, 1991, p. 11.

4 Robert E. Callahan, C. Patrick Fleeuor and Harry R. Kudson, **Understanding Organisational Behaviour,** Charles E. Merril Publishing, 1986, p. 5.

5 Joe Kelly, **Organisational Behaviour,** Irwin, Homewood, 1974, p. 30.

6 Stephen P. Robbins, **Organisational Behaviour,** Prentice Hall, New Delhi, 1994, p. 7

7 Fred Luthans, **Organisational Behaviour,** McGraw-Hill, New York, 1989, p. 9.

3. **Interdisciplinary Approach:** OB integrates the knowledge drawn from psychology, sociology, anthropology, etc. for organisational analysis. OB is an eclectic field of study, and a part of social science.
4. **Both Science and Art:** OB is a science as it contains systematic knowledge about human behaviour. But it is an inexact science because it does not provide specific answers to organisational problems. It is also not possible to predict exactly the behaviour of the people in organisations. It is called a social science because its main focus is on people and their behaviour.
5. **Multilayered:** OB involves analysis of human behaviour at three levels – individual, group and organisation. These levels interact with each other. Therefore, OB exists at multiple levels.
6. **Normative Discipline:** OB is value-oriented as it is based on the belief that human beings and their needs are important. It is humanistic and optimistic about the creative potential of people. This potential can be actualised by creating appropriate environment.
7. **Goal-oriented:** OB seeks to fulfil both organisational goals and individual needs. The main purpose of OB is to explain, predict and regulate human behaviour in organisations so as to achieve these goals and needs. OB is action-oriented as it seeks to balance human and technical aspects of work.
8. **Total Systems Approach:** As a system approach, OB takes into account all the variables that influence an organisation's functioning. Human behaviour is analysed keeping in view personal, social, cultural and other factors because human nature is quite complex.

15.3 ROLE OF ORGANISATIONAL BEHAVIOUR

The major applications of organisational behaviour are described below:

1. **Understanding Human Behaviour:** Behavioural sciences help a person understand himself and others better. Such understanding of self and others helps to improve interpersonal relations. The individual can shape his personality and deal effectively with others. Organisational behaviour is useful for understanding human behaviour in all the directions in which human beings interact. Human behaviour can be understood at the following levels:
   (i) **Individual Behaviour:** OB helps to analyse why and how an individual behaves in a particular way. A large number of psychological, social, cultural and other factors influence human behaviour. OB integrates these factors for better understanding of individual behaviour.
   (ii) **Interpersonal Behaviour:** Individuals interact with each other due to their natural desire of socialisation. OB provides means for understanding interpersonal relations in organisations. Analysis of attitudes, perception, reciprocal relationship, role analysis, transactional analysis, etc. facilitate understanding of interpersonal behaviour.
   (iii) **Group Behaviour:** Group norms and pressures modify an individual's behaviour Group dynamics helps in understanding how groups are formed, why people join groups and how groups exert pressures on individuals and management. The study

of group dynamics enables managers to improve leadership, communication and employee morale.

(iv) **Inter-Group Behaviour:** An organisation consists of several groups and there are complex relationships between them. Inter-group relationship may be in the form of cooperation or competition. OB provides means to achieve cooperative group relationships for attaining oganisational goals. Group interaction, rotation of members among groups, avoidance of win-lose situation, etc. can be used for this purpose.

2. **Directing and Controlling Behaviour:** Managers are expected to direct and control behaviour at all levels so that it conforms to standards meant for achieving organisational goals. OB helps managers in moulding behaviour in the following ways:

(i) **Motivation:** OB helps managers in understanding employee needs and desires. Suitable incentives can be used to satisfy these needs and thereby motivate people to work hard towards the attainment of organisational objectives.

(ii) **Use of Power and Sanction:** Managers can use power and sanction prescribed in the formal organisation to control behaviour. OB explains how various types of power and sanction can be used for simultaneous achievement of organisational and individual objectives.

(iii) **Leadership:** OB provides better understanding of leadership theory and practice. It explains various leadership styles and their appropriateness in different situations. Managers can use styles that are effective and thereby bring human behaviour consistent with the accomplishment of the organisation's objectives.

(iv) Communication: OB improves study of the communication process and factors affecting it. People come into contact with each other through communication. Effective communication is essential for organisational effectiveness. Analysis of communication process and how it works in interpersonal dynamics helps managers to make communication effective.

(v) **Organisational Climate:** OB suggests a total approach to organisational climate rather than merely improving physiological conditions and work process. Satisfactory working conditions, adequate compensation and necessary equipments for the job are viewed as only a small part of sound organisational climate. Effective supervision, participative leadership, two-way communication, congenial relations with others at the workplace, and opportunity for realisation of personal goals are of greater importance.

(vi) **Human Relations:** OB is useful in creating and maintaining cordial relations among people in the organisation. These relations are strained not only due to economic reasons. OB helps in understanding the real causes of poor relations and in taking suitable measures to improve them.

(vii) **Change and Adaptation:** Organisations must change and adapt themselves to changes in the external environment. But members of the organisation often resist change. OB helps in identifying need for change and in implementing change without adverse effects on people.

15.4 FOUNDATIONS OF ORGANISATIONAL BEHAVIOUR

Organisational behaviour is based upon certain basic concepts relating to the nature of man and the nature of organisation.

15.4.1 Concepts Relating to Nature of Man

(*i*) **Individual Differences:** OB is based on the assumption that every person is different from others. Individuals differ in physical attributes, intelligence, attitudes, skills, personality, etc. These differences influence the behaviour and performance of an individual. Therefore, everyone should be selected, trained, placed and treated on the basis of the kind of person he is.

The principle of individual differences also suggests that managers should be cautions while dealing with employees. Leadership and supervisory styles, motivation technique, etc. must satisfy the individual to secure his full cooperation. Thus, the principle of individual differences has wide application in different areas of management.

(*ii*) **The Whole Person:** According to this concept, an individual's behaviour cannot be studied in isolation. An individual comes to the workplace as a complete person. His background, emotions and sentiments cannot be separated from the skills used on the job. His behaviour and performance at the workplace are influenced by his private life and environment. Similarly, his working life influences his private life.

(*iii*) **Human Dignity:** A person has a mind which thinks and a heart which feels. He cannot be treated like raw materials or machinery. The organisation must respect his emotions and aspirations. Management must treat employees with respect and dignity, otherwise they feel dissatisfied and do not contribute their best towards the organisation.

(*iv*) **Causation:** Human behaviour is not spontaneous but is caused. It is a function of the interaction between personal characteristics of the individuals and environmental variables. Managers must understand the causes of behaviour before attempting to improve it. The factors influencing behaviour can be controlled to obtain the desired results from people.

15.4.2 Concepts Relating to Nature of Organisation

(*i*) **Social System:** An organisation is a social system and is a part of the society. It coordinates the activities of members for the accomplishment of common goals. Their behaviour is influenced by several factors inside and outside the organisation. Any change in these factors influences the behaviour of individuals and groups in the organisation. Therefore, organisational behaviour is dynamic in nature.

(*ii*) **Mutual Interest:** Individuals join an organisation to achieve their personal goals. An organisation, similarly, seeks to achieve its goals through the efforts of its members. Thus, there is mutuality of interest between an organisation and its members. In other words, organisations need people and people need organisations. Therefore, the goals of both must be achieved simultaneously.

15.5 CONTRIBUTION OF BEHAVIOURAL SCIENCES

As stated earlier, OB synthesises knowledge drawn from various behavioural and social sciences such as psychology, sociology, anthropology, political science, economics, etc. Behavioural science is the field of study which involves scientific investigation, analysis and understanding of human behaviour. Psychology, sociology and anthropology are behavioural sciences.

1. **Psychology:** The term 'psychology' is derived from the Greek word '*psyche*' which means soul or spirit. Psychology is a science of human behaviour. Its focus is on the factors that determine the behaviour of an individual. It involves the study of the types and processes of human behaviour such as perception, learning, attitudes, motivation, etc. A separate branch of psychology known as **industrial psychology** is concerned with behaviour in work oragnisations. Psychology has made considerable contribution to organisational behaviour by explaining **individual behaviour**.
2. **Sociology:** As an academic discipline, sociology makes use of scientific method in accumulating knowledge about the social behaviour of groups. It is specifically a study of social groups, social behaviour, society, customs, institutions, social classes, status, social mobility and prestige. It involves study of behaviour of people in groups. Sociology has enriched organisational behaviour through the study of group dynamics, leadership, formal and informal groups, communication and other dimensions of group behaviour.

Table 15.1: Contribution of Behavioural Sciences to OB

Psychology	Sociology
• Attitude analysis	• Group dynamics
• Personality analysis	• Formal organisation
• Learning theory	• Social stratification
• Perception and sensation	• Social institutions
• Scaling techniques	• Social values
• Motivational analysis	• Sociometry
• Projective techniques	• Role and status
• Rationality	• Morale
Anthropology	• Social change
• Organisation theory	• Environmental influences
• Cultural analysis	• Public opinion
• Ethnic relations	
• Status symbols	

3. **Anthropology:** The term anthropology is a combination of the Greek word '*anthropo*' which means man and 'logy' which means science. Therefore, anthropology may be defined as the science of man. It involves the study of origin and development of human cultures. Culture exercises significant influence on human behaviour. Anthropology contributes in understanding the cultural effects on organisational behaviour. Value systems, norms, sentiments, interactions, group cohesiveness are studied in anthropology.

In addition to these behavioural sciences, political science, economics and other disciplines have contributed to organisational behaviour. Political science is the study of the behaviour of individuals and groups within political environment. It provides clues to power and authority structure, coalition, conflict resolution, etc. Economics helps in understanding the decision process, allocation of scarce resources and the impact of economic policies on organisations.

15.6 MODELS OF ORGANISATIONAL BEHAVIOUR

Top management of every organisation develops a particular model within which behaviour of its members takes place. This model is developed on the basis of assumptions about human nature. These assumptions vary from one organisation and time period to others. Therefore, several OB models have emerged. Four main models of organisational behaviour are given below :[8]

1. **Autocratic Model:** This model is based on the assumption that employees have to be directed and pushed into performance and this is the task of management. Managers see authority as the only means to get things done. They decide what is the best course of action and employees are expected to follow orders. Strict and close supervision is exercised to obtain desired performance from employees. The managerial orientation is official authority. This authority is delegated by right of command over the people to whom it applies.

   Autocratic model represents conventional or traditional thinking or economic concept of man. Employees become dependent on the boss who has absolute power to hire and fire. Under this model employees perform reluctantly due to fear of punishment. Their morale and productivity tends to be low due to feelings of insecurity and frustration. However, autocratic model can be successful when workers are lazy and shirk work. It may be appropriate for blue collar workers who seek satisfaction of their physiological needs.

2. **Custodial Model:** This model depends on the economic resources of the organisation to pay wages and other benefits to the employees. The employees are able to satisfy their security needs. They become dependent on the organisation instead of on the boss. Employees feel satisfied and happy but are not motivated to work hard for the organisation. Custodial model is often used in family managed business organisations. Managers decide what is good for their employees and psychological needs of employees are not satisfied.

3. **Supportive Model:** This model depends on managerial leadership rather than on the use of power or money. Management provides a climate that helps employees grow and accomplish. The focus is on the participation and involvement of employees in the decision-making process. Supportive model is based on Likert's principle of supportive relationships. According to Likert, "The leadership and other processes of the organisation must be such as to ensure a maximum probability that in all interactions and

8 John W. Newstrom and Keith Davis, **Organisational Behaviour : Human Behaviour at Work,** McGraw-Hill, New York, 1997, p. 33.

all relationships with the organisation, each member will, in the light of his background, values and expectations, view the experience as supportive and one which builds and maintains his sense of personal worth and importance".[9]

Custodial model is an improvement over the earlier two models because it meets the psychological needs of employees. Under this model, employees feel a sense of task involvement and participation in the organisation. This model is effective with executive and professional employees who seek satisfaction of higher order needs.

Table 15.2: Models of Organisational Behaviour

	Autocratic	Custodial	Supportive	Collegial
Basis of model	Power	Economic resources	Leadership	Partnership
Managerial orientation	Authority	Money	Support	Teamwork
Employee orientation	Obedience	Security and benefits	Job performance	Responsible behaviour
Employee psychological result	Dependence on boss	Dependence on organisation	Participation	Self-discipline
Employee needs met	Subsistence	Security	Status and recognition	Self-actualisation
Performance result	Minimum	Passive cooperation	Awakened drives	Moderate enthusiasm

4. **Collegial Model:** The term 'collegial' means a body of persons having a common purpose. The collegial model is an extension of supportive model. It is based on the team concept wherein each employee has high degree of understanding towards others and shares common goals. The organisational climate is very conducive to self-fulfilment and self-actualisation. Self-discipline replaces direction and control from management.

The four models given above have been developed to meet different situations. There is no one best model applicable in all situations. These models are basically constructed around need hierarchy. Autocratic model uses carrot and stick approach to satisfy physiological needs. Custodial model makes use of incentives to meet security needs. Supportive model seeks to serve needs for affiliation and esteem. Collegial model attempts to fulfil self-actualisation needs. As the need hierarchy changes with the level of a person in the organisation, the suitability of a model also changes.

Therefore, a manager has two key tasks — to acquire a new set of skills as models evolve and to learn and apply the behavioural skills that are consistent with those values.[10]

15.7 DIFFERENCE BETWEEN ORGANISATION THEORY AND ORGANISATIONAL BEHAVIOUR

Organisation may be defined as the study of structure, functioning and performance of organisations. According to Robbins, "Organisation theory is the discipline that studies the

9 Rensis Likert, **New Patterns of Management,** McGraw-Hill, New York, 1961, pp. 102-103.
10 Newstrom and Davis, ***op. cit.,*** p. 25.

structure and design of organisations. It explains how organisations are actually designed and offer suggestions on how they can be constructed to improve organisational effectiveness."[11]

Organisation theory differs from organisational behaviour in the following ways :

1. **Nature:** Organisation theory is descriptive and predictive about a particular state of affairs in the organisation. On the other hand, organisational behaviour is prescriptive in nature. It provides ways of influencing human behaviour in certain directions on the basis of description and prediction. In the words of Davis, "From administrative point of view, organisational behaviour seeks to improve the people-organisation relationship in such a way that people are motivated to develop teamwork that effectively fulfils their needs and achieves organisational objectives."[12]
2. **Purpose:** Organisation theory seeks to improve organisation design and processes so that these can cope with the external environment. But the aim of organisational behaviour is to explain, predict and direct the behaviour of individuals and groups in the organisation.
3. **Perspective:** Organisation theory is macro analysis of organisations, that is, how the organisation structure can be designed to integrate people with the organisation. On the contrary, organisational behaviour involves micro analysis of organisations, that is, how to improve individual and group behaviour.
4. **Emphasis:** In organisation theory focus is on the sociology of organisations whereas organisational behaviour stresses upon the psychology of organisations.

15.8 DETERMINANTS OF ORGANISATIONAL BEHAVIOUR

Both internal and external factors influence the behaviour of individuals and groups in an organisation. These factors are as follows :

1. **Structure:** The structure refers to authority-responsibility relationships between people in the organisation. It defines the roles and relationships of people. Different people are given different tasks and roles through division of work. But all are related to each other and their activities are coordinated to achieve the desired goals. The structural design must be appropriate for people, technology used and the external environment. A sound structure helps in getting desirable behaviour from individuals and groups working in the organisation.
2. **Technology:** The nature of technology used in an organisation depends upon its nature and size. It may be batch/job production, assembly line or continuous manufacturing. Technology influences the working conditions and is an important determinant of organisation structure. It provides assistance to people in the form of machines, tools, work methods and procedures. But it also curtails their freedom.
3. **People:** Every organisation consists of people, both individuals and groups. People interact with each other and influence each other. They join the organisation to fulfil their needs and desires. The organisation seeks to achieve its goals through people.

11 Stephen P. Robbins, **Organisation Theory,** Prentice Hall, New Jersey, 1983, p. 7.

12 Keith Davis, **Human Behaviour at Work,** Tata McGraw-Hill, New Delhi, 1978, p. 5.

Management attempts to mould the behaviour of individuals and groups for attaining organisational goals.

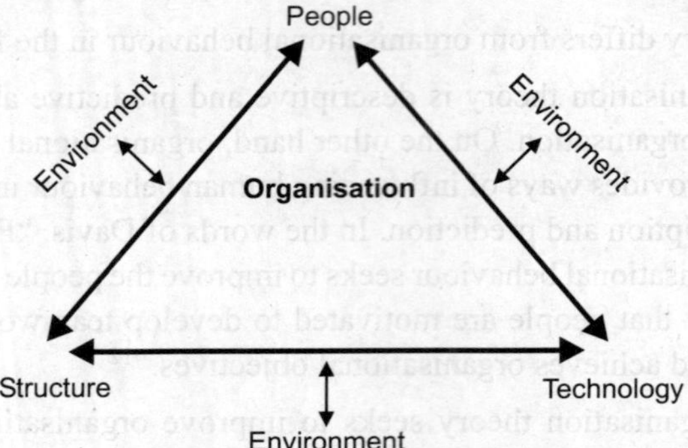

Fig. 15.1: Determinants of Organisational Behaviour

4. **Environment:** The external environment consists of economic, social, cultural, political, legal, natural and other forces. These forces exercise a significant influence on the perception, attitudes, motives of people in an organisation. For example, with the entry of several multinational corporations since 1991 in India and due to inflation, employees' expectations concerning pay and other benefits have increased.

TEST QUESTIONS

1. What is organisational behaviour? Why do managers need a conceptual framework for studying behaviour in organisations?
2. "Organisational Behaviour is a relatively young field of study that borrows many concepts and methods from the behavioural and social sciences." What advantages and disadvantages can you see in such youth and diversity?
3. What is OB? Discuss its nature. What are the contributing disciplines to organisational behaviour? List their contributions at individual, group and organisational levels.
4. Define OB. How does this compare with management? In what areas has psychology contributed to OB?
5. What is OB.? Briefly elucidate the following statements :

   (*a*) OB is situational.

   (*b*) OB represents a constant interaction between 'structure' and 'process' variables.

   (*c*) OB is an exciting field of study.
6. What are behaviour patterns A & B as identified by Chris Argyris? How are they related to theory *X* and theory *Y* of Douglas McGregor?
7. 'OB represents interaction among individuals, groups and organisation.' Elucidate this statement.
8. What is Organisational Behaviour? Distinguish between Organisation Theory and Organisational Behaviour.
9. "There is nothing as applied as a good theory." Explain how this statement is applicable to the study of Organisational Behaviour.

10. Explain the importance of study of organisational behaviour in the present context of liberalised economy. Are our industries geared up to take challenges in HR areas?
11. Define Organisational Behaviour and briefly explain the various models of Organisational Behaviour.
12. Define Organisational Behaviour. In your own words identify and summarise the various theoretical frameworks for understanding organisational behaviour.
13. "Organisational Behaviour is nothing but common sense, hence, there is no need to study it formally in a class." Critically examine the statement keeping in mind interaction among individual, group and the organisation.
14. "OB is a field of study that investigates the impact that individuals, groups and structure have on behaviour within an organisation." Comment and also use diagrammatical presentation of the OB Model.
15. "Organisational Behaviour is a field of study that has largely drawn from psychology and investigates the impact that individuals have on behaviour within the organisation." Comment. Also use diagram for the explanation.
16. "OB is a field of study that investigates the impact that structure and systems have on behaviour within an organisation." Comment and also use diagrammatical presentation of the OB Model.
17. Write a note on emerging issues in OB.
18. Explain the contribution of sociology and anthropology to the field of OB. To what extent is OB knowledge useful for managers in facing the emerging challenges?
19. "It is desirable but not necessary to study OB in an organisation particularly when the times are not good." Comment. Also discuss the challenges and opportunities for OB.
20. Explain the meaning and importance of organisational behaviour.
21. "OB is common sense". Comment. Explain the elements of OB.
22. Explain the relevance of supportive model of OB in modern setting.
23. Explain the challenges and opportunities for OB.
24. Define organisational behaviour. Point out the difficulties faced in the study of organisational behaviour.
25. What is the relevance of studying the organisational behaviour in modern business. Briefly describe the emerging trends in organisational behaviour.
26. Why is the study of organisational behaviour so important today? Discuss the latest developments in the field of organisational behaviour.
27. Explain the interdisciplinary nature of OB.
28. Explain the concept and determinants of organisational behaviour.
29. "OB is multidicisplinary in nature". Comment.
30. Analyse the impact of globalisation of business on organisational behaviour.
31. Define the systems dimension of organisational behaviour. Illustrate the impact of system on human behaviour in work organisations.

32. Discuss the basic philosophical concepts that form the foundation of organisational behaviour.
33. What is the subject matter of organisational behaviour? Why is the significance of OB increasing?
34. "Supportive model of organisational behaviour is suitable in all situations". Do you agree? Give reasons.

CASE STUDY

Jane wants to be a Manager, she enjoyed her accounting, finance and marketing courses. Each of these provided her with some clear-cut answers. Now, the professor informed her that there are really very few clear-cut answers to managing people. The professor has discussed some of the emerging environmental challenges and the historical background and says that behavioural science concepts play a big role in the course. Jane is very perplexed, she came to a business school to get answers on how to be an effective Manager, but this course surely does not seem to be heading in that direction!

Questions

(*a*) How would you relieve Jane's anxiety? How is a course in organisational behaviour going to make her a better manager?

(*b*) Why did the professor start off with a brief overview of emerging environmental challenges?

(*c*) How does a course in organisational behaviour differ from course in fields such as accounting, finance or marketing?

CHAPTER

16

ORGANISATIONAL GOALS

CHAPTER OUTLINE

16.1. Concept and Nature of Organisational Goals
16.2. Importance or Functions of Organisational Goals
16.3. Types of Organisational Goals
16.4. Goal Setting Process
16.5. Organisation as a Coalition
16.6. Influence of Environment on Organisational Goals
16.7. Goal Succession
16.8. Goal Distortion
16.9. Goal Displacement
16.10. Conflict between Organisational Goals and Individual Goals
16.11. Integration of Individual Goals and Organisational Goals
- **Test Questions**
- **Case Study**

16.1 CONCEPT AND NATURE OF ORGANISATIONAL GOALS

Every organisation is created to achieve some specific goals. According to Etzioni, "An organisational goal is something towards which the resources and efforts of the organisation are directed".[1] It is a desired and future state of affairs which the organisation attempts to realize. It represents the destination which an organisation wants to reach in future.

Some characteristics of organisational goals are as follows :

(*i*) Each and every organisation has some goals as without goals it would be purposeless and chaotic.

(*ii*) An organisation can have several goals such as earning a reasonable rate of return on investment, achieving a fair market share, etc.

(*iii*) It is the primary responsibility of every manager to establish appropriate goals.

1 Amitai Etzioni, **Modern Organisations,** Prentice Hall, New Delhi, 1965, p. 6.

(*iv*) The goals of many organisations are ambiguous because it is not possible to reduce everything in writing and interpret the same uniformly.

16.2 IMPORTANCE OR FUNCTIONS OF ORGANISATIONAL GOALS

Organisational goals perform the following functions :

1. **Legitimacy:** The goals of an organisation reflect the reasons for its existence. They indicate what it stands for so that people accept its existence and continuance. They help to justify the presence of the organisation.
2. **Direction:** Goals serve as guidelines for the activities of members of the organisation. They keep attention focussed on actions that are relevant for the organisation and guide decision-making. All the resources and efforts of the organisation are directed towards the achievement of goals.
3. **Coordination:** Goals make behaviour in organisations more rational. They help to keep activities on the right track. Everyone knows the accepted goals. The activities of all the people are directed towards common objectives. In this way goals serve as a binding force in the organisation.
4. **Motivation:** Goals are motivators because they make it clear to employees what they are supposed to do. When they know that achievement of organisational goals will fulfil their personal goals, they feel committed and work hard.
5. **Control:** Goals serve as the bench-marks or standards against which actual performance can be checked. Goals provide the yardstick for measurement of success.
6. **Interface with Environment:** The goals of an organisation influence its interaction with the environment. They determine the organisation's ability to receive inputs from the environment and thereby legitimise its existence. Goals also serve as the bases for specialisation of activities, flow of authority, communication networks and other structural relationships.

According to Glueck, organisational goals serve three purposes : (*i*) they define the organisation in its environment and justify its existence to various groups and to society at large; (*ii*) they provide for coordination and relate the diverse tasks performed in complex organisations; and (*iii*) they establish standards for evaluating the actual performance of individuals and groups.[2]

16.3 TYPES OF ORGANISATIONAL GOALS

Organisational goals may be classified into two broad categories — stated or official goals, and operative or real goals.

1. **Official or Stated Goals:** The stated or official goals are statements of desired results. They reflect what the organisation should do. These are normally expressed in writing and communicated to all employees.

---

2 William F. Glueck, **Business Policy : Strategy Formulation and Executive Action,** McGraw-Hill, New York, 1972, pp. 15-16.

Sometimes, an organisation may be pursuing something different from official goals. It may be applying its resources to unofficial goals. The goals which an organisation is actually pursuing are called **real or operative goals.** Official goals may be vague public relations gimmicks. The top management of an organisation defines official goals in vague terms such as achieving **'sufficient profits'** or **'market leadership'.** Sometimes, the official goals are so vague that nothing is intelligible. For example, "to provide quality goods at competitive price," or "to ensure that our activities do not damage the environment." These abstract phrases have to be converted into precise terms. These goals filter down through the organisation. At each successive level, managers assign 'real' meanings to the goals, and interpret them according to their perceptions. Operational goals specify the manner in which formal goals are to be attained. For example, profit goals can be achieved by pursuing operative goals such as competitive pricing, quality improvement, market penetration, etc. The study of operational goals helps in understanding :

(*a*) the criteria against which organisational performance is measured;

(*b*) the reasons for functioning of the organisation at less than optimum level; and

(*c*) the reasons for individual or group efforts to subvert the official goals.

Types of Operative Goals: Charles Perrow[3] has identified the following types of operative goals :

1. **Environmental Goals:** These goals are pursued by an organisation to satisfy various groups in its external environment. For example, a profit-making organisation may pursue customer satisfaction, environmental protection, social responsibility, etc.
2. **Output Goals:** These are related to the types of services or the product lines to be launched to meet the needs of customers. Target markets are identified to achieve the output goals. These goals serve as the basis of long-term planning.
3. **System Goals:** These are concerned with the survival of the organisation itself. Growth, profitability, stability and efficiency are examples of system goals.
4. **Product Goals:** These goals are related to the nature and quality of product to be offered to the customers. They define variety, style, quality, innovativeness and availability of products.
5. **Derived Goals:** These goals refer to the utilisation of the organisation's resources in the desired manner.

It is necessary to differentiate between official goals and operative goals. Official goals describe the policy frame of the organisation whereas the operative goals provide the action plans. For example, an organisation may define its official goal as efficiency and cost reduction. Then its operative goal can be how to increase efficiency and reduce costs. If official goals are the destination, operative goals can be considered as the milestones for reaching the destination.

16.4 GOAL SETTING PROCESS

According to the classical or traditional view, goals of an organisation are set by its top management. It is assumed that top management knows what is best and only they can see

3 Charles Perrow, "The Analysis of Goals in Complex Organisations", **American Sociological Review,** 26 (1961), p. 855.

the "big picture". From these goals, middle management develops secondary goals. The goals set at the lower level are the means for attainment of higher level goals. For example, the goal of earning a specified rate of return can be achieved when the production department focuses on production of quality products at reasonable cost. At the lowest level, factory workers focus on minimising waste and increasing productivity to reduce costs and improve quality. This hierarchy of objectives at various levels is known as **ends-means chain.** The goals set at the top level (*e.g.,* a specific return on investment) serve as the basis for setting goals at the middle level (*e.g.,* new product development) which in turn provide the basis for deciding goals at the lower level (*e.g.,* reducing waste and maintaining quality).

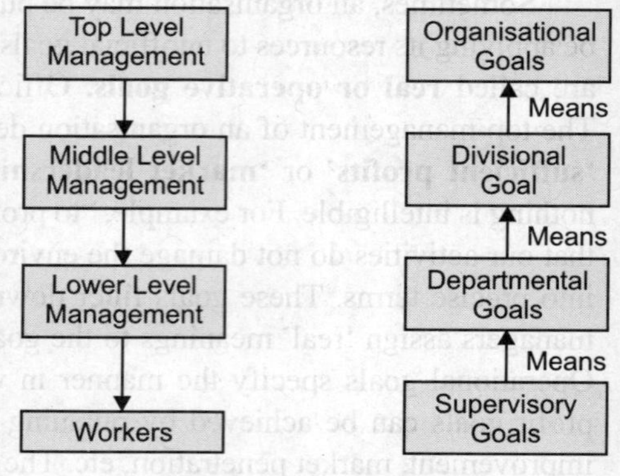

Fig. 16.1: Ends-Means Chain

The ends-means chain has several implications. **First,** goal setting is a top-down process. **Second,** each and every activity (means) should contribute to the achievement of goals. In other words, the concept of ends-means chain is useful in understanding the relationship between organisational goals and its activities.[4]

Under the classical approach, goal setting is a perfectly rational process and there is no reason for differences between stated and operational goals. But in real life, different units of an organisation disagree on the appropriate means for accomplishment of organisational goals. Personal values and interests of members and external forces also influence the goal setting process.

According to the behavioural theory, goal setting in modern organisations is a political process. The goals are the result of continuous negotiations or bargaining between various groups in the organisation. Every group in the organisation attempts to influence goal setting for its security, autonomy and prestige. The real goals are not clear from lofty policy statements of the organisation. Rather these can be judged from the functions/departments that receive the major share of resources, the behaviours that are rewarded most, etc. For example, the official goal of a hospital may be to provide quality healthcare to everybody. But the reality is different if the hospital refuses to admit patients who cannot afford to pay the costs of healthcare.

16.5 ORGANISATION AS A COALITION

According to the behavioural theory,[5] an organisation consists of several coalitions. A coalition is a temporary alliance of two or more individuals formed to pursue their common interests. The interests of these coalitions are not identical. Therefore, goals are the outcome of continuous bargaining between various coalitions or groups in the organisation. For example, managers, workers, customers, shareholders, suppliers have their coalitions. The dominant coalition exercises maximum influence over goal setting. Organisational goals represent compromises among coalitions. Every group in the organisation strives to influence goal setting

4 Joseph A. Litterer, **The Analysis of Organisations,** John Wiley, New York, 1973.
5 Richard M. Cyert and James G. March, **A Behavioural Theory of the Firm,** Prentice Hall, New Jersey, 1963, pp. 26-38.

through side payments (money, personal treatment, authority, etc.). These side payments offer security, autonomy and prestige in lieu of influence over goals. For example, to obtain support from production people, managers might commit the organisation to standardised products.

The negotiated order of objectives does not imply complete agreement among the members regarding organisational goals. For instance, production people might resent the high standards agreed upon earlier whereas quality control people may object to the deviations in quality standards. Each group may consider its own goal as the most important for the organisation. The side payments are incomplete as these do not anticipate all possible future situations. These are also inadequate because members' interests might change. An organisation solves this problem through **sequential attention.** It means attending the most important goals for the present and then turning to other goals to satisfy the interests of different groups in the organisation. For example, an organisation may sacrifice profits in the current year to increase advertising, research and development and employee remuneration.

The goals of an organisation do not remain static. They need to be reviewed and revised to cope with changes in the environment. Changes in the needs and preferences of members, consumer preferences, technology, government policies, etc. also change over a period of time. Necessary changes in organisational goals are made to fulfil the expectations of different groups inside and outside the organisation.

16.6 INFLUENCE OF ENVIRONMENT ON ORGANISATIONAL GOALS

An organisation is an open system and cannot survive without a healthy interaction with its environment. It must set and adjust its goals to meet challenges created by environmental challenges. For example, the goal of increasing profits may have to be modified due to pressure from trade unions (for higher wages), competitors (reduction in prices), suppliers (increase in prices of raw materials), Government (restrictions on exports), etc.

An organisation may adopt the following strategies to cope with environmental changes:[6]

1. **Competition:** Organisations compete for limited resources available in the environment. Technology, funds, talent, raw materials are examples of these resources. Such competition prevents a unilateral or arbitrary choice of organisational goals. In the long run, an organisation cannot survive by pursuing goals unacceptable to society.
2. **Bargaining:** The term 'bargaining' means negotiation or give and take for arriving at an agreement. An organisation is a coalition of different groups. Therefore, the final goals must be acceptable to all of them. In other words, goals are set through compromise and represent a common minimum programme. The group whose goals are not given due weightage may be offered side payments such as time-bound promotion for employees.
3. **Cooptation:** An organisation may absorb some elements in the environment into its policy-making structure in order to avert potential threats to its stability or existence. This is called cooptation. For example, a company may appoint representatives of creditors or employees on its board of directors. The employee director will support

6 J.D. Thompson and W.J. McEwen, "Organisational Goals and Environment : Goal Setting as an Interaction Process", **American Sociological Review,** February 1958, pp. 23-31.

implementation of the company's decisions. Cooptation, thus, acts as a 'safety valve' and integrates the interests of different elements in the environment. It also helps to identify mutually acceptable goals by checking arbitrary or unilateral goal setting.

4. **Coalition:** An organisation consists of several individuals and groups. A coalition refers to a temporary alliance between two or more persons or groups for the purpose of promoting a common interest. Bargaining between the coalition members may lead to a common minimum programme. As a compromise, an organisation may adopt multiple goals rather than a single goal. Differences between coalition partners threaten its existence and they agree upon goals acceptable to all.

16.7 GOAL SUCCESSION

Goal succession means substitution of new goals in place of old goals. It may involve multiplication or expansion of existing goals. An organisation may adopt new goals in addition to or in place of old goals. According to Etzioni, goal succession takes place when the old goals have been realised or cannot be attained. Usually, goal succession is a deliberate and intentional process. But sometimes changes in the environment may require it. The old goal may or may not be discarded but the organisation adopts new goals in order to survive. When the old goal has been achieved, a new goal is formulated to ensure the existence of the organisation. For example, Red Cross was established primarily to help those who suffered from war or any other casualty. But after World War 1 this was not very meaningful. Therefore, the goal of preserving and improving public health was adopted.[7]

Goal succession may be necessary in the following situations :

(*i*) The existing goals have been achieved and the organisation must adopt new goals for its survival.

(*ii*) The existing goals have become irrelevant and it is not desirable to pursue them due to changed circumstances. Therefore, the organisation must abandon the existing goals and adopt new goals.

(*iii*) It is not possible to realise the existing goals. The organisation must modify them or adopt new goals for its existence.

16.8 GOAL DISTORTION

Goal distortion refers to misunderstanding or misapplication of stated goals of the organisation. The real meaning of the organisational goals is misinterpreted or twisted. For example, a university may focus on higher pass percentage in the final examinations rather than the overall development of its students. Goal distortion occurs during the process of translating official goals into operating goals.

Goal distortion takes place due to the following reasons :

1. **Organisational Distance:** In a tall organisation structure, every piece of information has to travel a long distance to reach people at the operating level. People at each level

7 Amitai Etzioni, *op. cit.*, p. 13.

filter or modify the information. As a result lower level people do not have accurate understanding of organisational goals. Sometimes, the sender and the receiver attach different meanings to the message. Such blockages in communication lead to distortion of goals.

2. **Overemphasis of Quantitative Aspect:** In every organisation, there are some activities which are easily measurable (*e.g.,* output and sales) while others cannot be measured (*e.g.,* quality and customer satisfaction). When the measurable activities are overemphasised at the cost of non-measurable activities, goal distortion can occur. For example, the success of the training and development department may be measured in terms of the number of programmes rather than in terms of the impact of such programmes on employees and the organisation.
3. **Overcommitment to a Goal:** Every division or department has several goals. When a manager is overcommitted to a particular goal or a set of goals he ignores the other goals. Overcommitment blinds the manager to appreciate the significance of other goals. A manager may be overcommitted to a goal because its attainment will fulfil his personal goals. As a result, the manager's view of organisational goals becomes distorted.
4. **Inadequate Goal Formulation:** The official goals may be ambiguous or contradictory to one another. Frustration, anxiety and disillusionment occur if the stated goals make contradictory demands. Every manager interprets them in his own way to achieve clarity and specificity. Incorrect and biased interpretation causes goal distortion. Some goals may be too vague and difficult to measure.
5. **Remote View of Goals:** Employees at the operating level cannot see the "big picture". They interpret the organisational goals according to their understanding and to suit their convenience. They are not able to relate their own goals to the organisation.

16.9 GOAL DISPLACEMENT

Goal displacement occurs when an organisation pursues goals which are different from its official or stated goals. In other words, legitimate goals of the organisation are displaced or substituted by some other goals. In the words of Michels, "Goal displacement occurs when the organisation is pursuing a goal for which it was not established or for which resources were not allocated to it".[8] Goal displacement may be deliberate or unintentional. There is no change in official goals, but unofficial goals displace the official goals. For example, the head of a management institute may be more concerned with the employment of his relatives in the institute than with its official goal of high quality education and research. Goal displacement is, thus, an extreme form of goal distortion.

Goal displacement can occur in any organisation. But it is more common in bureaucratic organisations. In such organisations rigid adherence to rules and regulations takes precedence over goal attainment. Rules and regulations are only a means but these become an end. When means become the ends and ends become a means, goal displacement takes place.

8 Robert Michels, **Political Parties,** Dover, New York, 1959.

Goal displacement may occur due to the following causes :

1. **Reversal of Ends and Means:** An organisation may function in such a way that means themselves become the ends. The resources and activities of the organisation are directed towards the means rather than towards the ends. For example, the focus of a university may be on the number of graduates rather than on creating talent. This is the most common form of goal displacement. It may occur due to two reasons. **First,** a few influential people who control the organisation use its resources to perpetuate their hold over the organisation. This has been called the **Iron Law of Oligarchy.**[9] Such people use the organisation to achieve their personal goals thereby subverting the organisational goals. For example, the management of an educational institution may focus on raising funds (means) overlooking quality education (ends) for its students. **Second,** every organisation creates a set of procedures to achieve its goals. But people at lower levels consider the procedures as ends in themselves. Their activities focus on following the procedures rather than on attainment of organisational goals. For example, recruitment executives strictly follow the prescribed selection procedure overlooking the quality of people recruited.
2. **Preoccupation with Internal Matters:** In some organisations, such as government departments, the employees waste their time and efforts on transfer, promotion, pay revision, and other internal problems. As a result their attention is diverted from the stated goals of the organisation.
3. **Sub-optimisation on Overall Goals:** Sometimes, people in an organisation concentrate on achievement of a narrow operational goal instead of on the overall wider goals. For instance, a company may focus on the sales turnover rather than on its long-term financial health. This is like winning a battle but losing the war.
4. **Concentration on Measurable Aspects:** In most organisations, there is pressure to measure efficiency as it is considered rational behaviour. But the long-term goals are likely to be undermined in this process. According to Etzioni, "Frequent measuring can distort the organisational efforts because some aspects of its output are more measurable than the others. Frequent measuring tends to encourage over-production of highly measurable items and neglect of the less measurable ones".[10]
5. **Overemphasis on Rules and Regulations:** In bureaucratic organisations, strict adherence to rules and regulations is given priority over organisational goals. Such rule-oriented behaviour is dysfunctional for organisational goals.

Preventing Goal Displacement

Some of the steps that can be taken to check goal displacement are as follows :

1. **Management by Objectives:** Goals are often structured in a hierarchy in the form of ends-means chain. At one specific level, the goal and the means for its accomplishment can be easily identified. But, the overall goals of the organisation are not clearly understood at the operating level. Management by objectives (MBO) helps to translate the abstract or intangible goals into clear and meaningful terms. Under MBO, the goals of each position are defined in terms of the desired results. These expected results are

9 Robert K. Merton, **Social Theory and Social Structure,** The Free Press, New York, 1957.
10 Amitai Etzioni, *op. cit.,* p. 9.

used as the criteria for evaluation of performance of the position holder. As a result employees tend to focus on the results expected of them.

2. **Flexibility in Rules and Regulations:** Rigid rules and regulations and strict role prescriptions divert the time and efforts of employees away from organisational goals. Rules and regulations should be flexible and unintentional and desirable deviations from these should not be penalised. Moreover, rules, regulations and work procedures must be modified in the light of changes in the external environment.

16.10 CONFLICT BETWEEN ORGANISATIONAL GOALS AND INDIVIDUAL GOALS

An organisation is created to achieve some goals which cannot be achieved through individual action. Individuals join an organisation to achieve their personal goals such as survival, security, status, recognition, career advancement, etc. In other words, an organisation is a mechanism for the achievement of personal goals. At the same time, individuals contribute their time, effort and talent for achieving the organisational goals. A business organisation may have several goals such as market share, profitability and growth. In fact, both the organisation and its members have mutual expectations from each other. Thus, there is an exchange of relationship between an individual and an organisation which goes beyond the formal contract of service between the two. According to Schein[11], individual and organisation enter into some kind of **'psychological contract'**.

Now the question arises whether individual goals and organisational goals are compatible or contradictory. There are conflicting views on this issue.

Classical Viewpoint: Under the classical theory, it is assumed that organisational goals and individual goals are complementary. An individual contributes to organisational goals and the organisation, in turn, provides rewards to satisfy the individual's goals. In other words, there is no conflict between organisational goals and individual goals. In case there is any conflict, the organisational interest must prevail.[12]

Behavioural Viewpoint: According to the behavioural theory, organisational goals and individual goals are not always congruent or compatible. It is not easy to resolve the conflict between the two. There are three different viewpoints on the causes of conflict between organisational goals and individual goals.

(*a*) **Personality Advocates:** According to Chris Argyris[13], it is the organisation that is to be blamed for incongruency in goals. There is a built-in conflict or incompatibility between the demands of complex organisations and the needs of mature individuals. Over time, an individual moves from the passive, dependent and subordinate status of an infant to the active, independent and superior status of an adult. The structural elements of the formal organisation (specialisation, chain of command, authority structure and

---

11 Edgar H. Schein, **Organisational Psychology,** Prentice Hall, New Delhi, 1979, pp. 70-71.

12 Henri Fayol, **General and Industrial Management,** Sir Issac Pitman & Sons Ltd., London, 1949, p. 21.

13 Chris Argyris, "Personal versus Organisational Goals", in R. Dubin (ed.), **Human Relations in Administration,** Prentice Hall, New Delhi, 1974.

control) are not compatible with the needs of human personality for full development. The following properties of formal organisations create conflict between an individual and the organisation :

(*i*) **Rationality:** An organisation expects fully rational behaviour from its members. Taylor's **mental revolution** and Fayol's **esprit de corps** are examples of such rational behaviour. But, rationality is contrary to human nature. Man is a social animal and may not behave according to the norms of the organisation.

(*ii*) **Task Specialisation:** A formal organisation is characterised by high degree of specialisation of tasks. Work specialisation helps to increase efficiency. But narrow task specialisation makes jobs too dull and monotonous for the individual and restricts personality development. Task specialisation inhibits self-actualisation.

(*iii*) **Chain of Command:** Task specialisation results in segregation of the organisation into parts. A chain of superiors and subordinates is created to integrate these parts. Due to this chain of command, individuals lose control over their task environment. They are forced to be passive, dependent and subordinate to the boss.

(*iv*) **Unity of Direction:** The formal organisation is characterised by unity of direction. Under it, similar and interrelated activities are planned and controlled by a single boss. The work becomes meaningless to lower level persons due to goal setting by the top level. When the work goals do not match the individual's needs, there is **'psychological failure'** of the mature person. As a result, the individual feels alienated from the goals of the organisation.

Argyris[14] further contends that the incongruency between individual and formal organisation increases (*a*) with the increase in the maturity levels of individuals, (*b*) by making formal structure more tight and rule-bound emphasising dehumanisation, (*c*) as jobs become more and more mechanised, and (*d*) as one goes down the organisation. This lack of congruency results in frustration, failure, short-term perspective and conflict. Under these conditions, employees try to maintain self-integrity by resorting to such abnormal behaviours as leaving the organisation, regression, day dreaming, aggression, etc.

(*b*) **Organisation Advocates:** According to George Strauss[15], organisation is not responsible for conflict between the individual and the organisation. Every individual does not seek self-actualisation and money is an important motivator for people. Individuals can accommodate to the demands of formal organisation without much psychological damage or loss. Personality-organisation conflict is not that much frustrating for them. People at lower levels want to be directed and do not desire freedom. They can be motivated by good pay and status. Money also can satisfy status and other higher level needs of individuals. Job is not a source of self-actualisation for everyone. Many individuals depend on the job only for salary and other benefits. Moreover, the organisation expects only reasonable performance from people in return for the economic benefits.

---

14 Chris Argyris, **Integrating the Individual and the Organisation,** John Wiley & Sons, New York, 1964.

15 George Strauss, "Some Notes on Power Equalisation" in Harold J. Lewitt (ed.), **The Social Science of Organisations,** Prentice Hall, Englewood Cliffs, New Jersey, 1963.

(*c*) **Reconciliatory Viewpoint:** According to Dubin[16], the real problem lies neither in the personality nor the organisation, but rather in their **mutual adaptation**. An individual participates in several different institutions like family, church, club, workplace, etc. But the intensity of his participation in all these need not be same. An individual primarily concentrates only in one or some of these institutions. In others, he just participates in terms of minimum required behaviour. Those who are not primarily interested in workplace may just fulfil the minimum production requirements and may get the rewards. They may achieve "self-actualisation" in some other institutions. Thus, "organisations and individuals can survive happily even when incongruency between individual goals and organisational requirements exists."

16.11 INTEGRATION OF INDIVIDUAL GOALS AND ORGANISATIONAL GOALS

As stated earlier, a 'psychological contact' exists between the individual and the organisation. The process of fulfilling the mutual expectations of the two under this contract is known as **'reciprocation'**. The individual and the organisation become a part of each other under this process. The individual feels a part of the organisation and at the same time feels a representative of the organisation. This reciprocation or integration between individual and organisational goals can be achieved in the following ways :

1. **Fusion Process : Internalisation of Organisational Goals:** When the individual accepts organisational goals as his own and develops a personal commitment to them, there is internalisation of organisational goals. In other words, a **'fusion process'** occurs leading to the integration between organisational goals and individual goals.[17]

   The interaction between the individual and the organisation leads to two sub-processes, namely, (*i*) socialisation, and (*ii*) personalisation. **Socialisation** is the process through which the individual is made an agent of the organisation. **Personalisation** is the process through which the individual fulfils his personal goal of self-actualisation and the organisation is made an agent for the individual.[18]

   Both socialisation and personalisation occur simultaneously in an organisation. Socialisation process is stronger when organisational goals are being achieved without contribtuing much towards the achievement of individual goals. On the contrary, if individual goals are achieved without much contribution to the organisational goals, personalisation process is stronger. The aim of the fusion process is to maintain a balance or equilibrium between individuals, informal groups and the formal organisation. The individual as well as the organisation are benefited when the fusion process is strong.

2. **Inducement-Contribution Process:** According to March and Simon[19], inducement-contribution process operates as follows :

16 Robert Dubin (ed.), **Human Relations in Administration,** Prentice Hall, New Delhi, 1974.
17 E.W. Bakke, **The Fusion Process,** Yale University Press, New Haven, 1953, p. 20.
18 E.W. Bakke and Chris Argyris, **Organisation Structure and Dynamics,** Yale University Press, New Haven, 1954.
19 James G. March and Herbert A. Simon, **Organisations,** John Wiley & Sons, New York, 1958.

(*i*) Each participant or member of the organisation gets inducements for his contributions to the organisation.

(*ii*) Each participant continues to make contributions so long as the inducements offered are more or equal to his contributions.

(*iii*) The contributions of members and groups are the source from which the organisation offers inducements to them.

(*iv*) The organisation will continue to offer inducements and receive contributions so long as contributions are sufficient to give inducements.

Reciprocity between the individual and the organisation is the basis of the inducement–contribution process. A higher level of reciprocity leads to greater integration of their goals. Such integration in turn results in higher satisfaction of individuals and greater organisational effectiveness.

TEST QUESTIONS

1. What is meant by organisational goals? Explain their functions.
2. Describe and distinguish between official goals and real goals of an organisation.
3. Explain the goal setting process.
4. "Organisations are coalitions of individuals and groups". Comment. Does the coalition concept adequately explain goal setting in organisations?
5. Explain how does environment influence organisational goals.
6. Distinguish between goal succession and goal distortion. Why does goal distortion occur?
7. Discuss the concept and causes of goal displacement. How can goal displacement be checked?
8. "Organisation goals are often set in complicated power-play involving individuals and groups within and without the organisation." Discuss.
9. "The properties of formal organisations are such that incongruency between individual goals and organisation goals is inevitable". Explain this statement and suggest ways to achieve congruency between the goals of the two.
10. Explain the process of translation of general goals into operational goals in an organisation. How can it lead to goal distortion? Discuss with the help of some examples.
11. "Goal distortion occurs during the process of translation of stated goals into operational goals in an organisation". Explain.
12. Why does incongruency between organisational goals and individual goals occur?
13. "The properties of formal organisations are such that incongruency between individual objectives and organisational objectives is inevitable". Do you agree? Give reasons.
14. "The demands of the formal organisation are contrary to the needs of individuals". Critically examine this statement.

15. Write short notes on:
    (*a*) Ends-Means chain
    (*b*) Fusion Process
    (*c*) Inducement-Contribution Process
    (*d*) Goal Incongruency
    (*e*) Reconciliation of Individual and Organisational Goals.
16. "The dilemma between the needs of the individuals and the demands of the organisation is a basic, continual dilemma". Do you agree? Give reasons.

CASE STUDY

ABC Company produced several types of recreational products such as small pleasure boats, campers, and related accessories. Most of the operations were divided into two activities—manufacturing the various component parts and assembling these parts into finished products. There were eight different assembly lines in the plant which assembled twenty-seven different products. However, only eight different products could be produced at the same time. As seasonal demand for the various products changed, assembly lines were reconstituted. These tended to be little change in the staffing of these lines, since most of the work was of an assembly type nature and these skills were transferable between almost all products.

The general manager of ABC Company has recently attended some production management seminar in which the speakers made frequent reference to the 'Volvo Concept'. This concept referred to Volvo's move in one of its plants, from an assembly line operation to one designed around small work teams. Each of these teams was responsible for a significant portion of the final automobile (such as assembling an entire engine) and the groups were given considerable freedom to choose their own work methods and perform their own quality control functions. The work groups were also segregated from each other to increase the 'group feeling'. The general manager was seriously considering implementing the 'Volvo Concept' in his plant.

Questions

(*i*) What factors should be considered in deciding whether or not the idea should be used?

(*ii*) What problems would likely be encountered in implementing the 'Volvo Concept'?

CHAPTER

17

ORGANISATIONAL CHANGE

CHAPTER OUTLINE

17.1. Concept and Nature of Organisational Change
17.2. Factors or Forces in Organisational Change
  17.2.1 External Forces
  17.2.2 Internal Forces
17.3. The Process of Planned Change
17.4. Causes of Resistance to Change
  17.4.1 Individual Resistance to Change
  17.4.2 Group Resistance to Change
  17.4.3 Organisational Resistance to Change
17.5. Overcoming Resistance to Change
17.6. Group Dynamics for Change
17.7. Force Field Analysis
17.8. Change Agents
17.9. Organisational Growth and Change
- **Test Questions**
- **Case Study**

Change is inevitable and organisations must respond to it in order to survive and grow.

17.1 CONCEPT AND NATURE OF ORGANISATIONAL CHANGE

The term organisational change means any alteration in the overall work environment of an organisation. It involves alterations in structural relationships and role of people in the organisation. It requires a new equilibrium between different components of the organisation — job design, technology, structure and people.

Organisational change is **characterised** by the following features :

(*i*) Organisational change is a continuous or ongoing process.

(*ii*) Change is created by forces both inside and outside an organisation.

(*iii*) A change in any one part may affect the whole organisation.

(*iv*) Change occurs in all parts of the organisation but its speed and magnitude may vary from one part to another.

(*v*) Change may affect the structure, technology, people and other elements of the organisation.

(*vi*) Resistance to change is not always bad. It may provide an opportunity to the management to re-evaluate the change. It can suggest better ways to introduce change. It may help the organisation to prevent collapse.

(*vii*) When change takes place in any part of the organisation, it disturbs the existing equilibrium and requires a new equilibrium. The type of new equilibrium depends on the degree of change and its impact on the organisation. Evolutionary or incremental change may not require much alteration in the *status quo*. But revolutionary (sudden and rapid) change needs a new equilibrium.

Keith Davis explains the nature of work change by experimenting with an air-filled balloon. He argues, "When a finger (which represents change) is pressed against the exterior of the balloon (which represents the organisation) the contour visibly changes at the point of impact. The molecules of air in the balloon represent firm's employees. Repeated pressure at the point may unnecessarily weaken the balloon at that point. Pressure and motion create friction and heat. Eventually a rupture occurs, and the organisation collapses".[1] But an organisation is much more complex than the balloon, and the real people are quite different from molecules in the balloon. Just like molecules, an organisation also strives to achieve equilibrium. By equilibrium we mean that people learn to expect harmonious relationships within their working environment. When equilibrium exists, it becomes easier for people to adjust and adapt. Organisational change is so complex that management must convince employees to accept it. Change upsets personal and group relationships which must be adjusted and restored.

(*viii*) There is a dilemma of change. Organisations prefer a predictable and certain environment for day-to-day activities. But changes in external environment require change in *status quo*. Change is necessary to remain competitive in a changing environment. An organic organisation is oriented towards change while a mechanistic organisation is oriented towards stability. The uncertainty and unpredictability created by environmental changes can be reduced through planned change.

(*ix*) People respond to change either positively or negatively. These responses depend on how they perceive change — desirable or undesirable. Perception in turn depends on attitudes. Personal, social and psychological factors shape a person's attitude. Evaluation of change in the light of these factors leads to one of the four basic reactions — acceptance, tolerance, resistance and rejection. [Fig. 17.1]

If an employee perceives a change as beneficial and feels capable of adjusting to it, he may accept or tolerate change. On the other hand, if he feels change is harmful to him and he is incapable of adjusting to it, he may resist or reject change.[2]

---

1 Keith Davis, **Human Behaviour at Work,** Tata McGraw-Hill, New Delhi, 1975, pp. 154-155.

2 Arnold Judson, **A Managerial Guide to Making Changes**, John Wiley & Sons, London, 1966, pp. 41-43.

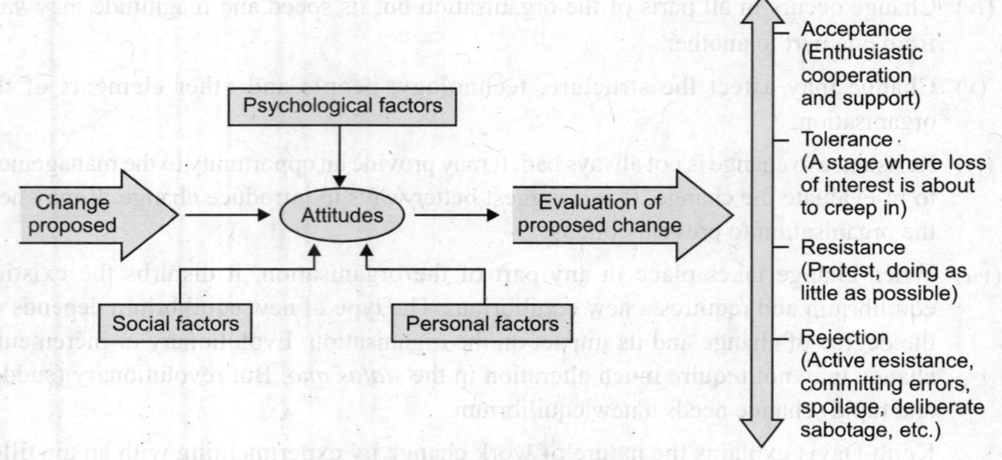

Fig. 17.1: Forces for Change

17.2 FACTORS OR FORCES IN ORGANISATIONAL CHANGE

Pressure for change arises from both external and internal forces.

17.2.1 External Forces

(*i*) **Technology:** It is a major external force which requires change. The rate of technological change is greater today than any time in the past. Technological changes are responsible for changing the nature of jobs performed at all levels in the organisation. Knowledge explosion, more particularly computer technology and automation, has made a remarkable impact on the functioning of organisations in the recent times.[3] Technological change has become increasingly rapid, diverse and complex. Therefore, managers must modify organisation structures and job designs, etc. to successfully meet the requirements of new technology.

(*ii*) **Market Situation:** Market conditions are changing rapidly. The needs, desires and expectations of customers change frequently. Moreover, competition in the market is increasing. New and innovative products and services are being launched. New media of advertising and publicity are being used to influence customers. All these changes create tremendous pressure on an organisation to develop new strategies.

(*iii*) **Social Changes:** Attitudes, customs and values of society are changing due to growing literacy and media exposure. Women empowerment, sexual harassment at work-place, environmental protection, etc. have created new challenges for management. Organisations must change their policies and practices to meet society's aspirations.

(*iv*) **Political Forces:** Political developments inside and outside the country have a major impact on organisations. The relationship between government and business has become quite complex. New laws and regulations affect the corporate sector. Business

3 Charles Handy, "The Changing Shape of Work", **Organisational Dynamics,** Autumn, 1980, p. 28.

organisations have no control over the political and legal forces. They have to adapt to meet the new requirements.

17.2.2 Internal Forces

(*i*) **Changes in Managerial Personnel:** New managers are replacing the old managers due to retirement, resignations, promotions and transfers. Each new manager brings his own ideas and working style in the organisation. Changes in the top management may lead to sweeping changes in the organisation. A new chief executive recruited from outside may modify the organisation structure, work allocation, reward and control system, etc.

(*ii*) **Changes in Workforce:** The nature of workforce is changing rapidly. The new generation of workers is better educated, more freedom loving and expect a humanitarian work culture. Their expectations are high and loyalty to the organisation is low. The organisation must handle them effectively.

(*iii*) **Deficiencies in Existing Structure:** Changes are also required to remove weaknesses in the existing structure and system. These deficiencies may be in the form of long chain of command, too narrow or too wide span of control, lack of coordination between departments, obstacles in communication, multiple committees, lack of uniformity in policies, etc. These deficiencies must be removed before they lead to a major crisis.

The Domino Effect: Another major source of change is the change itself. One change creates a chain of related and supporting changes. This is called domino effect. For example, creation of a new department may lead to introduction of new managerial posts, reallocation of work in other departments and so on. If managers overlook the potential domino effect of change, problems of coordination and control may arise. Therefore, undesirable chain reactions must be examined and evaluated before introducing a change.

Proactive and Reactive Change: A change initiated by an organisation on its own because it is considered desirable is known as **proactive change.** For example, the management of a company introduces an employee benefit scheme to improve the motivation and productivity of employees. Dynamic organisations anticipate the future and introduce changes to remain effective in future. On the other hand, a change implemented by an organisation due to pressure from environmental forces is **reactive change.** For example, a company introduces an employee benefit scheme due to strike from labour union. Reactive organisations stick to old policies and practices and remain out of step with changing times.

Successful organisations do not wait for the future. They make the future by planning and implementing change.

17.3 THE PROCESS OF PLANNED CHANGE

Planned change means a planned alteration in the existing structure, system, policies, practices or other elements of an organisation to achieve something. According to Bennis, "Planned change encompasses the application of systematic and appropriate knowledge to human affairs for the purpose of creating intelligent action and choices".[4] An organisation can achieve its goals rapidly through planned change. The main reasons for planned change are as follows[5]:

(*i*) to improve the means for satisfying economic needs of members;

(*ii*) to increase profitability;

(*iii*) to promote human work for human beings;

(*iv*) to contribute to individual satisfaction and social well-being. Systematic planning and implementation of change helps to overcome resistance to change on an enduring basis.

Kurt Lewin[6] has identified the following stages in the process of planned change :

1. **Unfreezing the Status Quo:** It means making people realize that the present behaviour is inappropriate, irrelevant, inadequate and, therefore, unsuitable to the changing demands of the situation. Unfreezing involves breaking down the existing habits, attitudes and ways of doing work. It requires discarding the current routines, work relationships and behaviour patterns. Rewards for willingness to change and punishment for unwillingness to change may be used for this purpose. It is the responsibility of managers, as change agents, to overcome complacency, self-righteousness and resistance on the part of employees. Discussions with subordinates can clear their doubts about the proposed change. Deficiencies in the present state of affairs, the need for change, the speed and magnitude of proposed change, the direction and implications of such change can be explained to them to ensure unfreezing.

2. **Moving or Changing:** Once the employees are convinced of the need for change, the proposed change is introduced in a systematic manner. During this phase, people learn to behave in new and better ways. Behavioural changes are difficult and several problems arise in their implementation. Employees may be offered alternatives out of which they choose. Moving phase involves[7]:

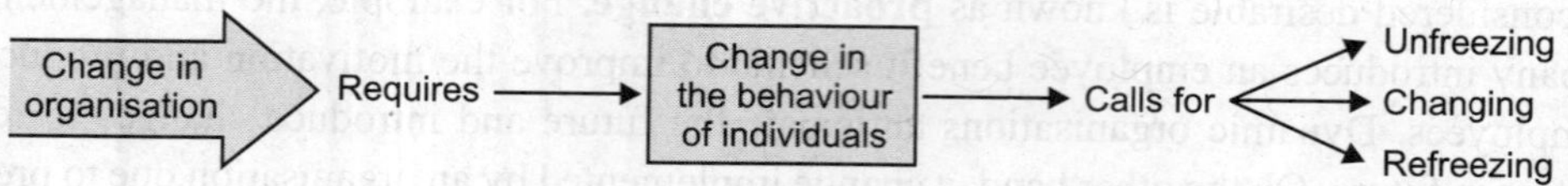

Fig. 17.2: The Change Process

(*a*) Compliance — individuals are forced to change by rewards or punishment.

(*b*) Internalisation — individuals are forced to face a situation that calls for new behaviour.

(*c*) Identification — individuals choose one among various models that is most suitable to their personality.

---

4 Warren Bennis, **The Planning of Change,** Harper & Row, New York, 1985.

5 Edgar Williams, "Changing System and Behaviour", **Business Horizons,** August 1969, pp. 53-58.

6 Kurt Lewin, "Frontiers in Group Dynamics : Concept, Methods, Reality in Social Sciences, Social Equilibrium and Social Change", **Human Relations,** June 1947, pp. 5-41.

7 H.C. Kolman, "Compliance, Identification and Internalisation: Three Phases of Attitude Change", **Conflict Resolution,** 1958 (2), pp. 51-60.

3. **Refreezing at the New Level:** During this phase, people internalise the new beliefs, attitudes and behaviour learned in the 'moving' phase. In other words, they accept these as a permanent part of their behaviour. The new roles, relationship and behaviour patterns must be stabilised through various types of reinforcements.

17.4 CAUSES OF RESISTANCE TO CHANGE

Resistance to change is one of the baffling problems faced by managers. Resistance may be overt or implicit or passive; or covert or explicit or active. Implicit resistance occurs in the form of tardiness, reduced motivation to work, increased absenteeism, request for transfer, etc. Explicit resistance takes place in the form of resignation, sabotage, violence, wild-cat strikes, etc. Change may be resisted at individual level, group level and organisation level.

17.4.1 Individual Resistance to Change

Individuals resist change due to several reasons :

1. **Economic Reasons:** These include :

   (*a*) Fear of technological unemployment, *i.e.,* loss of job due to new technology.

   (*b*) Fear of reduced work hours and consequently reduced pay.

   (*c*) Fear of demotion due to obsolescence of skills.

   (*d*) Fear of higher job standards and reduced incentive pay.

2. **Social Reasons:** These consist of :

   (*a*) People working together develop informal or social relationships. Introduction of change often disturbs or **interrupts these social relationships.** Employees dislike breakup of friendships with colleagues. They try to maintain friendship and fight **social displacement** by resisting change.

   (*b*) Sometimes an individual is willing to accept change but resists it due to **peer pressure.** His coworkers pressurise him to oppose change.

   (*c*) Individuals resist changes which are introduced **abruptly** without consulting them.

   (*d*) Changes are also resisted because workers fear that the **new social setup** will be less satisfying than the existing setup.

3. **Psychological Reasons:** These comprise :

   (*a*) Individuals attach great importance to **status quo**. Change creates uncertainty which is inconvenient and uncomfortable to them.

   (*b*) Change implies that the present behaviour is not adequate and suitable. Employees do not like such **criticism**.

   (*c*) Change is resisted due to the **fear of unknown.** People fear the consequences of change and therefore oppose it. For example, an employee may refuse promotion which requires transfer to an unknown place.

(*d*) Sometimes an individual resists change due to **ego-defensiveness.** For instance, a good suggestion made by a salesperson to increase sales is rejected by the sales manager who feels accepting the suggestion will hurt his ego.

17.4.2 Group Resistance to Change

Informal groups often resist change when they fear that it threatens their unity and existence. This is more likely when members have a strong sense of belonging to the group[8]. A study on the impact of technological change in the coal mining industry in England highlighted group resistance to change. Under the old system (shortwall method) miners worked in small independent teams. Each team was responsible for the total operation of cutting, loading and removing coal from a small section of coal face. The introduction of mechanical equipment for coal cutting and conveyors disrupted these small groups. The new system (longwall method) required large groups each consisting of 40 to 50 workers. The workers were so located that face-to-face relationship and communication was obstructed. Workers felt uprooted from their workgroup mooring, experienced loss of meaning in work and a sense of being unrelated to one another. They developed attitude of passivity and indifference and productivity suffered.[9]

17.4.3 Organisational Resistance to Change

Resistance to change may also occur at organisational level. Organisational resistance to change is caused by :

(*a*) **Threat to Power and Influence:** Top executives may resist a change which is a potential threat to their position and influence in the organisation. Novel ideas and new use of resources can disrupt power relationships.

(*b*) **Resource Constraints:** An organisation may resist change when it lacks resources which are essential for implementing the change. For example, a company may not have adequate funds needed to investment in new technology.

(*c*) **Sunk Costs:** The huge capital blocked in fixed assets may cause a problem in automation. Sunk costs are not restricted to physical assets. The knowledge and skills of employees may become redundant and retraining may be essential for introducing information technology.

(*d*) **Organisation Structure:** Some organisation structures have built-in mechanism for resistance to change. For example, in a typically bureaucratic structure jobs are narrowly defined, lines of authority are clearly spelled out and the flow of information is top to bottom. In such an organisation new ideas do not flow upwards the hierarchy. One study[10] of twenty companies in England revealed that 'mechanistic' organisations tend to resist change.

---

8 D.A. Trumbo, "Individual and Group Correlates of Attitudes Towards Work-related Change", **Journal of Applied Psychology,** 1961 (45), pp. 338-344.

9 E.L. Trist and K.W. Bamforth, "Some Social and Psychological Consequences of the Longwall Method of Coal-getting", **Human Relations,** 1951 (4), pp. 346-348.

10 Tom Burns and G.M. Stalker, **The Management of Innovation,** Tavistock Publication, London, 1961.

17.5 OVERCOMING RESISTANCE TO CHANGE

Managers can adopt the following techniques to overcome resistance to change by employees:

1. **Education and Training:** Many people resist change because they do not understand its consequences. Such misunderstanding can be removed by educating the people. Employees must be taught new skills and oriented in new relationships.
2. **Communication:** Communication helps people to understand the need and logic of change. It is an effective method when resistance is caused by inadequate or inaccurate information. Two-way communication is useful in removing fear and insecurity of employees. Managers should explain:
   (*a*) What the change is?
   (*b*) Why the change is needed?
   (*c*) How it will be implemented?
   (*d*) When it is to be introduced?
   (*e*) What will be its benefits to the employees?

   Once the employees are persuaded, they will help in the implementation of change. However, this method involves considerable time and effort.
3. **Participation and Involvement:** Employees can be actively involved in the design and implementation of change. A dialogue with the employees allows them to express their doubts and views. Such involvement and participation clears misunderstanding and satisfies the ego of employees. Labour leaders who are taken into confidence can convince the workers to accept change. Participation also increases commitment of those who have considerable power to resist change. The relevant information which they provide can be integrated into the change plan. But participation and involvement is very time-consuming.
4. **Facilitation and Support:** This method involves listening, providing emotional support, giving training in new skills and allowing employees time off after a difficult period. Support may be facilitative and emotional. Facilitative support implies removing physical barriers in implementing change by providing appropriate tools, materials, advice and training. Emotional support involves compassionate listening and helping people overcome their anxiety and stress. Facilitation and support are most helpful when resistance arises due to fear, anxiety and adjustment problems. But this method can be time-consuming and expensive with no guarantee of success.
5. **Negotiation and Agreement:** This method is helpful when the group has considerable power to resist change. It is relatively easy to avoid major resistance through negotiation and incentives.

   For example, agreement with labour union, promotion of union nominees and sharing gains of change with employees can overcome major resistance to change.
6. **Manipulation and Cooperation:** In rare cases managers may use covert methods to overcome resistance to change. Manipulation involves conscious structuring of events

and the very selective use of information. Under cooptation key persons are given a desirable role in design or implementation of change. This method is relatively quick and inexpensive. But it may backfire if people feel they are manipulated.

7. **Explicit or Implicit Coercion:** Managers may force people to accept change through explicit or implicit threats. Withholding promotion, dismissal, transfer are examples of such threats. This method is less time-consuming and is used when speedy implementation of change is essential.

   Managers often commit the mistake of using only one method. For example, a **people oriented** boss adopts participation and involvement while a **task oriented** boss often coerces people[11]. A combination of two or more methods may be more effective. But the combination or mix must be appropriate to the specific situation.

17.6 GROUP DYNAMICS FOR CHANGE

Group dynamics refers to the forces operating within a group. Hawthorne Experiments revealed that when a group opposes some change its members resist change. Any worker who deviated from the group norms was penalised by his co-workers. In the words of Kurt Lewin, "As long as group standards are unchanged the individual will resist changes more strongly the farther he is to depart from group standard. If group standard itself is changed, the resistance which is due to the relation between individual and group standard is eliminated."[12] Lewin's experiments also showed that group discussions are more effective in changing attitudes than lectures and one-to-one discussions.

Managers should, therefore, use the group as a medium of change. While using group as a means of overcoming resistance to change, the following characteristics[13] of group must be considered:

(i) **Strong Sense of Belonging:** When the members have a strong attachment, the group can be effectively used as an agent of change.

(ii) **Group Prestige:** The more cohesive is a group, the more effectively it can serve as a medium of change.

(iii) **Group Purpose:** A group can be more successful in changing the attitudes, values and behaviour of its members in the areas which are related to its purpose. For example, a labour union can exert influence over workers regarding strikes and lockouts.

(iv) **Individual Prestige:** The member who enjoys high prestige in the group can greatly influence other members.

---

11 John P. Kotter and Leonard A. Schlesinger, "Choosing Strategies for Change", **Harvard Business Review,** March-April, 1979.

12 Kurt Lewin, "Group Decision and Social Change" in G.E. Swanson, *et. al.* (eds.), **Readings in Social Psychology,** Holt Rinehart Winston, New York, 1952, p. 472.

13 Darwin Cartwright, "Achieving Change in People: Some Applications of Group Dynamics Theory, in I.L. Hechmann Jr. *et. al.* (eds.), **Human Relations in Management**, South-West Publishing, Cincinnati, 1960, pp. 404-467.

(*v*) **Group Norms:** Any change that requires members to deviate from the group's norms is strongly resisted. Therefore, the idea of homeostasis must be considered in group interactions.

(*vi*) **Shared Perception:** Change can be easily implemented if the group members share perception that change is needed. The source of pressure for change lies within the group.

(*vii*) **Shared Information:** When members of a group are well informed about the nature of and need for change, it becomes easy to implement the change.

17.7 FORCE FIELD ANALYSIS

Kurt Lewin has developed a model that contains a scientific and constructive approach for analysing the forces affecting change. These forces are of two types:

(*i*) **Driving forces** which push or favour the change.

(*ii*) **Restraining forces** which oppose change.

Change is a dynamic balance of these forces which move in opposite direction. Any behaviour is the outcome of an equilibrium between driving and restraining forces. If these forces are equal in strength there will be no change in the *status quo*. But when the forces are unequal in strength, existing equilibrium will be disturbed. In case diving forces dominate the restraining forces, desired change will be attained. On the other hand, when restraining forces dominate, there will be a downward change.

Force field analysis suggests that before deciding a change strategy, managers must properly identify and evaluate the strength of driving and restraining forces. Such analysis will enable them to remove the hindrances that block change efforts. At the same time, a manager should not waste his time and energy on those forces over which he has no control.

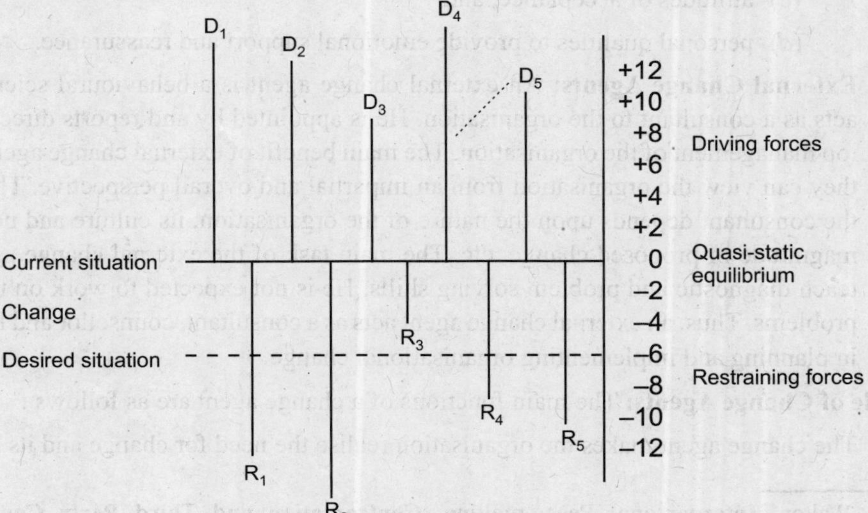

Fig. 17.3: Force Field Analysis

17.8 CHANGE AGENTS

Any planned change requires change agents. A change agent is a person who initiates change in the organisation. Change agents are of two types — internal and external.

1. **Internal Change Agents:** The managers of an organisation are the internal change agents. They are continuously involved in the process of change in the organisation. They not only initiate changes but also take steps to implement them. Internal change agents may be classified into two broad categories as follows:

   (*i*) **Chief Executive:** The chief executive sponsors the change and provides leadership and support to ensure its successful implementation. The role of the chief executive is crucial in the initial stage of change process. His personal commitment to the change programme and his conviction in its success is essential. As the change process gains momentum, heads of major units gradually take over the responsibility from the chief executive.

   (*ii*) **Change Advisors:** The key executives of the organisation who are selected to work in close harmony with the external change agent act as change advisors. They are trained by the external consultant for implementing the change. The change advisors educate the managers in the concepts and methods of various change techniques. They assist managers in developing appropriate skills and behaviour for the change process. The role of change advisors is persuading people to accept and internalise the values and practices needed for smooth implementation of change. An organisation must carefully select and train its change agents. Some of the qualities of change agents are as follows[14]:

   (*a*) diagnostic skills;

   (*b*) behavioural skills in breaking impasses and in interrupting repetitive interchange;

   (*c*) attitudes of acceptance; and

   (*d*) personal qualities to provide emotional support and reassurance.

2. **External Change Agents:** An external change agent is a behavioural scientist who acts as a consultant to the organisation. He is appointed by and reports directly to the top management of the organisation. The main benefit of external change agents is that they can view the organisation from an impartial and overall perspective. The role of the consultant depends upon the nature of the organisation, its culture and norms, the magnitude of proposed change, etc. The main task of the external change agent is to teach diagnostic and problem solving skills. He is not expected to work on the actual problems. Thus, an external change agent acts as a consultant, counsellor and facilitator in planning and implementing organisational change.

Role of Change Agents: The main functions of a change agent are as follows :

(*i*) The change agent makes the organisation realise the need for change and its benefits.

14 R. Walton, **Interpersonal Peace-making, Confrontation and Third Party Consultation,** Addison-Wesley, Reading Mass, 1969, p. 131.

(*ii*) The change agent diagnoses to identify the problems the organisation is likely to face during and after the change process.

(*iii*) The change agent prepares a blueprint of the actions to be taken for implementing the change.

(*iv*) Any change moves the organisation to a new equilibrium. The change efforts will fail unless the new equilibrium is maintained. The change agent helps the organisation in stabilising new behaviour and change.

(*v*) The change agent prepares the client organisation to take over and maintain the change effort itself.

The specific role and functions of a change agent may vary from one organisation to another depending upon the particular situation.

In the highly competitive and turbulent environment, organisations need to continuously rejuvenate and rebuild themselves. The following steps can help in achieving a lasting change:

1. **Establish a Sense of Urgency:** It is not easy to drive people out of their comfort zones. A sense of urgency makes the organisation initiate and gain momentum around change. The top management team must encourage employees to think differently, explore the unknown and experiment with new ideas.
2. **Be a Catalyst for Cultural Change:** Culture is the most difficult to change. To initiate and sustain cultural change, the management must create a 'shared' vision and make it a part of the organisation's DNA. Unless each artery/vein of the organisation carries the fresh blood, the vision will not be a shared one.
3. **Strong Teamwork:** Transforming an organisation is a massive combined effort. The team must adopt a solution-based approach. It is this teamwork that lays the foundation for cross-functional collaboration and develops an infectious energy to take the organisation beyond normal performance. Rules are re-written and average performers start to perform beyond expectations.

[Based on Aarif Aziz, "Three Steps to Scripting a Lasting Change", *Indian Management*, January, 2013, pp. 56-58]

17.9 ORGANISATIONAL GROWTH AND CHANGE

Growth of an organiastion is a type of change. But such change is neither smooth nor linear. Problems arise at different stages of growth and an organisation faces turmoil in its life. Managers face a great challenge in dealing with these problems. Greiner[15] has developed a model of organisational growth by making use of five key dimensions:

(*i*) **Age of the organisation:** Life span of an organisation is the key dimension.

(*ii*) **Size of the organisation:** With increase in size, the problems of an organisation tend to multiply. Problems of communication and coordination multiply as jobs become more interrelated and levels of management hierarchy increase.

---

15 Larry E. Greiner, "Evolution and Revolution as Organisations Grow", **Harvard Business Review,** July-August, 1972, pp. 36-46.

(*iii*) **Stages of Evolution:** The organisation that survives a crisis usually enjoys four to eight years of continuous growth without setback or severe internal disruption. These prolonged periods of growth are described as evolution.

(*iv*) **Stages of Revolution:** These are periods of substantial turmoil in the life of an organisation. These space between the smooth periods of evolution.

"Each evolutionary period is characterized by the dominant management style used to achieve growth, while each revolutionary period is characterised by the dominant problem that must be solved before growth will continue"[16]

(*v*) **Growth Rate of Industry:** It influences the speed at which periods of evolution and revolution occur.

Greiner's five stages of growth are as follows:

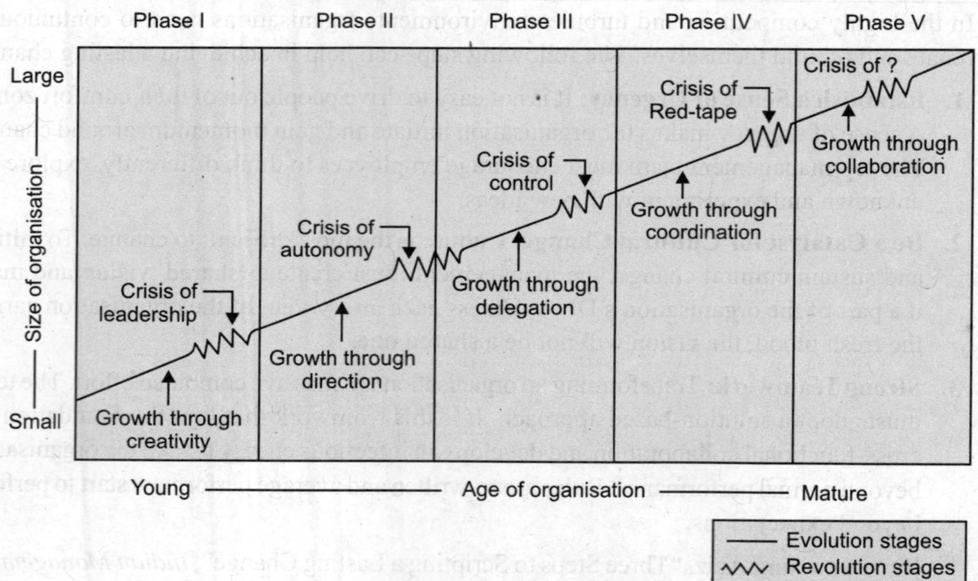

Fig. 17.4: Griener's growth model

1. **Creativity Stage:** During this stage, the emphasis is on creating both 'product' and 'market'. Generally, the founders have technical or entrepreneurial orientation. Their physical and mental energies are absorbed entirely in making and selling a new product. Communication among the employees is informal. As the organisation starts growing from its embryonic stage, problems crop up. For instance, increased number of employees cannot be managed exclusively through informal communication. New accounting procedures may be needed and additional capital must be raised: At this point a crisis of leadership occurs, which is the onset of the first revolution. The fundamental problem here is "who is to lead the company out of confusion and solve managerial problems confronting it"? The founders must choose and appoint competent managers who can pull the organisation together. The organisation survives through effective leadership and proceeds further.

16 *Ibid*, p. 40.

2. **Direction Stage:** At this stage, a functional structure, systematic accounting procedures, budgets and work standards are introduced. Communication becomes formal and leadership is task oriented. Professional managers at the top direct the operations and lower level managers act as functional specialists with little authority to take decisions. After a period of growth, lower level managers demand more autonomy in decision-making. A 'crisis of autonomy' occurs and further growth is hindered in the absence of adequate delegation of authority to the lower levels.
3. **Delegation Stage:** Top managers delegate authority which motivates lower levels. Greater authority and incentives enable lower level managers to penetrate large markets and develop new customers. The organisation expands in a decentralised structure. But top executives feel that they are losing control over highly diversified operations. A crisis of control arises.
4. **Coordination Stage:** The activities of various departments are coordinated to overcome the problem of control. Formal planning procedures are created, decentralised units are merged into product groups and technical functions such as data processing are centralised. However, the daily operating decisions remain decentralised. Top management imposes rules and regulations to ensure proper allocation and use of resources. With increase in size of the organisation, formal authority and rigid system eventually result in the crisis of red-tape.
5. **Collaboration Stage:** The crisis of red-tape and conflicts between line and staff are overcome through strong interpersonal collaboration. There is greater spontaneity in management action through teams and skilful handling of interpersonal differences. Social control and self-discipline replace formal control. At this stage top management adopts a more flexible and behavioural approach. Greiner did not identify the next period of crisis. However, he anticipated a 'psychological saturation of employees'. The employees grow emotionally and become physically exhausted due to the intensity of teamwork and the heavy pressure for innovative solutions.

Greiner's model takes into account the critical dimension of time while analysing the problems at different stages of growth. This model is typical for organisations with moderate growth over a long period of time. Fast growing companies experience the above five stages more rapidly. On the other hand, slow growing companies encounter only two or at the most three stages over many years.

TEST QUESTIONS

1. Explain the concept and nature of organisational change.
2. Describe the external and internal forces that create the need for change in organisations.
3. Why do people generally resist change? Identify the major factors which play a significant role in this process. Discuss, what are the common strategies for change and its management.
4. Discuss various strategies used in implementing organisational change in the context of a large public sector manufacturing organisation.
5. Identify some major characteristics found in successful organisational changes.
6. How does Lewin's model of change deal with the forces resisting changes?

7. Describe the techniques the organisational design specialists use to help bring out a change in organisations.
8. Why do people generally resist change? Do personal factors play a role in this process? Briefly discuss the common coping strategies for change.
9. "Organisations respond to their environment by developing many alternative strategies and corresponding structure." Explain this statement.
10. Change is highly important to the success of an organisation, but many people have the tendency, overtly or covertly, to resist it. How do you think resistance to change can be overcome?
11. Write notes on the following :
    (*a*) Force field analysis;
    (*b*) Stages in Lewin's model of change;
    (*c*) Stages in organisational growth.
    (*d*) The Domino Effect
12. How does change affect an organisation? Suggest a suitable approach for introducing change successfully in an organisation.
13. "Change and continuity are the dual realities of organisations which always move together." Discuss the relevance of this statement in the light of any major organisational change with which you are familiar. How do employees react to change in an organisation?
14. Explain what you believe are the most important features in the successful implementation of organisational change.
15. Why do individuals and organisations resist change? Explain instances of resistance to change in your own organisation and discuss critically the effectiveness of management actions to overcome the resistance.
16. Explain the role of external charge agent. What skills would you look for in a change agent?
17. Explain Kurt Lewin's model of organisational change. How does force field analysis help in the process of planned change?
18. Describe Greiner's model of organisational growth. What are the implications of this model for organisational change?
19. What are the reasons for resistance to change in organisations? What can management do to overcome such resistance?
20. "Change is a continuous process and not an end in itself". Examine this statement.
21. How far do you feel that managing change is an important part of maintaining organisational effectiveness?
22. "It is generally said that people resist change unless they are the creator of change." Critically evaluate the statement and discuss how one can overcome resistance to change.
23. As a result of economic reforms a large number of organisations in India are undergoing restructuring. Develop a change management programme for smooth restructuring.
24. (*a*) Compare the planned change model of change with Lewin's three-step model.
    (*b*) Identify the forces causing resistance to change programmes.
25. Discuss the reasons for organisational resistance to change. Suggest suitable strategies for overcoming resistance to change.
26. "Change in one part of the organisation affects the entire organisation". Comment.

27. "In our rapidly changing technological society, resistance to change is a normal result of psychological, economic or social factors or a combination of these three" (Jack Halloran). Comment.
28. Describe Greiner's model of organisational growth and change. For an organisation in which you have worked, can you identify a crisis described in the model that affected it? How was the crisis resolved?
29. Distinguish between reactive and proactive change.
30. Explain the process of planned change as suggested by Kurt Lewin.
31. To what extent group dynamics can be used to overcome resistance to change? Explain.
32. "People sometimes resist change for the sake of resistance". Explain.
33. "Several economic, social and psychological factors cause resistance to change". Elaborate.
34. "Change is highly important for the success of an organisation but people tend to resist it overtly or covertly". Explain in this context the reasons for resistance to change.
35. "Growing organisations move through relatively calm periods of evolution, each of which ends with a period of revolution and crisis." Explain the problems that managers face at different stages of organisational growth.
36. Discuss various traditional approaches to planned change. Give their advantages and limitations.
37. "Change for the sake of change is not change at all". Comment on this statement and show why change for the sake of change could be detrimental to the health of the organisation.
38. "For any change, there is always some resistance". Justify this statement and suggest strategies to make change effective for the organisation.
39. Explain systems theory of organisational change.
40. Describe in brief various theories of planned change. What are the limitations of these theories?

CASE STUDY

Strong Bond Company is a medium-sized enterprise which has followed a policy of growth through acquisitions. Six years ago, it took over Stickwell Adhesives as a subsidiary. Although Stickwell was the third largest adhesive manufacturer in the country, its sales and profits position had rapidly deteriorated. The management of Strong Bond felt that it was a good buy in the depressed condition and they were confident of turning it around.

The first new general manager of Strong Bond tried for five years to change the profit position, but he met with little success. Strickwell operates two plants, both in rural areas in the East and the South. Each plant employs approximately 800 people. At both the plants, the employees and management are very set in their ways and are non-receptive of new ideas. In fact last year at one plant, the workers almost rebelled against top management.

Questions

1. What are the barriers to change in this case?
2. How can new ideas become accepted at the plants?
3. Which techniques of change can be useful in this case?

CHAPTER

18

ORGANISATION DEVELOPMENT

CHAPTER OUTLINE

18.1. Concept of Organisation Development (OD)
18.2. Characteristics of Organisation Development
18.3. Difference between Organisation Development and Management Development
18.4. Objectives of Organisation Development
18.5. Benefits (Role) of Organisation Development
18.6. Limitations of Organisation Development
18.7. Assumptions of Organisation Development
18.8. Process of Organisation Development
18.9. Action Research Model of OD
18.10. OD Interventions or Techniques
18.10.1 Sensitivity Training
18.10.2 Grid Training
18.10.3 Survey Feedback
18.10.4 Process Consultation
18.10.5 Team Building
18.10.6 Management by Objectives
- **Test Questions**
- **Case Study**

A major problem in organisational change is alteration in everyone's entire set of formal and informal roles to support the change. Changing an individual alone creates role conflict because his peers, superiors and subordinates continue to expect the same roles from him. In order to change the entire role set, an integrated and comprehensive approach known as Organisation Development (OD) was developed in the 1960s.

18.1 CONCEPT OF ORGANISATION DEVELOPMENT

Some popular definitions of OD are given below:

"Organisation development is a planned process of change in an organisation's culture through the utilisation of behavioural science technology, research and theory."[1] — *Burke*

"Organisation development is a response to change, a complex educational strategy intended to change the beliefs, attitudes, values and structure of organisations so that they can better adapt to new technologies, markets and challenges, and the dizzing rate of change itself."[2] — *Bennis*

"Organisation development is a long range effort to improve an organisation's problem solving and renewal processes, particularly through a more effective and collaborative management of organisation culture — with special emphasis on the culture of formal work teams — with the assistance of a change agent or catalyst, and the use of the theory and technology of applied behaviour science including action research."[3]

— *French and Bell*

"Organisation development is an effort planned, organisation wide, and managed from the top to increase organisation effectiveness and health through planned interventions in the organisation's processes using behavioural science knowledge."[4] — *Beckhard*

18.2 CHARACTERISTICS OF ORGANISATION DEVELOPMENT

An analysis of the definitions given above reveals the following features of organisation development:

1. **Planned Change:** OD involves planned change for improvement of an organisation. It is different from haphazard and *ad hoc* change efforts which are frequently made by many organisations. OD requires planned interventions in the processes, structure, behaviour patterns, etc. of an organisation.
2. **Long Range:** OD is not meant to solve short-term, temporary or isolated problems. It is not a stop-gap measure. It is a long-term approach designed to elevate the organisation to a higher level of functioning by improving the performance and satisfaction of organisation members. An OD programme generally covers a period of three to five years.
3. **Comprehensive Strategy:** OD is broadbased and it involves change in the entire organisation. It is concerned with changes in the design, philosophy, technology, etc of the organisation as well as in the attitudes, skills and behaviour of its members. It involves organisation-wide efforts.

1 W, Warner Burke, **Organisation Development,** Little Brown, Boston, 1982, p. 10.

2 Warren G. Bennis, **Organisation Development : Its Nature, Origins and Prospects,** Addison-Wesley, Reading Mass, 1969, p. 2.

3 Wendell L. French and Cecil H. Bell, **Organisation Development,** Prentice Hall, New Delhi, 1978, p. 14.

4 R. Beckhard, **Organisation Development : Strategies and Models,** Addison-Wesley, Reading Mass, 1969, p. 9.

4. **Dynamic Process:** OD includes the efforts to guide and direct change as well as to cope with or adapt to imposed change. It recognises that the goals of an organisation change. Therefore, the methods of attaining them should also change. Thus, OD is not merely a one-shot deal, it is rather an ongoing, interactive and cyclical process.

5. **Systems Approach:** OD is based on systems thinking — open and adaptive systems concept. It recognises that an organisation is an interrelated whole and no part of the organisation can be changed without affecting other parts.

6. **Research-Based:** Under OD, change agents conduct surveys, collect data, evaluate and then decide the changes. Most of the OD interventions are research-based. Change agents are employed to carry out OD. There is a close working relationship between the change agent and the people who are being changed.

7. **Normative Educational Strategy:** OD is based on the principle that "norms form the basis for behaviour and change is a re-educative process of replacing old norms by new ones". It contains well-established principles regarding individual and group behaviours in the organisation. OD stresses human values and human side of organisational life.

8. **Managed from the Top:** OD efforts are initiated and controlled by top management of the organisation to bring about the desired change.

9. **Behavioural Approach:** OD involves use of knowledge drawn from behavioural sciences such as psychology, sociology and anthropology.

10. **Organisational Effectiveness:** The ultimate aim of OD is to increase the effectiveness of an organisation. OD techniques are designed to improve the problem-solving skills and adaptability of members of the organisation.

18.3 DIFFERENCE BETWEEN ORGANISATION DEVELOPMENT AND MANAGEMENT DEVELOPMENT

Organisation development differs from management development in several ways:

1. **Scope:** OD is a broader concept and management development is a part of it.

2. **Objective:** The primary objective of OD is to improve the total organisation while the objective of management development is to improve individuals (managers) so that they can discharge their responsibilities effectively.

3. **Time Span:** OD is a long-term strategy while management development is a short-term activity.

4. **Approach:** OD is a problem-solving approach but management development involves education and training. OD attempts to fit the organisation to the people whereas management development tries to fit the people to the existing organisation.

5. **Requirements:** OD requires the services of trained specialists. On the other hand, management development has no special requirements.

Management Development		Organisation Development
Objective:	Improving manager's contributions to goal accomplishment	Change the nature of the organisation.
Focus:	Train and equip employees and managers to perform better in existing organisation.	Focus on design, not on the manager, focus on achieving improvements in design.
Approach:	Education and training.	Problem-solving approach.
Time:	Short-range.	It is a long-range strategy for organisational innovation and renewal.
Specialist service:	No special requirements.	Trained specialists.

Source : Adapted from W.W. Burke and W.H. Schmidt, "Management and Organisation Development", *Personnel Administration,* March-April, 1971. pp. 46-52.

18.4 OBJECTIVES OF ORGANISATION DEVELOPMENT

Organisation development is designed to achieve the following objectives[5] :

(*i*) To increase the level of mutual trust and emotional support among all organisational members.

(*ii*) To increase the incidence of confrontation of organisational problems both within groups and among groups.

(*iii*) To create an environment in which authority of assigned role is augmented by authority based on knowledge and skill.

(*iv*) To increase the openness of communications, laterally, vertically and diagonally

(*v*) To increase the level of enthusiasm and personal satisfaction in the organisation.

(*vi*) To find synergistic solutions to problems with greater frequency.

(*vii*) To increase the level of self and group responsibility in planning and implementation.

18.5 BENEFITS (ROLE) OF ORGANISATION DEVELOPMENT

Organisation development offers the following benefits[6] :

1. Providing opportunities for people to function as human beings rather than as resources in the production process.
2. Providing opportunities for each organisation member, as well as for the organisation itself, to develop to his full potential.
3. Seeking to increase the effectiveness of the organisation in terms of all of its goals.
4. Attempting to create an environment in which it is possible to find exciting and challenging work.

---

5 Wendell French, "Organisation Development : Objectives, Assumptions and Strategies", **California Management Review,** 1969, pp. 23-46.

6 Newton Margulies and Anthony P. Raia, **Organisation Development : Values, Process and Technology,** McGraw-Hill, New York, 1972, p. 3.

5. Providing opportunities for people in organisations to influence the way in which they relate to work, the organisation, and the environment.
6. Treating each human being as a person with a complex set of needs, all of which are important in his work and in his life.

In the words of Davis, "OD tries to free up communication tightness by increasing the amount, trust and candour of communication. It seeks to build problem-solving capability of the organisation by improving group dynamics and problem confrontation. In short, it reaches into all aspects of organisation culture in order to make it more humanly responsive."[7]

18.6 LIMITATIONS OF ORGANISATION DEVELOPMENT

OD is criticised on the following grounds:

(*i*) OD attempts to create an ideal situation. But the internal and external conditions of an organisation may not allow to do so. OD does not take into account reality.

(*ii*) OD is based on the concepts of behavioural sciences. These sciences and consequently OD suffer from several limitations.

(*iii*) OD creates tremendous pressure for change. It may fail when there is considerable resistance to change.

(*iv*) OD requires trained specialists. Complacent and incompetent specialists may fail to initiate and implement the necessary changes.

(*v*) OD programmes are often costly without any guarantee of success. Only large organisations can afford such programmes.

(*vi*) OD may fail to motivate people who have low achievement motive. OD cannot be implemented in an organisation which is full of such people.

OD programmes have failed in several organisations mainly due to:

(*i*) failure of the consultant group to correctly tailor the programme to actual needs of the organisation;

(*ii*) failure to correctly model appropriate personnel behaviour in the programme; and

(*iii*) failure to increase employee motivation through participation and development of personal growth and self-esteem[8].

Some of the steps that can be taken to improve the success of OD efforts are as follows:

1. Top management of the organisation must provide genuine support to the OD programme.
2. The objectives of OD programme must be spelt out clearly and precisely.
3. Effects of OD programmes appear slowly. Therefore, adequate time should be allowed.
4. OD consultant must be fully competent and he must develop full understanding with internal change agents.

---

7 Keith Davis, *op. cit.,* p. 222.

8 M.G. Evans, "Failure in Organisation Development Programme: What Went Wrong", **Business Horizons,** April, 1974, p. 74.

5. Appropriate OD interventions should be used keeping in view the needs and problems of the organisation.

18.7 ASSUMPTIONS OF ORGANISATION DEVELOPMENT

Organisation development is based on the following assumptions[9] :

1. Most individuals have drives towards personal growth and development. However, the work habits are a response to work environment rather than personality traits. Accordingly, efforts to change work habits should be directed towards changing how the person is treated than towards attempting to change the person.
2. Highest productivity can be achieved when the individual goals are integrated with the organisational goals.
3. Cooperation is more effective than conflict. Conflict tends to erode trust, prohibit collaboration and eventually limit the effectiveness of the organisation. In healthy organisations, efforts are made at all levels to treat conflict as a problem subject to problem-solving methods.
4. Suppression of feelings adversely affects problem solving, personal growth and satisfaction with one's work. Accordingly, free expression of feelings is an important ingredient for commitment to work.
5. Growth of individuals is facilitated by relationships which are open, supportive, and trusting. Accordingly, the level of interpersonal trust, support and cooperation should be as high as possible.
6. The difference between commitment and agreement must be fully understood. Agreeing to do something is totally different from being committed to do something. Sense of commitment makes it easy to accept change and the implementation of change is even easier when this commitment is based upon participation in the process.
7. Organisation development must be reinforced by the organisation's total human-resource system.

18.8 PROCESS OF ORGANISATION DEVELOPMENT

The OD process involves the following phases:

1. **Identification and Diagnosis of the Problem:** The OD process begins with the identification of the problem in the organisation. Analysis of various overt and covert symptoms may help in identifying the problem. Diagnosis of the problem will identify its causes and suggest the future course of action. The analysis of the problem can reveal the variables that need to be altered, *e.g.*, organisation structure, leadership style, etc. Adequate information must be collected and an overall view of the situation must be adopted to find the real problem. Patience and sound judgement are necessary as otherwise OD programme may prove to be a self-defeating exercise.

9 Wendell L. French and Cecil H. Bell, *op. cit.*, pp. 65-72.

2. **Planning the Strategy for Change:** Once the problems are identified and diagnosed, the OD consultant (external change agent) and the management (internal change agent) jointly plan the change strategy. They attempt to transform diagnosis of the problem into a proper action plan involving the overall goals for change, determination of the basic approach for attaining these goals, and the sequence of detailed scheme for implementing the approach.[10]

3. **Implementing the Change:** It is relatively simple to identify change after it has occurred. But it is very difficult to influence the direction of change while it is underway. Planning and implementation of change are interrelated. The way in which a change is planned influences the manner in which it is carried out. Conversely, the problems of implementing change have an impact on the way in which it is planned. In case the change is not taking place in the desired direction, OD consultant intervenes by providing education, training, advice, etc. Implementation or intervention is the action phase in OD process.

4. **Evaluation and Feedback:** This phase involves monitoring the results of OD programme. OD is a very long process. Therefore, careful monitoring is necessary to obtain feedback regarding what is going on after the implementation of change. Such feedback will help in making suitable modifications whenever necessary. Several techniques such as critique sessions, comparison of pre- and post-training behavioural patterns, etc. are used for systematic appraisal of change efforts. Feedback should include the assessment of the change model itself. It is necessary to avoid emotional problems in feedback. For instance, when feedback contains criticism of the change agents, there may be resentment.

18.9 ACTION RESEARCH MODEL OF OD

The OD process can be conveniently presented in the form of action research model. Various steps of OD – as given above – are undertaken on continuous and cyclical basis. This cyclical process of using research to guide action is known as action research. According to French and Bell, "Action research is the process of systematically collecting research data about an ongoing system relative to some objective, goal, or need of that system; feeding these data back into the system; taking actions by altering selected variables within the system based both on the data and on hypothesis; and evaluating the results of actions by collecting more data."

Various steps involved in action research are shown in Fig. 18.1.

The action research model shows a continuous process of data collection and analysis, providing feedback to the client, discussion and determination of action at various stages. Action research is helpful both in diagnosis and in designing strategies for OD. To be specific, action research has the following **benefits**:

(*i*) It involves all those who take action or who are affected by change in the organisation. Therefore, change becomes more acceptable.

(*ii*) It accustoms the members of a group to work together effectively, paving the way for emotional and philosophical adjustments to change.

---

10 P.R. Lawrence and J.W. Lorsch, **Developing Organisation, Diagnosis and Action,** Addison-Wesley, Reading Mass, 1969, p. 89.

(*iii*) It rationalises the action by providing accurate knowledge of the context in which it occurs.

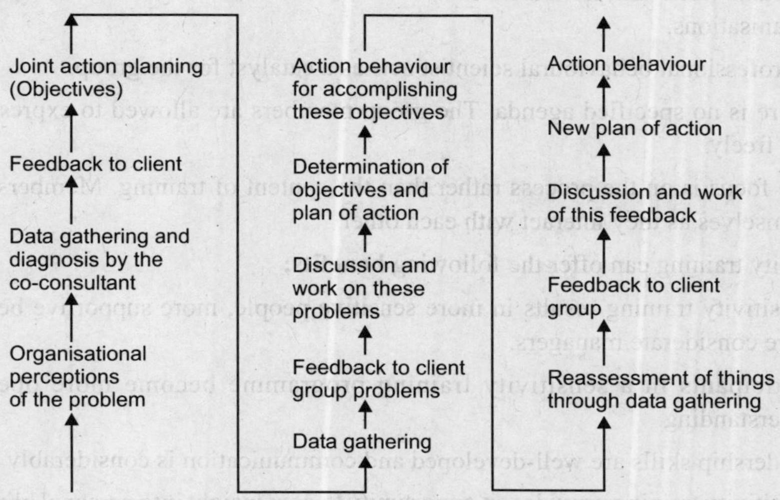

Fig. 18.1: Action Research Model of OD

18.10 OD INTERVENTIONS OR TECHNIQUES

OD interventions refer to various techniques of OD which are used for improving individuals, groups and the total organisation. According to French and Bell, OD interventions are "sets of structured activities in which selected organisational units (target groups or individuals) engage with a task or a sequence of tasks where the task goals are related directly or indirectly to organisational improvement. Interventions constitute the action thrust of organisation development; they make things happen."[11]

There is a wide range of OD interventions. French and Bell have suggested twelve types of OD interventions. The following OD interventions are described here:

1. Sensitivity Training.
2. Grid Training
3. Survey Feedback
4. Process Consultation
5. Team Building
6. Management by Objectives

18.10.1 Sensitivity Training

Sensitivity training is one of the popular techniques of OD. It is also known as T-group training (T stands for training). It is a method of improving interpersonal relations through unstructured interactions among members of a small group. The main **features** of sensitivity training are as follows:

11 Wendell L. French and Cecil H. Bell, *op. cit.*, p.134.

(*i*) A small group of ten to twelve persons is constituted. Its members may be drawn from the same work unit; from different work units in the same organisation; or from different organisations.

(*ii*) A professional behavioural scientist acts as a catalyst for the group.

(*iii*) There is no specified agenda. The group members are allowed to express their ideas and freely.

(*iv*) The focus is on the process rather than the content of training. Members learn about themselves as they interact with each other.

Sensitivity training can offer the following **benefits:**

(*i*) Sensitivity training results in more sensitive people, more supportive behaviour and more considerate managers.

(*ii*) Participants in a sensitivity training programme become more open and self-understanding.

(*iii*) Leadership skills are well-developed and communication is considerably improved.

(*iv*) Sensitivity training provides an opportunity to gain insight into personal blind spots. The participants become aware of group norms, role flexibility, and sense of belongingness.

Sensitivity training suffers from the following **drawbacks**:

(*i*) Many participants of sensitivity training have reported a feeling of humiliation, manipulation, decline in self-confidence, and psychological damage.

(*ii*) Sensitivity training incites anxiety with several harmful effects like frustration, unsettling and upset.

(*iii*) The increased sensitivity may be a containing source of frustration and problem if the participants return to their workplace in which openness, trust and sensitivity is frowned upon or repulsed.

Conditions for success of sensitivity training are as follows[12]:

(*i*) Careful selection of participants so that they have emotional stability, high tolerance and low anxiety.

(*ii*) Careful study of performance requirements.

(*iii*) Careful selection of the T-group leader.

(*iv*) Provision of precautionary procedure in case of failure of the programme. These may include alternative methods for coping with the desired changes, safety and well-being of the participants.

Problems in sensitivity training arise mainly due to two reasons. **First,** the participants and the leader are lacking the necessary qualities and the training is not conducted properly. **Second,** there is a mismatch between the work environment and the results of training. Sensitivity training requires organisations characterised by openness, trust, mutual cooperation and psychological safety. Sensitivity training focuses on group behaviour and it needs articulate and meaningful feedback.

---

12 Robert J. House, "T-Group Training : Good or Bad", **Business Horizons,** December 1969, pp. 69-77.

18.10.2 Grid Training

Grid training is based on the Managerial Grid developed by Blake and Mouton. It is a comprehensive, systematic and step-by-step approach. It helps individuals and groups to assess their own strengths and weaknesses, and to develop the knowledge and skills needed for effectiveness. The specific objectives of grid training are as follows[13]:

(*i*) To study the organisation as an interactive system and apply techniques of analysis in diagnosing its problems.

(*ii*) To understand the rationale and importance of systematic change.

(*iii*) To evaluate leadership styles and techniques of participation for creating desirable results.

The **process of grid training** involves the following steps:

1. **Laboratory-Seminar Training:** First of all, grid concepts are introduced to the managers. In a week-long seminar, each participant's leadership style is assessed and evaluated. After appropriate instructions, the key managers work to implement the grid programme throughout the organisation. They are educated about the desirability of a style of leadership.
2. **Team Development:** In this stage, the focus is on developing teamwork by analysis of team culture, traditions and alike. The aim is to improve superior-subordinate relationship and relationship among co-workers.
3. **Inter-Group Development:** During this phase, the focus is on improving inter-group behaviour and joint problem solving. The aim is to increase inter-group cooperation and coordination. Sources of inter-group conflict are carefully analysed and the typical win-lose mentality is changed to build inter-group relationships.
4. **Organisational Goal-Setting:** The participants discuss and agree upon the ideal model for their organisation. Action steps to achieve this model are decided by managers in cooperation with subordinates. Training is given to provide skills necessary for organisational excellence.

Evaluation
Goal attainment
Organisational goal setting
Inter group development
Team development
Laboratory seminar training
Organisation development
Management development

Fig. 18.2: Grid Training Process.

5. **Goal Attainment:** Managers attempt to achieve the goals set in the fourth phase. Each subunit examines how their activities should be carried out in order to achieve excellence. They proceed to take necessary corrective actions.
6. **Evaluation:** The results of all the earlier phases are evaluated to decide which areas of the organisation still need improvement or alteration. The grid training process may take three to five years.

Grid training helps participants in shifting towards the 9, 9 style. Thousands of organisations have used it. "Managerial and team effectiveness can be taught to managers without outside

13 Andrew J. Dubrin, **Foundations of Organisational Behaviour: An Applied Perspective,** Prentice Hall, New Jersey, 1994, p. 469.

assistance. Furthermore, it appears that this type of educational strategy can help to make significant contributions to organisational effectiveness."[14]

Grid training has been criticised as it overlooks the contingency approach and ignores reality by suggesting a single style as the best. The methodology of grid training is non-rigorous.

18.10.3 Survey Feedback

Survey feedback is a systematic and well-organised technique of OD. It is derived from a long and sound tradition of attitude measurement and survey research. The Institute for Social Research at Michigan University popularised survey feedback. The basic objectives of survey feedback are: (*a*) to assist the organisation in diagnosing its problems and developing action plan for problem solving, (*b*) to assist the group members to improve the relationships through discussion of common problems.

Survey feedback involves the following **steps**:

1. **Collection of Data:** First of all, a structured questionnaire is used to collect information. The questionnaire contains items relating to employee satisfaction, leadership styles, decision-making, communication, coordination and other aspects of the organisational climate. The questionnaire is administered in person either by the consulting firm or by members of the organisation. After collection, the data are classified, tabulated and analysed to arrive at useful conclusions.
2. **Feedback of Information:** Key findings of the survey are reported to the participants. The feedback may be given orally or in writing. In case of oral feedback, the consultant holds group discussions and problem-solving sessions with the participants. Feedback must be given in a constructive and suggestive manner so that the participants do not feel threatened or emotionally hurt. Written summary of findings may be given to avoid emotional problems.
3. **Developing Action Plan:** Survey feedback programme becomes meaningless without some action plan to overcome the problems. A straightforward and working plan is developed. The plan is based on the suggestions of the participants or participants are advised to develop their own action plans.
4. **Follow-up:** Follow-up is necessary to ensure that the action plan is being properly implemented.

Survey feedback has the following **advantages**:

(*i*) It is a cost-effective means of implementing a comprehensive programme which makes it a highly desirable technique.

(*ii*) It generates considerable amount of information efficiently and quickly. This information can be used in solving problems faced by the organisation and its members. The information serves as the basis for concrete plans to enhance organisational effectiveness.

(*iii*) It does not cause psychological damage to the participants because it does not involve high degree of soul searching.

---

14 Robert R. Blake and Jane S. Mouton, *op. cit.*, p. 155.

(*iv*) It has a wide coverage including all members of the organisation and emphasises two-way communication. It can meet both individual needs and organisational goals.

(*v*) It is flexible and can be applied to different problems and in different organisations.

(*vi*) It reduces resistance to change by involving employees in diagnosing problems and developing corrective actions.

(*vii*) It can improve the decision-making and problem-solving abilities of the organisation because it applies the knowledge and importance throughout the organisation.

Survey feedback can, however, prove counterproductive if the participants fail to decide and implement effective actions. Moreover, the success of this approach depends largely on the reliability of the information given by the participants. If there is bias in information then all attempts to diagnose the problems will fail.

To be successful, survey feedback requires the following conditions:

(*i*) Top management must have strong commitment and willingness to use the information.

(*ii*) The questionnaire must be valid and reliable.

(*iii*) The consultant conducting the programme must be competent at interpreting the data.

(*iv*) Employees must be honest and sincere in reporting their views and reactions.

(*v*) Each group must have sufficient discretion to consider and act upon the findings.

(*vi*) The participants must not feel manipulated and must trust each other.

(*vii*) The sessions must be conducted in a factual and solution-oriented environment.

18.10.4 Process Consultation

Under process consultation a consultant works with individuals and groups in the organisation to help them solve the problems. According to Edgar Schein, process consultation is "the set of activities on the part of the consultant which help the client to perceive, understand, and act upon the process events which occur in the client's environment".[15] Process consultation aims to improve organisational processes such as communication, group decision making and problem-solving, functional roles of members, group norms, leadership and authority, inter-group competition and cooperation.

Process consultation is based on the following **assumptions**[16]:

(*i*) Managers often need special diagnostic help in knowing what is wrong with the organisation.

(*ii*) Most managers have constant desire to increase organisational effectiveness, but they need help in deciding 'how' to achieve it.

(*iii*) Managers can be effective if they learn to diagnose their own strengths and weaknesses without exhaustive and time-consuming study of the organisation.

(*iv*) The outside consultant cannot learn enough about the culture of the organisation, to suggest reliable new courses of action. He should, therefore, work jointly with the members of the organisation.

---

15 Edgar Schein, **Process Consultation : Its Role in Organisation Development,** Addison-Wesley, Reading Mass, 1969, p. 9.

16 *Ibid.*

(*v*) The client must learn to see the problem for himself, understand the problem and suggest a remedy. The consultant should provide new and challenging alternatives for the client to consider. However, the decision-making authority on these alternatives about organisational change remains with the client.

(*vi*) It is essential that the process consultant is an expert in diagnosing and establishing effective helping relationships with the client. Effective process consultation involves passing those skills on to the client.

Steps in Process Consultation

Schein has suggested the following steps in process consultation:

1. **Initial Contact:** First of all, the client comes into contact with the consultant and specifies the problem that cannot be solved by the organisation through normal process and resources.
2. **Defining the Relationship:** The client and the consultant enter into an agreement. The formal agreement spells out the services, time and fees of the consultant. The client's expectations and desired results are also specified.
3. **Selecting the Work Method:** It involves a clear-cut understanding of where and how the consultant will do the job. The consultant is introduced to the members of the organisation so that they can help the consultant by providing the required information.
4. **Data Collection and Diagnosis:** The consultant collects the required information from various sources through observation, interview and questionnaire. The collected data are used to diagnose the causes underlying the problems.
5. **Intervention:** The consultant makes interventions such as agenda setting, feedback, coaching, structural change, etc. The solutions designed by the consultant are translated into actions in the organisation.
6. **Involvement Reduction and Termination:** When the programme is completed, the consultant leaves the organisation and formal agreement with the client is terminated.

Process consultation is relatively a traditional but an in-depth approach to OD in which the consultant plays a major role. It focusses attention on the interpersonal and inter-group problems. The professional consultant helps members of the organisation in changing attitudes, values, interpersonal skills, group norms and cohesiveness, etc. But the consultant may be unable to solve the organisation's problems. Another problem is that members may not inculcate the new culture and processes suggested by the consultant. Therefore, it is essential to select a competent consultant and to develop willingness to change among the members of the organisation.

18.10.5 Team Building

Team building is essentially an attempt to assist the work groups in becoming adept by learning how to identify, diagnose and solve its own problems. In a team building programme, members of work group diagnose how to work together effectively. The focus is on improving the effectiveness of work groups by allowing the group members to concentrate on :

(*a*) setting goals or priorities for the team.

(*b*) analysing the way the work is performed.

(*c*) examining the way the team is working.

(*d*) analysing how the team's goals and priorities are linked to those of the organisation.

(*e*) examining the relationships among the people doing the work[17].

In a typical team building programme, session starts with identification of problems such as ineffective policies, role ambiguity, etc. Members contribute information concerning their individual perceptions of problems, issues and relationships. After thorough discussions, actions for overcoming these problems are decided. The impact of these actions is assessed in the concluding session.

The team building process involves the following steps:

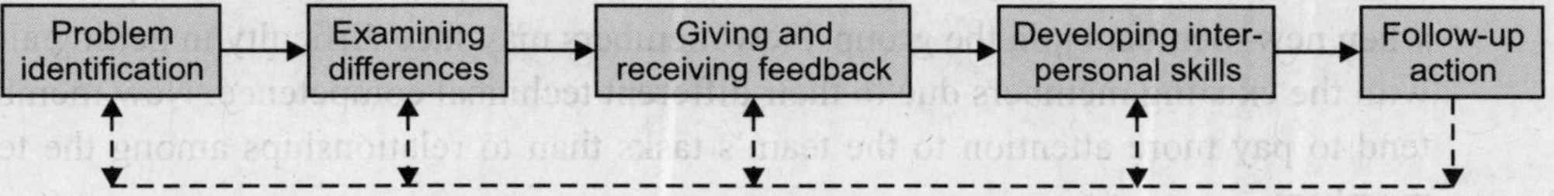

Fig. 18.3: Team Building Process

1. **Identifying the Problems:** First of all, members of the team identify the problems that are hindering its effectiveness. Every member expresses his views about what the real problems are. Such expression and discussion makes the members understand clearly the basic concepts of team building.
2. **Examining Differences:** Team members perceive the team's problems differently due to differences in their personality, attitudes and values. Open communication and training sessions help in clarifying the actual problems to the members.
3. **Giving and Receiving Feedback:** When perceptual differences become open to members some tension arises in the team. Members are given feedback about their feelings concerning the issue. Such feedback provides opportunity to members to understand themselves better.
4. **Developing Interpersonal Skills:** The basic objective of team building process is to improve members' ability to interact with each other and adopt positive behaviour. It is also necessary that members discard negative behaviour.
5. **Follow-up Action:** Finally, the total team is convened to review what has been learned and what more is needed. Responsibilities of each member are decided. Differences in perception are clarified and settled.

According to French and Bell, "Probably the most important single group of interventions in the OD are the team-building activities the goals of which are the improvement and increased effectiveness of various teams within the organisation".[18] This is so because in most organisations work is performed in groups or teams. The basic building blocks of an organisation are groups and, therefore, the basic units of change are also groups.

Team building has certain inherent **advantages**:

(*i*) Team building improves the decision-making and problem-solving skills of the organisation.

---

17 R. Bechard, "Optimizing Team Building Efforts", **Journal of Contemporary Business,** 1972 (3), pp. 23-32.

18 Wendell L. French and Cecil H. Bell, *op. cit.,* p. 119.

(*ii*) It results in effective interpersonal relationships through increased involvement and participation of people.

(*iii*) It helps in developing communication within the group and among groups.

(*iv*) It assists in improving job satisfaction and attitudes of employees.

Team building has been criticised due to its following **limitations:**

(*i*) It focusses only on work groups and does not pay attention to other organisational barriers such as structure, technology, etc.

(*ii*) Team building becomes a complicated exercise when there is frequent change in team members. Confusion arises in the roles and relationships among the group members when new members join the group. New members may face difficulty in getting along with the existing members due to their different technical competence. New members tend to pay more attention to the team's tasks than to relationships among the team members.

Despite these limitations, team building is one of the most powerful techniques of OD. It is helpful in changing both inputs (values, skills and needs) and processes (planning, leadership, group cohesiveness, communication) of the organisation.

Team building is likely to be more successful when there is task interdependence among group members and they understand and accept the group's goals.

18.10.6 Management by Objectives

The concept of management by objectives (MBO) was introduced by Peter Drucker[19] in 1954. Since then several organisations have used it to improve performance. MBO is a comprehensive system that involves joint goal setting and coordination of individual goals and organisational goals. It has been defined as follows:

"MBO is a result-centred, non-specialist, operational managerial process for the effective utilisation of material, physical and human resources of the organisation by integrating the individual with the organisation and organisation with the environment."[20]

The **key features** of MBO are as under:

(*i*) MBO is comprehensive approach to management that can be applied in all parts of the organisation.

(*ii*) The main focus of MBO is on objectives. Under it objectives are established at all levels of the organisation. The emphasis is on measurable and verifiable goals in key areas.

(*iii*) MBO involves participation of subordinates in both objective setting and performance reviews.

(*iv*) Periodic review of performance is another important feature of MBO. The review is future-oriented and serves as the basis for planning and corrective action.

(*v*) Resource allocation, delegation of authority, rewards and punishment are linked to the achievement of objectives.

---

19 Peter F. Drucker, **The Practice of Management,** William Heinemann, London, 1954.

20 S.K. Chakraborty, **Management by Objectives,** Macmillan, New Delhi, 1976, p. 5.

(*vi*) MBO has an operational thrust involving linkage between organisational goals and individual objectives.

(*vii*) MBO is an ongoing and cyclical process.

The **process of MBO** consists of the following steps.

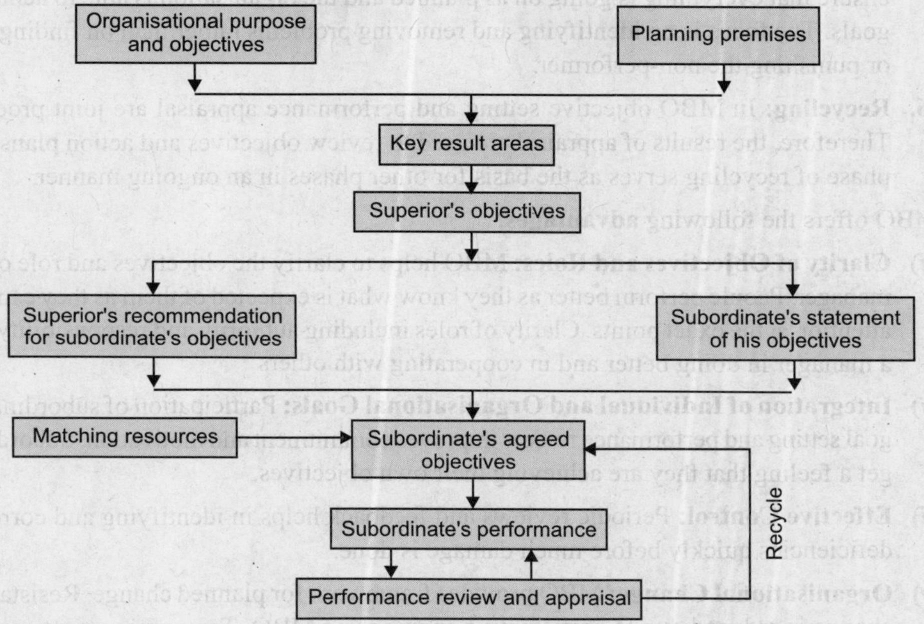

Fig. 18.4: Process of MBO

1. **Determining Organisational Objectives:** The MBO process begins with the setting of the organisation's purpose and objectives. In defining the purpose, answers are sought to questions such as "why does the organisation exist", "what business are we in", and "what should be our business". After this both strategic (long range) and operational (short range) objectives are defined. Usually object setting starts at the top level and moves downward to the lower levels of management.

2. **Identifying Key Result Areas (KRAs):** Organisational objectives, planning premises and expectations of stakeholders provide the basis for deciding the key result areas. These areas indicate priorities for performance. Drucker has identified eight key result areas : (*a*) profitability, (*b*) market standing, (*c*) innovation, (*d*) productivity, (*e*) worker performance, (*f*) financial and physical resources, (*g*) manager performance, and (*h*) public responsibility.

3. **Setting Subordinates' Objectives:** An organisation achieves its objectives through individuals. Therefore, the objectives of each individual are decided. The superior recommends the objective for his subordinate and the subordinate states his own objectives. Mutual negotiation between the two ultimately leads to an agreement on what the subordinate is expected to achieve.

4. **Matching Resources with Objectives:** An individual can achieve his objectives only when adequate resources are made available to him. Therefore, the superior

allocates resources commensurate with the subordinate's objectives. The allocation and mobilisation of resources is done in consultation with the subordinate.

5. **Performance Appraisal:** The superior and the subordinate jointly measure whether the subordinate has achieved his objectives or not. Appraisal is done continuously to ensure that everything is going on as planned and the organisation is able to achieve its goals. The focus is on identifying and removing problems rather than on finding faults or punishing the non-performer.

6. **Recycling:** In MBO objective setting and performance appraisal are joint processes. Therefore, the results of appraisal are used to review objectives and action plans. Each phase of recycling serves as the basis for other phases in an ongoing manner.

MBO offers the following **advantages:**

(*i*) **Clarity of Objectives and Roles:** MBO helps to clarify the objectives and role of each manager. People perform better as they know what is expected of them as they can focus attention at the exact points. Clarity of roles including authority and responsibility helps a manager in doing better and in cooperating with others.

(*ii*) **Integration of Individual and Organisational Goals:** Participation of subordinates in goal setting and performance review improves commitment and motivation. Subordinates get a feeling that they are achieving their own objectives.

(*iii*) **Effective Control:** Periodic reviews and feedback helps in identifying and correcting deficiencies quickly before much damage is done.

(*iv*) **Organisational Change:** MBO provides framework for planned change. Resistance to change is reduced due to participative approach of MBO. Top management can plan, initiate and control the direction and speed of change in the organisation.

(*v*) **Better Resource Utilisation:** In MBO, time and energy are put in key result areas. Moreover, resource allocation is linked to objectives at every level. The organisation can utilise its resources effectively in the context of changing environment.

(*vi*) **Satisfaction of Employees:** MBO provides adequate opportunity for personnel satisfaction. They feel that they are important to the organisation due to participation in goal setting and performance review. They also feel assured that managerial bias or prejudice will not affect appraisal of their performance.

(*vii*) **Executive Development:** Subordinate managers learn decision-making skills through participation in goal setting and performance appraisal. Continuous interactions with supervisors also help to develop their interpersonal skills.

Thus, MBO helps to improve planning, performance appraisal, interpersonal communication, superior-subordinate relations, employee attitudes towards organisational goals, coordination and control.

MBO suffers form several **drawbacks:**

(*i*) **Goal Setting Problems:** MBO needs verifiable objectives against which performance is to be measured. It is very difficult to set quantitative objectives in all areas of work. Moreover, participation of employees in goal setting may result in goal displacement. In some organisations there is too much focus on short-term results at the cost of long-term goals.

(*ii*) **Rigidity:** In a dynamic environment objectives need to be revised. But most managers tend to stick to the objectives set earlier. Therefore, MBO involves the possibility of creating inflexibility in the organisation.

(*iii*) **Time Consuming:** Implementation of MBO requires considerable time span ranging from two to five years. Many managers feel over-burdened and get frustrated due to lack of patience.

(*iv*) **Excessive Paperwork:** MBO involves a lot of paperwork because a large number of forms have to be designed and filled in. However, this problem disappears once MBO becomes a part of organisational life.

(*v*) **Lack of Understanding:** MBO is a new philosophy of managing. It requires rigorous analysis and thorough understanding. Often the database and the required expertise is not available. Managers who do not have a holistic view fail to introduce MBO.

(*vi*) **Confusion and Chaos:** When an organisation fails to implement MBO properly there is utter chaos. The organisation finds it difficult to work even with its old system. Introduction of MBO creates high expectation. When the expectations are not realised quickly there is disenchantment with MBO.

Thus, MBO is not a panacea for all organisational problems. Some problems are inherent in MBO system itself. But most of the problems arise due to faulty implementation of MBO.

Making MBO Effective

MBO is a philosophy rather than merely a technique of managing. Its successful use requires a basic change in the culture and environment of the organisation. An MBO programme can be successful when the following conditions are satisfied :

1. **Top Management Support:** Full commitment and involvement of top management is essential for the implementation of MBO. When subordinates feel that their superiors have full faith in MBO, the attitudes of subordinates become positive. MBO is an ongoing process rather than writing objectives once a year. Top management must develop participative leadership style. Every manager must (*a*) personally discuss with each subordinate the objectives, (*b*) evaluate progress towards these objectives, (*c*) assist and support the subordinates in overcoming the problems that hinder achievement. Managers at all levels must have sincere commitment to MBO.

2. **Clarity of Purpose:** The organisation must be fully clear about the purpose for which it is installing MBO programme. The contents and focus of the programme will vary from one organisation to another depending upon the purpose. For example, a company facing decline may use MBO to improve productivity and profitability. On the other hand, a prosperous company may adopt MBO for long range planning and management development. Unless the purpose is defined precisely, MBO may not produce the desired results.

3. **Training:** In most cases an MBO programme fails because managers do not have full understanding of MBO philosophy and procedure. Therefore, systematic training in the concepts and philosophy of MBO must be provided. When people do not understand why and how the programme will work they tend to fear and resist it. Training in interpersonal and inter-group relationships is also necessary to ensure that there is no personality clash between superiors and subordinates.

4. **Participation:** Success in a MBO programme is possible only when subordiantes at every level actively participate in all phases. But most organisations are highly structured and habituated to authoritarian system. It is very difficult and time-consuming to change management ideology and adopt participative style. Before installing MBO, an organisation must develop a climate and culture of participative management.
5. **Feedback for Self-Control:** Under MBO, a person can direct and control his own performance. But this requires adequate and timely feedback. The subordiante must be given periodic reports on his performance. Periodic counselling and support for removing obstacles is equally necessary.

TEST QUESTIONS

1. What do you mean by organisation development? Explain in brief the behavioural interventions of organisation development.
2. What are structural interventions? Explain how does MBO contribute to the development of an organisation.
3. Point out the conditions which enhance the likelihood that an OD effort will succeed.
4. "The concept of OD is based on the notion that people are capable of developing open, teaching and supportive relationships in work organisations." How realistic is this assumption for managerial situations in the Indian context? Discuss.
5. Explain various types of transactions under TA, giving two examples of each type.
6. What are the implications of Chris Argyris' behaviour patterns?
7. (*a*) What are the assumptions about people in an OD exercise?
   (*b*) What are the ideal organisational conditions for implementing successful OD interventions?
8. What styles change agents usually adopt in organisation development? Explain with reference to relationship between change agent and the client system.
9. Explain the interface between OD and HRD. What role can top management play in OD?
10. Write short notes on:
    (*a*) Action research
    (*b*) Institution building
    (*c*) Grid OD
    (*d*) OD skills
11. Describe organisation as a system that requires periodic interventions by forces that are inside or outside the organisation.
12. What are the characteristics of Organization Development? You have been appointed by your university as a consultant to prepare and execute an OD programme to tackle the existing problems. Draft an outline of your programme.
13. Describe the traditional techniques of Organization Development. Discuss their major advantages and limitations.

14. Outline some of the important modern OD techniques. How will you engage in a 'managerial grid' training programme?
15. "It has become fashionable now-a-days to talk about OD". Examine this statement.
16. Briefly explain the applications of OD. Comment on the state of OD in Indian companies.
17. Explain, in brief, various types of OD interventions. Discuss team building and inter-group interventions in detail.
18. "Five categories of ethical dilemmas in organisation development practice are existing". Illustrate the statement.
19. Do you think OD will be a major player in assisting organisations to shift to and sustain the new paradigms in the future? Discuss the contingencies that must be managed.
20. Discuss the process for evaluating OD. Why is such an evaluation necessary? Elaborate.
21. Explain the values and assumptions about people implicit in OD and examine their implications in dealing with individuals and groups in organisations.
22. "OD is a process that focuses on organisation culture, processes and structure utilising a total system perspective". Substantiate this viewpoint with the help of suitable examples.
23. Explain the contribution of any three behavioural scientists to the field of OD.
24. Examine the role of TQM and Reengineering in organisational transformation.
25. Comprehensive interventions are defined in lieu to the extent to which total organisation is involved and/or the depth of cultural change. Discuss any two of these comprehensive interventions, *viz.,* Beckhard's confrontation meeting. Grid OD, Schein's cultural analysis, survey feedback (linked by system 4T), transorganisational development (TD).
26. Describe the foundations that form important underpinnings of the field of OD and are used by OD practitioners to plan and implement effective change programmes for improving organisation performance and individual development.
27. Three components are basic to all OD programmes, *viz.,* Diagnosis, intervention and programme management. Discuss the factors that are considered while managing OD process.
28. Action Research is one of the cornerstones of OD underlying both the practice and theory of the field. Describe action research as a process and as an approach to OD.
29. OD interventions are the action component of OD. Give a scheme for classifying these OD interventions and what advice can you give to practitioners to structure activities in "better" ways?
30. Organization development has emerged largely from applied behavioural sciences and has four major streams: I-group and laboratory training. Survey feedback technology, action research and tavistock sociotechnical and socioclinical approaches. Describe the history of organisation development from the perspective of these four streams.
31. A set of values, assumptions and beliefs constitute an integral part of organisation development. Describe these and what are the implications of these for dealing with individuals, groups and organisations?
32. Teams and work groups are considered to be the fundamental units of organisations and also key leverage points for improving the functioning of the organization. Describe

briefly the interventions that have been developed to help teams become more effective while simultaneously addressing organisational problems and challenges.

33. Structural interventions seek a joint optimisation of social and technological systems of organisations. Discuss any three of these. Interventions viz., sociotechnical systems (STS), Self-managed teams, work redesign, MBO, Quality circles, quality of work life (QWL) programmes, parallel or collateral structures, physical settings, TQM, Reengineering and large-scale systems change.
34. Identify organisational development intervention techniques designed to affect the behaviour of individuals and groups.
35. Explain organisation development in right sizing scenario.
36. Define the term 'Organisation Development' and explain the major characteristics of the field.
37. What are the basic values and assumptions that underlie the organisation by development effort? What skills do OD change agents require?
38. What are the major components of the Organisation Development process? Describe.
39. Why are team-building interventions considered as the most important single group of interventions in OD? Describe briefly some popular team-building interventions.
40. "Grid organization development is a complete and systematic approach to organisation improvement". Explain this statement and briefly describe the various phases of the Grid OD programme.
41. What are the future directions in which organization development is likely to grow?
42. Write short notes on any two:
    (*a*) Sensitivity training
    (*b*) Sociotechnical systems
    (*c*) Role Analysis technique
43. Discuss the role of OD in organisational improvement.
44. What do you understand by OD interventions? Describe any four of them.
45. What are the focus areas of second-generation Organisation Development?
46. "The future of OD is bright but only if the field continues to evolve". Discuss.
47. Discuss the issues relating to consultant-client relationship in OD.
48. Explain how OD practitioners deal with power and politics in organisation.
49. What is second-generation OD? Discuss its scope and application.
50. Discuss various conditions and contingencies determining the future role of OD.
51. While utilising the services of a consultant, what are the major issues involved? Suggest ways to strengthen client-consultant relationship.
52. Describe the nature and utility of structural interventions for OD.
53. "OD is an applied behavioural science". Comment and explain the inter-disciplinary nature of OD.
54. "TQM appears to be highly congruent with OD approach and values". Discuss.
55. Explain the problems faced while conducting research in OD.

56. "Sound OD rests on action research model". Justify your answer with suitable examples from your classroom setting.
57. Illustrate various OD interventions and their relevance in the Indian context.
58. Critically evaluate the OD-HRD interface with suitable examples.
59. Discuss the elements of organisational diagnosis from the perspective of Weisbord's six-box model and McKinsey's 7 S Framework.
60. Discuss the various ways data can be gathered for the Family group diagnostic meeting for effective intervention.
61. Sketch the comparison between role negotiation technique and Gestalt method.
62. Describe the various steps involved in the confrontation meeting intervention for comprehensive intervention.
63. Discuss the application of TA and sensitivity to OD intervention at individual level.
64. "The number of OD interventions is quite large". Comment.
65. "Sensitivity training is the most controversial OD intervention". Do you agree? Give reasons in support of you answer.
66. "OD is not a panacea for all organisational problems". Explain.

CASE STUDY

The Pennathur Tyre Company (PTC) was set up in 1986 to fill what its founder Mr. Mani called a void that existed in the southern parts of India. According to Mani, who had worked for a foreign tyre company for nearly 15 years, there was no tyre company that had its major aim as producing tyres at the lowest cost and selling them to customers for a reasonable price. "The four-wheel vehicle owners pay through their nose for tyres, petrol and repairs. Anybody who owns a car spends at least 35 to 40 per cent of his salary on maintaining the vehicle and that is not how it should be!" Mani was often heard to say. Mr. Mani started the PTC in partnership with two of his close friends who also had extensive experience in the tyre business working for others. Mr. Mani was very actively involved with the business and was at work every day at the crack of dawn and never left the place before 8 p.m. Sometimes when work was heavy, Mani would stay as late as 10 p.m. at the shop. One of the other two partners owned another business and was, for all practical purposes, a sleeping partner in this firm, while the third partner was much less involved in the day-to-day operations of the company than Mr. Mani.

PTC, though a small partnership firm, had enormous backing from the business community because of their appreciation for the goals of the company, the extreme dedication of Mr. Mani, and the excellent abilities of the three partners. Thus. PTC was off to a good start. Being very cost-conscious, PTC set up a small Cost Analysis Department. As business began to expand, more customer services were added on and the company was known for its excellent wheel balancing services. Because of its reputation the company was given sole dealership in helmets as well. In 1988, just after two years of the initial start, the company had to expand its premises, operations, and personnel. With the expansion came the growing pains and Mr. Mani and the two partners had to encounter many small hurdles. Even as they were trying to solve one problem, several others seemed to crop up. Mr. Mani highlighted some of the more serious ones and described them to me as follows.

"Sometimes I wish we had never expanded our business. When we were merely selling tyres, we could easily handle the operations and the workmen and we, the partners, were all happy. At first, it was exciting to expand the operations and provide more services to our customers. The smile on the customers' faces as they drive their cars away is still very gratifying. But with our recruiting more and more people, we are beginning to lose control. Often, the customers are not served as effectively as they could be. The personalised touch that we used to give seems to be slowly slipping away. I have been telling the employees that they should be more customer-oriented, but they seem to be more concerned about their own inter-departmental problems and fights. For instance, last week, while a customer was patiently waiting, the mechanic who was to have changed the oil, was arguing for more than half an hour with the purchase clerk about some trivial matter. I almost lost my patience, and was about to give the mechanic a good yelling, when my partner took the mechanic aside and talked to him. The fact that customers are not serviced without delays, bothers me. I wonder if it bugs my partners as well! I have not discussed these kinds of issues with them since I don't want them to think that I am getting unduly worried about small matters.

"Another potential problem lies in the way some of the employees come across to the others in the company. For instance, we have a rather brash young engineer. He is thoroughly knowledgeable about his work and is extremely productive. However, he is always very serious and talks in a very abrupt, and sometimes, abrasive manner. Some of his mechanics have come and told me that they are scared of him. I have a set of capable workmen and don't want to lose any of them. I am at a loss to know how to handle this particular situation. I guess if I were this engineer's subordinate, I would be scared of him too; but the engineer is really a nice person, you know. The only problem is that he is too intense and comes across to others as a 'grouch'. We have a few others who are just the opposite; these guys are laughing and joking all the time and I sometimes wonder if their workers take them seriously at all!

"Something else is also engaging my thoughts. Ultimately, I would like to make each of the service departments, profit centres and share the additional profits with the workers. That, of course, is down the road; perhaps three to five years from now. I am thinking that if the employees have a stake in the profits, they will work hard and I will not have to put in so much time in supervising them. But then, these guys should all learn to work well together so that there is more collaboration and joint problem-solving rather than competition and dysfunctional conflicts. I would like them all to see themselves as one big family where everybody has to work together harmoniously to reap the full benefits. If, somehow, we can develop that spirit of friendliness and cooperation from now on, it would be great!

"Maybe, I am rambling too much, but these and other issues keep engaging my thoughts and I am wondering if you have any advice for me on how I should be handling some of these issues."

Questions

1. Clearly identify the problems in the case.
2. Recommend appropriate OD intervention strategies to resolve each of the issues.
3. Explain why do you make the particular recommendation and how it will resolve the problem.

CHAPTER

19

ORGANISATIONAL CLIMATE AND CULTURE

CHAPTER OUTLINE

19.1 Concept of Organisational Climate
19.2 Characteristics of Organisational Climate
19.3 Dimensions of Organisational Climate
19.4 Importance of Organisational Climate
19.5 Determinants of Organisational Climate
19.6 Improving Organisational Climate
19.7 Concept of Organisational Culture
19.8 Characteristics of Organisational Culture
19.9 Subcultures
19.10 Impact of Organisational Culture
19.11 Socialisation
- **Test Questions**
- **Case Study**

Organisational climate and culture is an important determinant of organisational behaviour. A sound climate is essential for the achievement of organisational goals.

19.1 CONCEPT OF ORGANISATIONAL CLIMATE

Some popular definitions of organisational climate are given below:

"Organisational climate is the summary of perception which people have about an organisation. In is, thus, a global expression of what the organisation is."[1]

"A relatively enduring quality of the internal environment that is experienced by its members, influences their behaviour, and can be described in terms of the values of a particular set of characteristics of the organisation."[2]

1 Benjamin Schneider and Rover A. Snyder, "Some Relationships Between Job Satisfaction and Organisational Climate," **Journal of Applied Psychology,** 60, No. 3 1975, p. 318.

2 Renate Tagiuri, "The Concept of Organisational Climate", in Renate Tagiuri and George H. Litwin (eds.), **Organisational Climate,** Graduate School of Business Administration, Harvard University, Boston, 1968 pp. 26-27.

"A set of characteristics that describe an organisation and that (*a*) distinguish one organisation from another, (*b*) are relatively enduring over a period of time, and (*c*) influence the behaviour of people in the organisation."[3]

19.2 CHARACTERISTICS OF ORGANISATIONAL CLIMATE

An analysis of the definitions given above reveals the following features of organisational climate:

1. **General Perception :** Organisational climate is the summary perception which people have about an organisation. It reflects the impression people have about what the organisation is.
2. **Qualitative Concept:** Organisational climate is an abstract and intangible concept. It is very difficult to explain its components in quantitative terms.
3. **Internal Environment:** Organisational climate represents the internal conditions of an organisation.
4. **Distinct Identity:** Organisational climate gives a distinct identity to the organisation. It indicates human organisation is different from other organisations. "Just as every individual has a personality that makes each person unique, each organisation has an organisational climate that clearly distinguishes its personality from other organisations."[4]
5. **Enduring Quality:** Organisational climate is a relatively enduring quality of the internal environment which is experienced by the members of the organisation. It develops over a long period of time.
6. **Multidimensional:** Organisational climate has several dimensions such as authority structure, individual autonomy, leadership style, communication pattern, degree of conflicts and cooperation, etc.

19.3 DIMENSIONS OF ORGANISATIONAL CLIMATE

The main diversions that together make up the climate of an organisation are as follows:

1. **Members' Orientation:** When the dominant orientation or concern for members is to adhere to the established rules and regulations, Organisational Climate is characterised by control. On the contrary, if the dominant orientation is to create excellence, the climate is characterised by achievement.
2. **Management Style:** The dominant style of managers may be task-oriented or relationship-oriented. In case the task orientation is predominant, the leadership style is autocratic. But if the relationship orientation is dominant, the leadership style is democratic.

---

3 G.A. Forehand and B. Von H. Gilmer, "Environmental Variations in Studies of Organisational Behaviour", **Psychological Bulletin,** 62, No. 6, 1964, p. 362.

4 G. James Francis and Gene Milbourn, Jr., **Human Behaviour in the Work Environment: A Managerial Perspective,** Goodyear Publishing Co., Santa Monica, California , 1980, p. 92.

3. **Type of Structure:** Organisation structure reflects who is to direct whom and who is responsible to whom. It also serves as the framework for superior-subordinate relations. When the authority is centralised at the top level subordinates do not participate much in decision-making. If authority is centralised, the climate will be characterised by participation in decision-making.

4. **Individual Freedom:** The climate of an organisation tends to be positive when its members are given sufficient autonomy to work. Such autonomy facilitates self-control and reduces the burden of higher level managers.

5. **Degree of Control:** A rigid control system creates a bureaucratic climate in the organisation and reduces individual freedom.

6. **Interpersonal Relationships:** When informal groups support the formal work groups, there is cooperation. On the other hand, powerful informal groups may create conflicts and goal displacement in the orgainisation.

7. **Communication Pattern:** In case the focus is on formal and downward communication, subordinates are not able to express their ideas and opinion. Such communication flow can cause frustration and low morale among employees.

8. **Reward System:** Merit-based reward creates healthy competition among employees. But when rewards depend on the superior's whims and fancies employees focus on pleasing the boss rather than on work performance.

9. **Mutual Trust:** Teamwork is possible only when there is mutual trust and cooperation between individuals, between groups, and between superior and subordinates.

10. **Conflict Handling:** In an organisation differences often arise among individuals and groups. Effective management of conflicts maintains cooperation while suppression of conflicts creates distrust.

11. **Risk Taking:** Innovation is necessary for success in a fast changing and competitive environment. If management allows employees to try new ideas without fear of failure and punishment, innovations become easy.

19.4 IMPORTANCE OF ORGANISATIONAL CLIMATE

A sound climate is essential for the survival and growth of organisations. The study of organisational climate helps in understanding cooperation, creativity, communication, employee satisfaction, morale and other important dimensions. It also provides insight into the attitudes of people towards the organisation. An organisation tends to attract and retain people who fit its climate, so that its patterns are perpetuated.

An organisation's climate affects the behaviour of its members in several ways. **First,** it defines the stimuli for them. **Second,** it places constraints upon their freedom of choice. **Third,** it provides source of rewards and punishments. A sound organisational climate (two-way communication, cooperative relationships, etc.) is helpful in improving employee morale and jobs satisfaction and productivity.

Fig. 19.1 shows the relationship between organisational climate and organisational effectiveness. The variables given in column I (organisation structure, employee attitudes, managerial policies, leadership style, communication system, mutual trust, conflict handling, interpersonal relations, etc.) constitute organisational climate. These in turn influence morale, job satisfaction, commitment and productivity of employees (Column II) which determine the effectiveness of the organisation (Column III).

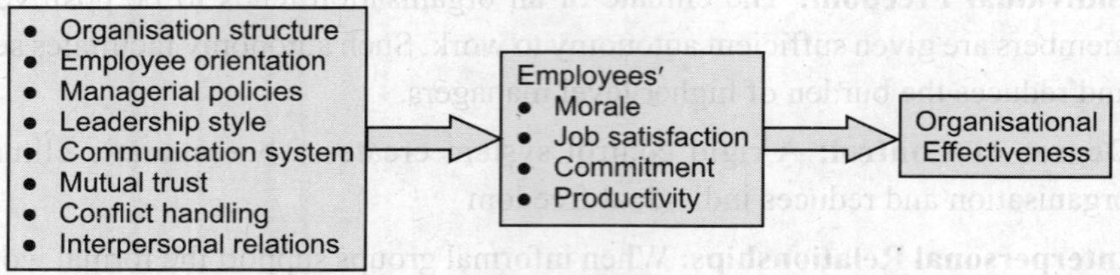

Fig. 19.1: Organisational Climate and Effectiveness

19.5 DETERMINANTS OF ORGANISATIONAL CLIMATE

The major factors influencing organisational climate are given below[5]:

1. **Organisational Context:** The mission, goals, objectives and policies together constitute the organisational context. The management philosophy of an organisation is reflected in its policies, rules, regulations and practices. The reaction of employees and the degree to which they agree with management philosophy is a major determinant of organisational climate. Similarly, managers' attitudes towards employees influence an organisation's climate. If management is able to reconcile employees' goals to organisational goals, it can create a favourable climate.

2. **Organisation Structure:** It refers to the network of authority-responsibility relationships in the organisation. If there is high degree of decentralisation, it facilitates participative decision making and employee development. But if the top management prefers consistency in decisions making and close control over decisions, the structure will be centralised.

3. **Leadership Process:** In any organisation, leadership styles, communication, decision-making and related processes exercise considerable influence on climate. The effectiveness of a leadership style depends on the particular situation. Therefore, the leadership style must suit the given situation. When employees are dissatisfied with the managers' leadership style, their morale, satisfaction and productivity go down.

4. **Physical Environment:** The working conditions and characteristics of physical space also affect organisational climate. Employees working in a clean, quiet and safe environment perceive the organisation favourably. Size and location of office, nature of city and other external factors are also important. However, an employee working in a small town may be happy because his place of work is near his residence and the life is slow and peaceful. Office size, office decor and the physical space allotted to

5 Lawrence R. James and Allan P. Jones, "Organisational Climate, A Review of Theory and Research", **Psychological Bulletin,** 81, December, 1974, p. 1098.

an employee influence his attitude towards the job. For example, high level of noise creates frustration, nervousness and aggression which have a negative impact on the organisation's climate.

5. **Organisational Values and Norms:** These consist of conformity, legality, impersonality, reciprocity, etc. Every organisation has its own values and norms, which indicate desirable behaviour. For example, styles of dress, interaction between man and woman, manner of speaking to seniors, punctuality, etc. are all guided by values and norms of the organisation. If these values and norms are good and employees observe them the organisational climate becomes positive.

19.6 IMPROVING ORGANISATIONAL CLIMATE

Managers play a dominate role in shaping the climate of an organisation. They determine the values, norms, goals, structure, communication system, decision-making process, etc. of the organisation. Management also has direct control over the physical environment in which employees work. Managers can improve the organisational climate through the following techniques:

1. **Concern for People:** The climate of an organisation is likely to be sound when the management improves working conditions and works for employee welfare. A genuine concern and respect for employees will develop positive attitudes towards the organisation.
2. **Sound Policies:** Appropriate changes in policies, procedures and rules can win loyalty and commitment of employees. But their implementation must be unbiased and fair.
3. **Open Communication:** A two-way communication system provides an opportunity to employees to know what is going on and react to it.
4. **Participative Decision Making:** Employees tend to be cooperative and loyal when they are involved in setting goals and in taking decisions influencing them.
5. **Physical Changes:** Improvement in working conditions and work methods are also helpful in improving organisational climate. But these changes should be carried out in consultation with the employees.

19.7 CONCEPT OF ORGANISATIONAL CULTURE

Culture means a set of values, beliefs, customs, habits, preferences, art, etc., which members of a community share in common. Culture determines the identity of a society just as personality creates the identity of an individual. The concept of culture is applicable to organisations because an organisation is a social system that operates within the framework of its cultural environment. Moreover, people in an organisation come from different cultural backgrounds.

"Organisation culture is the set of assumptions, beliefs, values and norms that are shared by an organisation's members."[6]

---

6 Charles O'Reilly, "Corporations, Culture and Commitment: Motivation and Social Control in Organisation", **California Management Review,** Summer, 1989, pp. 9-25.

The set of assumptions that the members of an organisation share in common is known as organisation culture. These assumptions may be abstract and internally oriented (values, beliefs attitudes, feelings, etc.) and material or externally oriented (buildings, products, dresses, etc.). The main elements of organisational culture are as follows[7]:

- Shared things (*e.g.,* the way people dress).
- Shared saying (*e.g.,* let's go to work).
- Shared actions (*e.g.,* a service-oriented approach).
- Shared feelings (*e.g.,* hard work is rewarded here).

Each and every organisation has its own culture which gives it a distinct identity and differentiates it from other organisations. Culture of an organisation changes slowly and in doing so it ensures stability and security to its members. In other words, the cultural characteristics of an organisation are relatively enduring over time and relatively static in their propensity to change.

Organisational culture consists of two main components — material culture, and non-material culture.

(*i*) **Material Culture:** It includes all the man-made objects. Food, clothing, housing, tools, modes of transportation and communication are such objects. These material objects of culture are relevant to the creation and operation of organisation. For example, in several business organisations, office staff wears white dress while factory workers wear blue dress.

(*ii*) **Non-Material Culture:** It comprises intangible objects such as values, beliefs, norms, customs, habits, etc. Rituals (for example, farewell party for a retiring employee), taboos (*e.g.,* no one calls the boss by his first name, no gifts from suppliers, etc.) and jargon (*i.e.,* the special language used by employees) are other important aspects of non-material culture in organisations.

19.8 CHARACTERISTICS OF ORGANISATIONAL CULTURE

According to Campbell and others, organisation culture is characterised by the following features[8].

1. **Individual Autonomy:** The degree of responsibility and freedom and opportunities of exercising initiative that individuals have in the organisation.
2. **Structure:** The rules and regulations and the amount of direct supervision that is used to oversee and control employee behaviour.
3. **Support:** The degree of assistance and warmth provided by managers to their subordinates.
4. **Identity:** The degree to which members identity with the organisation as a whole rather than with their work groups or field of professional expertise.

7 Vijay Sathe, **Culture and Related Corporate Realities,** Richard D. Irwin, Homewood, Ill. 1985, p. 18.

8 John P. Campbell, Marvin D. Dunnette, Edward E. Lawler III and Kail K. Weick, **Managerial Behaviour, Performance and Effectiveness,** McGraw-Hill, New York, 1970, p. 393.

5. **Performance Reward:** The degree to which rewards system (*e.g.,* salary increments, promotion) in the organisation are based on employee performance.
6. **Conflict:** The degree of conflict present between peers and work groups as well as the willingness to be honest and open about differences.
7. **Risk Tolerance:** The degree to which employees are allowed to be innovative and risk-taking.

In essence, culture is what blood is to a human body — it keeps all the organs functioning and alive. It is the most fundamental component which gives an organisation its identity and form.

19.9 SUBCULTURES

An organisation culture is composed of two subcultures.

1. **Institutional Subculture:** It refers to the cultural pattern of a particular unit (*e.g.,* division, department) in the organisation. For example, a company may put considerable emphasis on employee safety and accident prevention. People ingrained with this value will wear safety devices before operating a machine or equipment. Similarly, quality of work may be a dominant value in an institutional subculture. Members of another organisation may place high value and work even during lunch break.
2. **Professional Subculture:** It means the values, norms, etc. associated with a particular professional or occupational group within an organisation. For example, accountants have their own code of conduct. When employees belonging to a particular profession give priority to professional subculture over instructional subculture, there may be conflict in the organisation. Professional culture is sometimes called horizontal culture because members sharing it are at the same level.

19.10 IMPACT OF ORGANISATIONAL CULTURE

Culture of an organisation influences the behaviour of its members which in turn has an impact on its processes.

1. **Goal Setting:** People are the basic building blocks of an organisation. Culture moulds people and regulates their thinking on the objectives to be pursued. That is why one organisation aims at profit-maximisation whereas another organisation considers it an unworthy objective.
2. **Work Ethic:** Culture determines the moral principles to be followed at work. The ethical standards of an organisaiton and its members are derived from its culture.
3. **Motivational Pattern:** Cultural values determine what motivates the members of an organisation. For example, in an achievement-oriented culture, employees find it quite motivating to put their time and effort in work. On the other hand, in the absence of such culture, high achievement-oriented employees get frustrated and leave the organisation.
4. **Work Processes:** Decision-making, communication, controlling and other processes in an organisation are influenced by its culture. Bhattacharya[9] has analysed how corporate

9 S.K. Bhattacharya, "Organisational Culture: An Indian Perspective", **Business World,** February 1-14, 1988, pp. 48-49.

culture influences professionally managed and family managed companies in India [Table 19.1]

Table 19.1: Impact of Culture on Two Groups of Organisations

Dimensions of Corporate Culture	Professionally-managed Companies	Family-managed Companies
1. Nature of desired managerial skill.	Emphasis on professional qualifications and rank.	Emphasis on demonstrated skills, depth, quality and knowledge.
2. Actual performance.	Emphasis on conformity to organisational values, loyalty and relative fit with the position.	Emphasis on originality of action and thinking, innovation and upgradation of knowledge and skills.
3. Style of planning and decision-making.	Emphasis on information gathering, bureaucratic mode of function, risk aversion and non-entrepreneurial decision-making.	Emphasis on selective information usage, intuitive, and qualitative decision-making of entrepreneurial nature.
4. Management systems adopted.	Emphasis on use of elegant, scientific, sophisticated and rational system.	Emphasis on reliance on business sense and no frills, systems, geared to quick action.
5. Nature of management control.	Comprehensive, formal and written reporting.	Emphasis on primary use of verbal reporting and remedial action.

19.11 SOCIALISATION

Socialisation is the process of indoctrinating the new employees into the culture of an organisation. It consists of the steps taken by the organisation to get them adapt to its existing culture. Socialisation is a process of adaptation by which employees come to understand the basic values, norms and customs for becoming the accepted members of the organisation, and assuming organisational roles. Employees who do not learn to adjust to the organisation's culture are labelled as 'rebels' or 'non-conformists' and may even be expelled from the organisation. Socialisation performs two functions — *(a)* it creates uniform behaviour in members, increases understanding in communication and reduces conflicts, and *(b)* it reduces role ambiguity of employees by indicating what is expected of them, and creates a feeling of security among them.

According to Mannen and Schein[10] socialisation process consists of the following three stages:

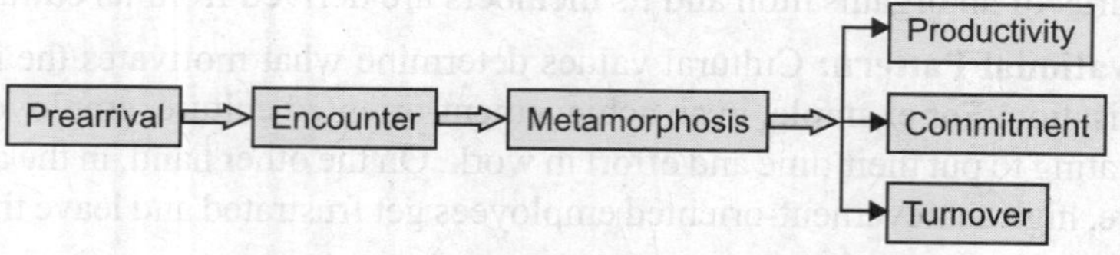

Fig. 19.2: The Process of Socialisation

10 John Van Mannen and Edgar H. Schein, "Career Development", in J.R. Hackman and J.C. Suttle (eds.), **Improving Life at Work,** Goodyear Publishing Co., California, 1977, pp. 58-62.

1. **Pre-Arrival:** Each individual arrives in an organisation with a particular set of values, attitudes and expectations. The organisation must keep this in mind while selecting employees so that people who fit into its existing culture are selected. The candidates must be made aware of the organisation's values and expectations during the selection process. This will help to create a cultural fit between the organisation and the new employees.
2. **Encounter:** In this stage, the new employees may face some dichotomy between their expectations and the organisation's requirements. If this is so the new employees must be oriented to the organisation's culture. In case the new employee is unable to adapt to the requirements of the organisation, he might have to resign.
3. **Metamorphosis or Transformation:** In due course of time, the new employees learn to adjust to the values, norms and requirements of the organisation. When they internalise the organisation's culture they get accepted by the existing employees and their confidence increases. As a result they feel committed to the organisation and their performance improves. They do not look for work in other organisations. Otherwise, they lack commitment, feel frustrated and may leave the organisation.

TEST QUESTIONS

1. What is organisation culture? Describe the relationship between organisational culture and organisational effectiveness.
2. Explain the significance of organisational culture and the role of top management in the creation and sustenance of the same.
3. What are terminal values and instrumental values? Assume a situation where they are at conflict with each other and you have to practise one of them. Give reasons for your answer.
4. "If so much diversity exists among segments of a single culture, then even more diversity is likely to exist among the members of two or more cultures". Explain the similarities and diversity in adopting strategies.
5. "The study of culture is a challenging task because its primary focus is on the broadest component of social behaviour — an entire society". Explain the concept of culture with particular emphasis on the role it plays in influencing employee behaviour.
6. "Organisational Cultures have great impact on performance and satisfaction in an organisation." Elucidate with suitable examples.
7. How is organisational culture created and maintained?
8. How is organisational culture transmitted in an organisation? Discuss its impact on organisation.
9. (*a*) Elucidate some important characteristics of organisational culture. How do organisations go about maintaining their culture?

   (*b*) Outline strategies for improving quality of work life in an organisation.
10. What are the various determinants of organisational culture? How does leadership influence the culture of an organisation?

11. Define Organisational Culture. Use suitable examples to discuss Hofstede's classification of corporate culture.
12. Identify the critical barriers to advancement by women in Indian organisations today. What attempts are being made by organisations as well as by individuals to overcome these barriers?
13. Discuss the relationship between organisational, national and global culture. How can different aspects of culture be both functional and dysfunctional? Give examples.
14. Consider the dimensions on which national cultures differ. Select any two of those dimensions. Discuss consequences in the workplace if someone from another culture differing on the dimensions from the United States were to take a job in a U.S. company. Then indicate what steps (policies, practices, training etc.) you believe the U.S. company should take to help accommodate the differences.
15. Write short notes on the following :
    (*a*) Gender issues in management
    (*b*) Key variables shaping customer-responsive cultures.
16. How do organisational cultures develop? Describe the steps of organisational, cultural socialisation process.
17. Explain the socialisation process in context of familiarising the organisational culture.
18. Briefly describe the Terminal Values and Instrumental Values with five examples of each. Also give one example of a situation where they are in conflict with each other and one example where they are in line with each other.
19. Analyse the challenges in cross-cultural communication in the light of high and low context cultures with two suitable examples.
20. XTC (a transport corporation) is said to be at the verge of collapse. The prevailing organisational culture is found to be one of the major factors responsible for this situation. As a management consultant suggest a strategy for development of positive organisational culture.
21. "Culture is not learnt but acquired from circumstances". Do you agree? Give reasons.

CASE STUDY

Indo Industrial Engineers (IIE) is a manufacturing unit producing auto components and is an OEM (Original Equipment Manufacturer) of Maruti Udyog Limited. The company is very successful and is ISO certified for quality and environment. The systems in the company seem to be matured and everything is moving as per plans.

The company recently conducted an Organisational Culture Survey in which it was found that the scores of openness, transparency, confrontation are on a higher side whereas experimentation score is the lowest. This opened the eyes of the top management in the light of the fact that Tata Motors has announced that it will produce a car of ₹ 1,00,000 with four doors. Since the company is OEM to Maruti Udyog Limited (MUL) which is going to face this competition in the market and is likely to pass this to their OEMs as they have done in the past. Indo Industrial Engineers have faced situations in the past that the price reduction has been executed from the Buyer's side which they were supposed to execute being an OEM of MUL. The top management remembers the good time when they use to just pass on the price rise in the production to the customer very easily following the cost plus model. But now those days are gone and the market governs the price and the manufacturer is required to manufacture with the price specified by the market. There is complete shift in the paradigm from the suppliers market to a buyers market. The Research and Development is very weak in IIE which is reflected in the low score of experimentation in the organisation culture survey. It was also found in the research survey that the top management is concerned about the lack of leadership qualities amongst the managerial cadre of the organisation.

The top management is in a fix as the challenge of competition is going to be stiffer particularly in the light of Tata Motors announcement of producing the cheapest car.

Questions

(*a*) Discuss the main issues of the case. What does the Research Survey on Organisational Culture indicate?

(*b*) What leadership qualities are required to be developed amongst the employees of Indo Industrial Engineers?

CHAPTER

20

ORGANISATIONAL CONFLICT

CHAPTER OUTLINE

20.1. Concept of Organisational Conflict
20.2. Nature of Organisational Conflict
20.3. Stages in Organisational Conflict
20.4. Changing Views of Organisational Conflict
20.5. Functions (Positive Outcomes) of Organisational Conflict
20.6. Dysfunctions (Negative Effects) of Organisational Conflict
20.7. Levels of Organisational Conflict
- 20.7.1 Intra-Individual Conflict
- 20.7.2 Interpersonal Conflict
- 20.7.3 Intra Group Conflict
- 20.7.4 Inter-Group Conflict
- 20.7.5 Intra Organisation Conflict
- 20.7.6 Inter-Organisation Conflict

20.8. Management of Organisational Conflict
- 20.8.1 Stimulation of Conflict
- 20.8.2 Resolution of Conflict
- **Test Questions**
- **Case Study**

Conflict is an inevitable feature of organisational life. The very nature of organisations makes conflict unavoidable. An organisation consists of people having divergent personalities, values and perceptions. Members of an organisation are assigned different jobs and have different degrees of status. Individuals and groups in an organisation compete for scarce resources. In any organisation conflicts assume different forms and arise from several sources. Successful managers must understand the nature, consequences and causes of conflict. They must deal with conflict so as to achieve both organisational and individual goals.

20.1 CONCEPT OF ORGANISATIONAL CONFLICT

In the literal sense conflict implies opposition, controversy, friction, strife, disagreement or clash. But in management, "conflict is a process in which an effort is purposefully made by one person or unit to block another that results in frustrating the attainment of the other's goals or the furthering of his or her interests."[1]

In broad terms conflict may be viewed "as a breakdown in the standard mechanism of decision-making."[2] For example, an employee gets a promotion but has to relocate to an unknown city. He is in a state of dilemma and is not able to make any decision.

Another view is that "conflict is any situation in which two or more parties feel themselves in opposition. It is an interpersonal process that arises from disagreement over the goals or the methods to accomplish those goals."[3] For example, marketing department in a company wants more funds for advertising but the finance department does not accept the demand citing shortage of funds.

One expert has used the term conflict to describe: (*i*) antecedent conditions, *e.g.,* scarcity of resources, policy differences among individuals, etc; (*ii*) effective states of the individuals involved, *e.g.,* stress, tension, hostility, anxiety, etc., (*iii*) cognitive states of individuals, *i.e.,* their perception or awareness of conflicting situations; and (*iv*) change in behaviour ranging from passive resistance to overt aggression."[4]

These four states may be viewed as different stages in the conflict process. A conflict occurs when these is a difference of opinion or a clash of interests.

20.2 NATURE OF ORGANISATIONAL CONFLICT

The main characteristics of conflict in organisations are as follows:

(*i*) Conflict arises due to incompatibility of two or more aspects of something. It may be goals, values, perceptions, interests, work methods, etc.

(*ii*) Conflict occurs when an individual is unable to choose among the available courses of action.

(*iii*) Conflict must be perceived and expressed by the parties to it. If no one is aware of a conflict, the conflict does not exist even if there is some incompatibility.

(*iv*) Conflict is a dynamic process because it consists of a series of interlocking events.

(*v*) Conflict represents deliberate behaviour. If interference is accidental there is no conflict.

(*vi*) Conflict can exist at both overt (latent) and covert levels.

(*vii*) Conflict is different from competition. In competition both sides try to win but neither side actively interferes with the other. On the other hand, in a conflict one party interferes in the other's efforts.

(*viii*) Conflict is inevitable. It is inherent in all social relations.

1 Stephen P. Robbins, **Managing Organisational Conflict : A Non-Traditional Approach,** Prentice-Hall, New Jersey, 1974.

2 Louis R. Pondy, "Organisational Conflict: Concepts and Models", **Administrative Science Quarterly,** Sept. 1967, p. 297.

3 John W. Newstrom and Keith Davis, **Organisational Behaviour: Human Behaviour at Work,** Tata McGraw-Hill, New Delhi, 2005, p. 312.

4 Louis R. Pondy, *op.cit.,* pp. 298-299.

(*ix*) Conflict is not abnormal. It is a fact of organisational life.

(*x*) Conflict is not always bad. Sometimes, it may be desirable.

(*xi*) Conflict is not always caused by trouble makers. Structural factors like too many levels of authority may also lead to conflict.

20.3 STAGES IN ORGANISATIONAL CONFLICT

There are five stages in a conflict episode. These are as follows[5]:

1. **Latent:** A conflict episode begins when conflict occurs in the sub-conscious mind but is not apparent or clear. Antecedent conditions exist but the conflict has not yet emerged. Competition for scarce resources, divergence of sub-unit goals, competition for positions in the organisation, ambiguities in roles are examples of antecedent conditions.

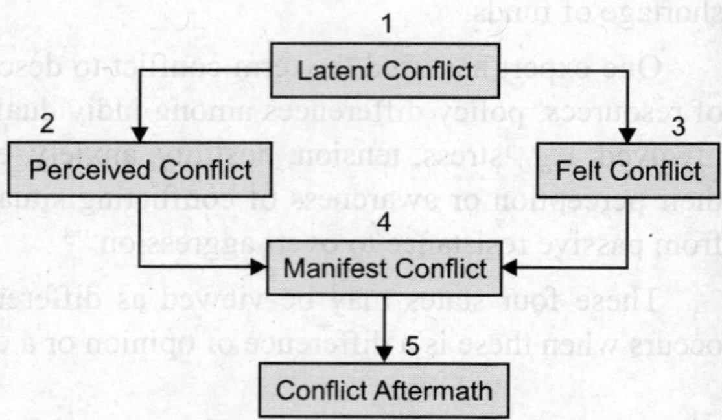

Fig. 20.1: Conflict Process

2. **Perceived Conflict:** A conflict may be perceived even if conditions of latent conflict do not exist. Perceived conflict occurs because the parties misunderstand each other's true position. Such a conflict can be resolved by improving communication between the parties involved in conflict.

3. **Felt Conflict:** When the differences between the parties become personalised or internalised, felt conflict occurs. Conflict becomes personalised when the parties develop hostile feelings towards each other. For example, A and B are aware that they seriously disagree on something. But none of them is tense and their relationship is not affected. Here conflict is not felt. Both organisational and extra-organisational factors may lead to internalisation. Inconsistency in demand from the organisation and needs and involvement of an individual's whole personality in the relationship are such factors.

4. **Manifest Conflict:** At this stage there is open confrontation between the parties. Manifest conflict may occur in the form of open aggression, sabotage, apathy, withdrawal, perfect obedience to rules. In extreme cases there may be violence.

5. **Conflict Aftermath:** A conflict may have positive or negative consequences for the organisation depending on how the conflict is resolved. If the conflict is genuinely resolved to the satisfaction of both the parties, there can be more enduring and cooperative relationship between them. But in case the conflict is merely suppressed and not resolved, the latent conditions may be aggravated. Later on these may explode in a more serious form. This legacy of conflict is known as "conflict aftermath".

5 Louis R. Pondy, *op. cit.,* pp. 298-299.

20.4 CHANGING VIEWS OF ORGANISATIONAL CONFLICT

There are three different views of conflict. These are given below:

1. **Classical or Traditional View:** According to the classical approach, conflict is abnormal phenomenon and is always undesirable. It induces negative outcomes such as anger, resentment, confusion, lack of cooperation, etc. It disrupts the smooth functioning of an organisation and creates chaos or disorder. Therefore, conflict must be avoided at all costs.

   The classical writers believed that conflict is inherently bad or harmful. It indicates malfunctioning in the organisation. For example, Fayol[6] suggested that whenever there is a clash between the interest of the organisation and that of individuals, the interest of the organisation must be given priority. Thus, classical approach presents a very conservative and negative view of conflict.

2. **Behavioural View:** The human relations experts believed that conflict is a natural phenomenon in organisation. It is inevitable because an organisation is composed of people having different values, goals, and perceptions. But conflict is harmful and should be resolved amicably to maintain good human relations.

3. **Interactionist or Modern View:** According to the modern writers, conflict is not only inevitable but also necessary for the effectiveness of an organisation. An organisation void of some conflict lacks diversity, excitement and viability. Conflict prevents stagnation and apathy and stimulates curiosity and creativity. It provides an opportunity to people to express their differences, anxiety and claims. Conflict is needed for personal and social change. It is the task of the group leader to allow conflicts to happen to keep the group viable, self-critical and creative[7]. However, he must keep conflicts under control to avoid their harmful consequences.

20.5 FUNCTIONS (POSITIVE OUTCOMES) OF ORGANISATIONAL CONFLICT

Conflicts can provide the following benefits:

1. **Release of Tension:** Conflict provides an opportunity to the members of a group to express their fears, doubts, differences of opinion, etc. This leads to reduction of stress which might otherwise remain suppressed. A good fight clears accumulated ill-feelings and tensions.

2. **Stimulant for Change:** Conflict highlights and clarifies problems. It initiates a search for ways to improve goals, work methods and attitudes. Conflict is integral to the process of change.

3. **Creativity and Innovation:** Open confrontation puts pressure on people to search for imaginative solutions to problems. It encourages them to learn and develop. Absence of conflict may make people lethargic and non-creative.

---

6 Henri Fayol, **General and Industrial Management,** Sir Issac Pitman & Sons Ltd; London, 1949.

7 Stephen P. Robbins, **Organisational Behaviour,** Prentice Hall of India, New Delhi, 1994, p. 446.

4. **Identification of Weaknesses:** A conflict helps in identifying deficiencies in the system and process of the organisation. Managers can then take steps to remove these deficiencies.
5. **Avoidance of Group-think:** Strong vocal disagreement helps to avoid group-think. When all members of a group think in the same way, the group fails to make rational decisions.
6. **Group Cohesiveness:** Competition and conflict between group members create solidarity among them. They unite to face external pressures and become more loyal to the group. They forget their differences and the group becomes more cohesive. For example, petty conflicts between members of a cricket team are put aside before a big match. Similarly, occasional flare-up serves to balance power relationships between departments. It facilitates internal stability in the organisation.
7. **Challenge:** Conflict tests the abilities and capacities of both individuals and groups. It creates challenge for them to improve their knowledge and skills for facing problems and for working in cooperation.

20.6 DYSFUNCTIONS (NEGATIVE EFFECTS) OF ORGANISATIONAL CONFLICT

Too much conflict is dangerous and can lead to the following undesirable consequences:

1. **Stress:** Prolonged conflict generates feelings of anxiety, guilt, frustration and hostility. These spoil the physical and mental health of the parties involved in the conflict.
2. **Lack of Mutual Trust:** Conflict may create a climate of suspicion and distrust among people in an organisation. People develop negative feelings towards one another and try to avoid interactions. Discord replaces cooperation.
3. **Dissatisfaction:** Conflict creates discontentment for the losing side. The loser waits for an opportunity to settle the score with the winner.
4. **Diversion of Time and Efforts:** Individuals and groups focus their time and energy on winning the conflict rather than on achieving organisational goals. Personal problems and interests become more important than organisational goals. Some sort of goal displacement occurs.
5. **Instability and Chaos:** Intense conflicts create social distance between different units of the organisation leading to communication breakdowns. The normal workflow is disrupted and the moral fabric of the people is torn apart. Competent and key personnel leave the organisation. In extreme cases, sabotage and illegal activities may occur. All these weaken the organisation and its survival is in danger.

20.7 LEVELS OF ORGANISATIONAL CONFLICT

Conflict in organisations can occur mainly at three levels :

1. Individual Level
   (*a*) Intra-individual Conflict
   (*b*) Interpersonal Conflict

2. Group Level
   (*a*) Intra-group Conflict
   (*b*) Inter-group Conflict
3. Organisational Level
   (*a*) Intra-organisation Conflict
   (*b*) Inter-organisation Conflict

20.7.1 Intra-individual Conflict

The conflict which arises within an individual is known as intra-individual conflict. The individual faces a conflict within himself. Inter-individual conflict is of two types:

1. **Goal Conflict:** Goal conflict arises when the individual is attempting to achieve a goal that has both positive and negative features or when the individual faces two or more competing goals. The individual feels dissatisfied as his expectations are not met. This may lead to incongruency between the individual goals and organisational goals. Goal conflicts are of three types:

   (*a*) **Approach-Approach Conflict:** This type of goal conflict arises when a person has to choose from two or more equally attractive goals. For example, a person may have to choose between two lucrative job offers.

   (*b*) **Approach-Avoidance Conflict:** In this form of conflict, a person attempts to achieve a goal that has both positive and negative consequences. For example, a person may get a promotion but he has to work far away from his home town.

   (*c*) **Avoidance-Avoidance Conflict:** Such conflict occurs when an individual has to choose between two equally unattractive alternatives. For example, an employee dislikes his present job but the alternative of resigning and looking for another job is equally unattractive.

2. **Role Conflict:** A role is a set of activities expected of a person holding a particular position in the organisation[8]. There are three types of roles — expected, perceived and enacted. The expected role is what others expect from a person. The perceived role is what the person thinks he should perform or behave. The enacted role is how the person actually behaves. When the role expectations are not clear, role ambiguity arises.

   Role ambiguity means an individual is unclear about the job duties and responsibilities expected from him. As a result the individual experiences difficulty in enacting his expected role and his job performance suffers. Role conflict may lead to decline in job satisfaction, motivation, self-confidence and performance as it creates tension, anxiety and has an adverse impact on the individual's mental and physical health: Open communication, joint problem solving and participative decision making help to resolve role conflict. There are four forms of role conflict.

   (*a*) **Person-Role Conflict:** This kind of conflict arises when the behaviour expected from a person is incompatible with his own value system. For example, a company

8 Theodore R. Sarbin, "Role Theory", in Gardener Lindzey (ed.), **Handbook of Social Psychology,** Addison-Wesley, Cambridge Mass, 1954, pp. 223-258.

asks its marketing manager to secure purchase order from Government officials by bribing them. The manager does not want to do so on moral grounds.

(*b*) **Inter-Role Conflict:** Such conflict occurs when an individual is supposed to play multiple roles which are divergent. For instance, a manager asks his assistant to work overtime while the assistant's family expects him to spend more time with them.

(*c*) **Intra-Sender Role Conflict:** This form of conflict occurs when an individual is expected to perform a task which he is not capable of doing due to lack of adequate time and resources. For example, a librarian is asked to purchase rare books from approved bookstores but the books are available only with roadside book sellers.

(*d*) **Inter-Sender Role Conflict:** Such conflict arises when an individual faces conflicting expectations from different groups. For example, management expects the factory supervisor to exercise strict control while the workers expect him to be liberal with them.

20.7.2 Interpersonal Conflict

Conflict between two or more individuals is called interpersonal conflict. Two men vying for the same woman and two employees competing for the same position, are examples of interpersonal conflict. The main causes of interpersonal conflict are as follows:

1. **Personality Differences:** When an outgoing (extrovert) and an in-going (introvert) persons interact, conflict can arise between them.
2. **Perceptual Differences:** Two or more individuals may perceive the same issue in opposite ways. Such differences in perception lead to conflict between them. For instance, the marketing head of a company may believe that the market share of its products is declining due to severe competition whereas the production head feels it is because of inadequate efforts on the part of the sales team.
3. **Differences in Value Systems:** Conflict between individuals may also arise due to clash of values. For example, the chief engineer emphasises quality, design and durability whereas the production manager stresses upon simplicity and low manufacturing costs. The reaction of the engineer is "we shall lose on reputation if we do it your way", while the production manager says "it is too expensive to do it your way",
4. **Differences in Power and Status:** Interpersonal conflicts arise from unequal distribution of power and status. For example, conflict may occur when a low status waitress in a restaurant gives orders to a high status cook.
5. **Scarcity of Resources:** When two or more persons compete for scarce resources, conflict occurs. For example, when three qualified heads of department compete for the chief executive's post which has fallen vacant conflict may arise between them. Similarly, a common company vehicle, limited space, scarcity of funds may be source of conflict between individuals.

20.7.3 Intra-Group Conflict

Intra-group conflict means conflict between members of the same group. It is similar to interpersonal conflict except that the persons involved in the conflict belong to a common group. Individuals are usually members of different groups for different purposes. Therefore, interpersonal conflicts may gradually result in intra-group conflict. When an intra-group conflict becomes serious or intense, the group may become divided into two subgroups. As a result, intra-group conflict may lead to inter-group conflict. According to Kelly[9], intra-group conflict may arise due to the following reasons:

(*i*) When the group faces a novel problem
(*ii*) When new values are imported from the social environment into the group
(*iii*) When a person's extra-group role comes into conflict with his intra-group role.

20.7.4 Inter-Group Conflict

Inter-group conflict refers to conflict between different groups in the organisation. The most common example of inter-group conflict is conflict between production department and marketing department. The main sources of inter-group conflict are as follows:

1. **Incompatible Goals:** When the achievement of one group's goals interferes with the attainment of another group's goals, a conflict arises between the two groups. Conflict between management and labour is due to incompatibility of goals.

2. **Task Interdependence:** In an organisation, one group or unit often depends on another for information and resources. As this interdependence increases the possibility of conflict increases. Thompson[10] has identified three types of interdependence between groups. Pooled interdependence exists when groups have little interaction with each other. For example, a branch in Delhi need not interact with a branch in Chandigarh. The only linkage between them is that both contribute to organisational goals. When the output of one group is the input of another group, it is called **sequential interdependence**. For example, interdependence between sugar mill and confectionary unit is sequential. In this case one unit cannot start its work until the other unit completes its task. **Reciprocal interdependence** exists when two groups are mutually interdependent in accomplishing the task. It requires continuous interaction. For example, the relationship between nursing staff, surgeons and anesthesiology staff is reciprocal. Conflict potential is greatest in such interdependence.

3. **Resource Sharing:** Conflict between groups often arises when they compete for a larger share of scarce resources. Each group wants a bigger slice out of the common pool of resources but the total amount of resources is not adequate to meet the demand of all the groups. Resources are not only means of achieving goals but also symbolise power and influence.

4. **Reward System:** When incentives are based on individual group performacne but tasks are interdependent, different groups may come into conflict. If departments are rewarded for departmental performance, departments may try to excel at each other's expense. If the reward system allows only one group to accomplish its goal at the expense of other groups there are bound to be conflicts and even power struggle among the groups. For example, if only the sales team is rewarded for high sales volume, advertising group and production team are likely to become jealous and may sabotage the efforts of sales team in future.

9 Joe Kelly, **Organisational Behaviour,** Richard D. Irwin, Homewood, 1974, p. 565.
10 Edgar H. Schein, *op. cit.,* p. 98.

5. **Differences in Values and Attitudes:** Different groups may have different values and attitudes and such differences can lead to conflict between them. Attitudes of distrust and suspicion between groups can cause conflict. Work orientation of different groups differ. For example, finance department may stress conservation of funds while advertising section desires to be liberal in spending money.
6. **Distortions in Communication:** When communication between groups is blocked misunderstanding and clash arise between them. Jurisdictional disputes can arise when the areas of authority and responsibility of different departments are not clearly defined.
7. **Joint Decision Making:** Higher level coordination requires joint decision-making by different departments. Their differences come into the open and conflict may arise when these departments are not able to work together in cooperation.

20.7.5 Intra-Organisation Conflict

There can be three types of conflict within an organisation:

1. **Horizontal or Functional Conflict:** Conflict between employees or departments at the same level of authority is called horizontal conflict. Each department may try to achieve its own goals at the expense of other departments. For example, production department may prefer long production runs while sales department may insist on quick delivery.
2. **Vertical or Hierarchical Conflict:** It means conflict between superiors and subordinates. Vertical conflict arises because superiors attempt to control subordinates and subordinates resist control to maintain their freedom of action.
3. **Line and Staff Conflict:** Such conflict is basically a clash of domains. The main sources of line and staff conflict are as follows[11]:
   (*i*) Line managers dislike to take advice from younger staff specialists.
   (*ii*) Line managers consider staff as unnecessary impediments. The staff, in turn, view themselves as experts.
   (*iii*) Line managers feel that staff oversteps its authority.
   (*iv*) Line people resent staff's highly academic and untested ideas.
   (*v*) Staff people feel that line managers are bull-headed and do not clothe staff with enough authority and resist new ideas.

20.7.6 Inter-Organisation Conflict

Conflict between two or more organisations is known as inter-organisational conflict. Such conflict promotes unity among members of an organisation. It simplifies the objectives of an organisation. It makes the members aware of the strategy and tactics of the opponent. Inter-organisational conflict can arise only when (*a*) each organisation is considering the other organisation in decision-making, and (*b*) the two organisations affect each other.

---

11 M. Dalton, "Conflict between Staff and Line Managerial Officers", **American Sociology Review,** 1905 (15), pp. 342-351.

Inter-organisational conflict is of the following types[12]:

(i) **Management-Government:** Conflict between business and government can arise over consumer protection, labour exploitation, fair trade, bribery, political contributions, etc.

(ii) **Management-union:** Conflict between management and labour can occur in the form of strikes, go slow, sabotage, lockout, etc.

(iii) **Inter-management:** Managements of different organisations may compete against each other to enhance their respective positions in the industry. Disputes over patents, advertisements, price wars are examples of such conflict.

(iv) **Inter-union:** Unions may compete for recognition, jurisdiction, jobs for their members, etc.

(v) **Union-government:** Unions may face action from government due to illegal activities such as discrimination, illegal strikes, violence, etc.

20.8 MANAGEMENT OF ORGANISATIONAL CONFLICT

Conflict has both constructive and destructive consequences. Therefore, every conflict must be analysed and managed carefully. Constructive conflict should be stimulated and destructive conflict must be amicably resolved. "The way conflict is managed rather than suppressed, ignored or avoided, contributes significantly to an organisation's effectiveness."[13]

20.8.1 Stimulation of Conflict

Robbins[14] has suggested the following strategies for stimulating constructive conflict:

1. **Communication:** Management can send ambiguous or threatening messages to encourage conflict. For example, management may spread the message that a department (division) branch is to be closed down. This can reduce apathy, force employees to forget their differences, stimulate new ideas, and force reevaluation of existing practices. But such messages or rumours must be planted intelligently in the informal channels so as to serve a useful purpose. Sometimes, a manager can also redirect messages and alter communication channels to encourage conflict.
2. **Encouraging Competition:** Well-designed incentives such as bonus, awards for outstanding performance, etc. can stimulate healthy competition between individuals and groups. One individual or group will struggle hard to outperform the other.
3. **Restructuring the Organisation:** Management can reorganise work groups, increase interdependence between work groups and alter rules and regulations to disrupt the *status quo*. As employees try to adjust to the new situation, there will be improvement in the methods of operations.
4. **Bringing in Outsiders:** In order to 'shake up' or bring back life in a stagnant group, management can bring in new employees whose values, attitudes, background differ

---

12 R. Stagner and H. Rosen, **Psychology of Union-Management Relations,** Books/cole, Belmont, Califf, 1965, p. 91.

13 Joe Kelly, **Organisational Behaviour,** *op. cit.,* p. 568.

14 Stephen P. Robbins, *op. cit.,* pp. 59-89.

from those of existing employees. This will disturb the *status quo* due to divergent opinions and innovative ideas.

20.8.2 Resolution of Conflict

Some of the strategies that can be used to resolve conflicts are given below:

1. **Avoidance or Withdrawal:** In this strategy, parties to conflict avoid dealing with conflict and pretend that conflict does not exist. They become indifferent, evasive, apathetic, and depend on fate. They may withdraw or detach themselves from the conflict. They ignore disagreement, take no position on the issues involved and do not talk about the situation. This strategy is useful when the differences are irrelevant for the organisation. For example, individuals may differ on religion, politics, sports, etc. These differences may not affect cooperation and work performance.
2. **Smoothing (Accommodation) :** In this approach, the conflicting parties play down their differences and highlight similarities and areas of agreement. Management tries to appease group members whose feelings have been hurt or down-plays the significance of the issue. The purpose is to reduce the intensity of the conflict and avoid its escalation into open hostility.

   Smoothing does not tackle the real issues which are likely to resurface soon. But smoothing is a more sensitive approach than withdrawal. Smoothing can be used as a stop-gap measure to let the parties cool down and reduce the conflict to a manageable level. For example, when a controversial issue is being discussed in a meeting, tempers often run high and people show hostile behaviour. Then the chairman intervenes to cool down tempers.
3. **Compromising (Bargaining):** This is a traditional method of resolving conflicts. Each party makes some concession so that a compromise or agreement is reached. It is a give and take process and involves negotiation. Bargaining leads to a mutually acceptable agreement. But it is not in the long-term interest because the basic problem is not solved rationally. The party which has least bargaining power comes out to be a loser as it has to make the biggest sacrifice. This strategy is used commonly where the conflict arises due to differences in values, attitudes or goals. It can be effective when the desired goals (*e.g.,* resource sharing) can be divided.
4. **Competition:** This strategy involves direct attack to gain control over others. Parties to the conflict fight it out using arguments, and intimidation to overpower each other. This approach may aggravate the situation and create ill-will unless one party is strong enough to punish or dominate others. One party's gain is another's loss. Therefore, confrontation should be used with great care.
5. **Problem Solving:** Conflict usually creates feelings of resentment, hostility and frustration. Under problem-solving approach, attempt is made to convert these negative feelings into positive ones. The time and energy of the parties are channelised into finding a rational solution to the problem. The management clarifies the issue, encourages communication, maintains relationship between the parties. There is a complete rethinking of the conflict situation. Parties share information, listen to each other with empathy and depersonalise the issue.

Problem solving is a constructive approach and creates a win-win situation. An organisation may seek the help of an outside consultant to establish initial trust between the conflicting sides and to lay down ground rules for open discussions.

6. **Dominance (Repression):** The simplest approach is forcing the conflicting parties to accept the solution developed by the boss. A higher-level manager asks the conflicting sides to drop their fight and get on with the job. People in the organisation recognise and accept the authority of their superior. Dominance is an autocratic approach and may prove ineffective in the long run. The conflict may recur in a more violent form and the peace may be temporary. This is because the real issue is not tackled. A formal procedure for redressing grievances also involves an appeal to higher authority who arrives at a solution.

7. **Reducing Interdependence:** The scope for conflict is high when two departments are interdependent and share scarce resources. Conflict can be reduced by reducing such interdependence and providing resources independently to each. But it can increase costs due to duplication of resources.

8. **Physical Separation:** Sometimes, a conflict can be resolved temporarily through physical separation. The conflicting parties are not allowed to interact with each other. Separation provides enough time for lasting solution of the problem later on. It helps to prevent more damage being done as the escalation of conflict is avoided for the time being. For example, a trouble-making employee may be transferred to a different location.

9. **Rotation of People:** Rotation of employees makes them understand the problems and functioning of different branches of factories or departments. They also learn different roles.

10. **Liaison Group or Intermediaries:** A liaison group or an intermediary may be appointed to iron out differences between two warring factions. The intermediary uses expertise and persuasion to achieve cooperation and coordination between them. He must understand each side's problems and viewpoint and rally them toward a mutually acceptable solution. Such a third party is considered to be unbiased without a vested interest in either party. Such a human relations expert can change attitudes and resolve conflicts.

11. **Superordinate Goals:** A superordinate goal is a common goal that appeals to all the parties and cannot be achieved by the resources of any single party. Such a goal requires cooperation between the parties. The conflicting parties sink their differences and cooperate with each other to achieve the overriding goal. Threat to the survival is a superordinate goal. For example, when the existence of a company is under threat due to severe competition, different departments work unitedly to overcome the threat. A strong common enemy is a great unifying force. In the face of an overriding common purpose or threat, individuals and groups come together to ensure victory. For instance, the threat of Hitler led to an alliance between Western nations and Russia. The alliance fell apart as soon as the common threat disappeared.

TEST QUESTIONS

1. Define organisational conflict. Explain the sources of conflict with suitable illustrations.
2. Under what conditions does it become imperative to stimulate conflict in an organisation? Briefly discuss the techniques of conflict management in an organisational set-up.

3. How do Traditional, Behavioural and Interactionist views explain the process of conflict? Evaluate the changes which take place within and between the groups as a result of long-standing inter-group conflict.
4. Describe conflict avoidance, conflict diffusion and conflict confrontation strategies with the help of suitable examples.
5. "Both too low and too high levels of conflict have deleterious effects on organisational performance." Discuss.
6. Distinguish between avoidance and repression as conflict handling strategies.
7. What consequences can result from extremely high or low levels of conflict? How can managers maintain an optimal level of conflict?
8. Identify major sources of conflict in an organisation. What approaches will you suggest for managing conflict in a service organisation in today's context?
9. "Conflict in organisations is inevitable and to some extent even desirable." Elucidate. Explain briefly the three major forms of conflict management.
10. Write notes on the following:
    (*a*) Interpersonal conflict;
    (*b*) Role conflict;
    (*c*) Interactionist view of conflict.
11. Discuss the reasons for various types of conflicts in an organisation. Suggest measures to resolve interpersonal conflicts.
12. What are the styles for handling interpersonal conflicts? Give examples of situations in which each style would be appropriate.
13. "Most severe conflict between groups arises when there is a Win-Lose Orientation". Do you agree?
14. In the context of the above statement, discuss the Forcing and Pressure tactics of conflict management. Also, enumerate the role of collaboration (Integrative Problem Solving) in resolving inter-group conflict.
15. What are the sources of interpersonal conflict?
16. What is the difference between functional and dysfunctional conflict? Enumerate conflict management techniques.
17. How do groups in conflict behave? What are the four strategies that can be used to manage inter-group conflict effectively?
18. (*a*) Discuss the Nine classifications of conflict resolution.
    (*b*) How can organisations deal with inter-group conflicts?
19. "Conflict is not always bad". Comment.
20. "The best way to deal with conflict is to avoid the conflict." Critically evaluate the statement in the light of various modes of handling conflict with the help of a diagram. Give at least one example in each case where that mode of handling conflict is suitable.

21. "Different conflict resolution strategies have their own strengths and weaknesses." Do you agree? In the context of a conflict between the management and the trade union, which strategy would you recommend and why?
22. What implications does the modern view of conflict have for the managers?
23. Explain the differences between functional and dysfunctional conflicts.
24. Explain the attributes of an effective conflict resolution process.
25. Distinguish between intra-group and inter-group conflict.
26. "Inter-group conflicts can lead to group cohesiveness". Comment.
27. "Even organisations which are considered to be ideal ones are not free from conflicts". Explain.

CASE STUDY

Two union representatives Sharma and Verma have totally different approaches to representing their members' interests when negotiating workplace changes with their respective managers. In the opening stages of negotiation. Verma's style is to try to get the manager to show his hand about what he wants and how much ground he is prepared to give, but without revealing anything to the manager. When things have progressed a little, he also tends to be quite pushy. For example, to get his point over, he attempts to shout the manager down, and doggedly refuses to give ground until it is clear that an impasse has been reached.

Sharma also tends to stand his ground, but in a different way. He always knows clearly what he wants to achieve before negotiation starts, but is prepared to be quite open about this in return for the manager being equally open. By doing this he is often able to get the manager to be clear about the overall result the manager wants to achieve. Using this as a criterion, Sharma is then able to say "Look-in overall terms, you have told me what you want to achieve, and so if I can show you another way to achieve the same outcome in a way that also enables my members to get what they want — are you prepared to explore ways in which we can both get what we want?"

Questions

(*a*) How would you characterise the conflict handling styles of Sharma and Verma?

(*b*) Discuss some functional and dysfunctional outcomes of conflict based on research evidence.

CHAPTER

21

ORGANISATIONAL EFFECTIVENESS

CHAPTER OUTLINE

21.1. The Concept of Organisational Effectiveness
21.2. Effectiveness Versus Efficiency
21.3. Measurement of Effectiveness
21.4. Approaches to Organisational Effectiveness
21.4.1 Goal Attainment Approach
21.4.2 Systems Approach
21.4.3 Strategic Constituencies Approach
21.4.4 Behavioural Approach
21.5. Factors Influencing Organisational Effectiveness
21.6. Likert's Model of Effectiveness
21.7. Adaptive Coping Cycle
• **Test Questions**
• **Case Study**

Organisational effectiveness is one of the essential issues in organisation theory and behaviour.

21.1 THE CONCEPT OF ORGANISATIONAL EFFECTIVENESS

Organisational effectiveness is the extent to which an organisation, given certain resources and means, achieves its objectives without placing undue strain on its members[1]. An organisation is said to be effective when it is able to achieve its goals.

The main features of organisational effectiveness are as follows.

(*i*) Organisational effectiveness is a multidimensional concept. It means different things to different people. To a financial analyst, it means the return on investment; to a production manager it means the quantity of output while to a marketing manager it means the sales turnover or market share. There is no single criterion to measure effectiveness.

1 Basil Georgopolous and Arnold S. Tannenbaum, "A Study of Organisational Effectiveness", **American Sociological Review,** 22 (1957), pp. 535-536.

(*ii*) Organisational effectiveness is a relative term or a matter of degree depending upon the organisation's capacity and potential. An organisation with huge capacity and high potential can be called effective only when it achieves comparatively higher goals.

(*iii*) The effectiveness of an organisation is the outcome of effectiveness of individuals and groups working in it [Fig.21.1]

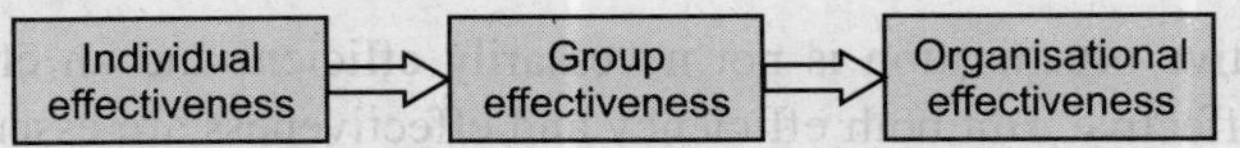

Fig. 21.1. Perspectives of Effectiveness

Individual effectiveness refers to task performance of organisational members. It depends on physical attributes, personality traits, motivation and morale etc. of the individual. Group effectiveness means the performance of various groups in the organisation. It depends on leadership, communication, socialization, etc. Organisational effectiveness depends on technology, personal competence of managers and employees, environmental constraints, etc.

According to Lawless[2], group effectiveness is not necessarily the sum of individual effectiveness. Similarly, organisational effectiveness may be more than the sum of individual and group effectiveness. An organisation may be able to obtain higher levels of performance than the sum of its parts due to synergistic effects. The relationship among these three depends on the type of organisation, the task and the level of technology used in the organisation.

21.2 EFFECTIVENESS VERSUS EFFICIENCY

Effectiveness is the degree to which predetermined goals are achieved. On the other hand, efficiency refers to the manner in which resources are used for achieving objectives. Effectiveness is a broad concept and it takes into account a large number of factors both inside and outside the organisation. But efficiency is a narrow concept that pertains to the internal working of the organisation. The focus of effectiveness is more on the human side of the organisation whereas the focus of efficiency is more on the technological side.

Some organisations are effective but highly efficient while others are highly efficient but ineffective. For example, a factory exceeds its target of producing 1000 cars per year. But the cost of production per car is unreasonably high. The factory is effective (goal attainment) but inefficient (uneconomical utilisation of resources). In another factory, the cost of production per car is the lowest possible but the factory fails to achieve the target of producing 15,000 cars in the year. The second factory is highly efficient but inefffective. According to Chester Barnard, "When unsought consequences are trivial, effective action is efficient, when unsought consequences are not trivial effective action is inefficient."[3]

Effectiveness is a multidimensional concept and cannot be measured by a single criterion. But efficiency is unidimensional and can be measured by the ratio of input to output. In the words of Barnard, "Organisational effectiveness is the degree to which operational goals have

2 David Lawless, **Effective Management: Social and Psychological Approach,** Prentice Hall, New Jersey, 1972, pp 391-399.

3 Chester I. Barnard, **Functions of the Executive,** Harvard University Press, Cambridge Mass, 1938, pp. 19-20.

been attained while the concept of efficiency represents the cost/benefit rate incurred in the pursuit of these goals."[4] According to Jackson and others, "Effectiveness is commonly referred to as the degree to which predetermined goals are achieved. Efficiency refers to the economical manner in which goal-oriented operations are carried out — something of an input/output ratio."[5]

Thus, an effective organisation is not necessarily efficient and an efficient organisation is not necessarily effective. But both efficiency and effectiveness are essential for the success and growth of an organisation in the long run. Efficiency may help an organisation to become effective.

Distinction Between Efficiency and Effectiveness

Basis of Distinction	Efficiency	Effectiveness
1. Meaning	Economical use of resources	Degree of goal attainment
2. Nature	One-dimensional concept	Multidimensional concept
3. Scope	Narrow concept	Wide concept
4. Measurement	Input/output ratio — *e.g.,* output per labour hour	No single criterion
5. Environmental interface	Does not involve organisation-environment interface	Considers organisation-environment interface
6. Focus	On technical and economic aspects	On human side of the organisation

21.3 MEASUREMENT OF EFFECTIVENESS

The concept of effectiveness appears to be simple but it is very difficult to measure effectiveness due to the following reasons:

(*i*) There is no single unanimons criteria to measure effectiveness. Campbell after reviewing thirty different criteria for measuring effectiveness concluded, "Since an organisation can be effective or ineffective on a number of different facets that may be relatively independent of one another, organisational effectiveness has no operational definition."[6] Similarly, Steers[7] reviewed seventeen different approaches to the study of effectiveness and found a general absence of agreement among them. The four top ranking evaluation criteria in his study are adaptability-flexibility, productivity, job satisfaction and profitability. Most suprisingly, 'survival' and 'growth' are least important factors in his study. Steers reached the conclusion that there is little agreement among analysts concerning what criteria should be used to assess current levels of effectiveness.

4 Chester I. Barnard, **Functions of the Executive,** Harvard University Press, Cambridge, 1938, p. 7.

5 John H. Jackson, Cyril P. Morgan and Joseph G. Puolillo, **Organisation Theory: A Macro Perspective for Management,** Prentice Hall, New Jarsey, 1986. p. 24.

6 John P. Campbell, "On the Nature of Organisational Effectiveness", in P.S. Goodmann and J.M. Pennings (eds.), **New Perspectives on Organisational Effectiveness.**

7 R.M. Steers, "Problems in the Measurement of Organisational Effectiveness", **Administrative Science Quarterly,** 20 (1975), pp. 546-558.

(*ii*) Effectiveness is usually defined in terms of goal achievement. But an organisation and its management generally have multiple and conflicting goals. When there is no agreement on goals, measurement of goal attainment is impossible. Different groups (*e.g.*, employees, investors, customers, etc.) interpret organisation goals in different ways. The tendency to focus on measurable goals leads to neglect of non-measurable goals. Moreover, the same yardstick cannot be used to judge the effectiveness of different types of organisations. For example, profitability which is often used to judge effectiveness of business firms is not applicable in case of social organisations such as universities, NGOs, self-help groups, etc.

21.4 APPROACHES TO ORGANISATIONAL EFFECTIVENESS

21.4.1 Goal Attainment Approach

Every organisation exists to attain certain goals. Goal attainment is probably the most widely used criterion of organisational effectiveness. According to Barnard, "What we mean by effectiveness … is the accomplishment of recognised objectives of cooperative effort. The degree of accomplishment indicates the degree of effectiveness."[8] Organisational effectiveness is judged in terms of the accomplishment of ends rather than means.

The goal attainment approach is a traditional view of effectiveness. It is based on three **assumptions:** (*i*) each organisation strives to achieve an ultimate goal; (*ii*) the goal is clearly defined and well understood by all members of the organisation; and (*iii*) progress towards the goal can be measured.

Three main research studies on the goal attainment approach are as follows:

1. **Price's Conceptual Study:** Price has developed a model comprising five independent variables and five intervening variables that influence organisational effectiveness [Fig. 21.2].

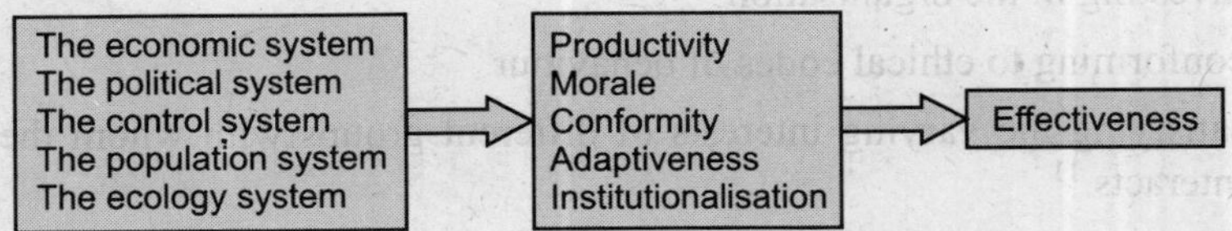

Fig. 21.2: Variables Influencing Effectiveness

Price concludes: "Organisations which have a high degree of division of labour, a high degree of vertical communication, and a high degree of authority are more likely to have a high degree of effectiveness."[9]

2. **Empirical Study of Mahoney and Weitzel:** There are three sets of criteria in determining organisational effectiveness — ultimate, intermediate, and immediate. The first one is the achievement of final goal whereas the second and third are mid-range criteria used to assess short-run effectiveness. These researchers have developed models

8 Chester I. Barnard, *op. cit.*, p. 21.

9 James L. Price, **Organisational Effectiveness,** Irwin, Homewood Ill, 1968.

for two types of organisations — business organisations and research & development organisations. In business organisations the variables useful for predicting effectiveness are: productivity, support and utilisation, planning reliability and initiation. Profitability, productivity, and efficiency are the ultimate goals of business organisations.[10]

3. **Gross's Activities Model:** According to this model, the basic activities in which an organisation must engage help determine what the organisational goals might be and therefore what effectiveness must be. These activities are as follows:

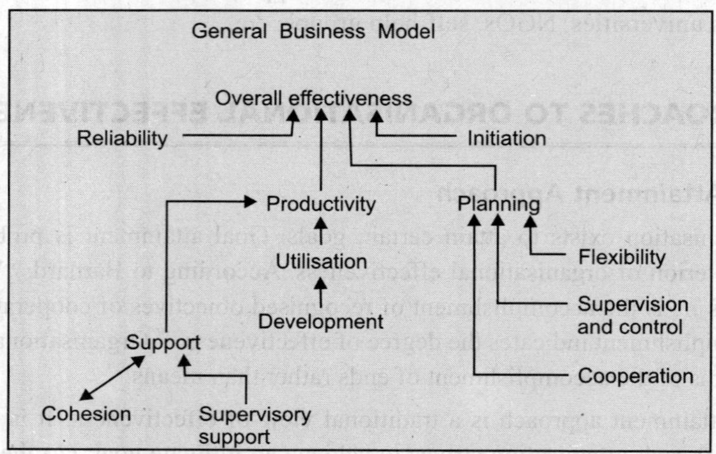

Fig. 21.3: Effectiveness Criteria

(*a*) procurement of resources
(*b*) efficient use of resources
(*c*) producing goods or services
(*d*) rational performance of technical and administrative tasks
(*e*) investing in the organisation
(*f*) conforming to ethical codes of behaviour
(*g*) satisfying the varying interests of different groups with whom the organisation interacts.[11]

Limitations of Goal Attainment Approach: The goal approach has widespread commonsense and practical appeal. It is very popular for measuring organisational effectiveness because goals are the basic reasons for the existence of an organisation. However, this approach suffers from the following problems:

(*i*) Goal approach is based on the assumption that there is consensus on organisational goals. But such consensus is rare because different groups interpret the goals to serve their self-interests.

(*ii*) Most organisations have multiple goals. These goals compete with each other and sometimes are even incompatible. For example, low cost of production and high quality

10 A. Mahoney and William Weitzel, "Managerial Models of Organisational Effectiveness", **Administrative Science Quarterly,** 1969, pp. 357-365.

11 R.M. Gross, "Where Are Your Organisation's Objectives: A General Systems Approach to Planning," **Human Relations,** 18 (August 1965), pp. 195-216.

may be incompatible goals. It is not possible to pursue all the goals simultaneously. The question arises, "whose goals should be given priority?"

(*iii*) It is not always possible to measure the performance of different individuals and groups. This creates a serious problem in judging organisational effectiveness.

(*iv*) Realistic assessment of goals as ideal states is not possible. Goals, as cultural entities, arise outside the organisation as a social system. These cannot arbitrarily be attributed as properties of the organisation itself.[12]

(*v*) It is very difficult to apply goal attainment approach in service organisations (clubs, hospitals, schools, etc.) which do not produce tangible outputs.

Goal Optimisation: As against the traditional approach of goal maximisation, Steers[13] has suggested goal optimisation. He gives the following arguments in support of his theory:

1. Goal maximisation might be detrimental to the well-being and survival of the organisation. Sometimes, goals may be conflicting, *e.g.,* productivity and job satisfaction. Goal optimisation provides a compromise, *i.e.,* to achieve an optimum level of both in such a situation. Thus, optimisation approach recognises multiple and conflicting goals of an organisation.
2. Through optimisation, managers can assign differential weightage to various goals. For example, profitability goal may be given three weights as against one to job satisfaction.
3. There are several constraints in goal maximisation. Optimisation is the best alternative in the presence of unavoidable constraints.
4. Goal optimisation is a flexible criteria as it reflects the changing goals and needs of the organisation.
5. Goal optimisation is helpful in long-range planning. Computer simulations can be used to develop optimal allocation of resources.

21.4.2 Systems Approach

Under the systems approach, an organisation is considered an open system. It consists of several interrelated and interacting elements (called subsystems). It continuously interacts with the environment (called supra system). During such interaction, the organisation takes inputs from its environment, transforms them into outputs and returns these outputs to the environment. An organisation is said to be effective when it uses its inputs in an efficient manner and contributes to the larger system. Its effectiveness is dependent on the performance of its subsystems – economic, technical and social.

According to Seashore and Yuchtman, the resources in the environment are limited. Therefore, organisations compete with each other for these resources. The bargaining position of an organisation to obtain the resources and the efficiency in using them indicates its effectiveness. "The highest level of organisational effectiveness is reached when the organisation maximises

12 Amitai Etzioni, "Two Approaches to Organisational Analysis: A Critique and a Suggestion", **Administration Science Quarterly,** Sept. 1960, p. 258.

13 R.M. Steers, "When is an Organisation Effective", **Organisation Dynamics,** Autumn, 1976.

its resource procurement … optimum is the point beyond which an organisation endangers itself because of depletion of its resource producing environment or the devaluation of the resource, or because of the stimulation of countervailing within that environment."[14]

Bennis has suggested the following criteria to judge the effectiveness of the organisation as a system:

(*i*) Adaptability or ability to solve problems and to react with flexibility to change.

(*ii*) A sense of identity which represents insight on the part of the members about the organisational goals and how outsiders perceive them.

(*iii*) Capacity to test reality which means ability to search out, accurately perceive and correctly interpret the environment.

(*iv*) State of integration among the sub-parts of the total organisation such that various parts are not working at cross purposes.[15]

The systems approach presents a more comprehensive view of organisational effectiveness. It considers the total input-process-output cycle rather than viewing effectiveness merely in terms of output or goal attainment. The systems approach also takes into account interface between organisation and environment. In order to ensure regular availability of inputs and acceptance of its outputs, an organisation must have favourable relations with its environment. Flexible response to the changing environment is necessary for developing such relations. Management of the organisation must understand the environment and speedily adapt its structure, technology, policies, etc. to the changing environment.

Limitations of Systems Approach: Though the systems approach is an improvement over the goal attainment approach, it suffers from the following drawbacks:

(*i*) The focus of the systems approach is on means rather than ends

(*ii*) It is difficult to measure flexibility of response to the environment and other qualitative variables related to the acquisition of resources.

(*iii*) The official goals of the organisation are the basis for acquisition of resources from the environment. But these goals may be vague or overshadowed by operative goals.

21.4.3 Strategic Constituencies Approach

The strategic constituencies approach is somewhat similar to the systems approach but with a slightly different focus. Like the systems view, it also considers the interdependence among different subsystems in the organisation. But the strategic constituencies approach is concerned with only those elements of the environment that can pose threat to the survival of the organisation. An effective organisation is one that satisfies the demands of those constituencies in its environment from which it requires support for its continued existence.[16]

---

14 Stanley E. Seashore and Ephraim Yuchtman, "A Systematic Resource Approach to Organisational Effectiveness", **Administrative Science Quarterly,** Dec. 1967, pp. 377-395.

15 W.G. Bennins, "Toward a Truly Scientific Management: The Concept of Organisational Health", **General Systems Year Book,** 7 (1962).

16 Jeffrey Pfeffer and Gerald Salanick, **The External Control of Organisations,** Harper and Row, New York, 1978.

The strategic constituencies approach is an integration of goal approach and systems approach. It considers the attainment of objectives of all the relevant constituencies and the elements of the environment which supply the resources needed by the organisation. It is based on the assumption that an organisation faces competing demands from various groups (constituencies) both within and outside the organisation. Management must take the following steps:

(*a*) identify the constituencies in the environment on which the survival of organisation depends.

(*b*) evaluate the relative power of each constituency in terms of the organisation's dependence on it.

(*c*) identify the expectation of each constituency.

(*d*) rank the constituencies in order of their power and expectations.

(*e*) the ability of the organisation to satisfy the ranked constituencies indicates its effectiveness.

Limitations of Strategic Constituencies Approach: The main weaknesses of the strategic constituencies approach are as under:

(*i*) It is very difficult to select the strategic constituencies. These change with changes in the environment.

(*ii*) It is equally difficult to rank these constituencies in terms of the organisation's dependence on them.

(*iii*) The expectations of these constituencies from the organisation cannot be identified and measured.

21.4.4 Behavioural Approach

An organisation's response to the environmental demands depends upon the behaviour of its members. If the members wholeheartedly accept the organisational goals, there is perfect integration of individual and organisational goals which leads to high degree of organisational effectiveness. But this ideal situation is rare in real life. Quite often there is a gap between organisational goals and individual goals. Greater is this gap, lower is the degree of organisational effectiveness [Fig. 21.4].

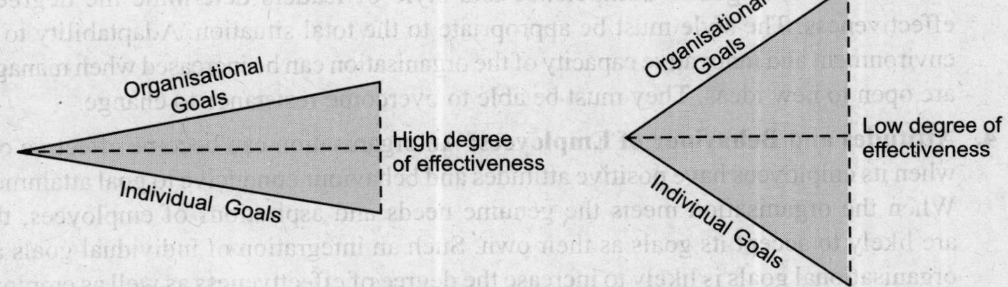

Fig. 21.4: Integration of Goals and Degree of Effectiveness

In between the two extremes given above, there may be several combinations of goal congruency. When there is conflict between organisational goals and individual goals, the organisation becomes ineffective [Fig. 21.5].

21.5 FACTORS INFLUENCING ORGANISATIONAL EFFECTIVENESS

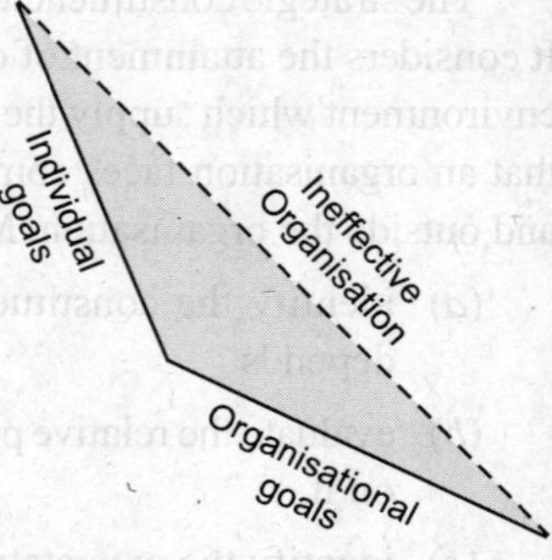

Fig. 21.5: Ineffective Organisation

Some important determinants of organisational effectiveness are given below:

1. **Organisation Structure:** Various aspects of organisation structure exercise considerable influence on effectiveness. Task specialisation, span of control, decentralisation, large size and formalisation tend to improve productivity and effectiveness.
2. **Type of Technology:** Capital-intensive technology is helpful in increasing organisational effectiveness. Technology and organisational structure are interrelated. A shift to sophisticated technology requires changes in span of control, delegation of authority and other dimensions of structure. Unless the structure is changed to meet the needs of technology, the organisation may not be effective.
3. **Managerial Policies and Practices:** These relate to strategic planning, resource acquisition and utilisation, work environment, leadership, adaptation and innovation, etc. When the **goals** set by the management are: (*a*) in accordance with the capacity of employees and the available resources, and (*b*) acceptable to the employees, effectiveness is likely to be high. Similarly, if the management is able to acquire the right quantity and quality of resources at the right time and cost, organisation can be effective. Proper allocation of resources among different departments and their efficient utilisation increases the degree of effectiveness. Proper policy guidelines and effective control are needed for this purpose.

   Employees can perform well only when the management creates and maintains proper environment. Work environment for high level of performance can be created through effective systems of : (*a*) employee selection and induction, (*b*) training and development, and (*c*) performance appraisal and rewards.

   Dynamic leadership is needed for execution of decisions that lead to attainment of organisational goals. Competence and style of leaders determine the degree of effectiveness. The style must be appropriate to the total situation. Adaptability to the environment and innovative capacity of the organisation can be increased when managers are open to new ideas. They must be able to overcome resistance to change.
4. **Attitudes and Behaviour of Employees:** An organisation can become effective only when its employees have positive attitudes and behaviour conducive to goal attainment. When the organisation meets the genuine needs and aspirations of employees, they are likely to accept its goals as their own. Such an integration of individual goals and organisational goals is likely to increase the degree of effectiveness as well as employee satisfaction.
5. **External Environment:** Effective organisations are able to forecast changes in their environment with reasonable accuracy and respond properly to these changes. Increasing complexity and uncertainty in the external environment act as constraints on organisational effectiveness.

21.6 LIKERT'S MODEL OF EFFECTIVENESS

Rensis Likert[17] has identified three variables which determine effectiveness. These variables are as follows:

1. **Causal Variables:** These are the independent factors which influence the course of development within an organisation. These include managerial strategies, organisation structure, managerial skills, and policies, leadership styles, etc. These are within the control of the organisation.
2. **Intervening Variables:** These factors represent the internal state of an organisation. Employee motivation and morale, decision-making and problem-solving techniques, communication are examples of intervening variables. Causal variables like leadership style influence the intervening variables.
3. **End-Result or Output Variables:** These are the dependent variables and represent the accomplishments of the organisation.

The interrelationship between the three sets of variables is shown in Fig. 21.6.

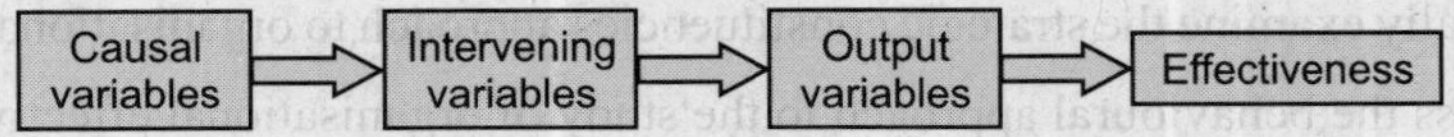

Fig. 21.6: Relationship between Variables

Causal variables act as stimuli upon the intervening variables which create certain responses or end results. The end results represent effectiveness of the organisation. Three points are notable in this connection. **First,** the efforts to improve the intervening variables directly will be less successful than when they are improved through modifying causal variables. **Second,** efforts to improve the end result variables by modifying the intervening variables will be less effective than changing the causal variables. **Third,** intervening variables should not be overlooked. In the short run, higher output may be achieved by neglecting them (*e.g.,* employee morale) but this is not possible in the long run.

21.7 ADAPTIVE COPING CYCLE:

The systems approach to organisational effectiveness suggests that effective organisations adapt their structure, policies, technology, etc. to changes in the environment. Edgar Schein has suggested the concept of **adaptive coping cycle** for this purpose. This concept refers to "the sequence of activities … process which begins with some change in some part of the internal or external environment and end with more adaptive dynamic equilibrium for dealing with change."[18]

Adaptive coping cycle consists of the following stages:

(*i*) sensing a change in some part of internal or external environment.

(*ii*) importing the relavaent information about the change into those parts of the organisation that can act upon it.

(*iii*) changing transformation process inside the organisation according to the imported information.

17 Rensis Likert, **The Human Organisation,** McGraw-Hill, New York, 1967, pp. 27-29.

18 Edgar Schein, **Organisational Psychology,** Prentice-Hall, New Delhi, 1973.

(*iv*) stabilising internal change while reducing undesired.

(*v*) exporting new outputs that are more consistent with the perceived changes in the environment.

(*vi*) obtaining feedback about the acceptability of new outputs by the environment.

According to Schein, the effectiveness of an organisation depends on its ability to collect and use the feedback from the environment.

TEST QUESTIONS

1. What is organisational effectiveness? Explain its relationship with individual effectiveness and group effectiveness.
2. "Measuring effectiveness is crucial but very difficult". Explain.
3. "There seems to be little agreement on the criteria to judge organisational effectiveness". Explain in this context problems involved in measurement of organisational effectiveness.
4. How will you judge the effectiveness of an organisation?
5. Critically examine the strategic constituencies approach to organisational effectiveness.
6. Discuss the behavioural approach to the study of organisational effectiveness.
7. Explain the factors influencing the effectiveness of an organisation.
8. Discuss Rensis Likert's model of organisational effectiveness.
9. Define organisational effectiveness. How do you differentiate effectiveness from efficiency? Comment critically with suitable examples from Indian organisations.
10. Explain the systems approach to organisational effectiveness. What are its limitations?
11. Evaluate the various criteria of organisational effectiveness.
12. Discuss goal attainment approach to organisation effectiveness. How does the degree of integration of individual and organisational goals affect organisational effectiveness?
13. "Organisational theory is the study of how organisations function and how they affect and are affected by the environment in which they operate." Elaborate this statement and differentiate between organisational theory and organisational behaviour.
14. "Job related attitudes are significant for understanding organisational behaviour." Explain this statement.
15. What behavioural predictions will you make if you know an employee has:
    (*i*) An External Locus of Control;
    (*ii*) 'Type A' Personality;
    (*iii*) A low Mach Score.
16. Explain the characteristics of effective organisations.
17. Write notes on:
    (*a*) Goal optimisation
    (*b*) Adaptive coping cycle.

CASE STUDY

In August 2008. Wal-Mart Stores announced that its profit rose 17 per cent in the second quarter and that it is raising its full-year forecast. In a challenging economy, the world's largest retailer benefited from low prices and its moves to cut costs. Wal-Mart's President and Chief Executive Lee Scott said that, "While current economic crisis is pressuring suppliers, retailers and customers worldwide, we're confident that Wal-Mart is well positioned for this economy." Chief Financial Officer Tom Schoewe attributed the better second-quarter profits to tighter inventory controls, which led to fewer markdowns on merchandise. One of Wal-Mart's goals – which it successfully met – was keeping inventory growth at half the rate of its sales growth. In contrast, sales at department stores and specially retailers were lagging behind.

What is the key to such good results? Wal-Mart overhauled its strategy. Instead of announcing any price increases to cope with the tough economy, the company slashed its expansion plans. It refocused on lower prices, improved the mix of merchandise offered, cleaned up its stores and provided friendlier and faster customer service. But there is more to Wal-Mart's success over the years than just tighter inventory controls and lower prices.

Wal-Mart is truly a great company. A strong organisational culture is the foundation for making a good company a great one. The secret to Wal-Mart's success has long been attributed to its strong culture. Analysts like Jim Collins believe that Wal-Mart had the kind of 'cult-like' culture that is shared by all great companies. Wal-Mart employees are referred to as 'Walmartians' which is a sign of a unique culture shared by them. This culture is responsible for a company of this magnitude to be able to sustain its entrepreneurial spirit decade after decade.

Since its early days, Wal-Mart achieved remarkable growth rates and was the first trillion dollar company in the world. In 1999, Wal-Mart became the largest private employer in the US with 1,140,000 Associates. But with amazing success also came criticism. Wal-Mart was sued many times and even held the record for being sued the maximum at one time. Its practices and culture were held responsible for killing small local retailers. It was also criticised for gender-based discrimination, its overtime policies and using sweatshop products.

Questions

(*a*) Identify the major factors contributing to the success of Wal-Mart in tough times.

(*b*) What new initiatives Wal-Mart should take in the light of the current economic crisis to maintain the growth of the organisation?

(*c*) What steps for each type of problem should be taken to reduce the law suits against the company keeping in mind the behavioural dimensions?

NOTES

NOTES

NOTES